SUICIDE SQUAD

THEIR GREATEST SHOTS

JOHN OSTRANDER ADAM GLASS
ALES KOT ROB WILLIAMS WRITERS

LUKE MCDONNELL FERNANDO DAGNINO
PATRICK ZIRCHER PHILIP TAN GUS VAZQUEZ
TONY S. DANIEL STJEPAN ŠEJIC
PHILIPPE BRIONES PENCILLERS

BOB LEWIS FERNANDO DAGNINO
PATRICK ZIRCHER JONATHAN GLAPION
SCOTT HANNA SANDU FLOREA
CARLOS RODRIGUEZ STJEPAN ŠEJIC
PHILIPPE BRIONES INKERS

JULIANNA FERRITER MATT YACKEY JASON KEITH
ALEX SINCLAIR GABE ELTAEB TOMEU MOREY
STJEPAN ŠEJIĆ COLORISTS

TODD KLEIN JARED K. FLETCHER TRAVIS LANHAM
NATE PIEKOS OF BLAMBOT PAT BROSSEAU LETTERERS

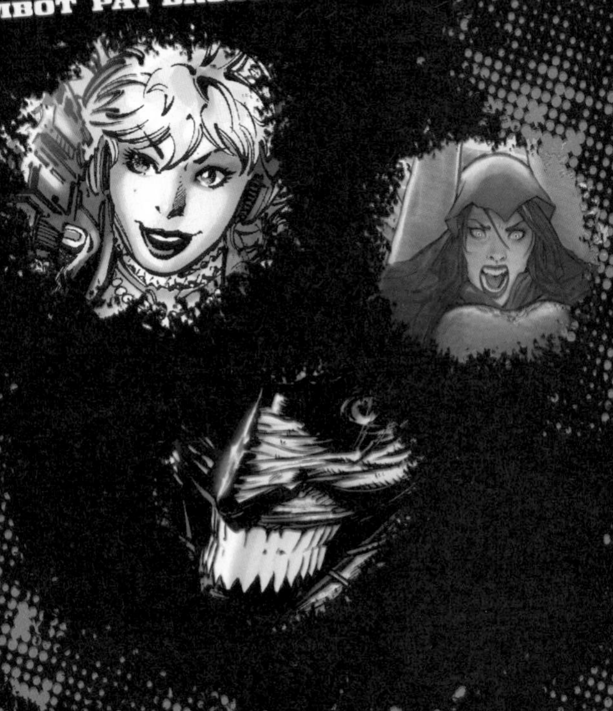

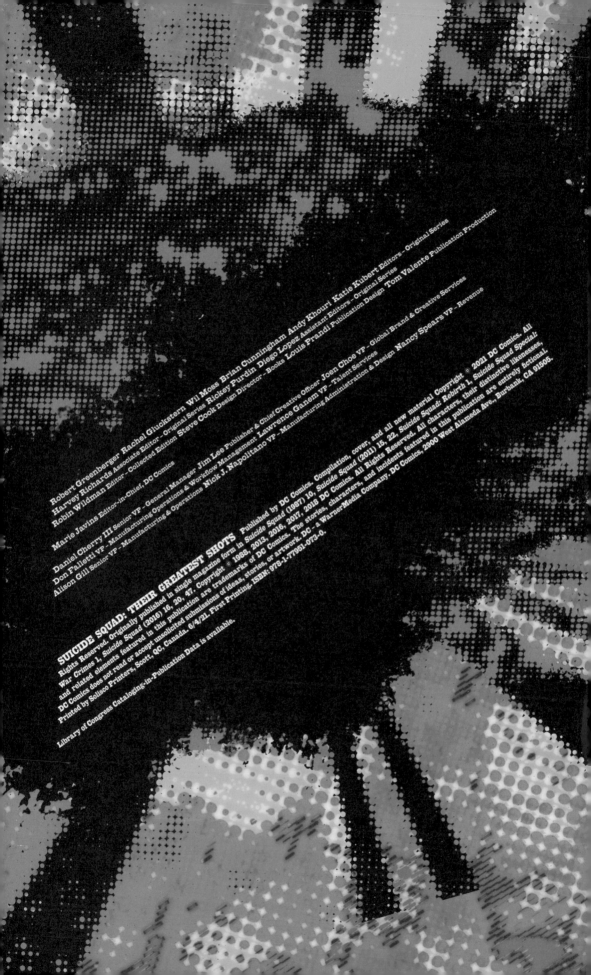

Robert Greenberger Rachel Gluckstern Wil Moss Brian Cunningham Andy Khouri Katie Kubert Editors – Original Series
Harvey Richards Associate Editor – Original Series Rickey Purdin Diego Lopez Assistant Editors – Original Series
Robin Wildman Editor – Collected Edition Steve Cook Design Director – Books Louis Prandi Publication Design Tom Valente Publication Production

Marie Javins Editor-in-Chief, DC Comics

Daniel Cherry III Senior VP – General Manager Jim Lee Publisher & Chief Creative Officer Joen Choe VP – Global Brand & Creative Services
Don Falletti VP – Manufacturing Operations & Workflow Management Lawrence Ganem VP – Talent Services
Alison Gill Senior VP – Manufacturing & Operations Nick J. Napolitano VP – Manufacturing Administration & Design Nancy Spears VP – Revenue

SUICIDE SQUAD: THEIR GREATEST SHOTS Published by DC Comics. Compilation, cover, and all new material Copyright © 2021 DC Comics. All Rights Reserved. Originally published in single magazine form in *Suicide Squad* (1987) 10, *Suicide Squad* (2011) 15, 22, *Suicide Squad: Rebirth* 1, *Suicide Squad Special: War Crimes* 1, *Suicide Squad* (2016) 16, 20, 47. Copyright © 1988, 2013, 2016, 2017, 2018 DC Comics. All Rights Reserved. All characters, their distinctive likenesses, and related elements featured in this publication are trademarks of DC Comics. The stories, characters, and incidents featured in this publication are entirely fictional. DC Comics does not read or accept unsolicited submissions of ideas, stories, or artwork. DC – a WarnerMedia Company. DC Comics, 2900 West Alameda Ave., Burbank, CA 91505. Printed by Solisco Printers, Scott, QC, Canada. 6/4/21. First Printing. ISBN: 978-1-77951-073-0.

Library of Congress Cataloging-in-Publication Data is available.

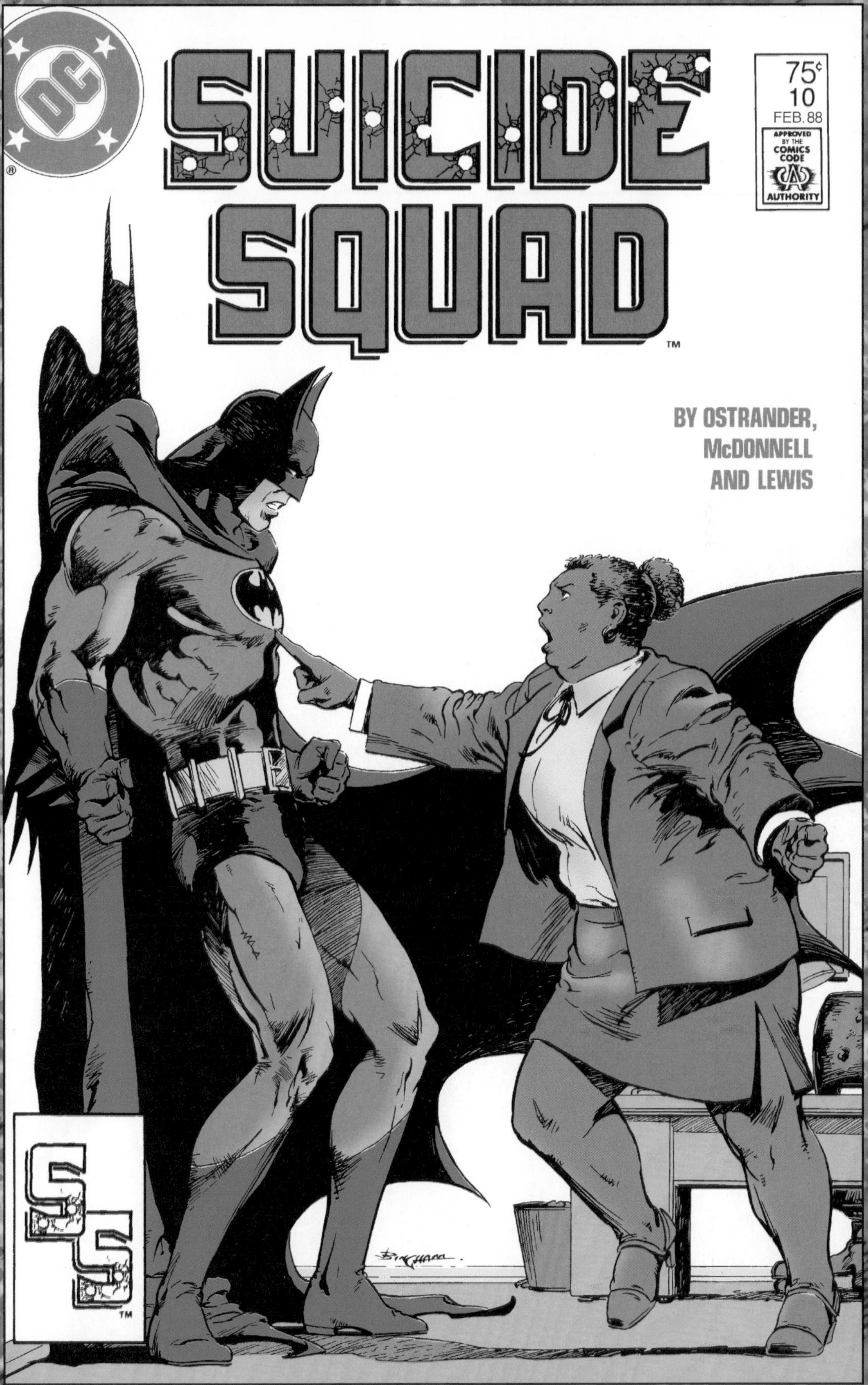
SUICIDE SQUAD
75¢
10
FEB. 88
APPROVED BY THE COMICS CODE AUTHORITY
BY OSTRANDER, McDONNELL AND LEWIS
SS

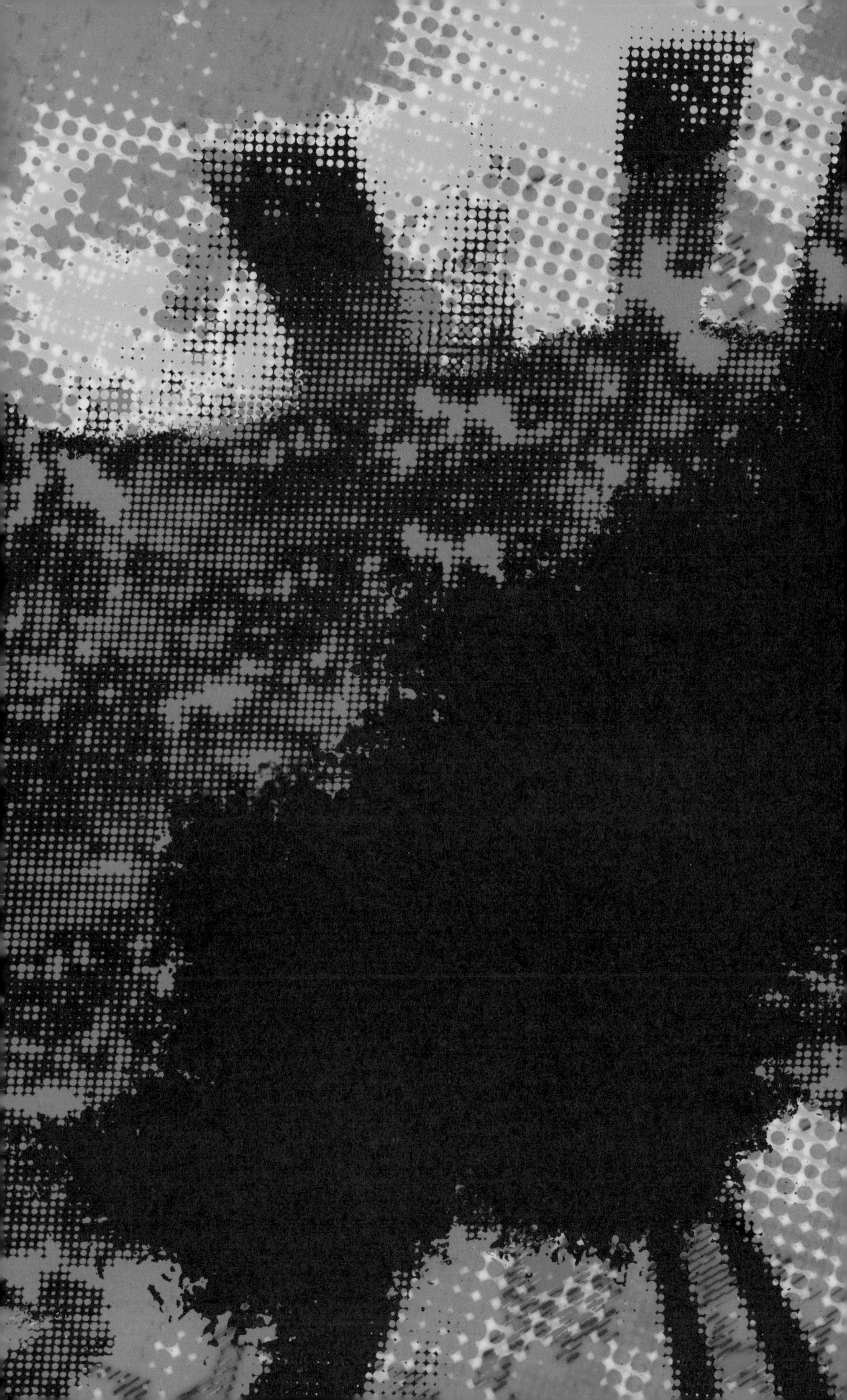

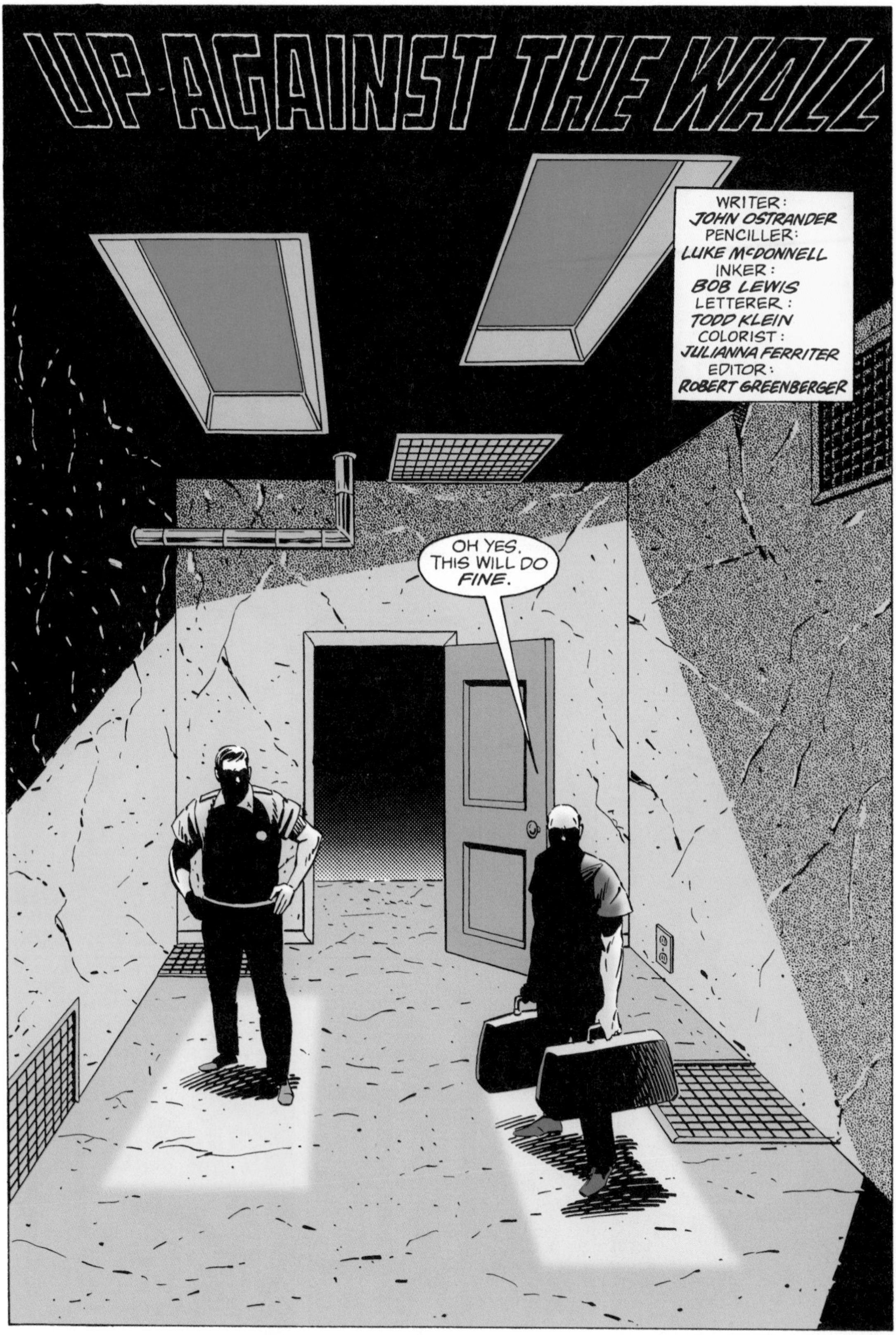

UP AGAINST THE WALL
WRITER: JOHN OSTRANDER
PENCILLER: LUKE McDONNELL
INKER: BOB LEWIS
LETTERER: TODD KLEIN
COLORIST: JULIANNA FERRITER
EDITOR: ROBERT GREENBERGER
OH YES, THIS WILL DO FINE.

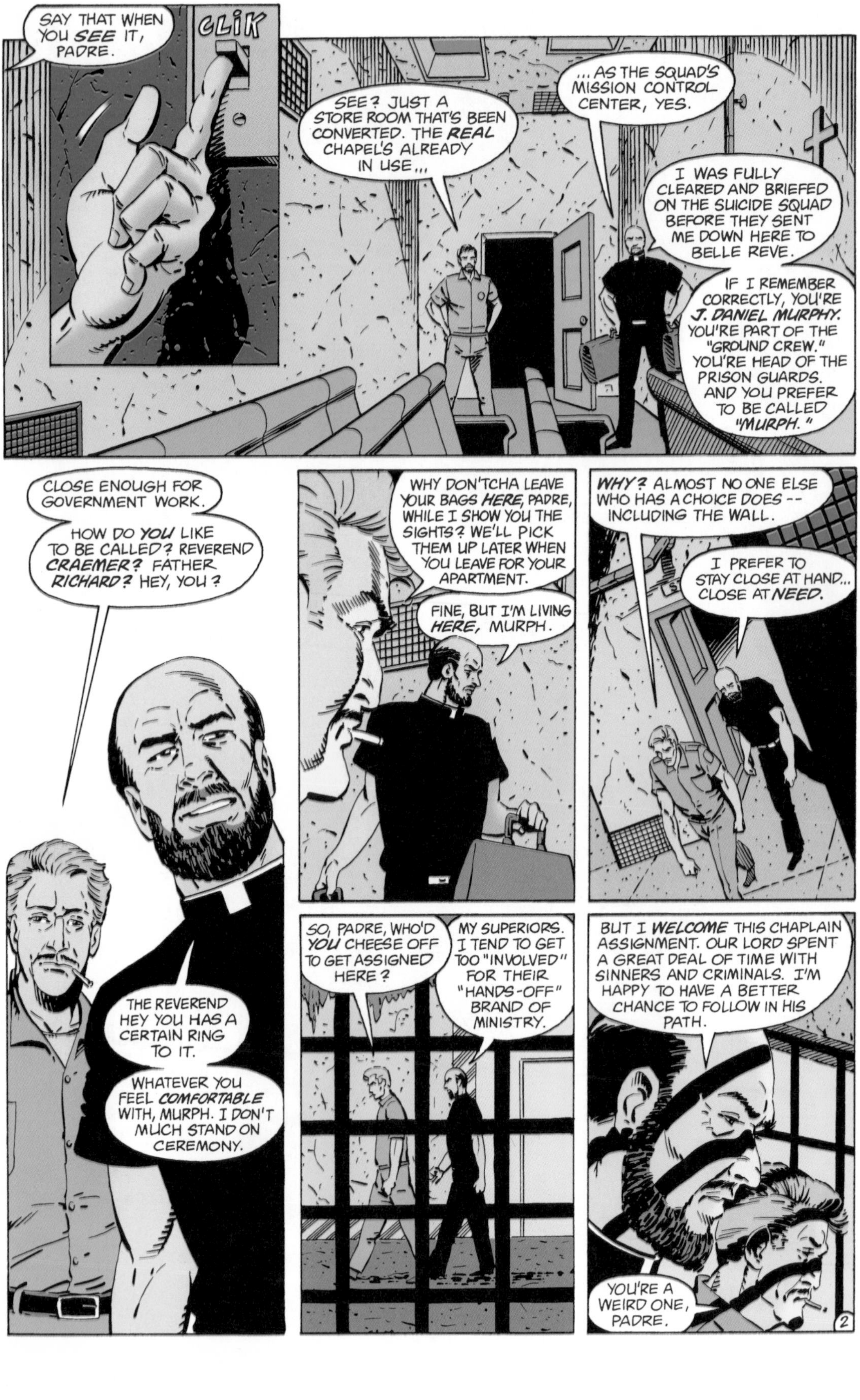

SAY THAT WHEN YOU SEE IT, PADRE.
CLIK
SEE? JUST A STORE ROOM THAT'S BEEN CONVERTED. THE REAL CHAPEL'S ALREADY IN USE...
...AS THE SQUAD'S MISSION CONTROL CENTER, YES.
I WAS FULLY CLEARED AND BRIEFED ON THE SUICIDE SQUAD BEFORE THEY SENT ME DOWN HERE TO BELLE REVE.
IF I REMEMBER CORRECTLY, YOU'RE J. DANIEL MURPHY. YOU'RE PART OF THE "GROUND CREW." YOU'RE HEAD OF THE PRISON GUARDS. AND YOU PREFER TO BE CALLED "MURPH."
CLOSE ENOUGH FOR GOVERNMENT WORK.
HOW DO YOU LIKE TO BE CALLED? REVEREND CRAEMER? FATHER RICHARD? HEY, YOU?
THE REVEREND HEY YOU HAS A CERTAIN RING TO IT.
WHATEVER YOU FEEL COMFORTABLE WITH, MURPH. I DON'T MUCH STAND ON CEREMONY.
WHY DON'TCHA LEAVE YOUR BAGS HERE, PADRE, WHILE I SHOW YOU THE SIGHTS? WE'LL PICK THEM UP LATER WHEN YOU LEAVE FOR YOUR APARTMENT.
FINE, BUT I'M LIVING HERE, MURPH.
WHY? ALMOST NO ONE ELSE WHO HAS A CHOICE DOES -- INCLUDING THE WALL.
I PREFER TO STAY CLOSE AT HAND... CLOSE AT NEED.
SO, PADRE, WHO'D YOU CHEESE OFF TO GET ASSIGNED HERE?
MY SUPERIORS. I TEND TO GET TOO "INVOLVED" FOR THEIR "HANDS-OFF" BRAND OF MINISTRY.
BUT I WELCOME THIS CHAPLAIN ASSIGNMENT. OUR LORD SPENT A GREAT DEAL OF TIME WITH SINNERS AND CRIMINALS. I'M HAPPY TO HAVE A BETTER CHANCE TO FOLLOW IN HIS PATH.
YOU'RE A WEIRD ONE, PADRE.
2

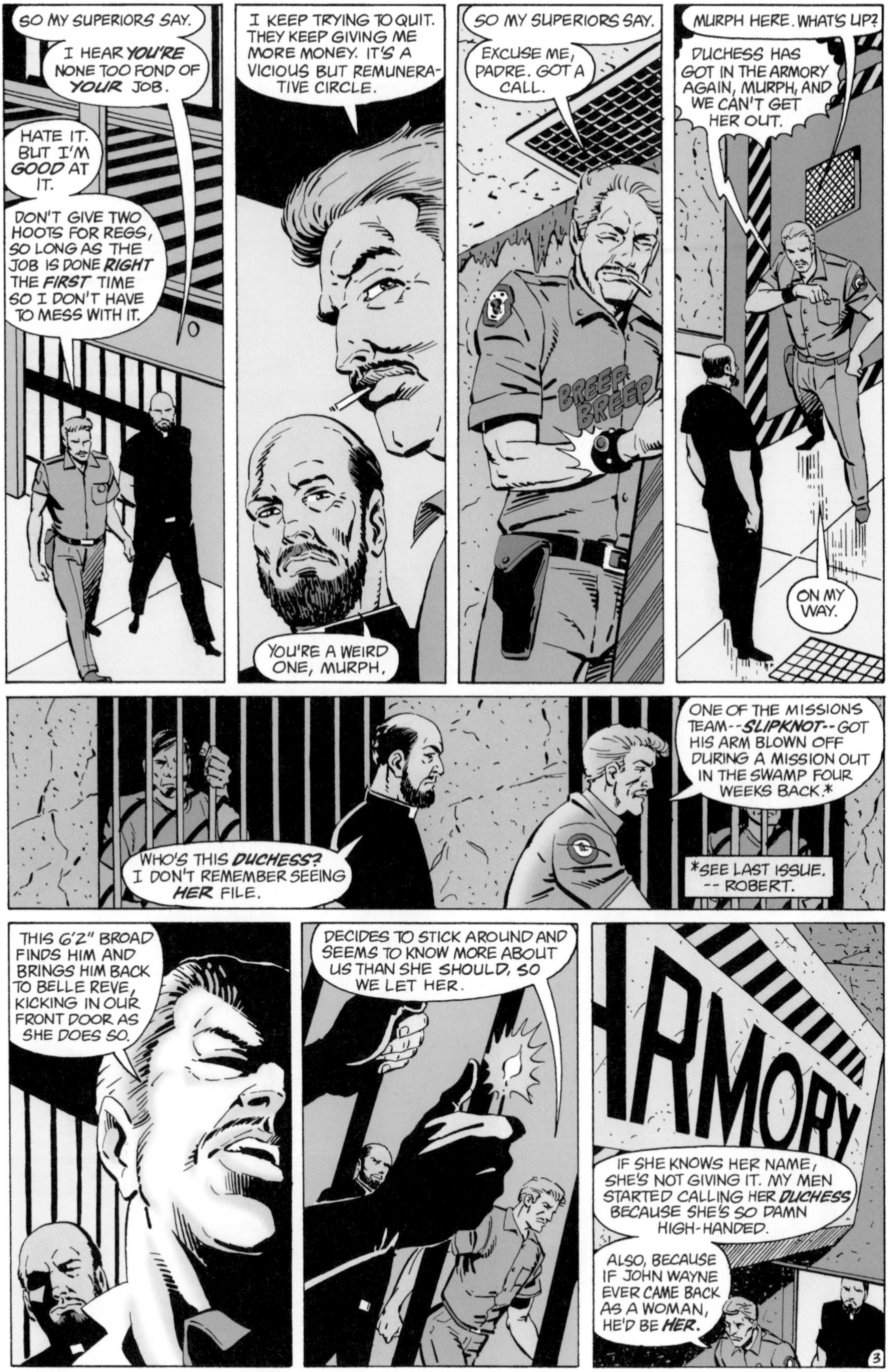

SO MY SUPERIORS SAY.
I HEAR YOU'RE NONE TOO FOND OF YOUR JOB.
HATE IT. BUT I'M GOOD AT IT.
DON'T GIVE TWO HOOTS FOR REGS, SO LONG AS THE JOB IS DONE RIGHT THE FIRST TIME SO I DON'T HAVE TO MESS WITH IT.
I KEEP TRYING TO QUIT. THEY KEEP GIVING ME MORE MONEY. IT'S A VICIOUS BUT REMUNERATIVE CIRCLE.
YOU'RE A WEIRD ONE, MURPH.
SO MY SUPERIORS SAY.
EXCUSE ME, PADRE. GOT A CALL.
BREEP BREEP
MURPH HERE. WHAT'S UP?
DUCHESS HAS GOT IN THE ARMORY AGAIN, MURPH, AND WE CAN'T GET HER OUT.
ON MY WAY.
WHO'S THIS DUCHESS? I DON'T REMEMBER SEEING HER FILE.
ONE OF THE MISSIONS TEAM--SLIPKNOT--GOT HIS ARM BLOWN OFF DURING A MISSION OUT IN THE SWAMP FOUR WEEKS BACK.*
*SEE LAST ISSUE. -- ROBERT.
THIS 6'2" BROAD FINDS HIM AND BRINGS HIM BACK TO BELLE REVE, KICKING IN OUR FRONT DOOR AS SHE DOES SO.
DECIDES TO STICK AROUND AND SEEMS TO KNOW MORE ABOUT US THAN SHE SHOULD, SO WE LET HER.
RMORY
IF SHE KNOWS HER NAME, SHE'S NOT GIVING IT. MY MEN STARTED CALLING HER DUCHESS BECAUSE SHE'S SO DAMN HIGH-HANDED.
ALSO, BECAUSE IF JOHN WAYNE EVER CAME BACK AS A WOMAN, HE'D BE HER.

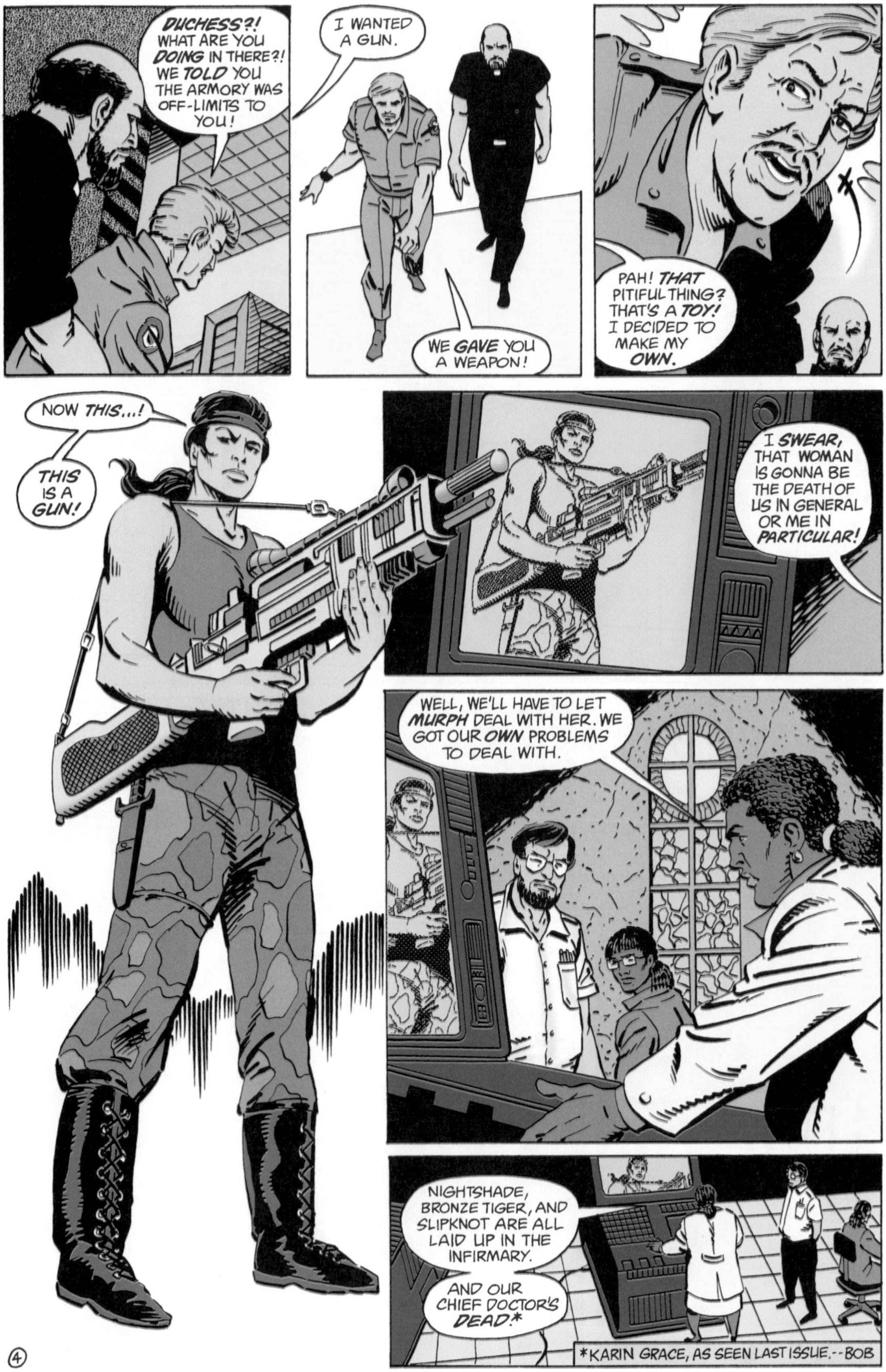
DUCHESS?! WHAT ARE YOU DOING IN THERE?! WE TOLD YOU THE ARMORY WAS OFF-LIMITS TO YOU!
I WANTED A GUN.
WE GAVE YOU A WEAPON!
PAH! THAT PITIFUL THING? THAT'S A TOY! I DECIDED TO MAKE MY OWN.
NOW THIS...!
THIS IS A GUN!
I SWEAR, THAT WOMAN IS GONNA BE THE DEATH OF US IN GENERAL OR ME IN PARTICULAR!
WELL, WE'LL HAVE TO LET MURPH DEAL WITH HER. WE GOT OUR OWN PROBLEMS TO DEAL WITH.
NIGHTSHADE, BRONZE TIGER, AND SLIPKNOT ARE ALL LAID UP IN THE INFIRMARY.
AND OUR CHIEF DOCTOR'S DEAD!*
*KARIN GRACE, AS SEEN LAST ISSUE.--BOB
4

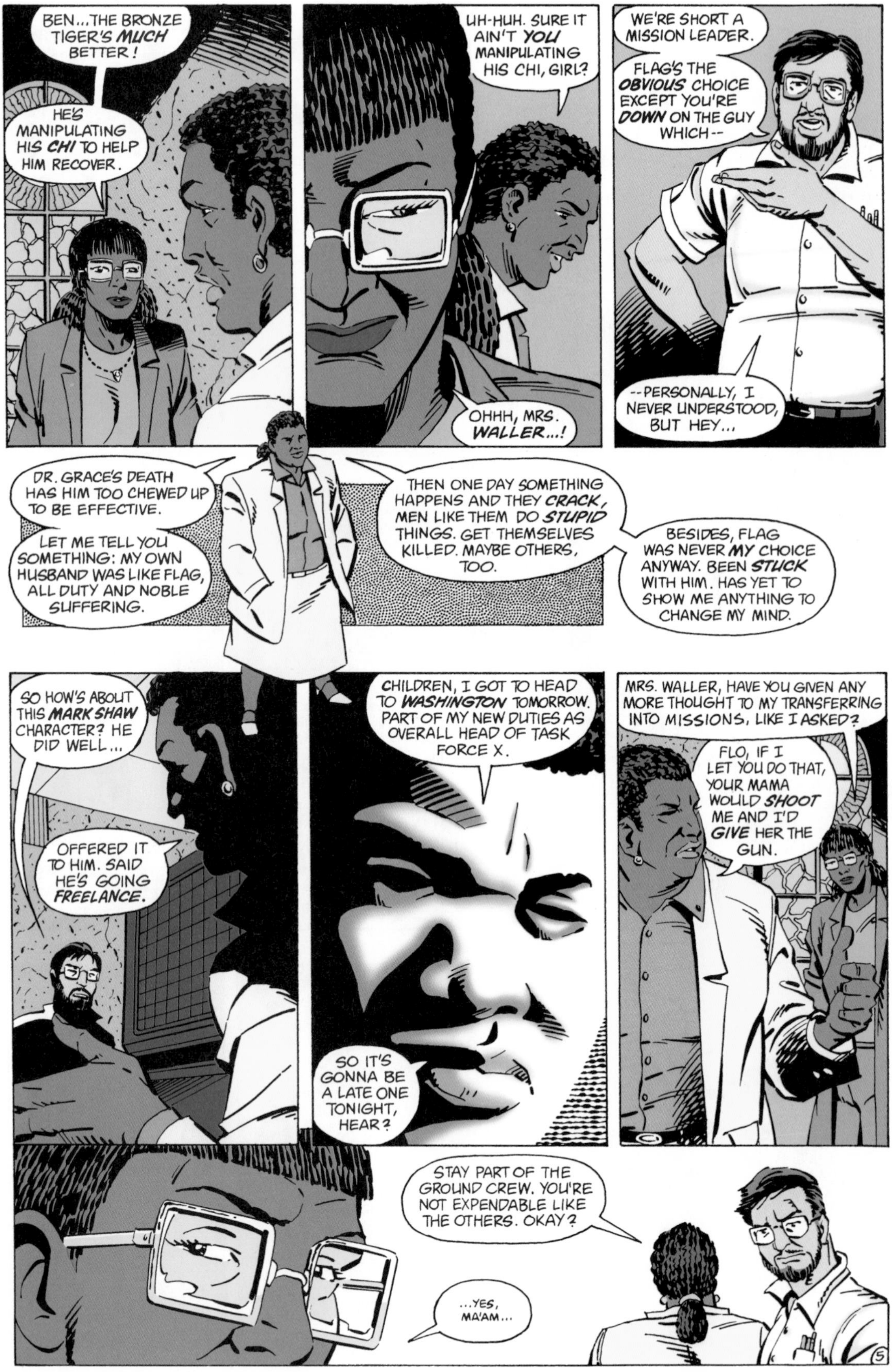

BEN...THE BRONZE TIGER'S MUCH BETTER!
HE'S MANIPULATING HIS CHI TO HELP HIM RECOVER.
UH-HUH. SURE IT AIN'T YOU MANIPULATING HIS CHI, GIRL?
OHHH, MRS. WALLER...!
WE'RE SHORT A MISSION LEADER.
FLAG'S THE OBVIOUS CHOICE EXCEPT YOU'RE DOWN ON THE GUY WHICH--
--PERSONALLY, I NEVER UNDERSTOOD, BUT HEY...
DR. GRACE'S DEATH HAS HIM TOO CHEWED UP TO BE EFFECTIVE.
LET ME TELL YOU SOMETHING: MY OWN HUSBAND WAS LIKE FLAG, ALL DUTY AND NOBLE SUFFERING.
THEN ONE DAY SOMETHING HAPPENS AND THEY CRACK, MEN LIKE THEM DO STUPID THINGS. GET THEMSELVES KILLED. MAYBE OTHERS, TOO.
BESIDES, FLAG WAS NEVER MY CHOICE ANYWAY. BEEN STUCK WITH HIM. HAS YET TO SHOW ME ANYTHING TO CHANGE MY MIND.
SO HOW'S ABOUT THIS MARK SHAW CHARACTER? HE DID WELL...
OFFERED IT TO HIM. SAID HE'S GOING FREELANCE.
CHILDREN, I GOT TO HEAD TO WASHINGTON TOMORROW. PART OF MY NEW DUTIES AS OVERALL HEAD OF TASK FORCE X.
SO IT'S GONNA BE A LATE ONE TONIGHT, HEAR?
MRS. WALLER, HAVE YOU GIVEN ANY MORE THOUGHT TO MY TRANSFERRING INTO MISSIONS, LIKE I ASKED?
FLO, IF I LET YOU DO THAT, YOUR MAMA WOULD SHOOT ME AND I'D GIVE HER THE GUN.
STAY PART OF THE GROUND CREW. YOU'RE NOT EXPENDABLE LIKE THE OTHERS. OKAY?
...YES, MA'AM...
5

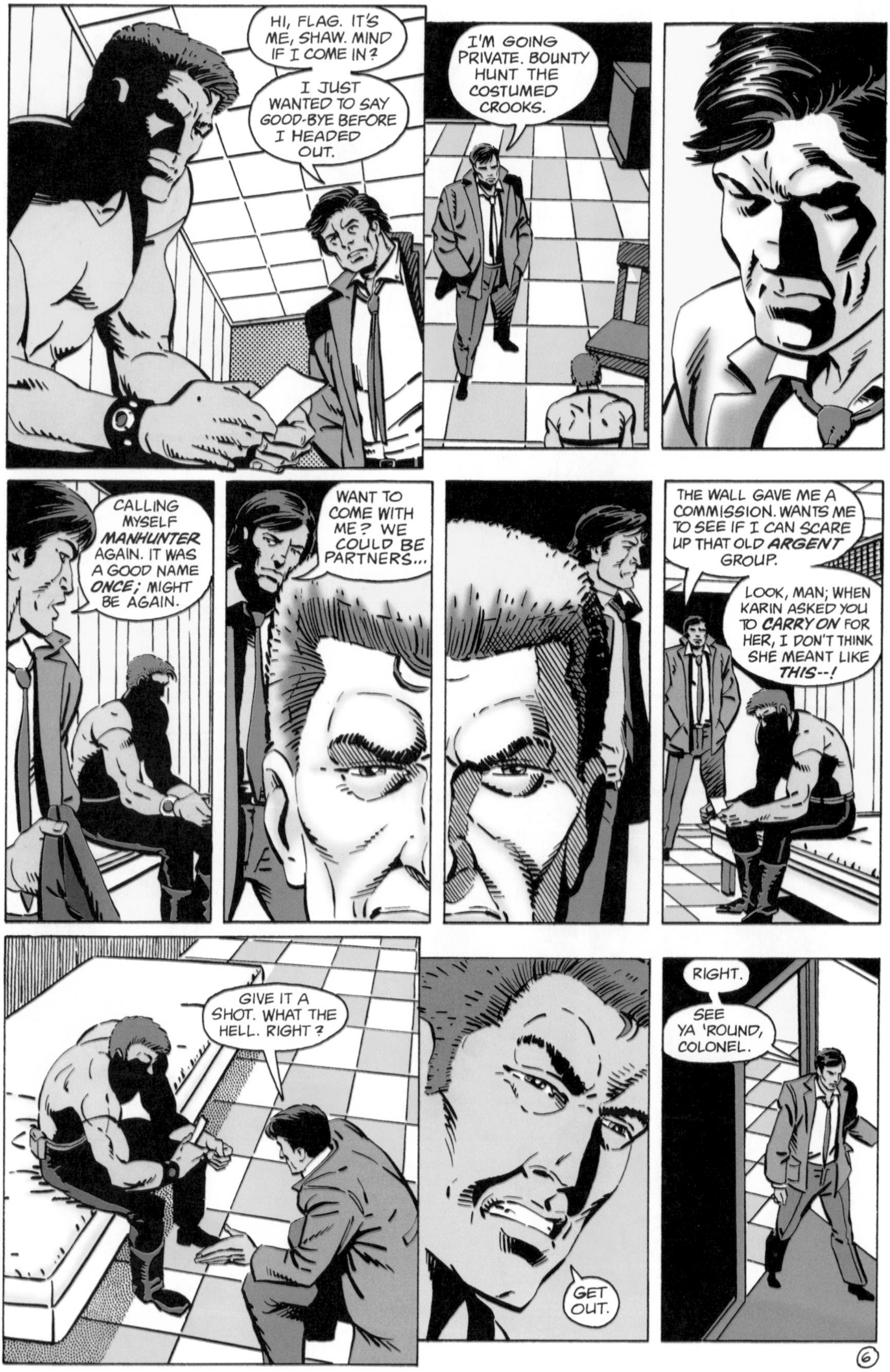

HI, FLAG. IT'S ME, SHAW. MIND IF I COME IN?
I JUST WANTED TO SAY GOOD-BYE BEFORE I HEADED OUT.
I'M GOING PRIVATE. BOUNTY HUNT THE COSTUMED CROOKS.
CALLING MYSELF MANHUNTER AGAIN. IT WAS A GOOD NAME ONCE; MIGHT BE AGAIN.
WANT TO COME WITH ME? WE COULD BE PARTNERS...
THE WALL GAVE ME A COMMISSION. WANTS ME TO SEE IF I CAN SCARE UP THAT OLD ARGENT GROUP.
LOOK, MAN; WHEN KARIN ASKED YOU TO CARRY ON FOR HER, I DON'T THINK SHE MEANT LIKE THIS--!
GIVE IT A SHOT. WHAT THE HELL. RIGHT?
GET OUT.
RIGHT.
SEE YA 'ROUND, COLONEL.

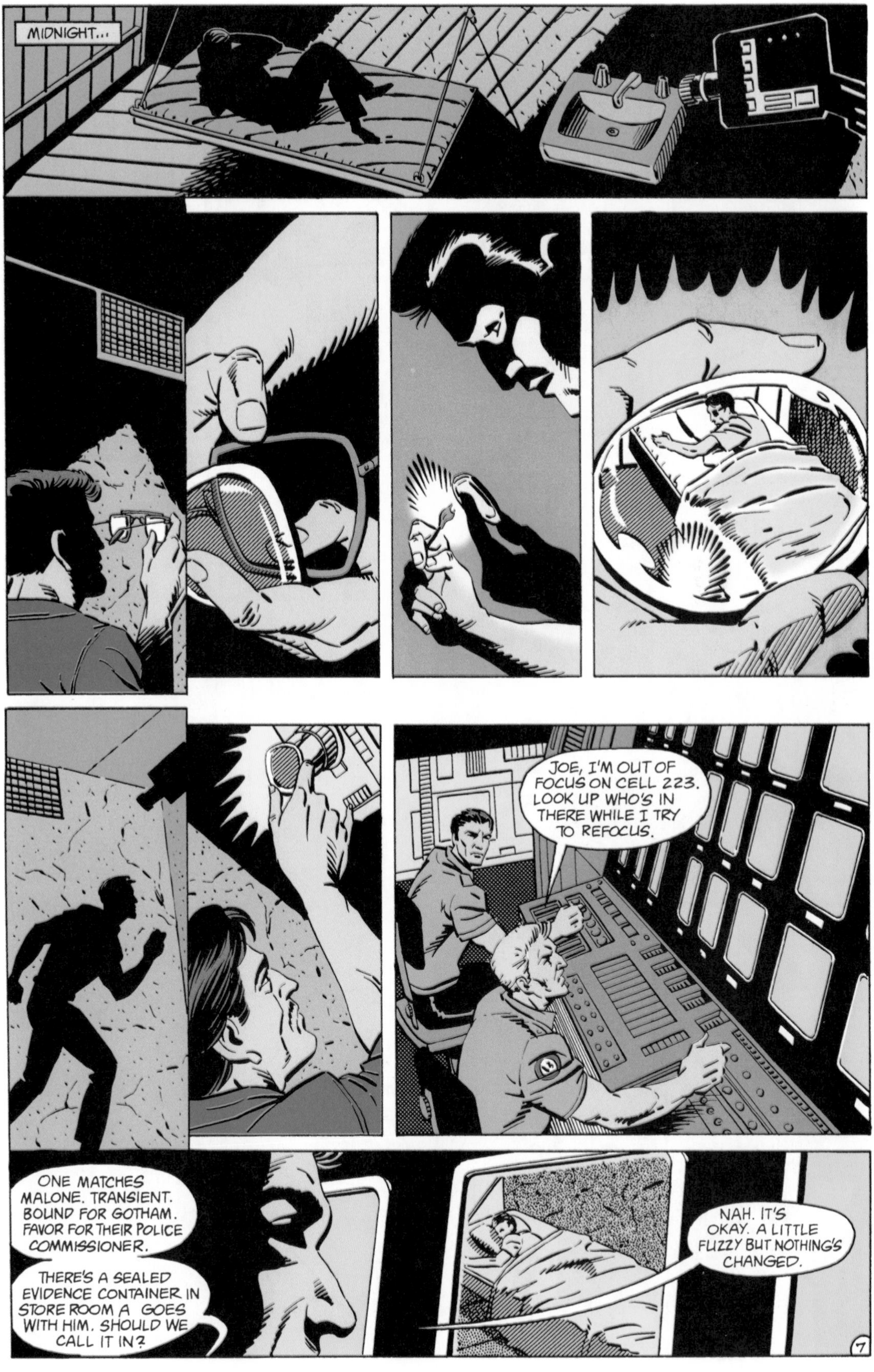
MIDNIGHT...
JOE, I'M OUT OF FOCUS ON CELL 223. LOOK UP WHO'S IN THERE WHILE I TRY TO REFOCUS.
ONE MATCHES MALONE. TRANSIENT. BOUND FOR GOTHAM. FAVOR FOR THEIR POLICE COMMISSIONER.
THERE'S A SEALED EVIDENCE CONTAINER IN STORE ROOM A GOES WITH HIM. SHOULD WE CALL IT IN?
NAH. IT'S OKAY. A LITTLE FUZZY BUT NOTHING'S CHANGED.
7

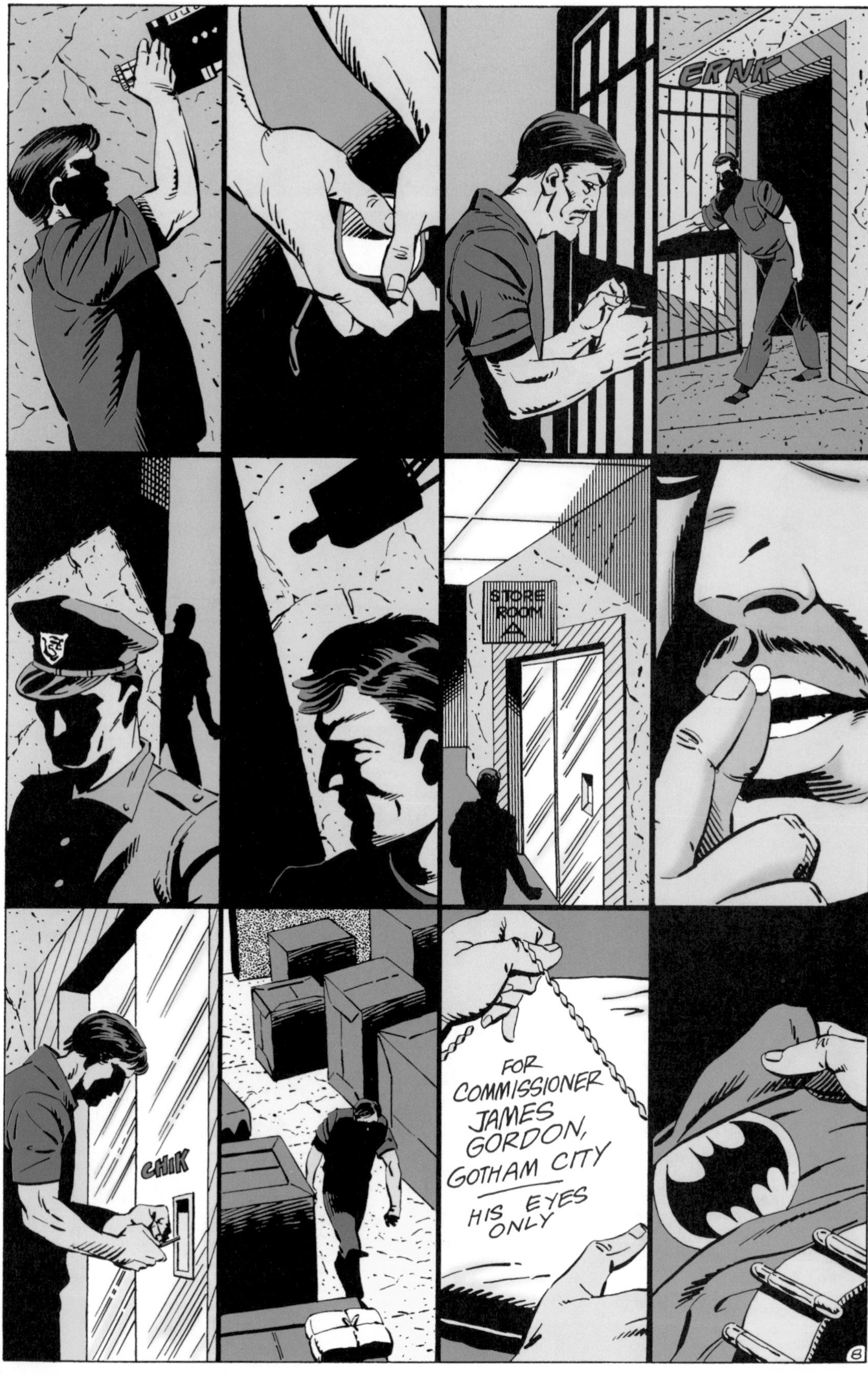

ERNK
STORE ROOM
CHIK
FOR COMMISSIONER JAMES GORDON, GOTHAM CITY
HIS EYES ONLY

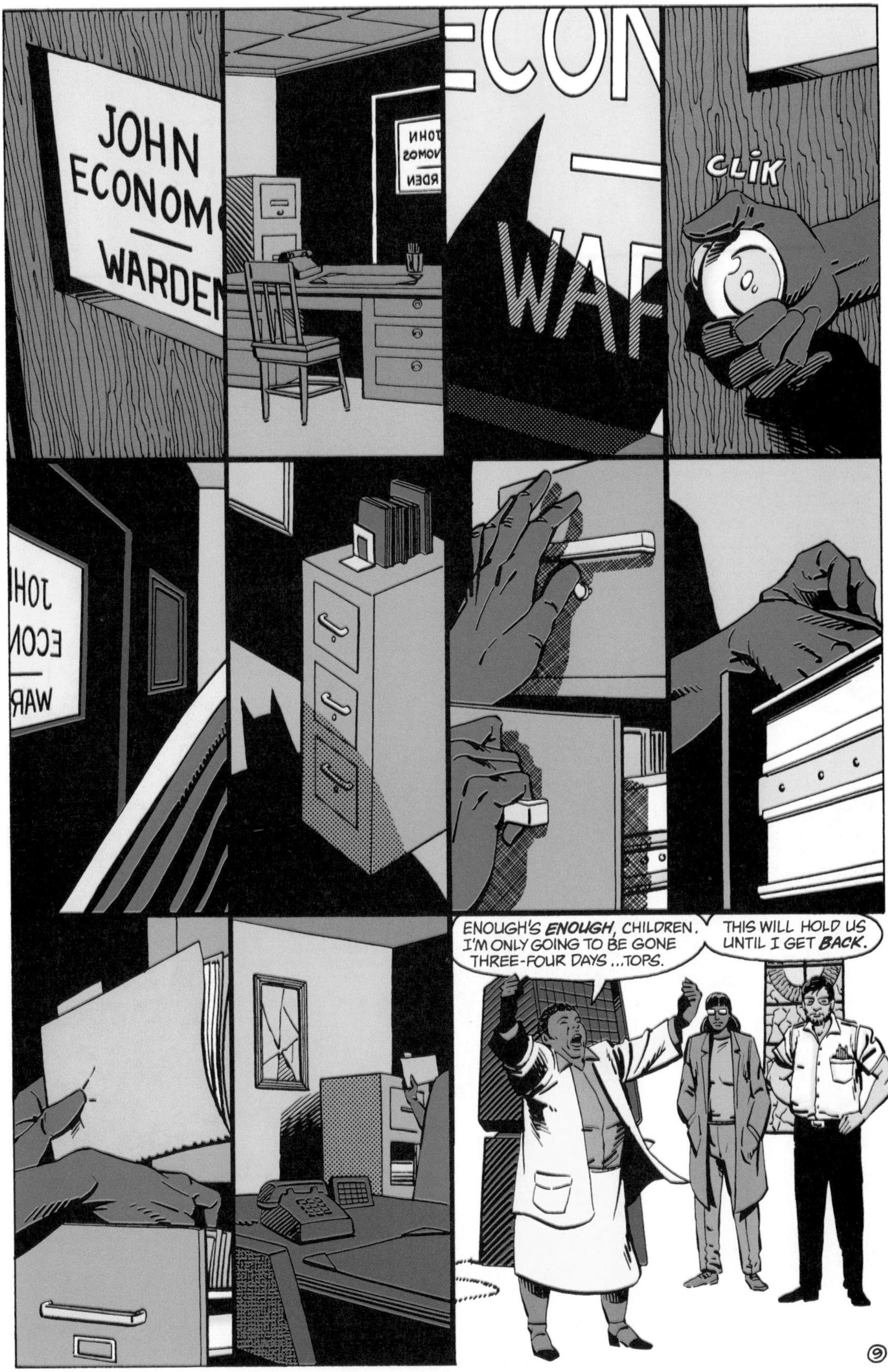
JOHN
ECONOM
WARDEN
ECON
WAR
CLIK
ENOUGH'S ENOUGH, CHILDREN. I'M ONLY GOING TO BE GONE THREE-FOUR DAYS ...TOPS.
THIS WILL HOLD US UNTIL I GET BACK.

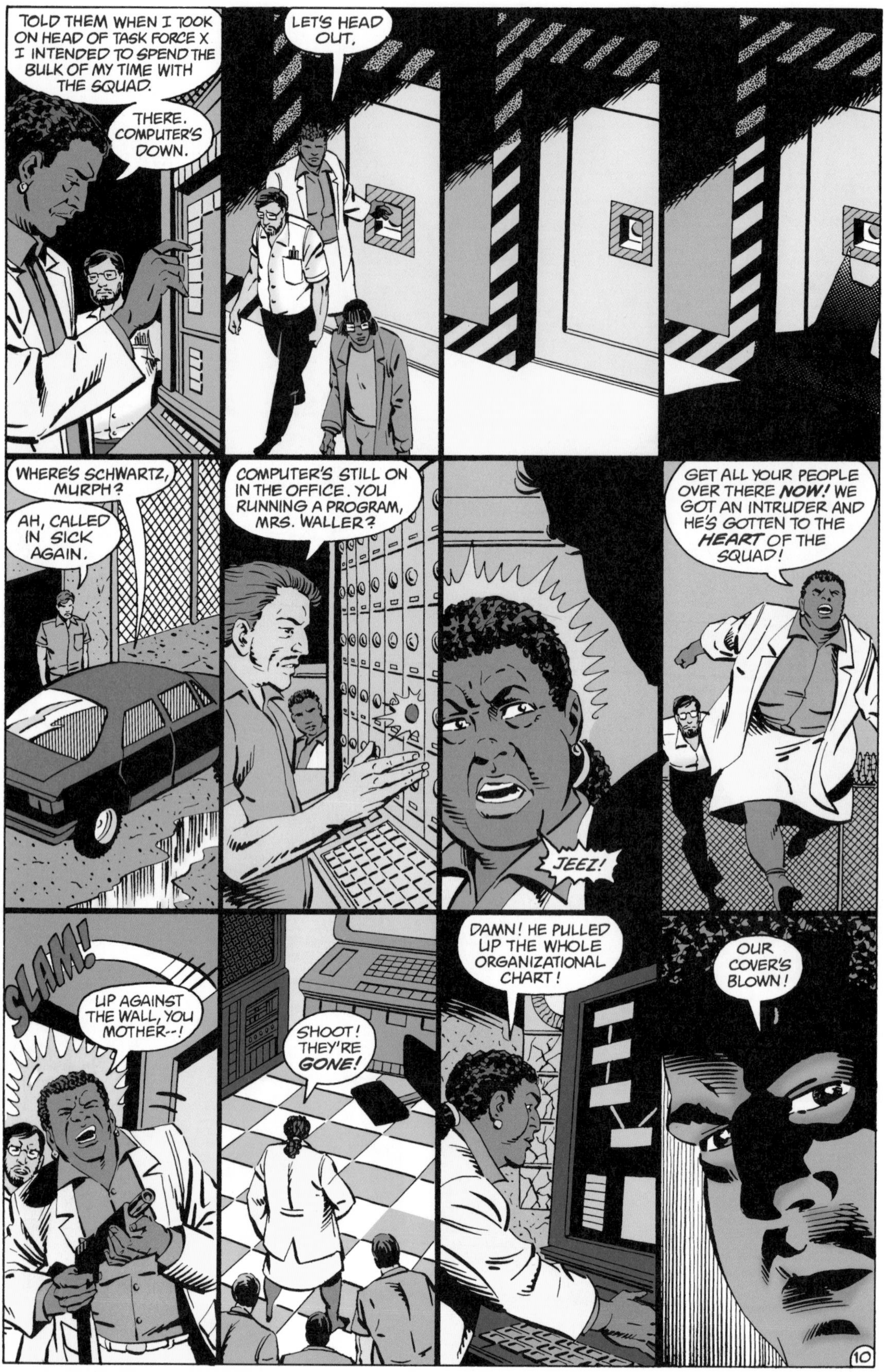
TOLD THEM WHEN I TOOK ON HEAD OF TASK FORCE X I INTENDED TO SPEND THE BULK OF MY TIME WITH THE SQUAD.
THERE. COMPUTER'S DOWN.
LET'S HEAD OUT.
WHERE'S SCHWARTZ, MURPH?
AH, CALLED IN SICK AGAIN.
COMPUTER'S STILL ON IN THE OFFICE. YOU RUNNING A PROGRAM, MRS. WALLER?
JEEZ!
GET ALL YOUR PEOPLE OVER THERE NOW! WE GOT AN INTRUDER AND HE'S GOTTEN TO THE HEART OF THE SQUAD!
SLAM!
UP AGAINST THE WALL, YOU MOTHER--!
SHOOT! THEY'RE GONE!
DAMN! HE PULLED UP THE WHOLE ORGANIZATIONAL CHART!
OUR COVER'S BLOWN!
10

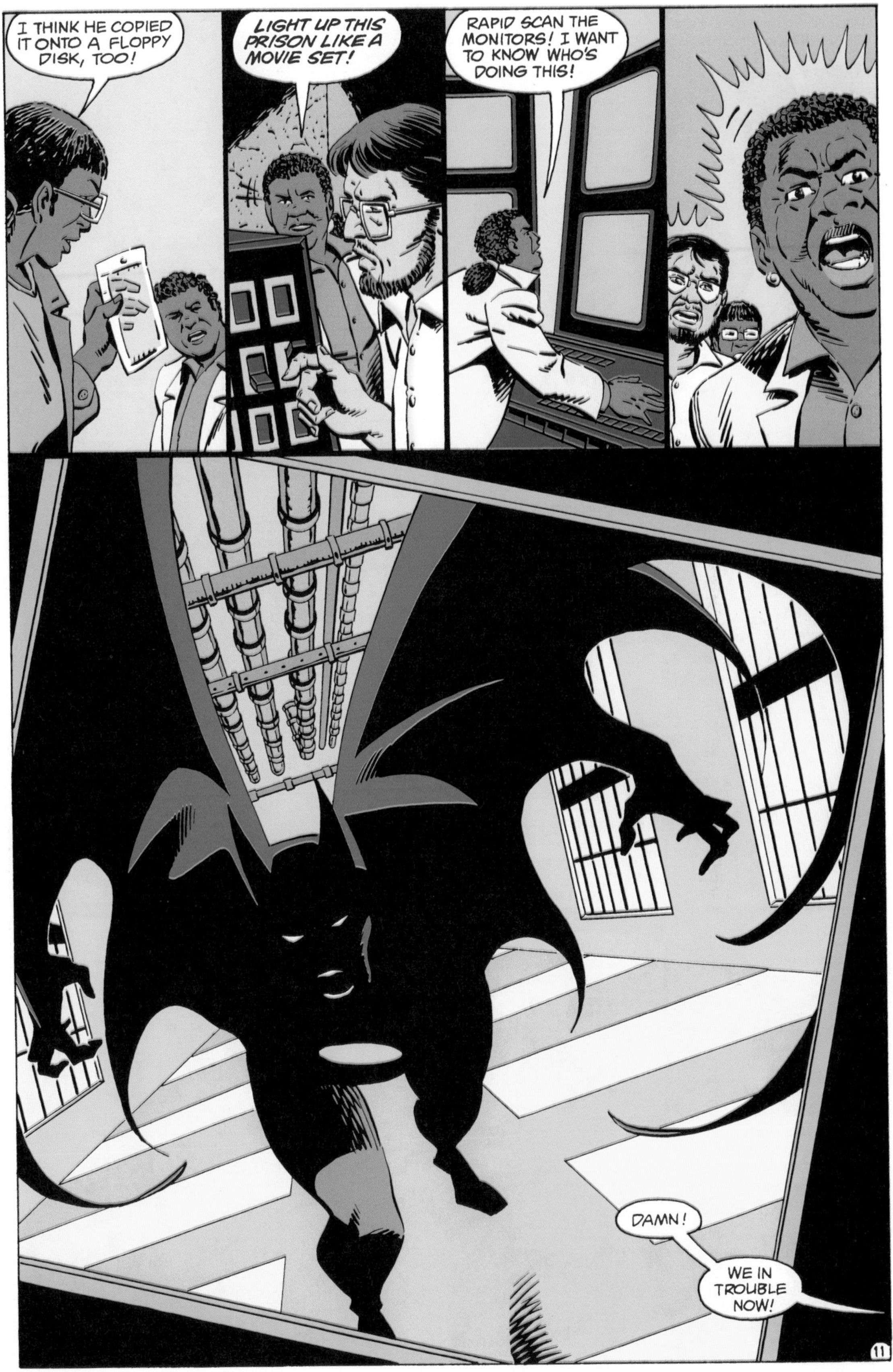
I THINK HE COPIED IT ONTO A FLOPPY DISK, TOO!
LIGHT UP THIS PRISON LIKE A MOVIE SET!
RAPID SCAN THE MONITORS! I WANT TO KNOW WHO'S DOING THIS!
DAMN!
WE IN TROUBLE NOW!

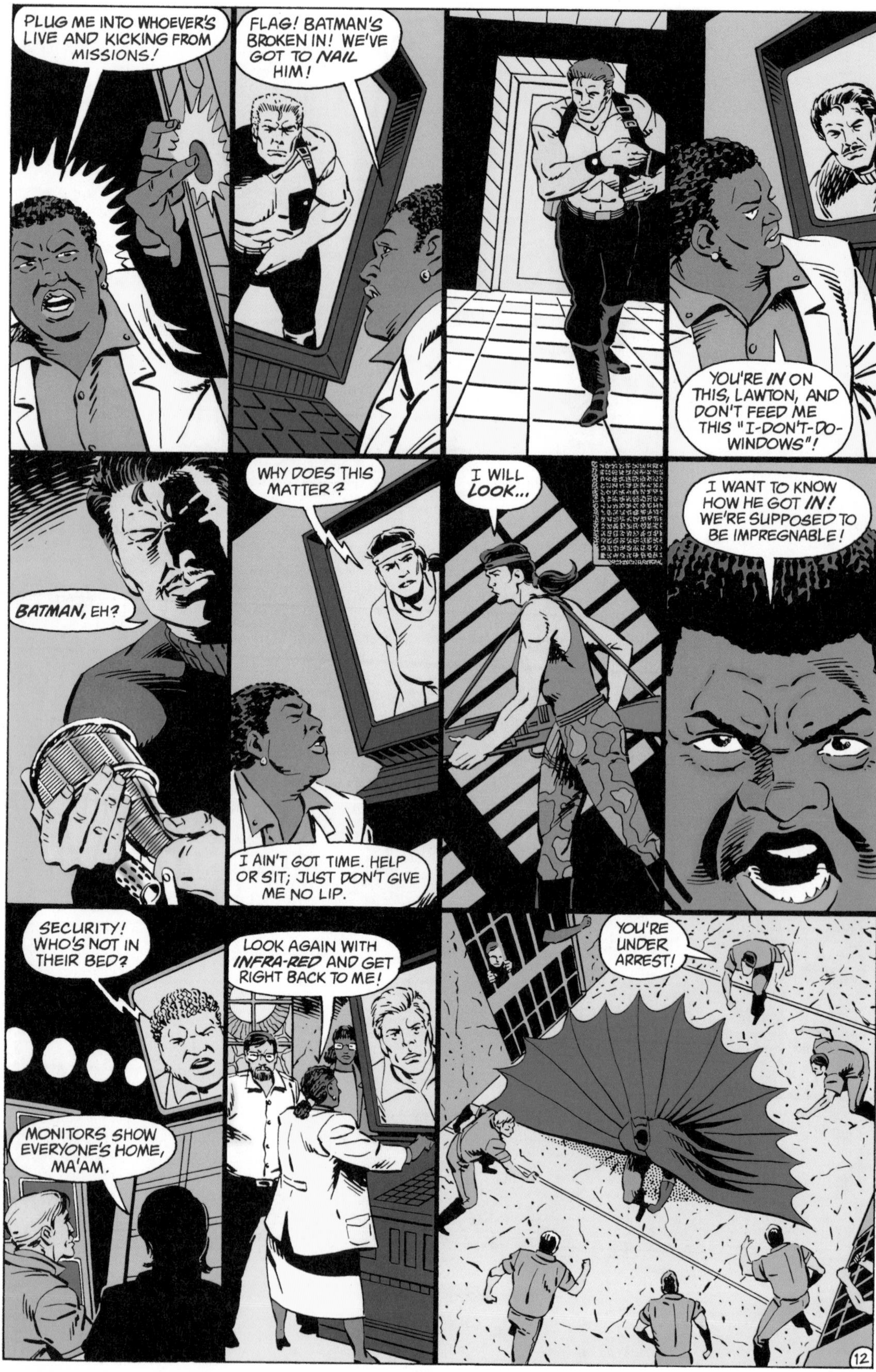
PLUG ME INTO WHOEVER'S LIVE AND KICKING FROM MISSIONS!
FLAG! BATMAN'S BROKEN IN! WE'VE GOT TO NAIL HIM!
YOU'RE IN ON THIS, LAWTON, AND DON'T FEED ME THIS "I-DON'T-DO-WINDOWS"!
BATMAN, EH?
WHY DOES THIS MATTER?
I AIN'T GOT TIME. HELP OR SIT; JUST DON'T GIVE ME NO LIP.
I WILL LOOK...
I WANT TO KNOW HOW HE GOT IN! WE'RE SUPPOSED TO BE IMPREGNABLE!
SECURITY! WHO'S NOT IN THEIR BED?
MONITORS SHOW EVERYONE'S HOME, MA'AM.
LOOK AGAIN WITH INFRA-RED AND GET RIGHT BACK TO ME!
YOU'RE UNDER ARREST!

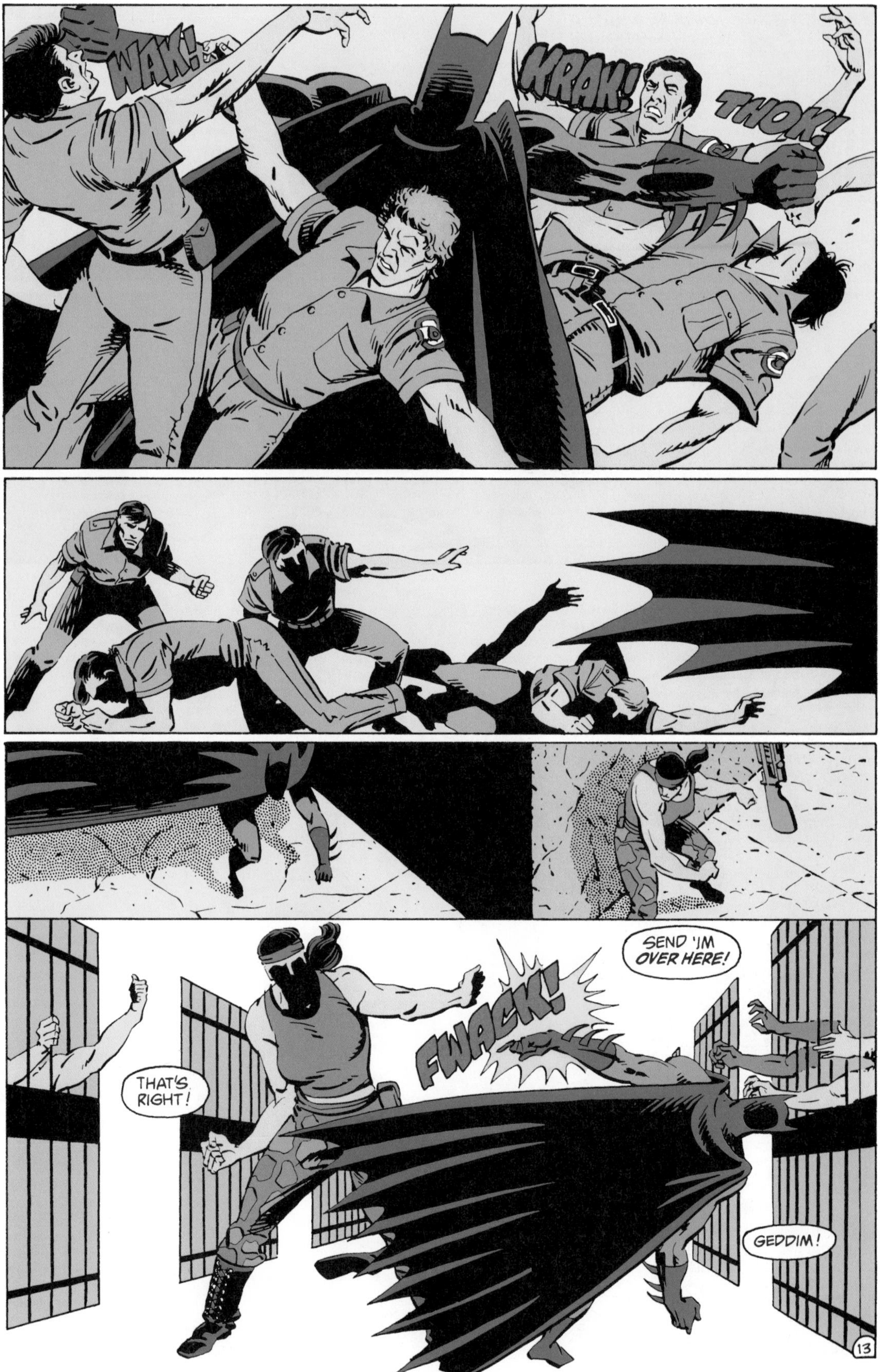
WAK!
KRAK!
THOK!
SEND 'IM OVER HERE!
FWACK!
THAT'S RIGHT!
GEDDIM!
13

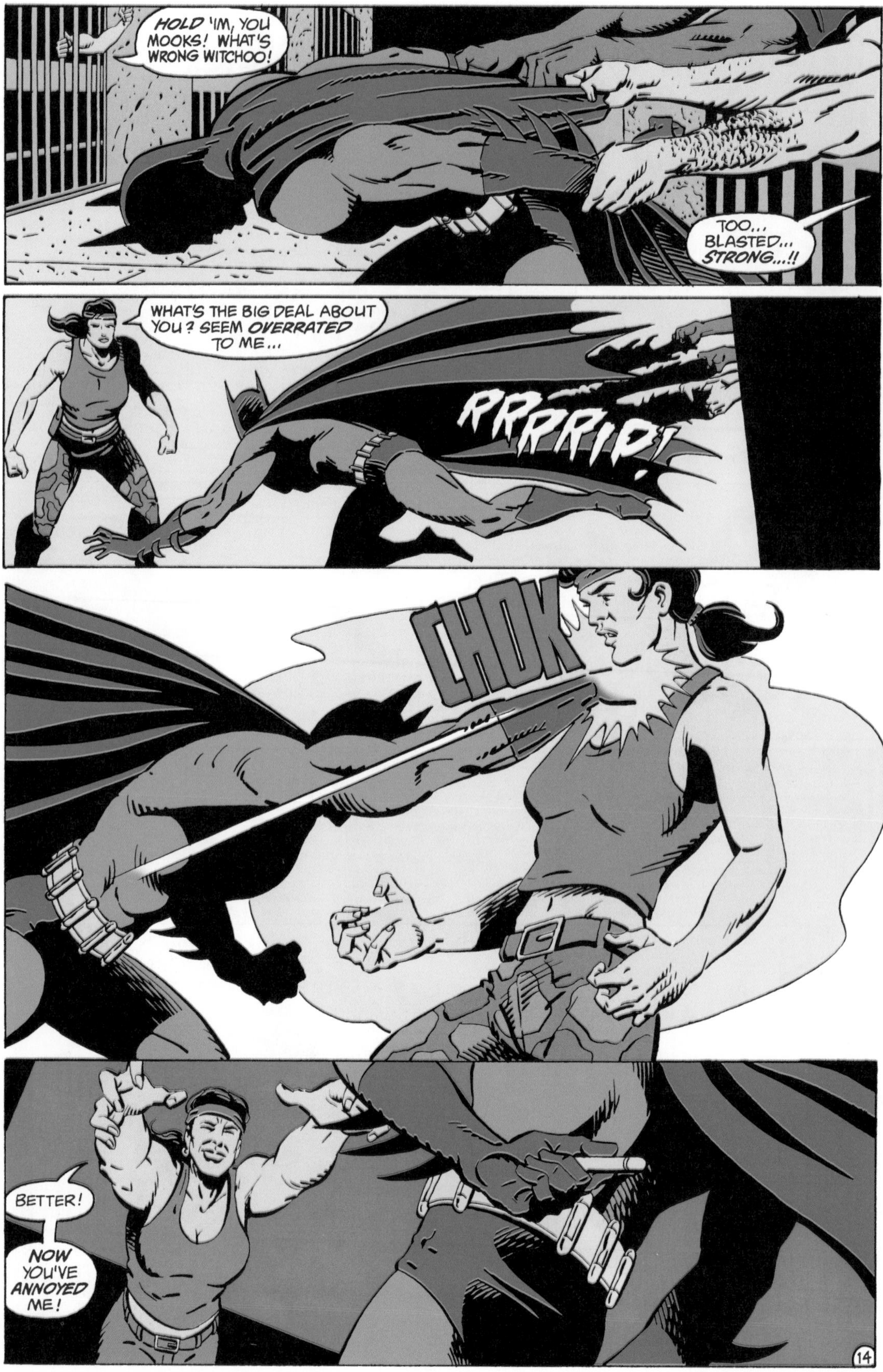

HOLD 'IM, YOU MOOKS! WHAT'S WRONG WITCHOO!
TOO... BLASTED... STRONG...!!
WHAT'S THE BIG DEAL ABOUT YOU? SEEM OVERRATED TO ME...
RRRRIP!
CHOK
BETTER!
NOW YOU'VE ANNOYED ME!

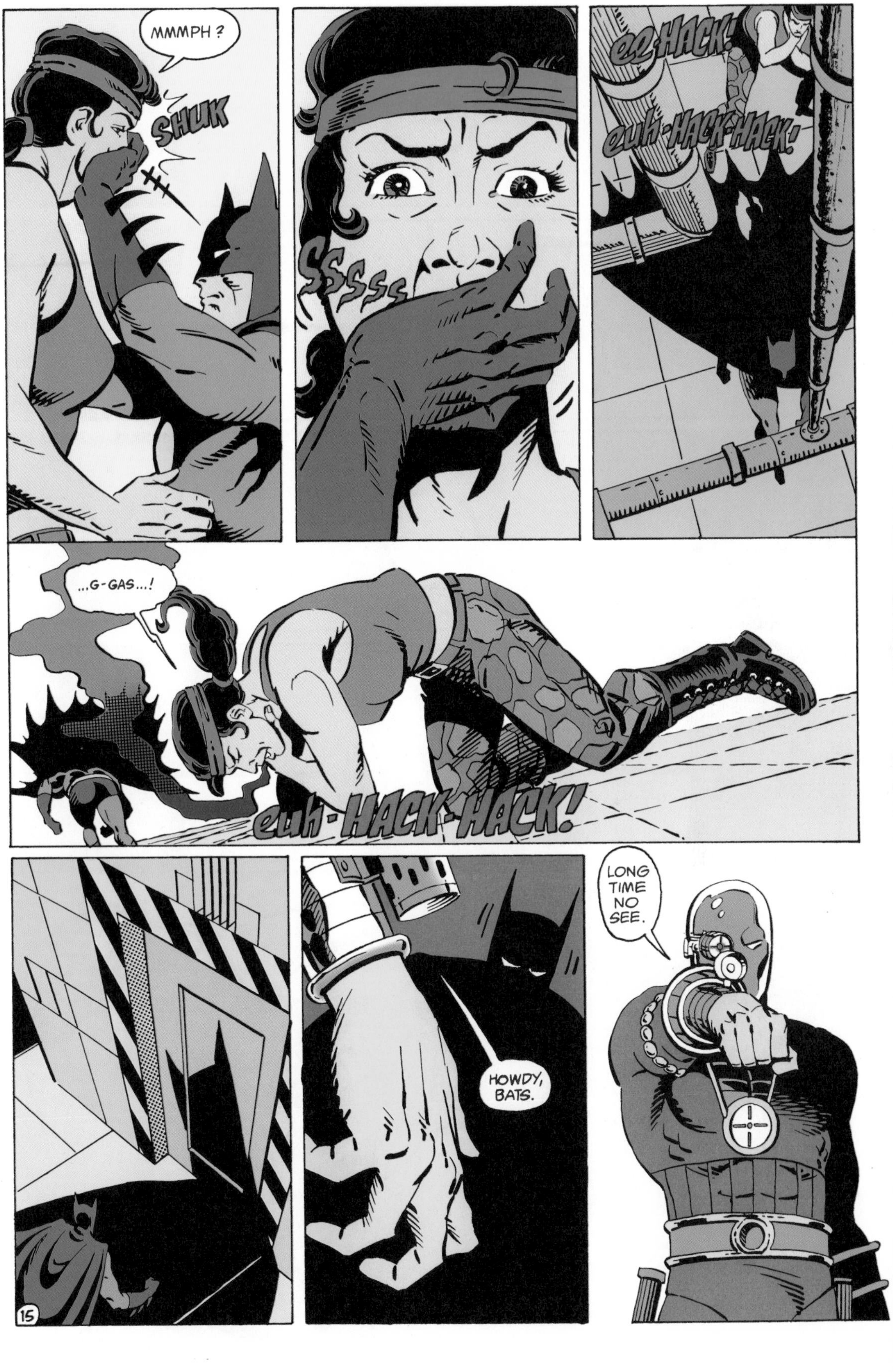
MMMPH ?
SHUK
SSsss
ee-HACK!
euh-HACK-HACK!
...G-GAS...!
euh-HACK-HACK!
HOWDY, BATS.
LONG TIME NO SEE.
15

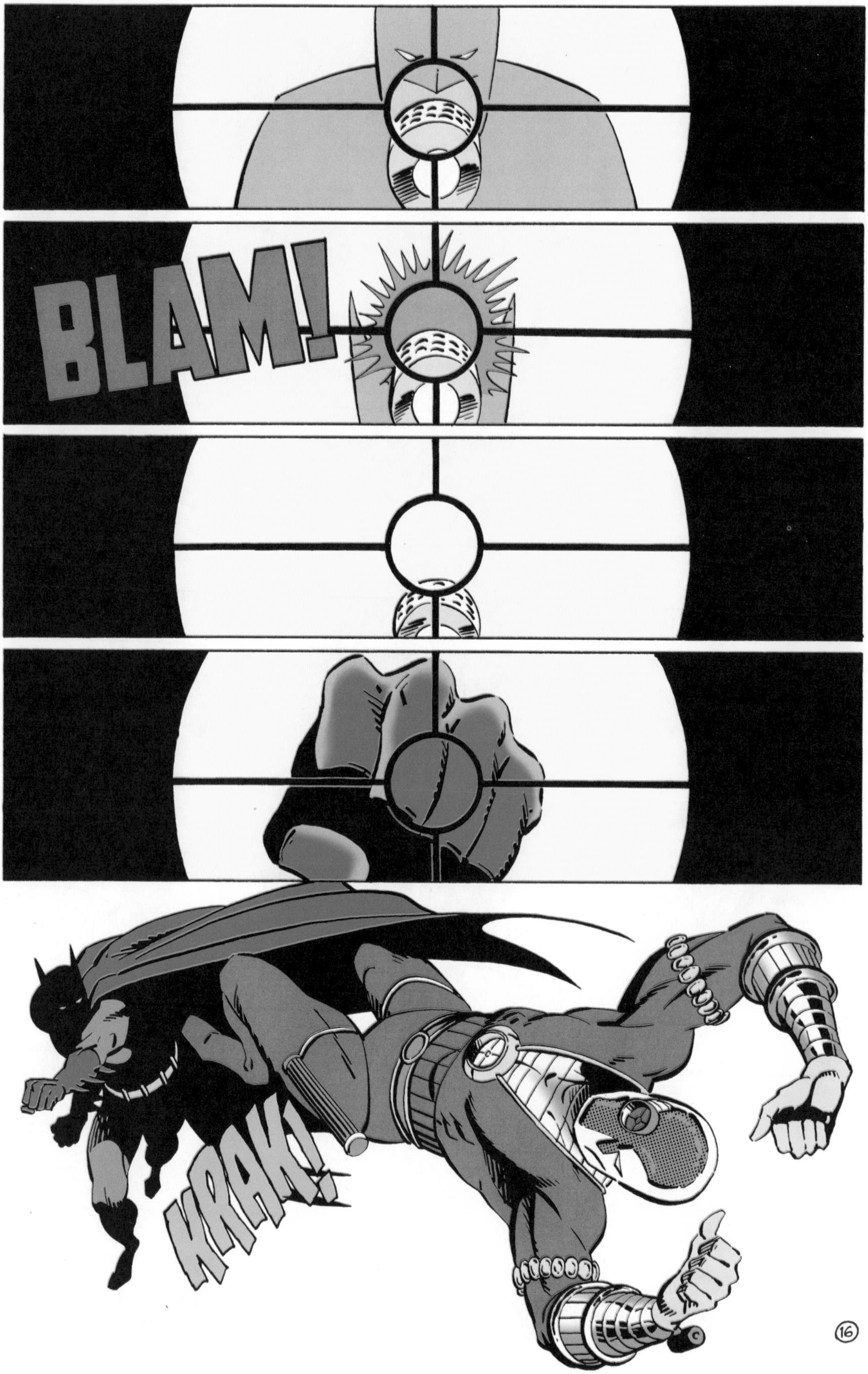
BLAM!
KRAK!

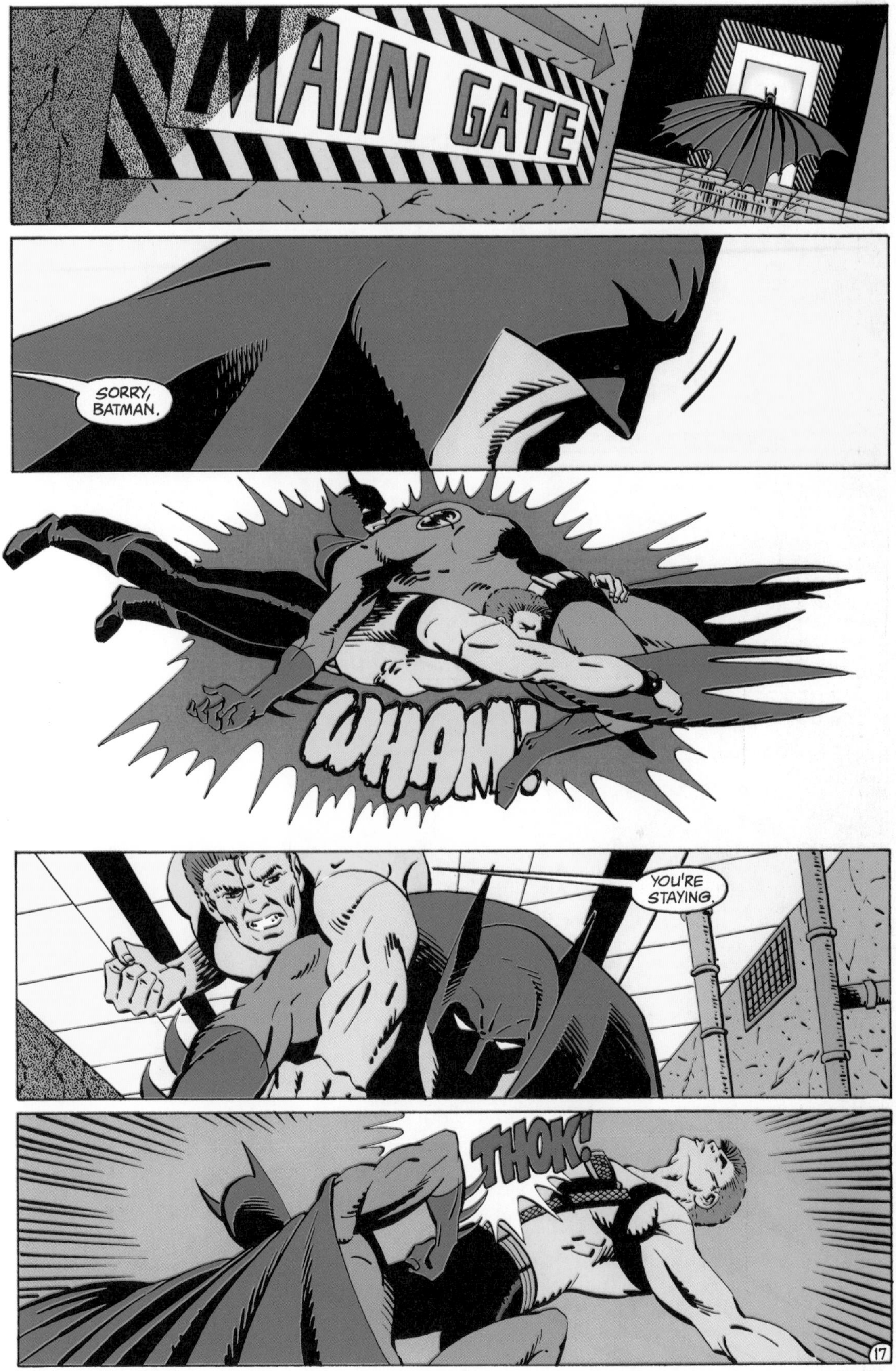
MAIN GATE
SORRY, BATMAN.
WHAM!
YOU'RE STAYING.
THOK!

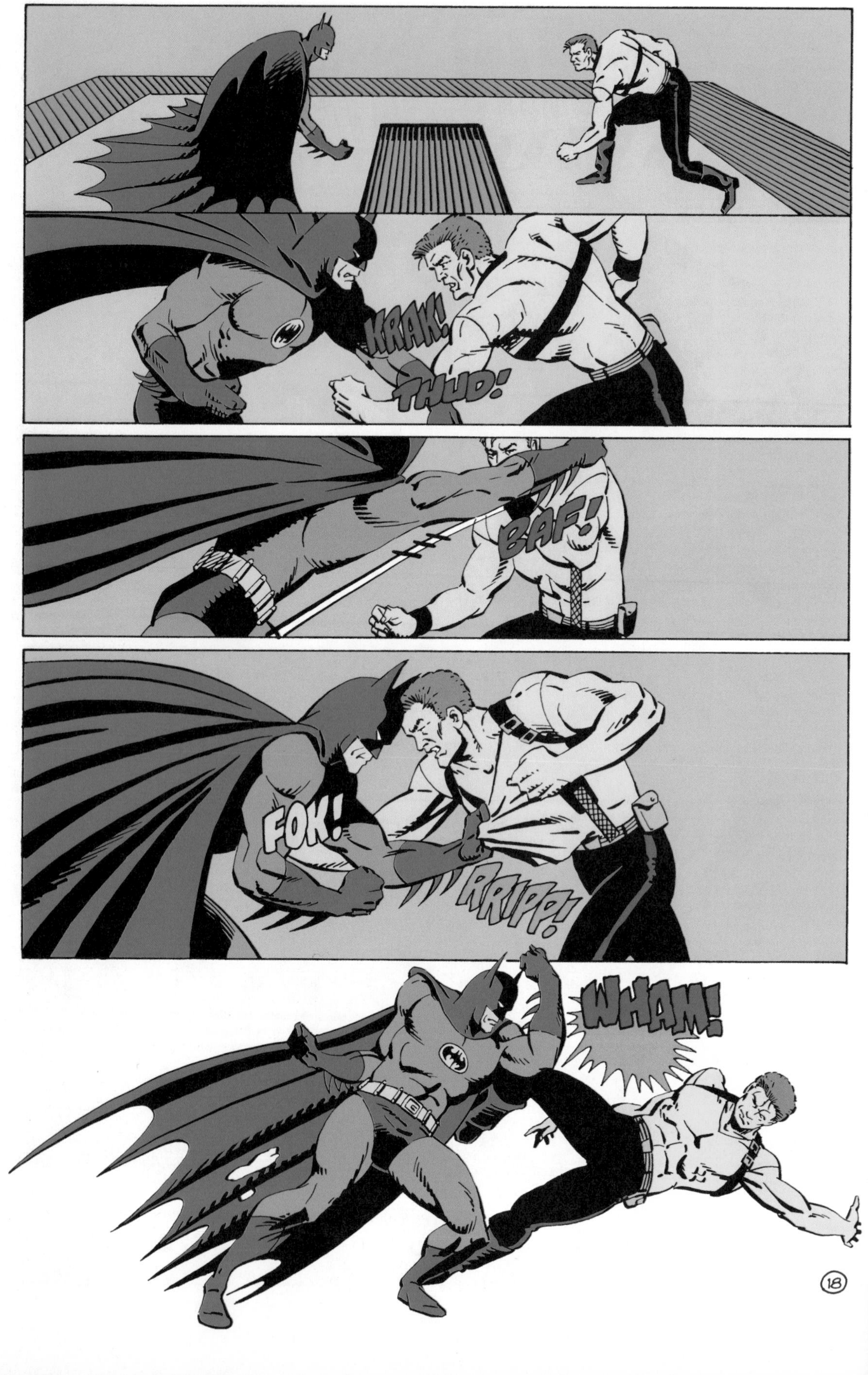
KRAK!
THUD!
BAF!
FOK!
RRIPP!
WHAM!

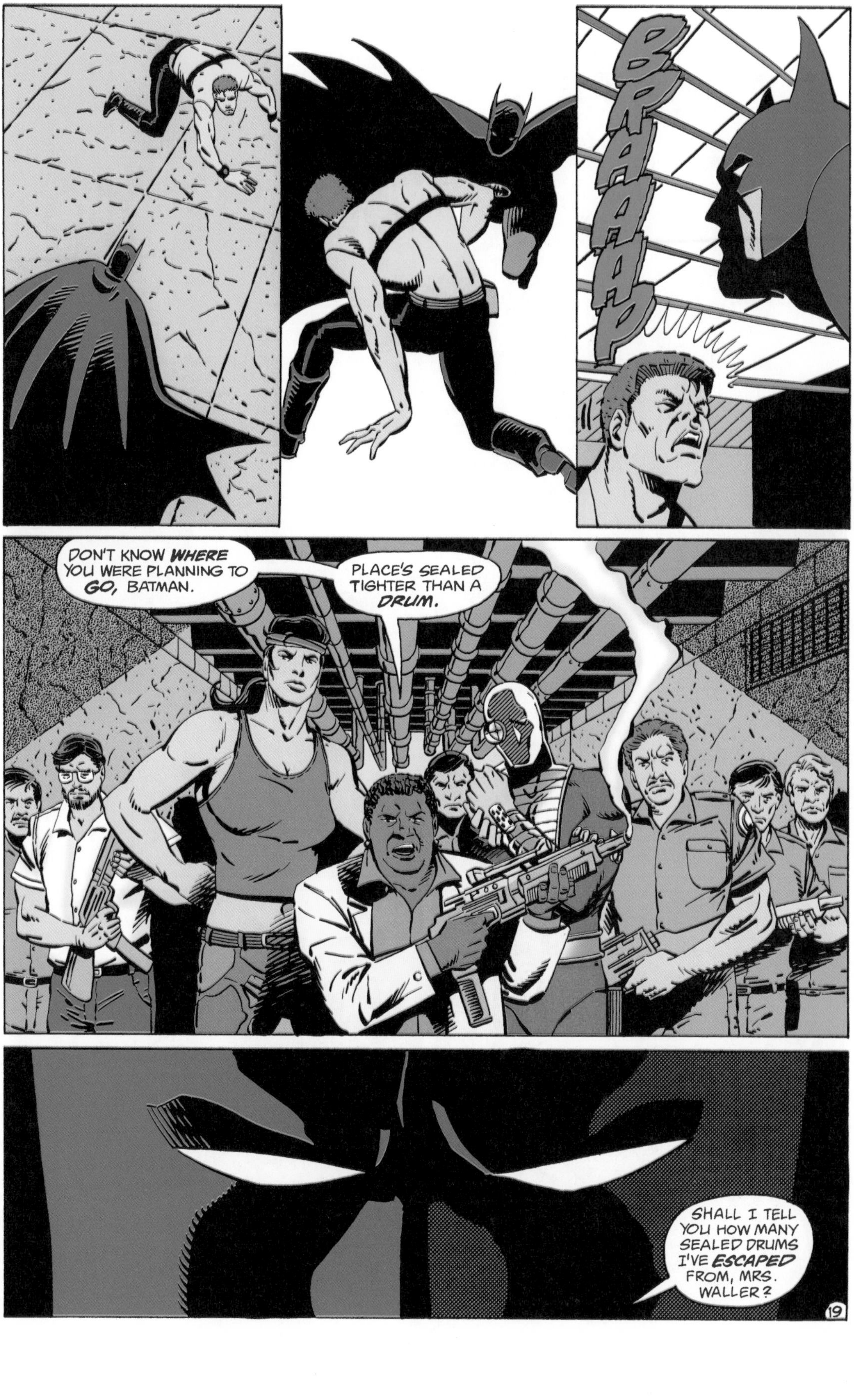
BRAAAP
DON'T KNOW WHERE YOU WERE PLANNING TO GO, BATMAN.
PLACE'S SEALED TIGHTER THAN A DRUM.
SHALL I TELL YOU HOW MANY SEALED DRUMS I'VE ESCAPED FROM, MRS. WALLER?

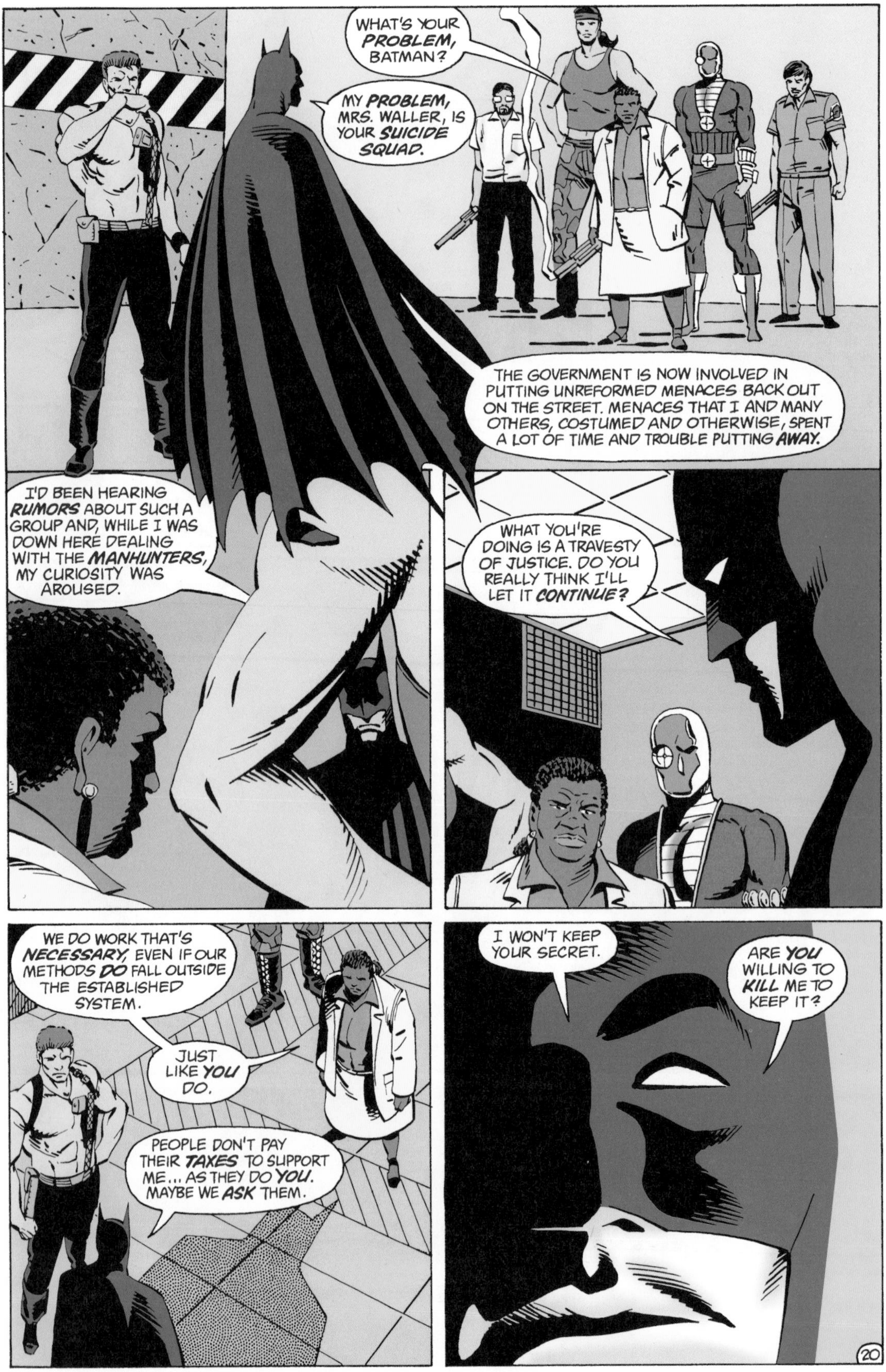
WHAT'S YOUR PROBLEM, BATMAN?
MY PROBLEM, MRS. WALLER, IS YOUR SUICIDE SQUAD.
THE GOVERNMENT IS NOW INVOLVED IN PUTTING UNREFORMED MENACES BACK OUT ON THE STREET. MENACES THAT I AND MANY OTHERS, COSTUMED AND OTHERWISE, SPENT A LOT OF TIME AND TROUBLE PUTTING AWAY.
I'D BEEN HEARING RUMORS ABOUT SUCH A GROUP AND, WHILE I WAS DOWN HERE DEALING WITH THE MANHUNTERS, MY CURIOSITY WAS AROUSED.
WHAT YOU'RE DOING IS A TRAVESTY OF JUSTICE. DO YOU REALLY THINK I'LL LET IT CONTINUE?
WE DO WORK THAT'S NECESSARY, EVEN IF OUR METHODS DO FALL OUTSIDE THE ESTABLISHED SYSTEM.
JUST LIKE YOU DO.
PEOPLE DON'T PAY THEIR TAXES TO SUPPORT ME... AS THEY DO YOU. MAYBE WE ASK THEM.
I WON'T KEEP YOUR SECRET.
ARE YOU WILLING TO KILL ME TO KEEP IT?
20

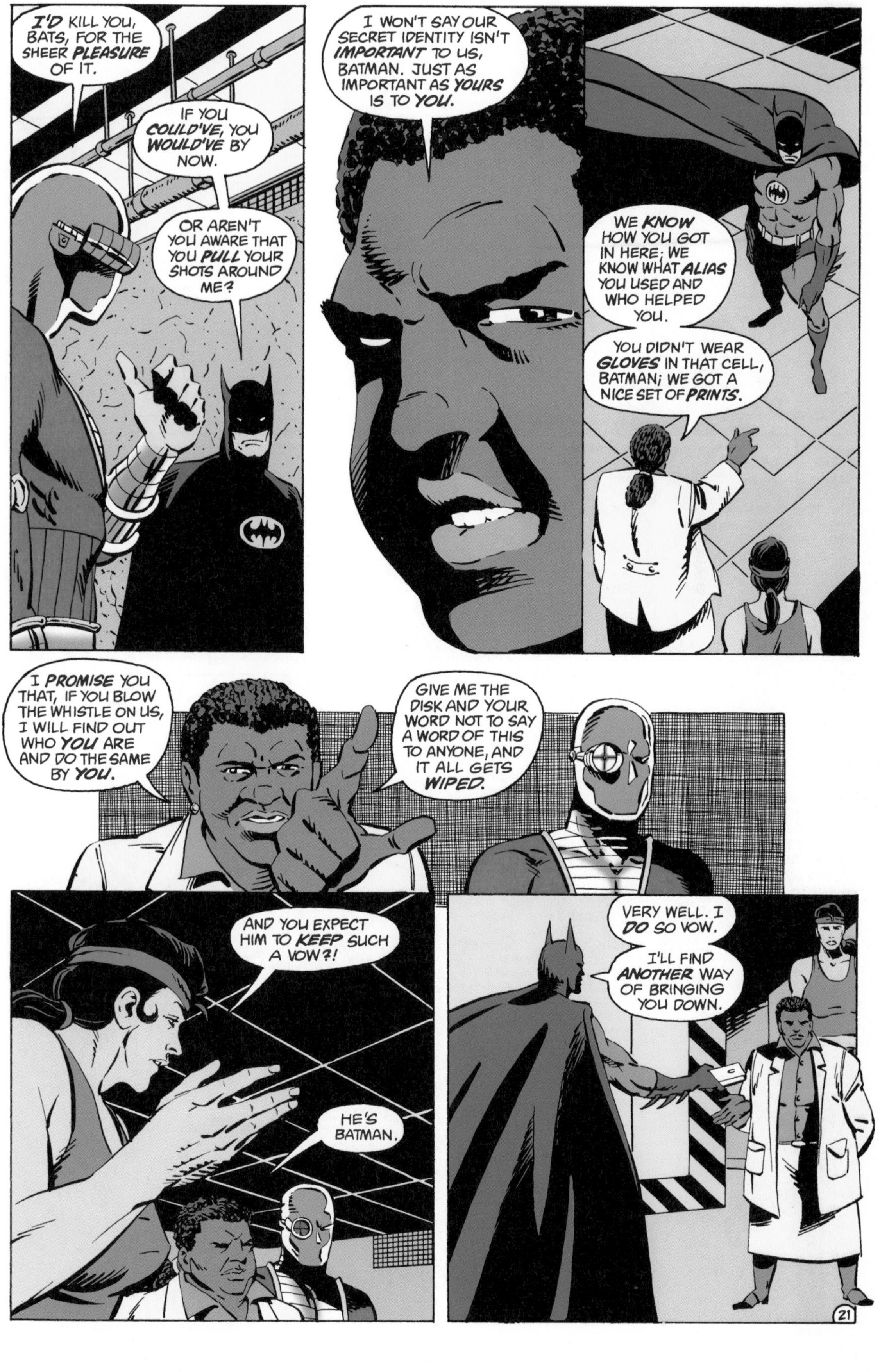
I'D KILL YOU, BATS, FOR THE SHEER PLEASURE OF IT.
IF YOU COULD'VE, YOU WOULD'VE BY NOW.
OR AREN'T YOU AWARE THAT YOU PULL YOUR SHOTS AROUND ME?
I WON'T SAY OUR SECRET IDENTITY ISN'T IMPORTANT TO US, BATMAN. JUST AS IMPORTANT AS YOURS IS TO YOU.
WE KNOW HOW YOU GOT IN HERE; WE KNOW WHAT ALIAS YOU USED AND WHO HELPED YOU.
YOU DIDN'T WEAR GLOVES IN THAT CELL, BATMAN; WE GOT A NICE SET OF PRINTS.
I PROMISE YOU THAT, IF YOU BLOW THE WHISTLE ON US, I WILL FIND OUT WHO YOU ARE AND DO THE SAME BY YOU.
GIVE ME THE DISK AND YOUR WORD NOT TO SAY A WORD OF THIS TO ANYONE, AND IT ALL GETS WIPED.
AND YOU EXPECT HIM TO KEEP SUCH A VOW?!
HE'S BATMAN.
VERY WELL. I DO SO VOW.
I'LL FIND ANOTHER WAY OF BRINGING YOU DOWN.

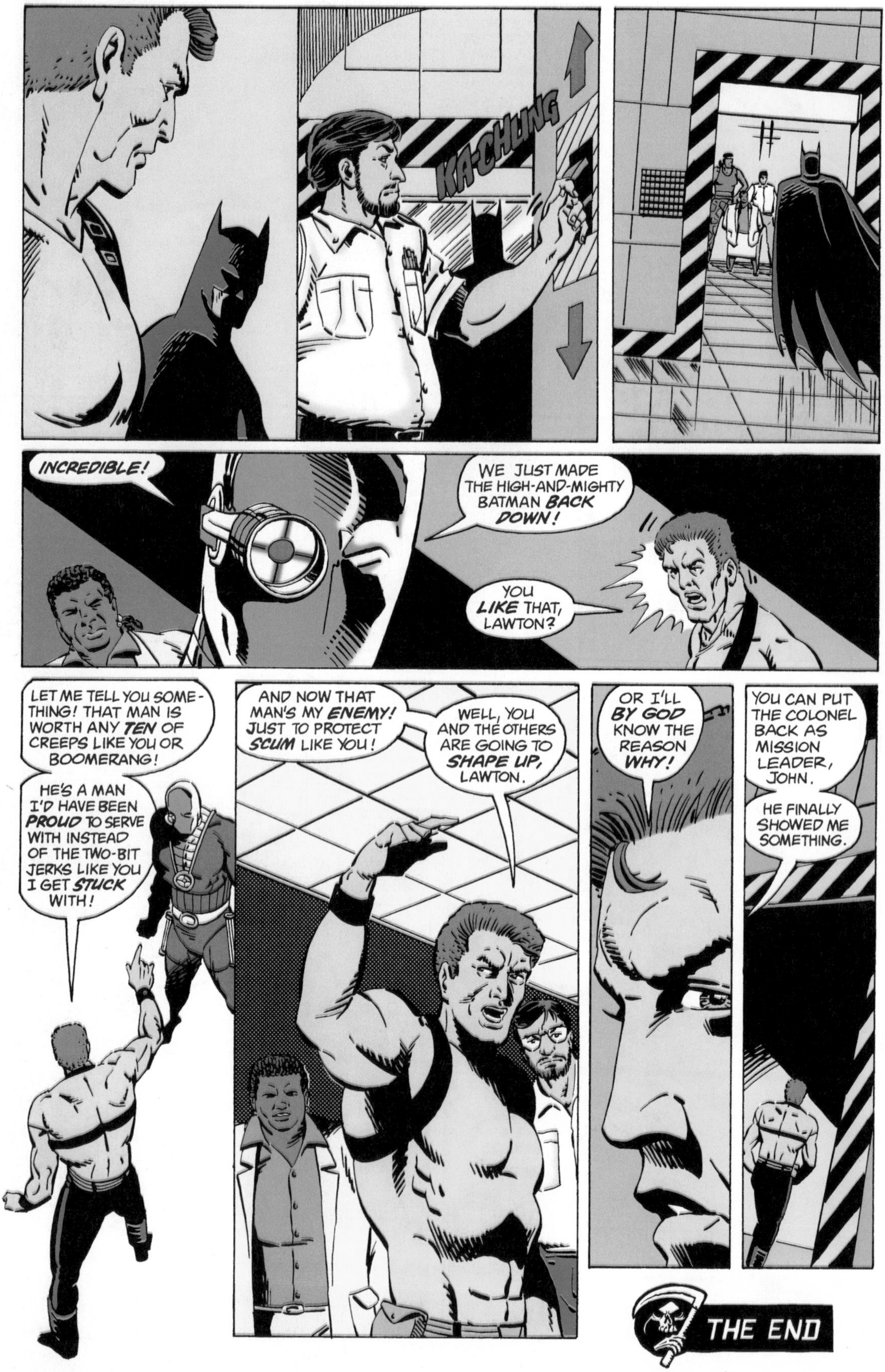
KA-CHUNG
INCREDIBLE!
WE JUST MADE THE HIGH-AND-MIGHTY BATMAN BACK DOWN!
YOU LIKE THAT, LAWTON?
LET ME TELL YOU SOME-THING! THAT MAN IS WORTH ANY TEN OF CREEPS LIKE YOU OR BOOMERANG!
HE'S A MAN I'D HAVE BEEN PROUD TO SERVE WITH INSTEAD OF THE TWO-BIT JERKS LIKE YOU I GET STUCK WITH!
AND NOW THAT MAN'S MY ENEMY! JUST TO PROTECT SCUM LIKE YOU!
WELL, YOU AND THE OTHERS ARE GOING TO SHAPE UP, LAWTON.
OR I'LL BY GOD KNOW THE REASON WHY!
YOU CAN PUT THE COLONEL BACK AS MISSION LEADER, JOHN.
HE FINALLY SHOWED ME SOMETHING.
THE END

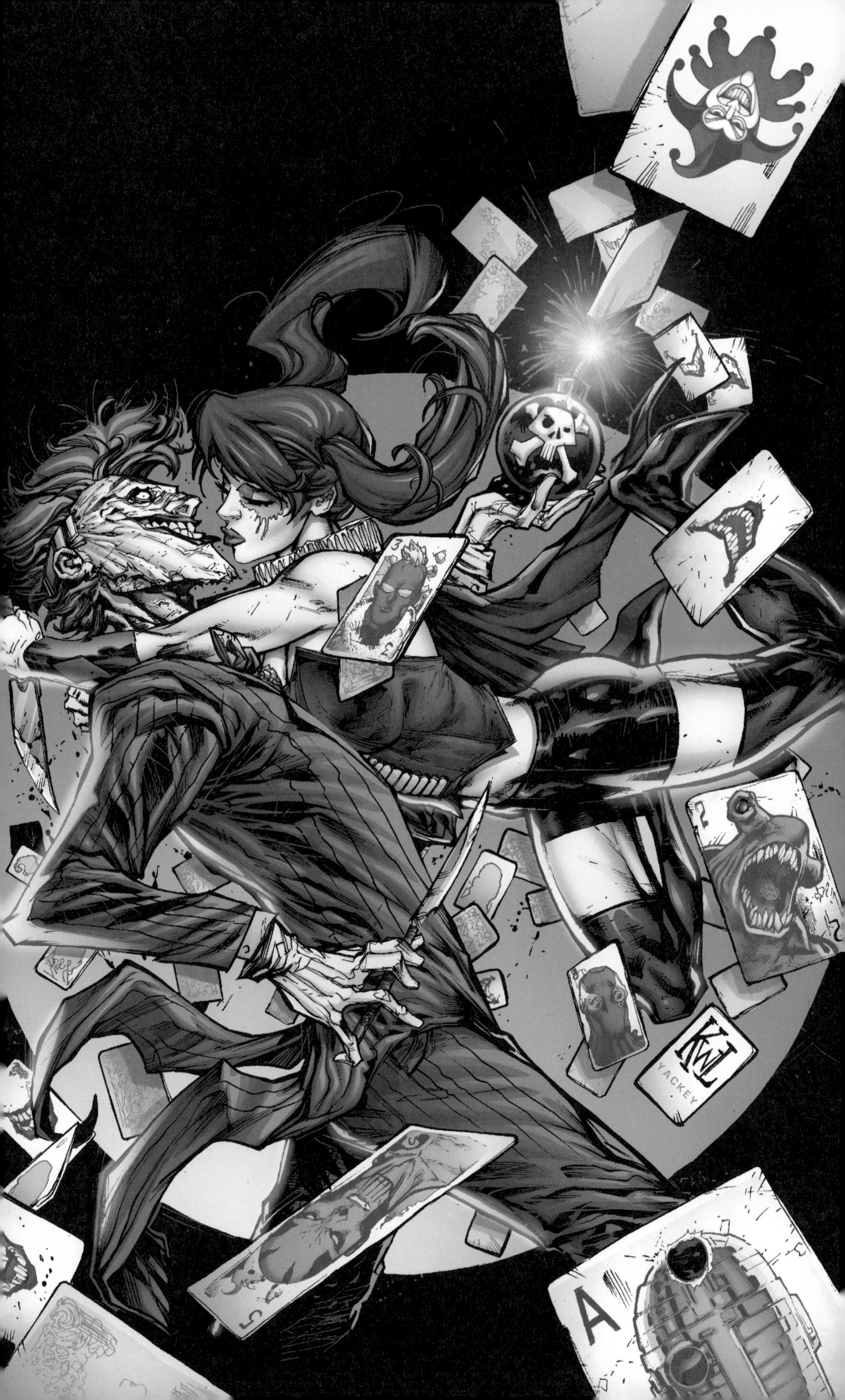
YACKEY

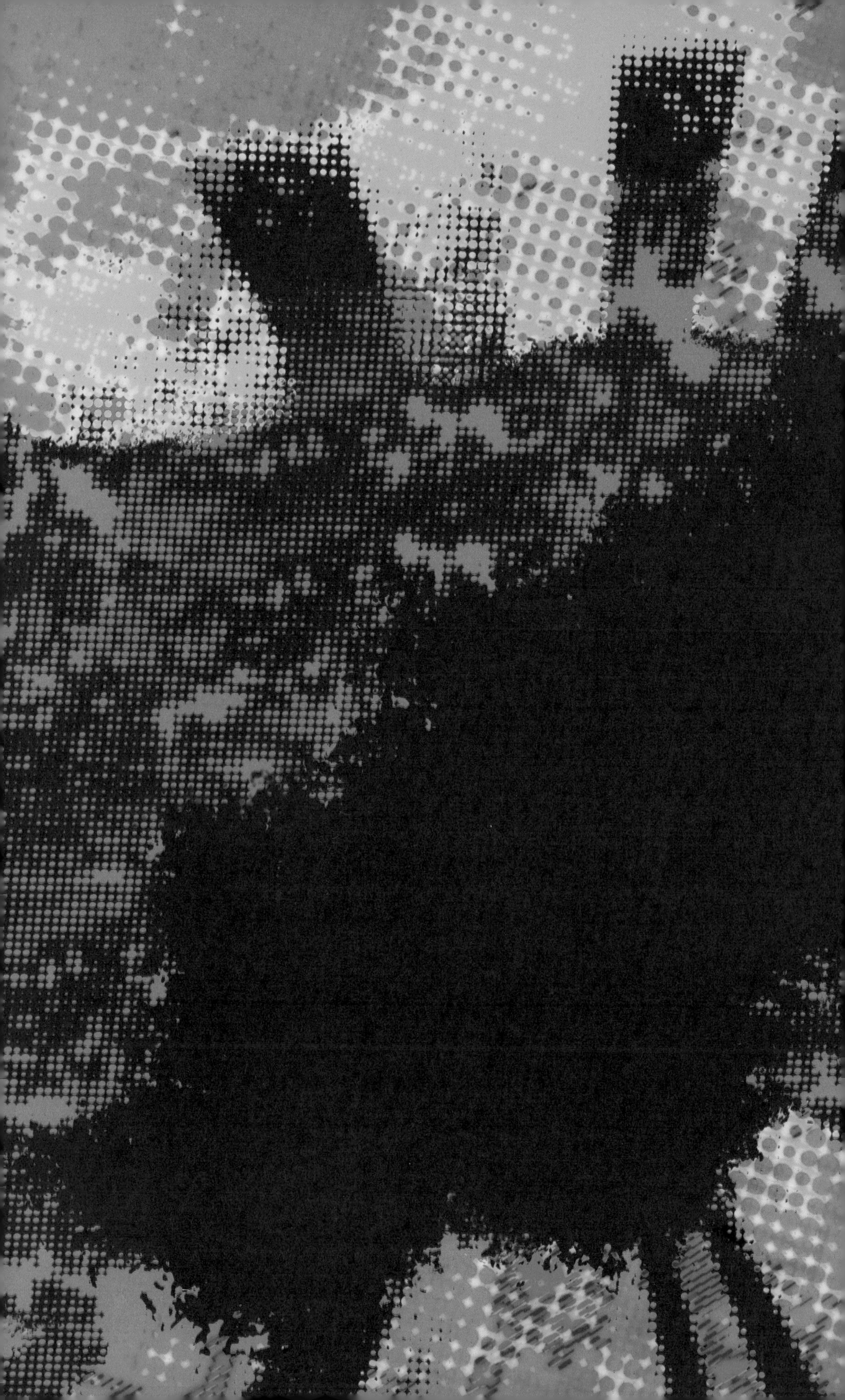

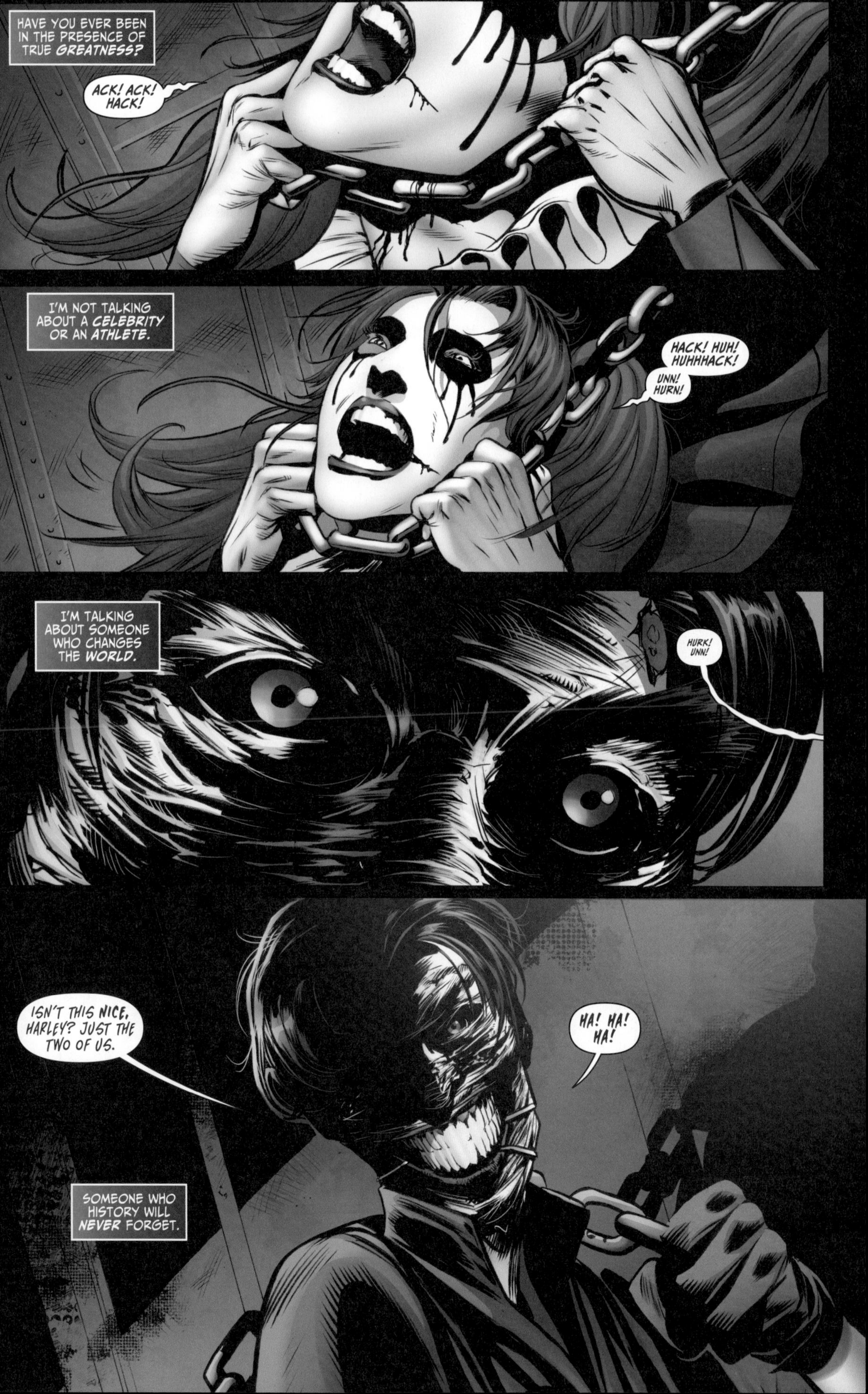
HAVE YOU EVER BEEN IN THE PRESENCE OF TRUE GREATNESS?
ACK! ACK! HACK!
I'M NOT TALKING ABOUT A CELEBRITY OR AN ATHLETE.
HACK! HUH! HUHHHACK!
UNN! HURN!
I'M TALKING ABOUT SOMEONE WHO CHANGES THE WORLD.
HURK! UNN!
ISN'T THIS NICE, HARLEY? JUST THE TWO OF US.
HA! HA! HA!
SOMEONE WHO HISTORY WILL NEVER FORGET.

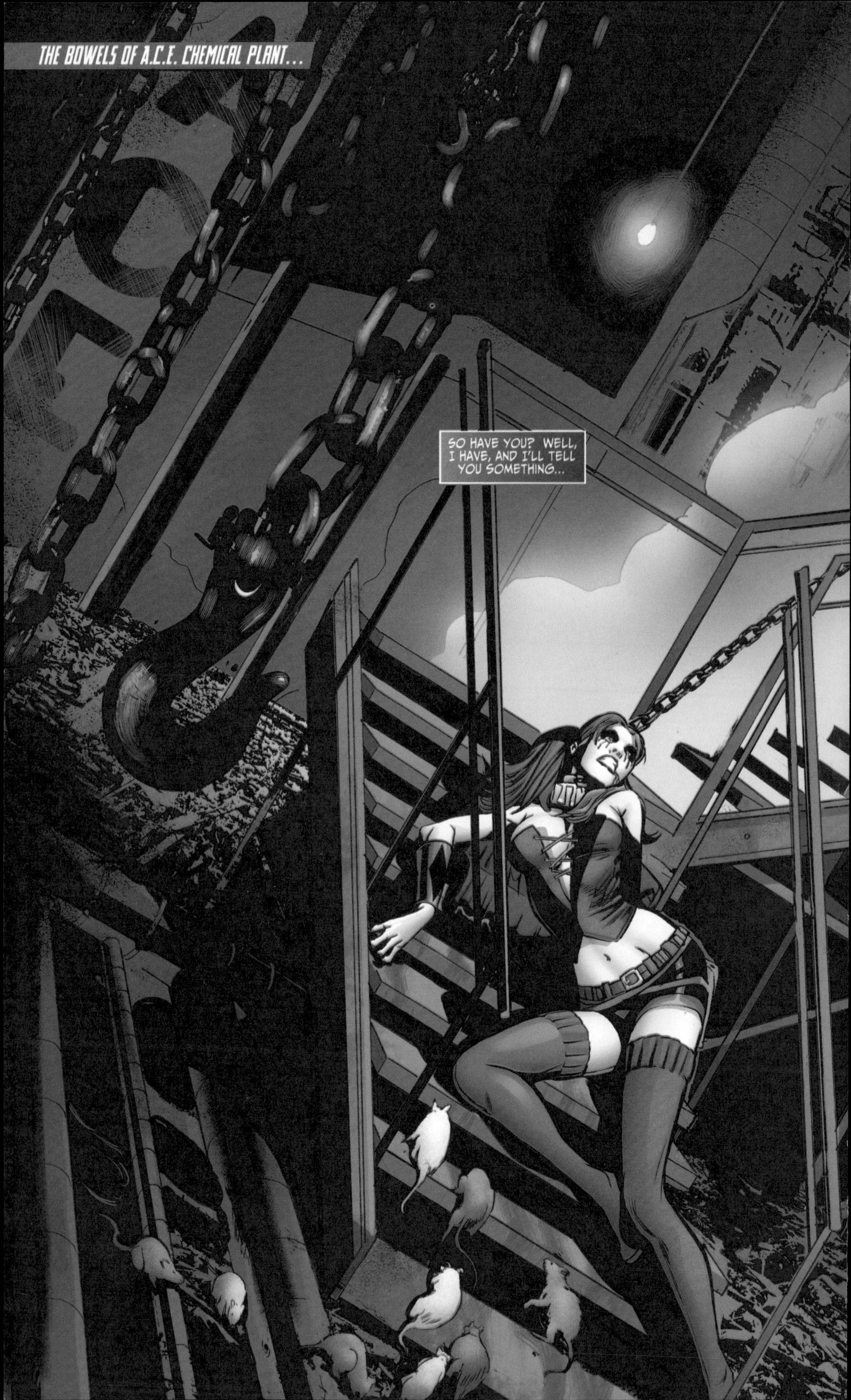
THE BOWELS OF A.C.E. CHEMICAL PLANT...
SO HAVE YOU? WELL, I HAVE, AND I'LL TELL YOU SOMETHING...

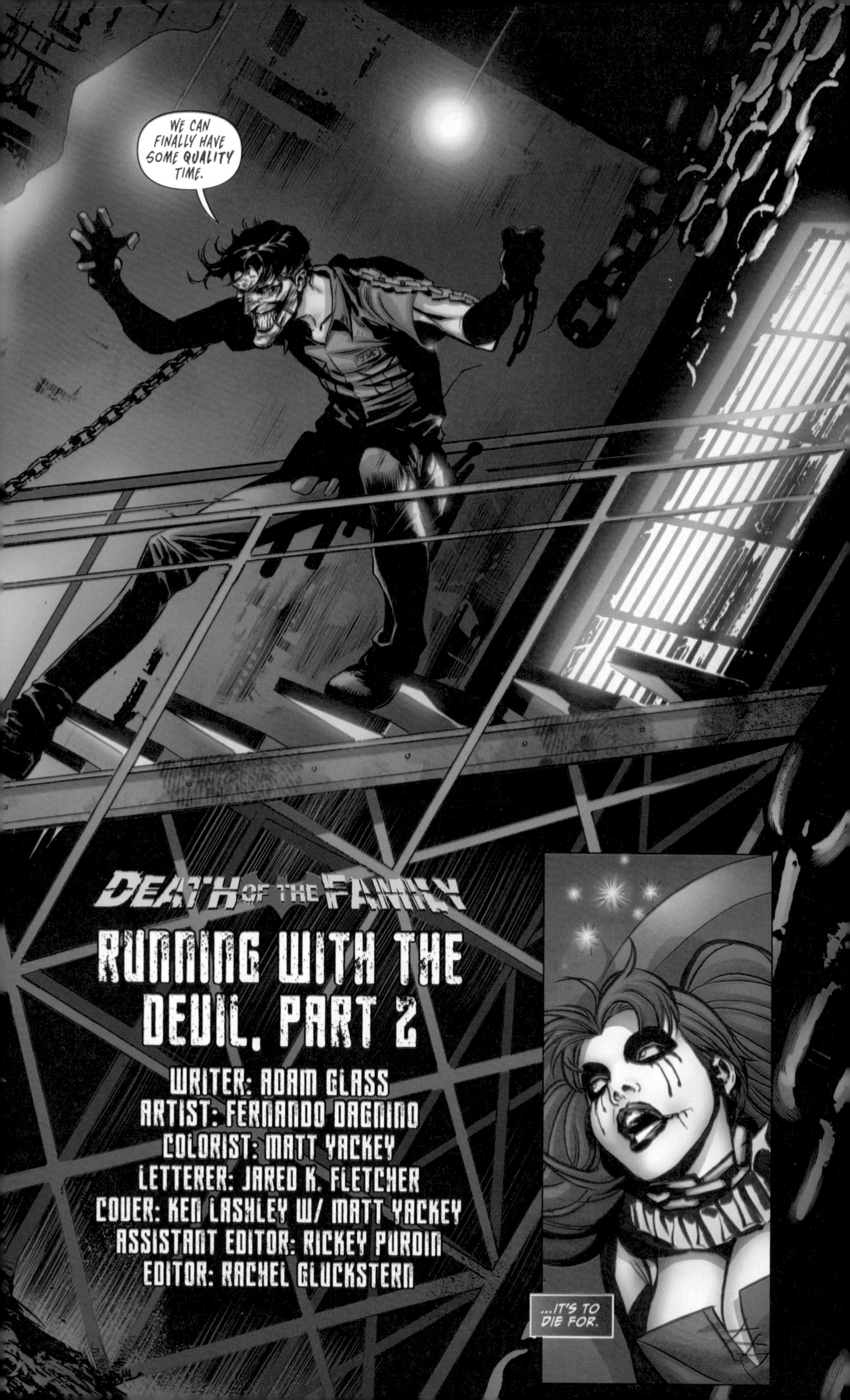
WE CAN FINALLY HAVE SOME QUALITY TIME.
DEATH OF THE FAMILY
RUNNING WITH THE DEVIL, PART 2
WRITER: ADAM GLASS
ARTIST: FERNANDO DAGNINO
COLORIST: MATT YACKEY
LETTERER: JARED K. FLETCHER
COVER: KEN LASHLEY W/ MATT YACKEY
ASSISTANT EDITOR: RICKEY PURDIN
EDITOR: RACHEL GLUCKSTERN
...IT'S TO DIE FOR.

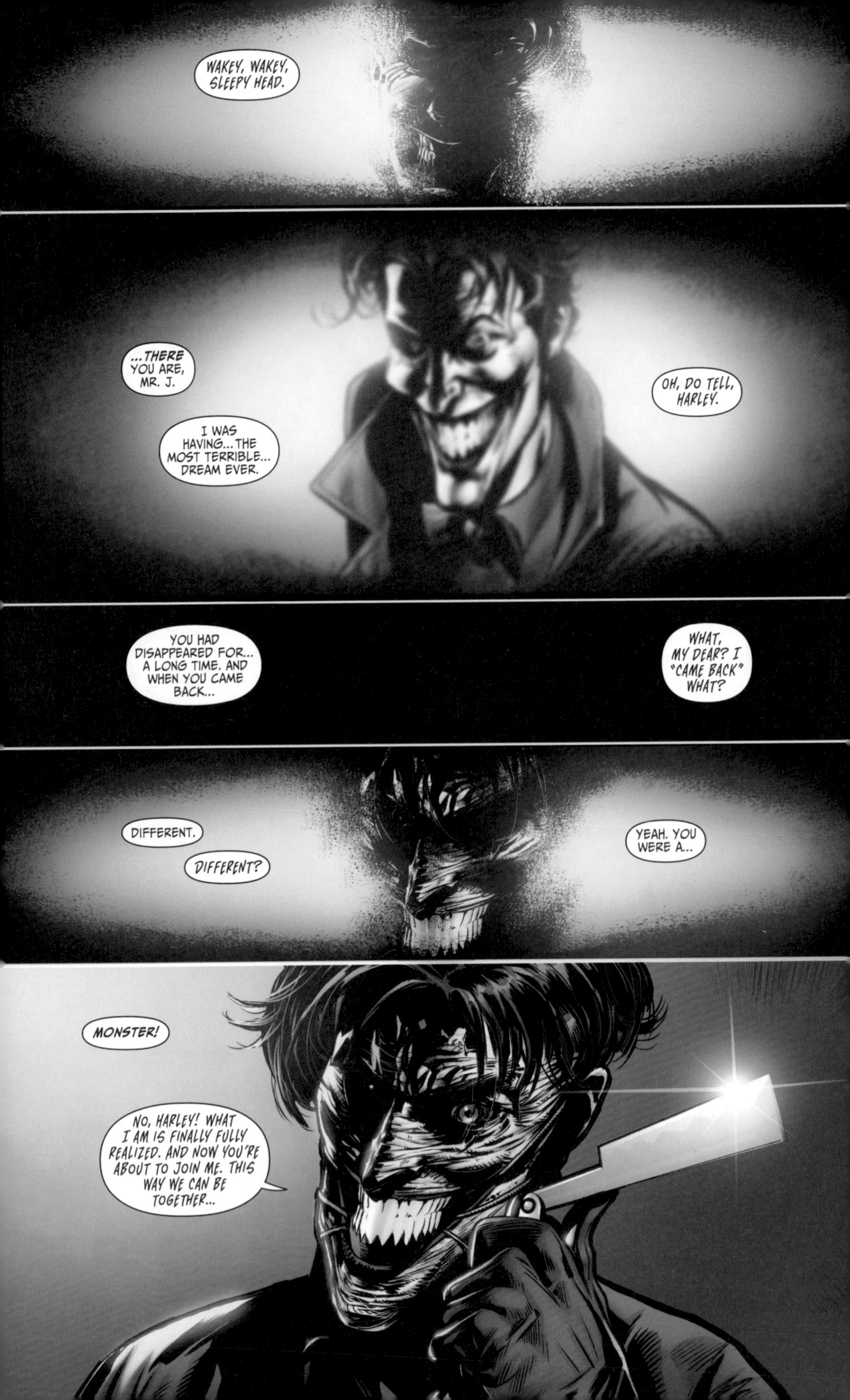
WAKEY, WAKEY, SLEEPY HEAD.
...THERE YOU ARE, MR. J.
I WAS HAVING... THE MOST TERRIBLE... DREAM EVER.
OH, DO TELL, HARLEY.
YOU HAD DISAPPEARED FOR... A LONG TIME. AND WHEN YOU CAME BACK...
WHAT, MY DEAR? I "CAME BACK" WHAT?
DIFFERENT.
DIFFERENT?
YEAH. YOU WERE A...
MONSTER!
NO, HARLEY! WHAT I AM IS FINALLY FULLY REALIZED. AND NOW YOU'RE ABOUT TO JOIN ME. THIS WAY WE CAN BE TOGETHER...

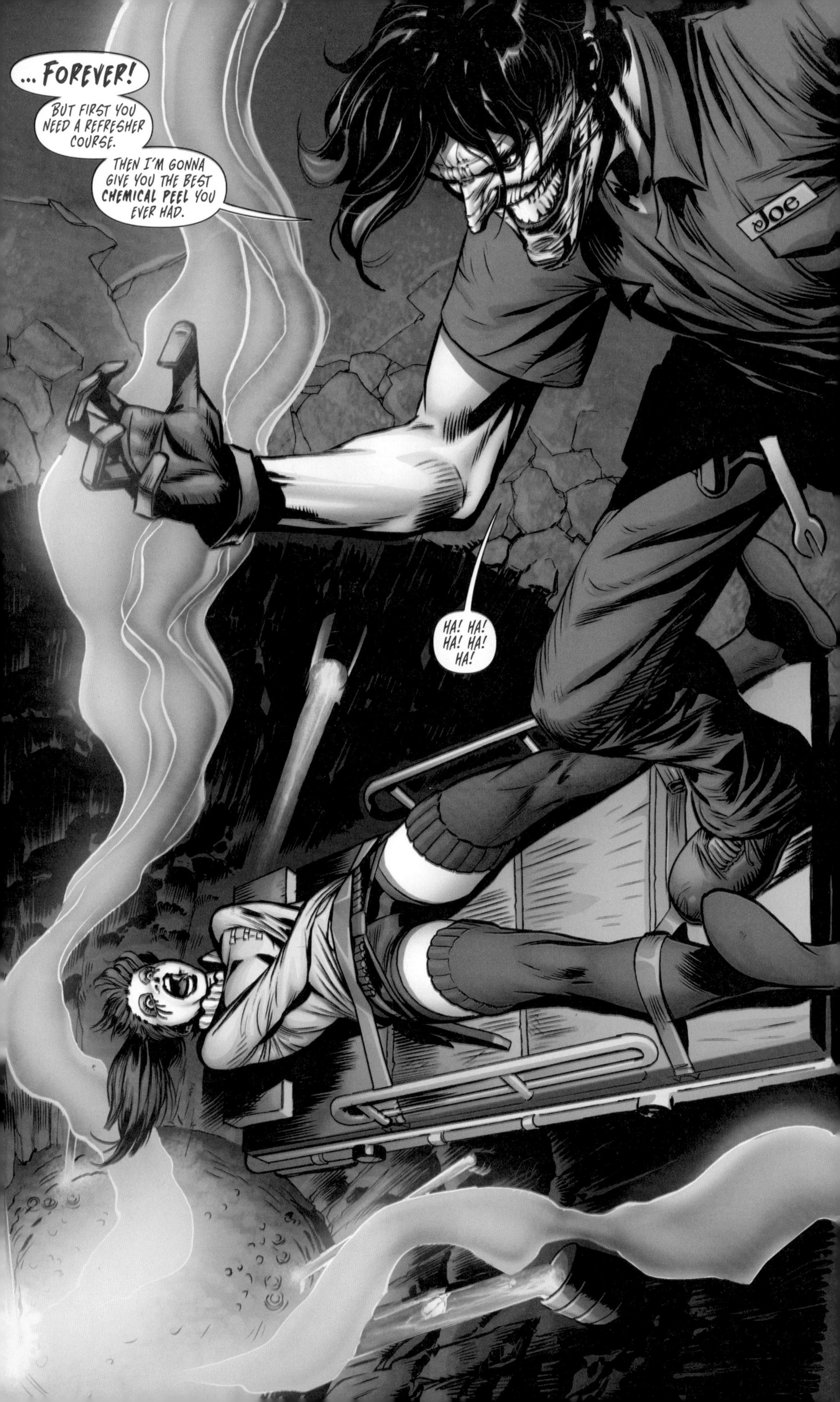
...FOREVER!
BUT FIRST YOU NEED A REFRESHER COURSE.
THEN I'M GONNA GIVE YOU THE BEST CHEMICAL PEEL YOU EVER HAD.
HA! HA! HA! HA! HA!
Joe

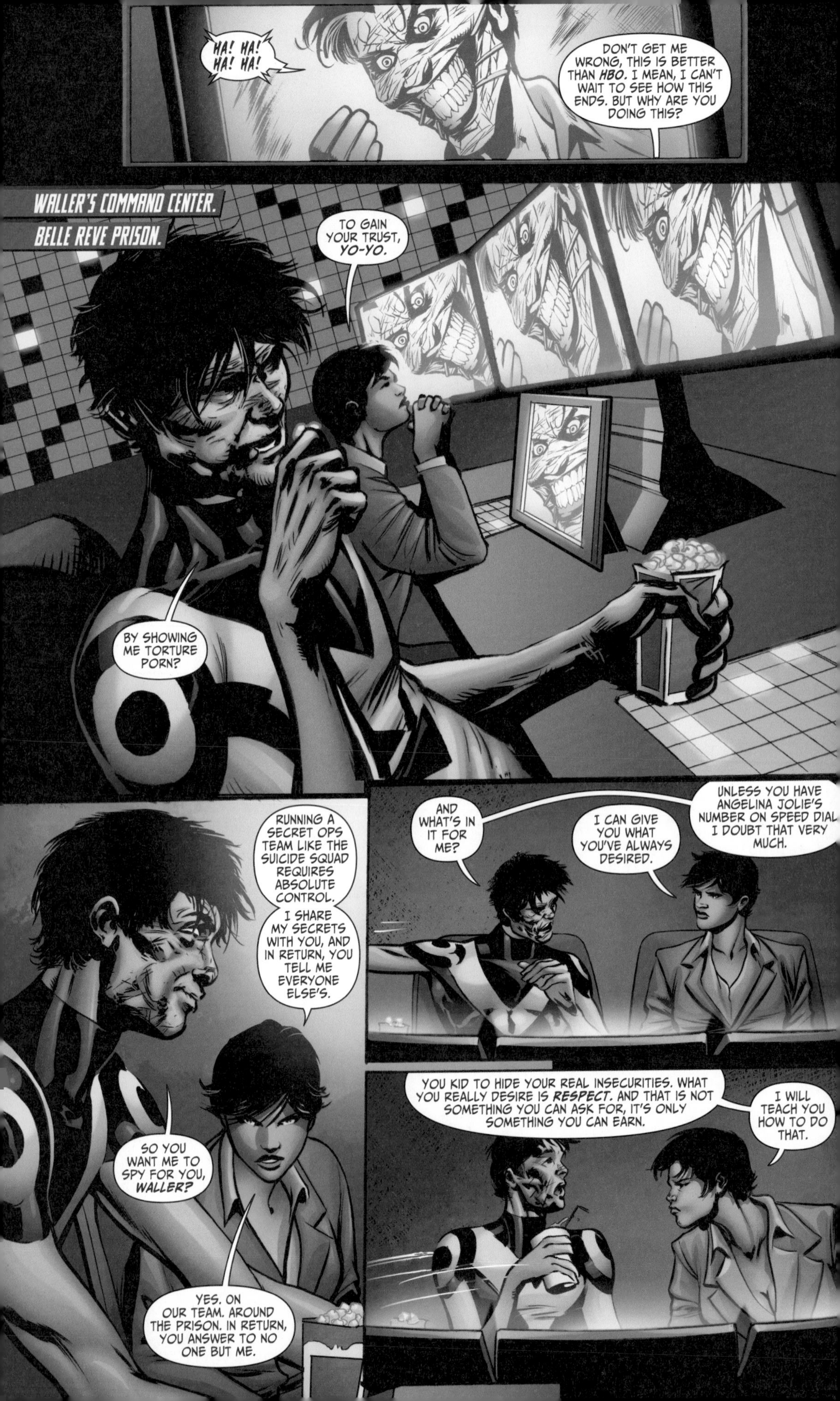
HA! HA! HA! HA!
DON'T GET ME WRONG, THIS IS BETTER THAN HBO. I MEAN, I CAN'T WAIT TO SEE HOW THIS ENDS. BUT WHY ARE YOU DOING THIS?
WALLER'S COMMAND CENTER.
BELLE REVE PRISON.
TO GAIN YOUR TRUST, YO-YO.
BY SHOWING ME TORTURE PORN?
RUNNING A SECRET OPS TEAM LIKE THE SUICIDE SQUAD REQUIRES ABSOLUTE CONTROL.
I SHARE MY SECRETS WITH YOU, AND IN RETURN, YOU TELL ME EVERYONE ELSE'S.
SO YOU WANT ME TO SPY FOR YOU, WALLER?
YES. ON OUR TEAM. AROUND THE PRISON. IN RETURN, YOU ANSWER TO NO ONE BUT ME.
AND WHAT'S IN IT FOR ME?
UNLESS YOU HAVE ANGELINA JOLIE'S NUMBER ON SPEED DIAL I DOUBT THAT VERY MUCH.
I CAN GIVE YOU WHAT YOU'VE ALWAYS DESIRED.
YOU KID TO HIDE YOUR REAL INSECURITIES. WHAT YOU REALLY DESIRE IS RESPECT. AND THAT IS NOT SOMETHING YOU CAN ASK FOR, IT'S ONLY SOMETHING YOU CAN EARN.
I WILL TEACH YOU HOW TO DO THAT.

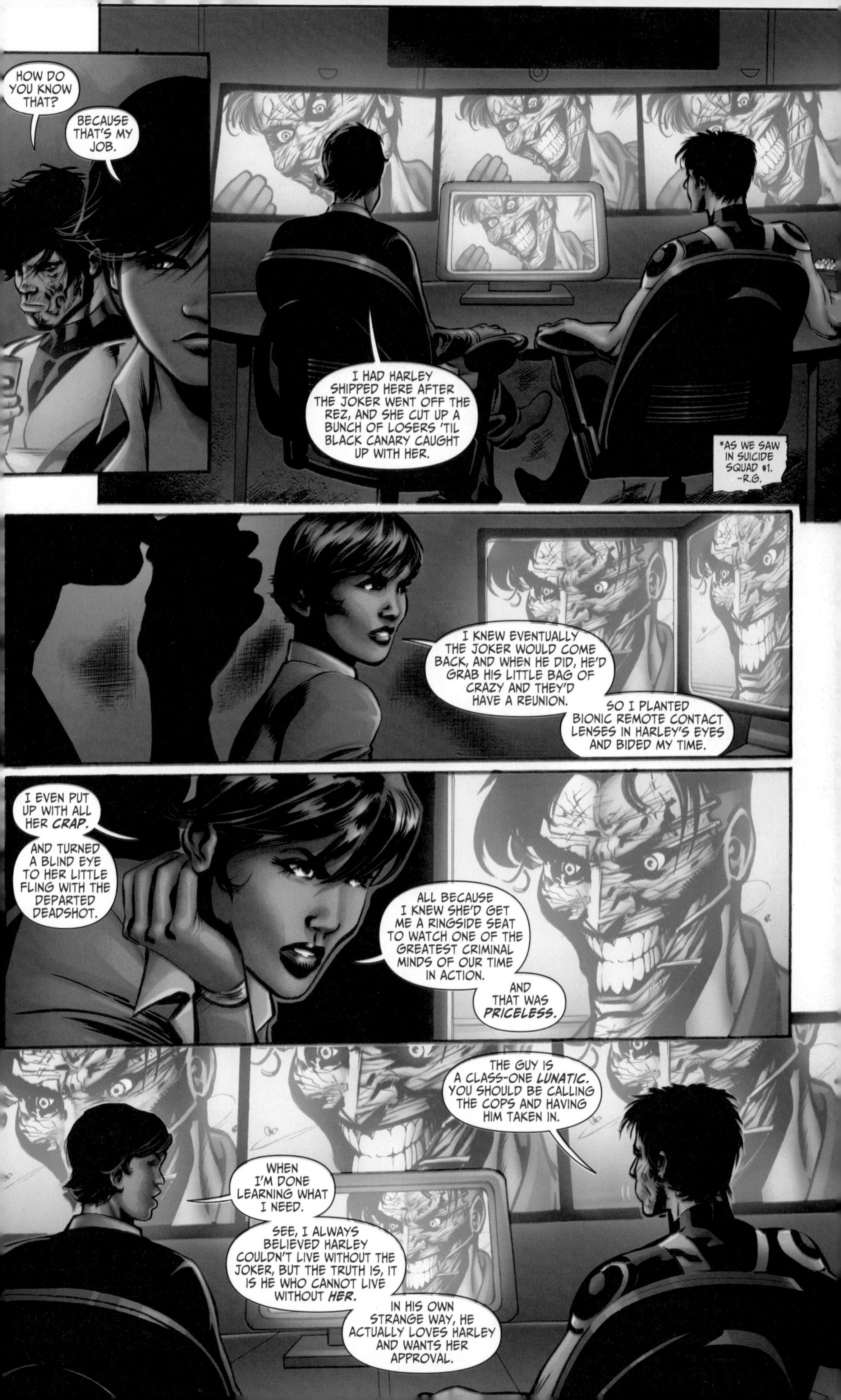

HOW DO YOU KNOW THAT?
BECAUSE THAT'S MY JOB.
I HAD HARLEY SHIPPED HERE AFTER THE JOKER WENT OFF THE REZ, AND SHE CUT UP A BUNCH OF LOSERS 'TIL BLACK CANARY CAUGHT UP WITH HER.
*AS WE SAW IN SUICIDE SQUAD #1. -R.G.
I KNEW EVENTUALLY THE JOKER WOULD COME BACK, AND WHEN HE DID, HE'D GRAB HIS LITTLE BAG OF CRAZY AND THEY'D HAVE A REUNION.
SO I PLANTED BIONIC REMOTE CONTACT LENSES IN HARLEY'S EYES AND BIDED MY TIME.
I EVEN PUT UP WITH ALL HER *CRAP.*
AND TURNED A BLIND EYE TO HER LITTLE FLING WITH THE DEPARTED DEADSHOT.
ALL BECAUSE I KNEW SHE'D GET ME A RINGSIDE SEAT TO WATCH ONE OF THE GREATEST CRIMINAL MINDS OF OUR TIME IN ACTION.
AND THAT WAS *PRICELESS.*
THE GUY IS A CLASS-ONE *LUNATIC.* YOU SHOULD BE CALLING THE COPS AND HAVING HIM TAKEN IN.
WHEN I'M DONE LEARNING WHAT I NEED.
SEE, I ALWAYS BELIEVED HARLEY COULDN'T LIVE WITHOUT THE JOKER, BUT THE TRUTH IS, IT IS HE WHO CANNOT LIVE WITHOUT *HER.*
IN HIS OWN STRANGE WAY, HE ACTUALLY LOVES HARLEY AND WANTS HER APPROVAL.

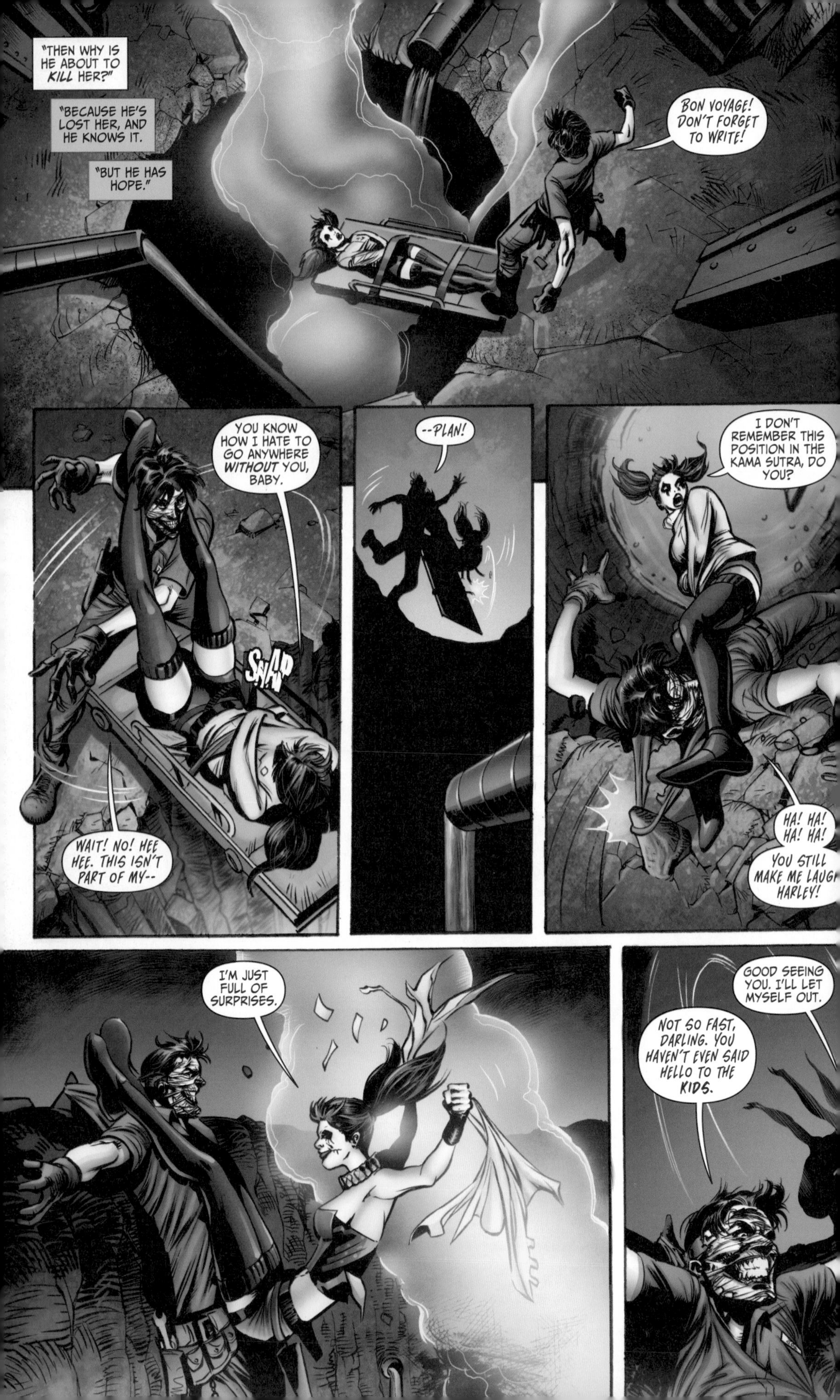
"THEN WHY IS HE ABOUT TO KILL HER?"
"BECAUSE HE'S LOST HER, AND HE KNOWS IT.
"BUT HE HAS HOPE."
BON VOYAGE! DON'T FORGET TO WRITE!
YOU KNOW HOW I HATE TO GO ANYWHERE WITHOUT YOU, BABY.
SNAP
WAIT! NO! HEE HEE. THIS ISN'T PART OF MY--
--PLAN!
I DON'T REMEMBER THIS POSITION IN THE KAMA SUTRA, DO YOU?
HA! HA! HA! HA!
YOU STILL MAKE ME LAUGH, HARLEY!
I'M JUST FULL OF SURPRISES.
GOOD SEEING YOU. I'LL LET MYSELF OUT.
NOT SO FAST, DARLING. YOU HAVEN'T EVEN SAID HELLO TO THE KIDS.

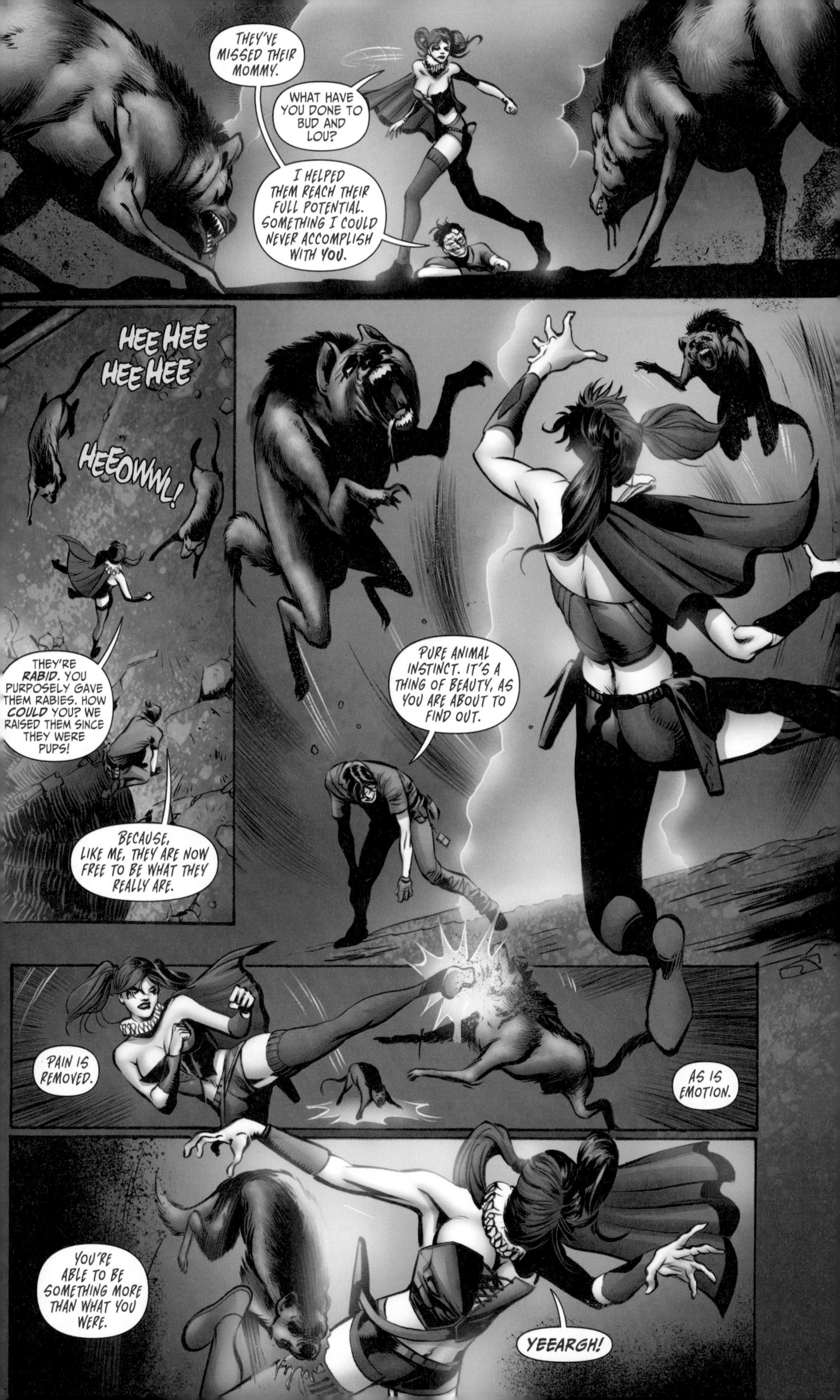
THEY'VE MISSED THEIR MOMMY.
WHAT HAVE YOU DONE TO BUD AND LOU?
I HELPED THEM REACH THEIR FULL POTENTIAL. SOMETHING I COULD NEVER ACCOMPLISH WITH YOU.
HEE HEE HEE HEE
HEEOWWL!
THEY'RE RABID. YOU PURPOSELY GAVE THEM RABIES. HOW COULD YOU? WE RAISED THEM SINCE THEY WERE PUPS!
BECAUSE, LIKE ME, THEY ARE NOW FREE TO BE WHAT THEY REALLY ARE.
PURE ANIMAL INSTINCT. IT'S A THING OF BEAUTY, AS YOU ARE ABOUT TO FIND OUT.
PAIN IS REMOVED.
AS IS EMOTION.
YOU'RE ABLE TO BE SOMETHING MORE THAN WHAT YOU WERE.
YEEARGH!

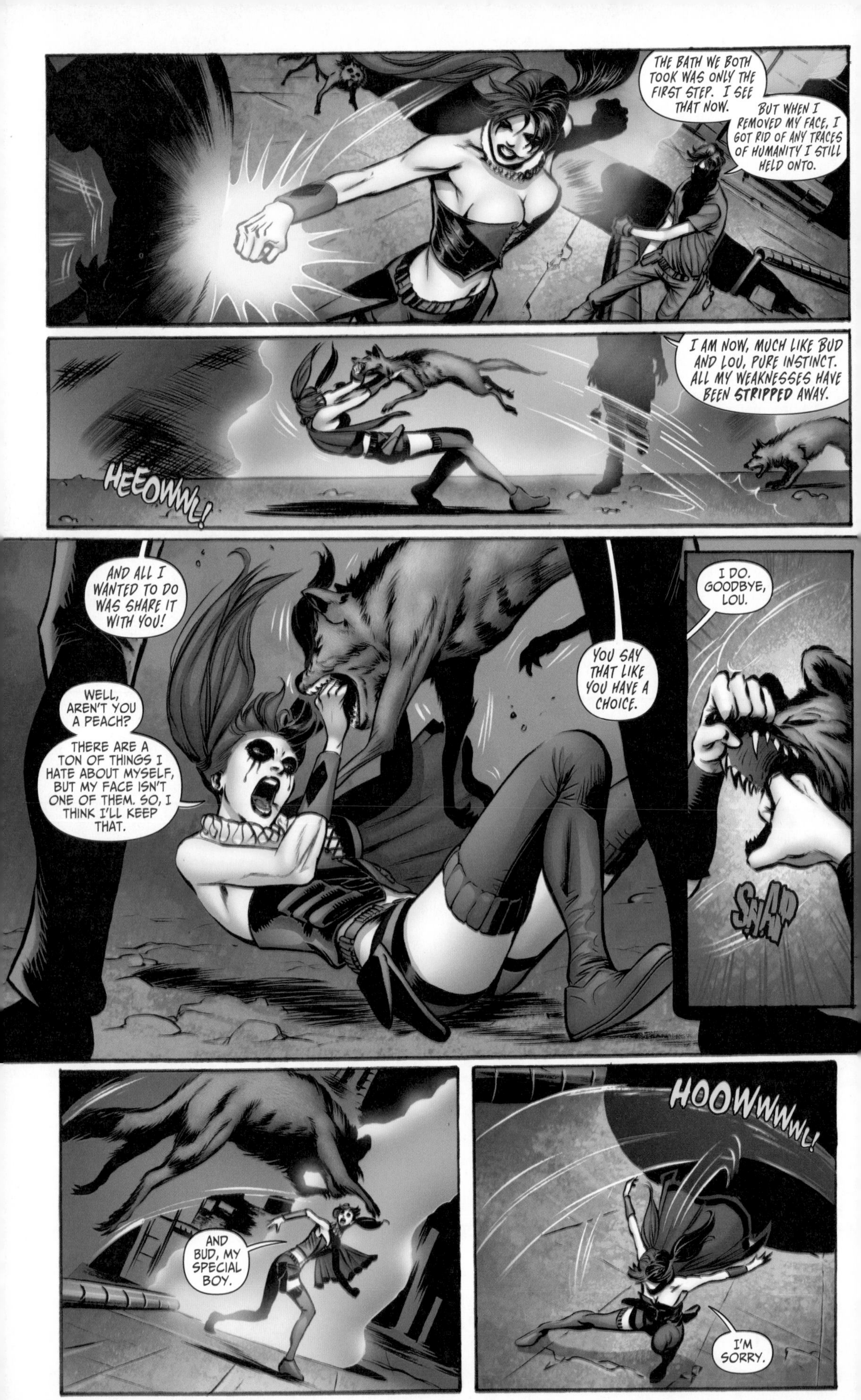

THE BATH WE BOTH TOOK WAS ONLY THE FIRST STEP. I SEE THAT NOW.
BUT WHEN I REMOVED MY FACE, I GOT RID OF ANY TRACES OF HUMANITY I STILL HELD ONTO.
I AM NOW, MUCH LIKE BUD AND LOU, PURE INSTINCT. ALL MY WEAKNESSES HAVE BEEN STRIPPED AWAY.
HEEOWWL!
AND ALL I WANTED TO DO WAS SHARE IT WITH YOU!
WELL, AREN'T YOU A PEACH?
THERE ARE A TON OF THINGS I HATE ABOUT MYSELF, BUT MY FACE ISN'T ONE OF THEM. SO, I THINK I'LL KEEP THAT.
YOU SAY THAT LIKE YOU HAVE A CHOICE.
I DO. GOODBYE, LOU.
SNAP
AND BUD, MY SPECIAL BOY.
HOOWWWWL!
I'M SORRY.

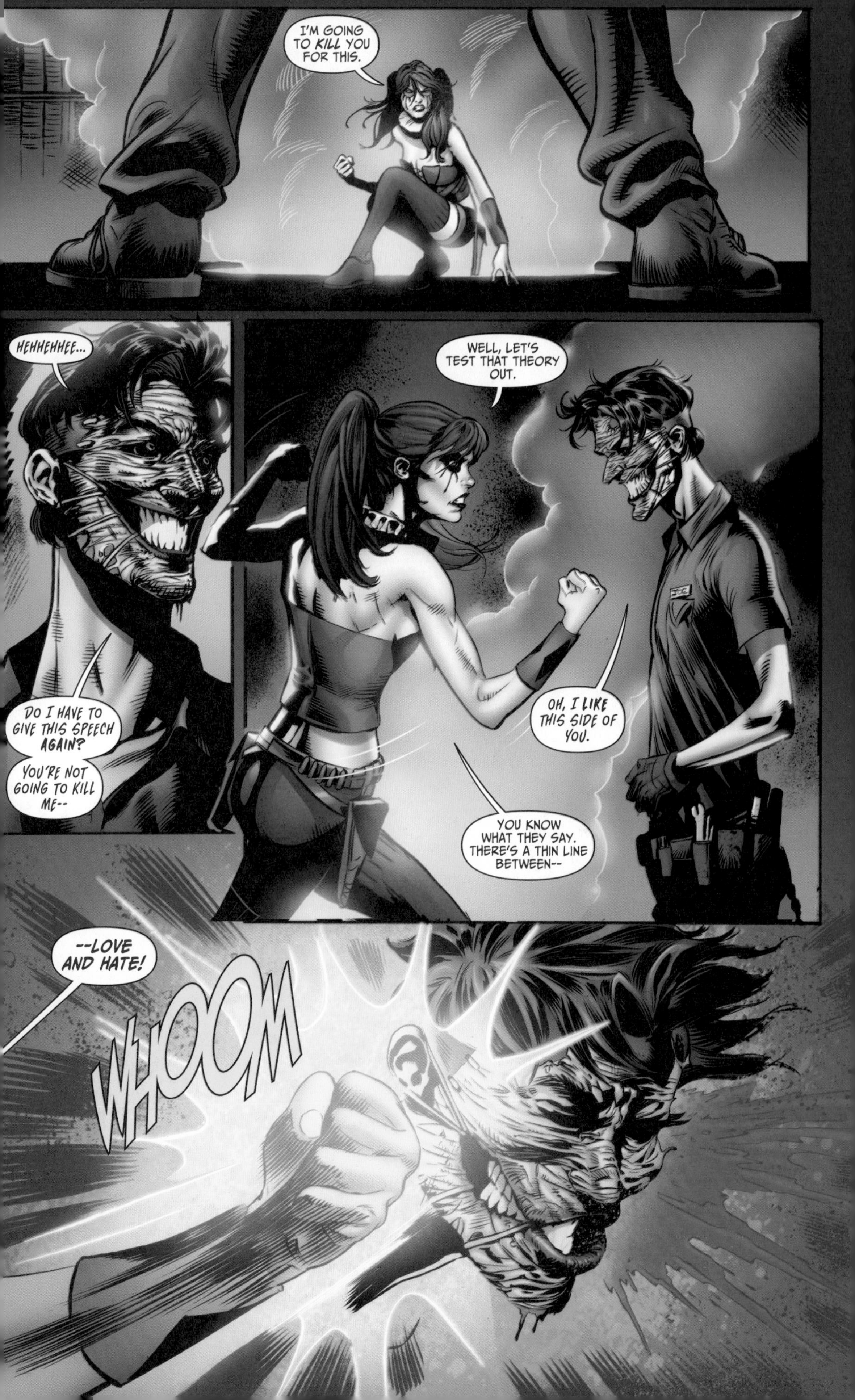
I'M GOING TO KILL YOU FOR THIS.
HEHHEHHEE...
DO I HAVE TO GIVE THIS SPEECH AGAIN?
YOU'RE NOT GOING TO KILL ME--
WELL, LET'S TEST THAT THEORY OUT.
OH, I LIKE THIS SIDE OF YOU.
YOU KNOW WHAT THEY SAY. THERE'S A THIN LINE BETWEEN--
--LOVE AND HATE!
WHOOM

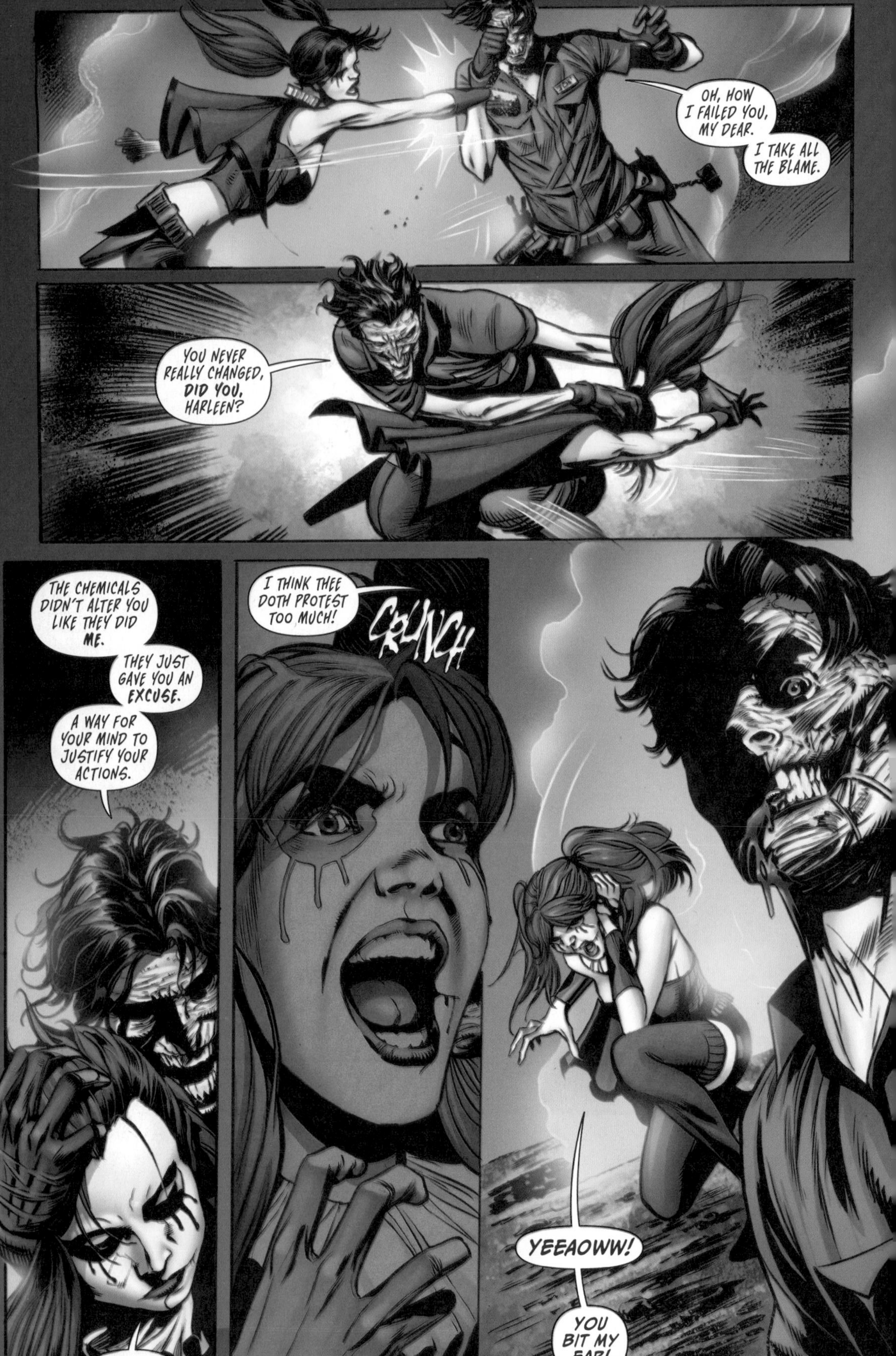
OH, HOW I FAILED YOU, MY DEAR.
I TAKE ALL THE BLAME.
YOU NEVER REALLY CHANGED, DID YOU, HARLEEN?
THE CHEMICALS DIDN'T ALTER YOU LIKE THEY DID ME.
THEY JUST GAVE YOU AN EXCUSE.
A WAY FOR YOUR MIND TO JUSTIFY YOUR ACTIONS.
NO! THAT'S NOT TRUE!
I THINK THEE DOTH PROTEST TOO MUCH!
CRUNCH
YEEAOWW!
YOU BIT MY EAR!

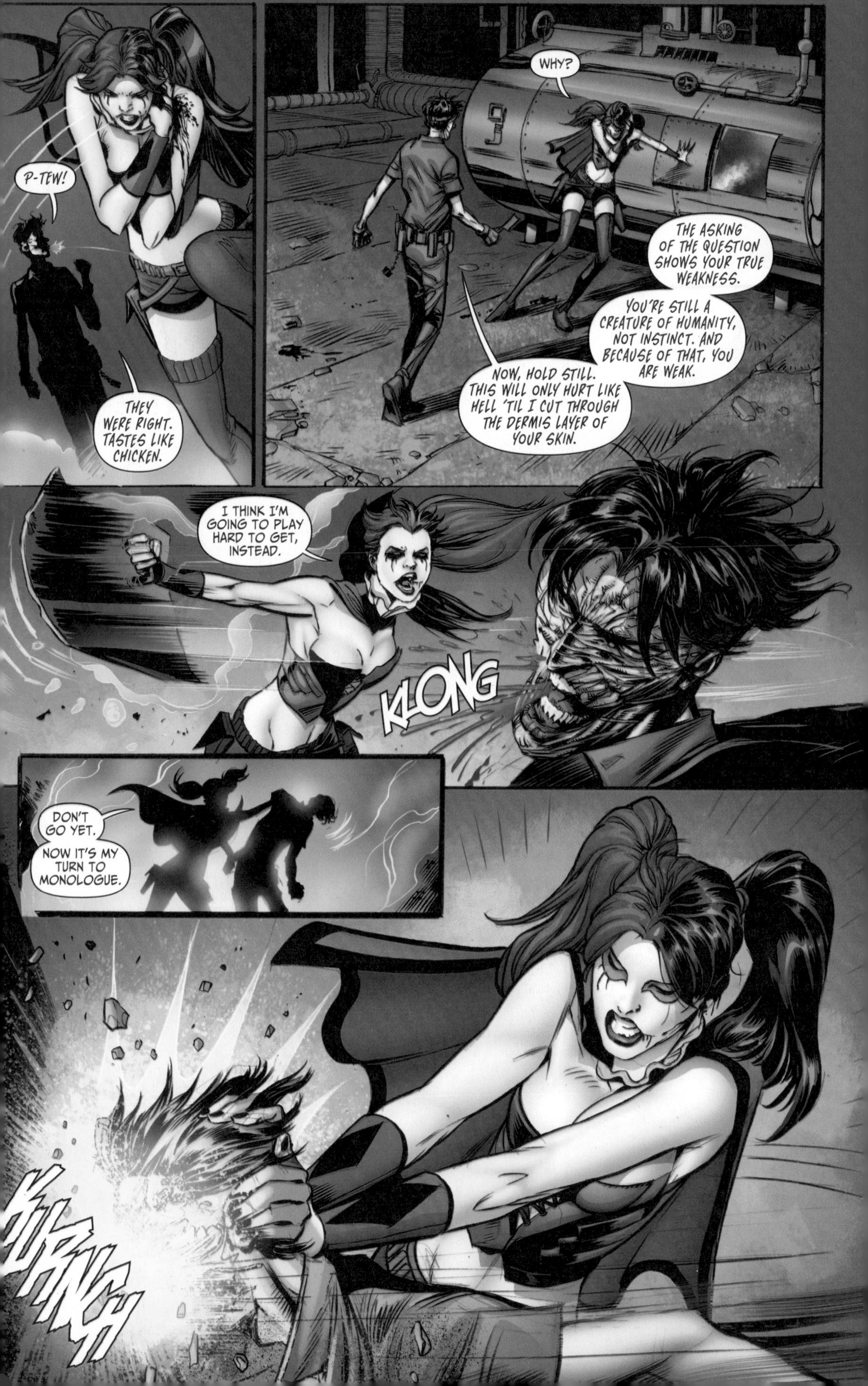
P-TEW!
THEY WERE RIGHT. TASTES LIKE CHICKEN.
WHY?
THE ASKING OF THE QUESTION SHOWS YOUR TRUE WEAKNESS.
YOU'RE STILL A CREATURE OF HUMANITY, NOT INSTINCT. AND BECAUSE OF THAT, YOU ARE WEAK.
NOW, HOLD STILL. THIS WILL ONLY HURT LIKE HELL 'TIL I CUT THROUGH THE DERMIS LAYER OF YOUR SKIN.
I THINK I'M GOING TO PLAY HARD TO GET, INSTEAD.
KLONG
DON'T GO YET.
NOW IT'S MY TURN TO MONOLOGUE.
KRUNCH

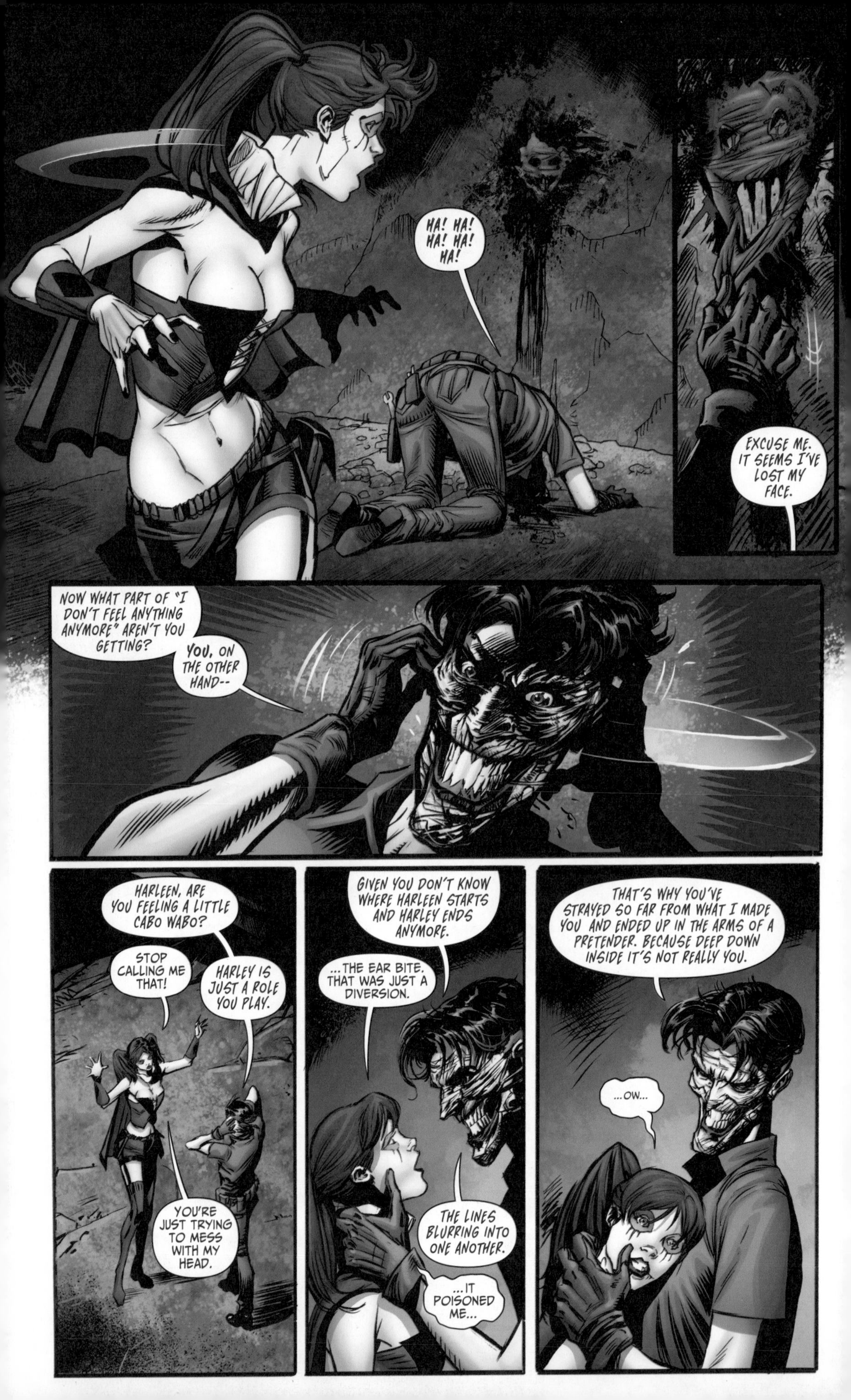
HA! HA! HA! HA! HA!
EXCUSE ME. IT SEEMS I'VE LOST MY FACE.
NOW WHAT PART OF "I DON'T FEEL ANYTHING ANYMORE" AREN'T YOU GETTING?
YOU, ON THE OTHER HAND--
HARLEEN, ARE YOU FEELING A LITTLE CABO WABO?
STOP CALLING ME THAT!
HARLEY IS JUST A ROLE YOU PLAY.
YOU'RE JUST TRYING TO MESS WITH MY HEAD.
GIVEN YOU DON'T KNOW WHERE HARLEEN STARTS AND HARLEY ENDS ANYMORE.
...THE EAR BITE. THAT WAS JUST A DIVERSION.
THE LINES BLURRING INTO ONE ANOTHER.
...IT POISONED ME...
THAT'S WHY YOU'VE STRAYED SO FAR FROM WHAT I MADE YOU AND ENDED UP IN THE ARMS OF A PRETENDER. BECAUSE DEEP DOWN INSIDE IT'S NOT REALLY YOU.
...OW...

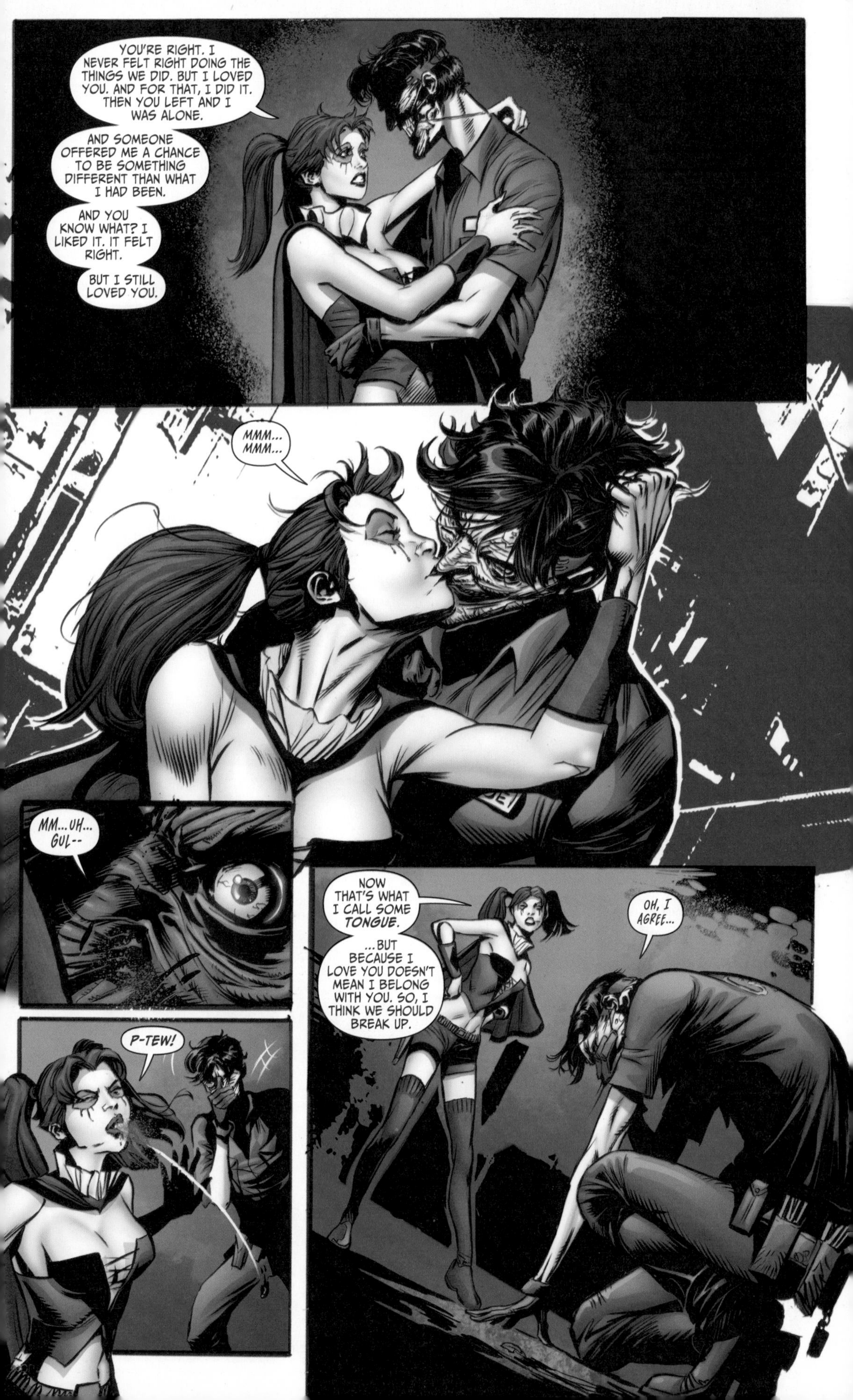

YOU'RE RIGHT. I NEVER FELT RIGHT DOING THE THINGS WE DID. BUT I LOVED YOU. AND FOR THAT, I DID IT. THEN YOU LEFT AND I WAS ALONE.
AND SOMEONE OFFERED ME A CHANCE TO BE SOMETHING DIFFERENT THAN WHAT I HAD BEEN.
AND YOU KNOW WHAT? I LIKED IT. IT FELT RIGHT.
BUT I STILL LOVED YOU.
MMM... MMM...
MM...UH... GUL--
P-TEW!
NOW THAT'S WHAT I CALL SOME *TONGUE*.
...BUT BECAUSE I LOVE YOU DOESN'T MEAN I BELONG WITH YOU. SO, I THINK WE SHOULD BREAK UP.
OH, I AGREE...

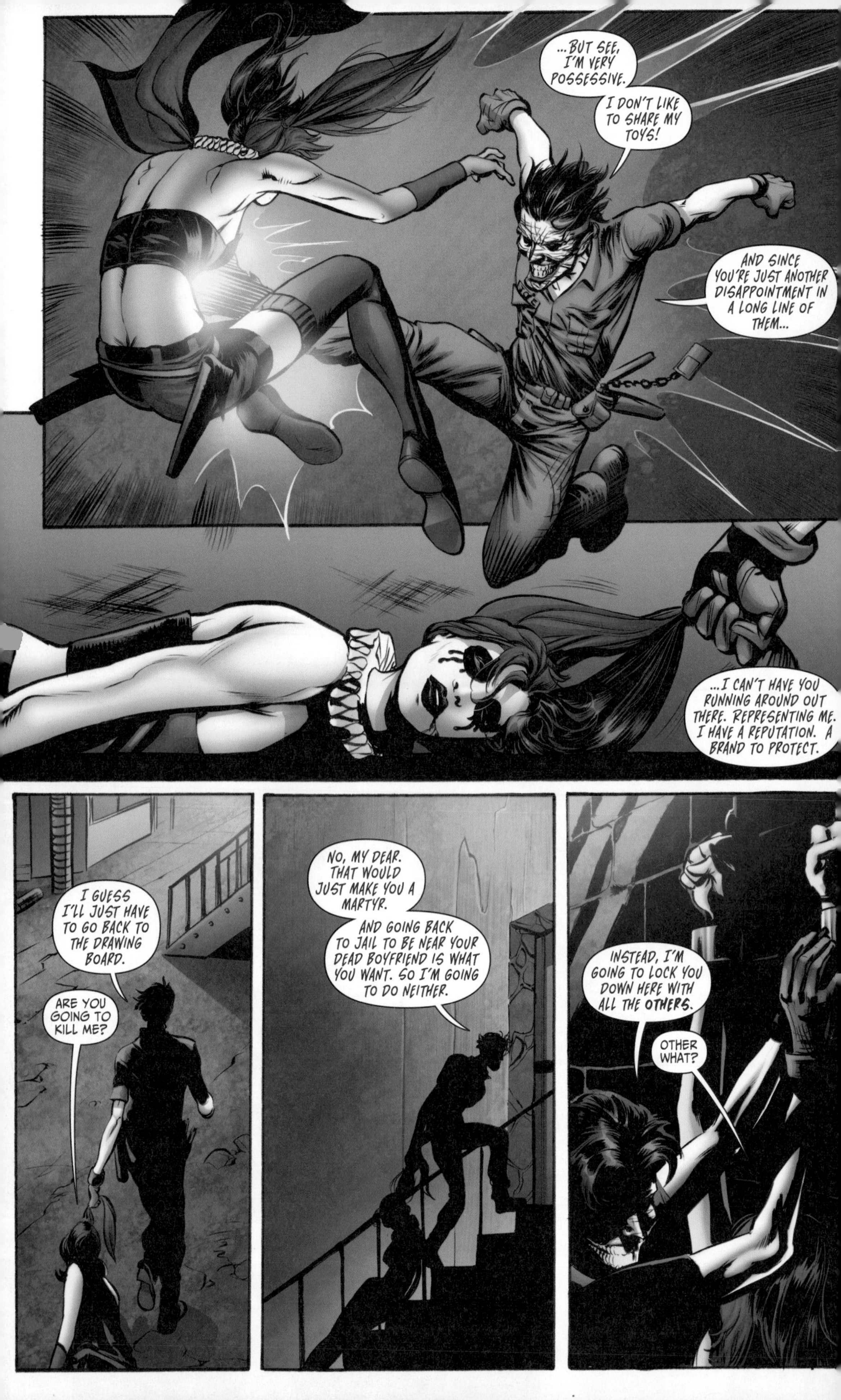
...BUT SEE, I'M VERY POSSESSIVE.
I DON'T LIKE TO SHARE MY TOYS!
AND SINCE YOU'RE JUST ANOTHER DISAPPOINTMENT IN A LONG LINE OF THEM...
...I CAN'T HAVE YOU RUNNING AROUND OUT THERE. REPRESENTING ME. I HAVE A REPUTATION. A BRAND TO PROTECT.
I GUESS I'LL JUST HAVE TO GO BACK TO THE DRAWING BOARD.
ARE YOU GOING TO KILL ME?
NO, MY DEAR. THAT WOULD JUST MAKE YOU A MARTYR.
AND GOING BACK TO JAIL TO BE NEAR YOUR DEAD BOYFRIEND IS WHAT YOU WANT. SO I'M GOING TO DO NEITHER.
INSTEAD, I'M GOING TO LOCK YOU DOWN HERE WITH ALL THE OTHERS.
OTHER WHAT?

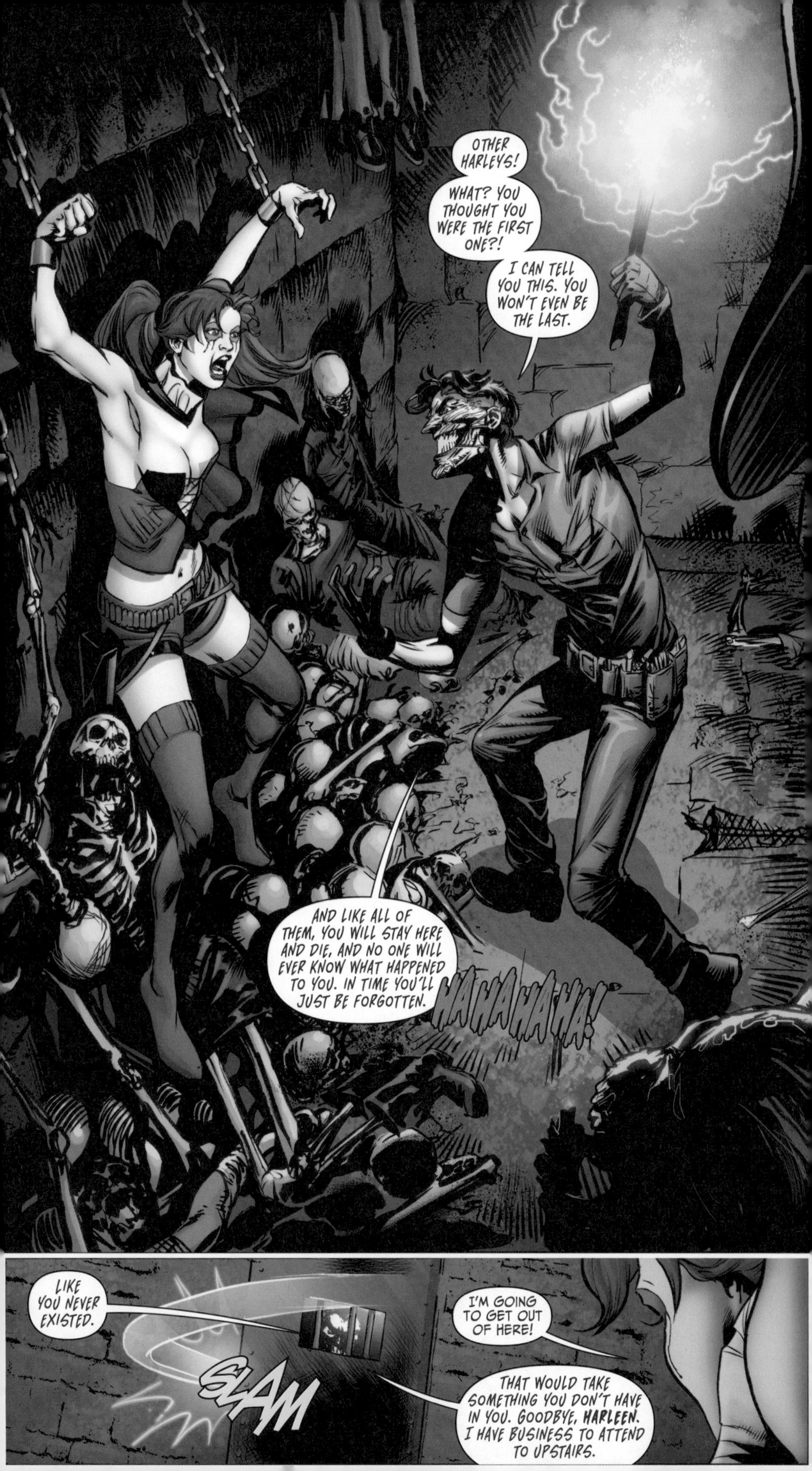
OTHER HARLEYS!
WHAT? YOU THOUGHT YOU WERE THE FIRST ONE?!
I CAN TELL YOU THIS. YOU WON'T EVEN BE THE LAST.
AND LIKE ALL OF THEM, YOU WILL STAY HERE AND DIE, AND NO ONE WILL EVER KNOW WHAT HAPPENED TO YOU. IN TIME YOU'LL JUST BE FORGOTTEN.
HAHAHAHAHA!
LIKE YOU NEVER EXISTED.
SLAM
I'M GOING TO GET OUT OF HERE!
THAT WOULD TAKE SOMETHING YOU DON'T HAVE IN YOU. GOODBYE, **HARLEEN.** I HAVE BUSINESS TO ATTEND TO UPSTAIRS.

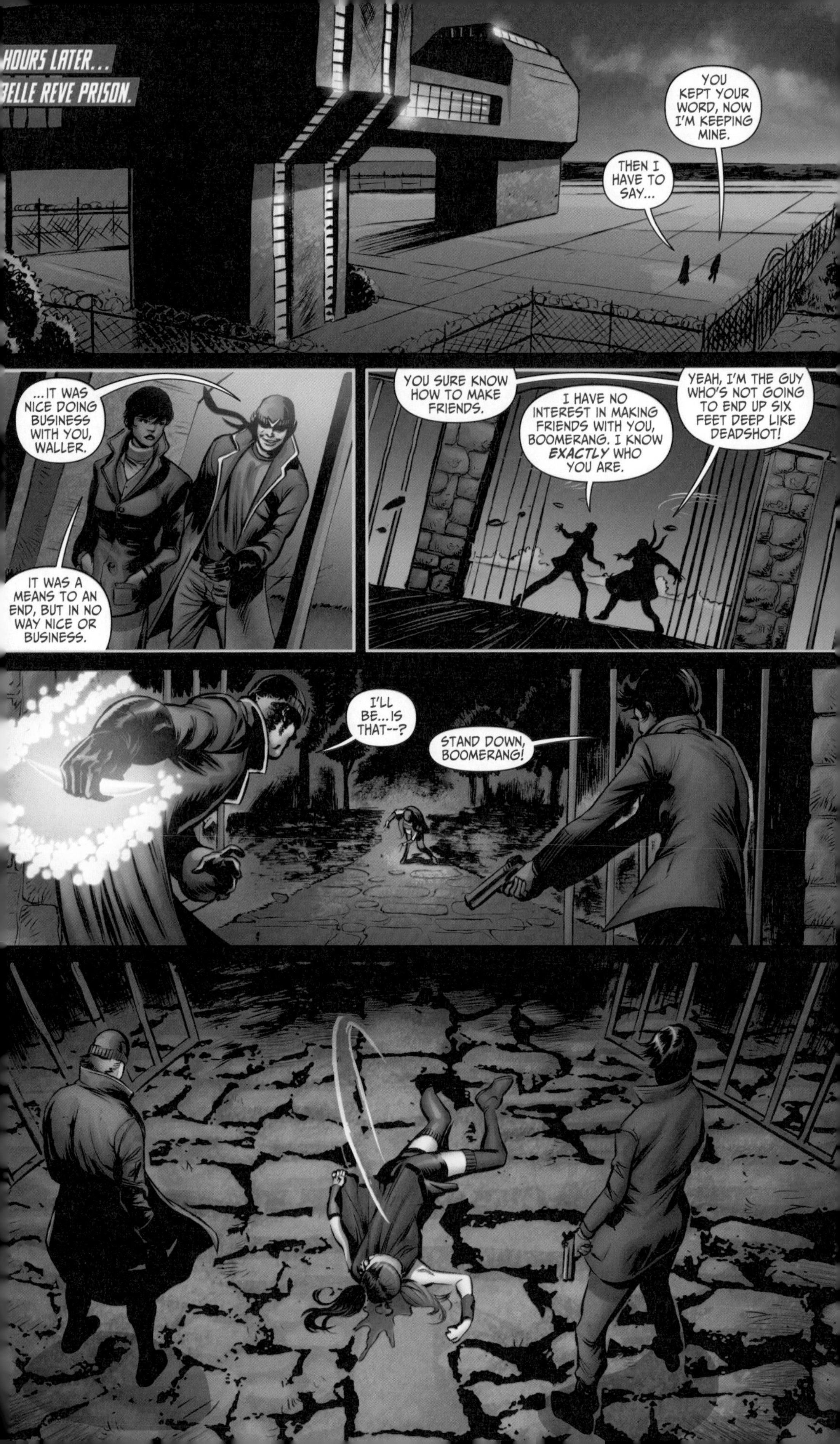
HOURS LATER...
BELLE REVE PRISON.
YOU KEPT YOUR WORD, NOW I'M KEEPING MINE.
THEN I HAVE TO SAY...
...IT WAS NICE DOING BUSINESS WITH YOU, WALLER.
IT WAS A MEANS TO AN END, BUT IN NO WAY NICE OR BUSINESS.
YOU SURE KNOW HOW TO MAKE FRIENDS.
I HAVE NO INTEREST IN MAKING FRIENDS WITH YOU, BOOMERANG. I KNOW EXACTLY WHO YOU ARE.
YEAH, I'M THE GUY WHO'S NOT GOING TO END UP SIX FEET DEEP LIKE DEADSHOT!
I'LL BE...IS THAT--?
STAND DOWN, BOOMERANG!

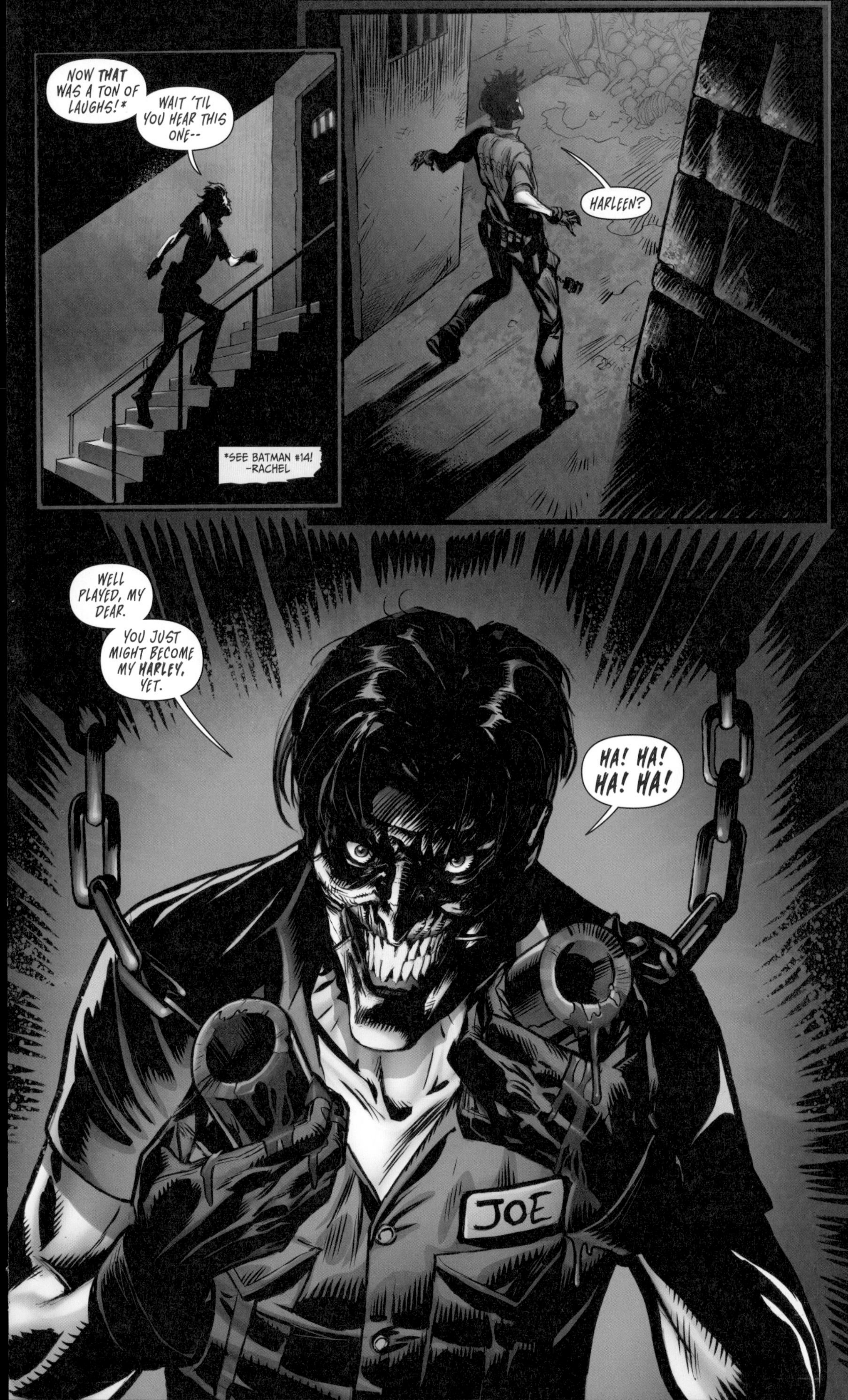

NOW THAT WAS A TON OF LAUGHS!*
WAIT 'TIL YOU HEAR THIS ONE--
*SEE BATMAN #14! -RACHEL
HARLEEN?
WELL PLAYED, MY DEAR.
YOU JUST MIGHT BECOME MY HARLEY, YET.
HA! HA! HA! HA!
JOE

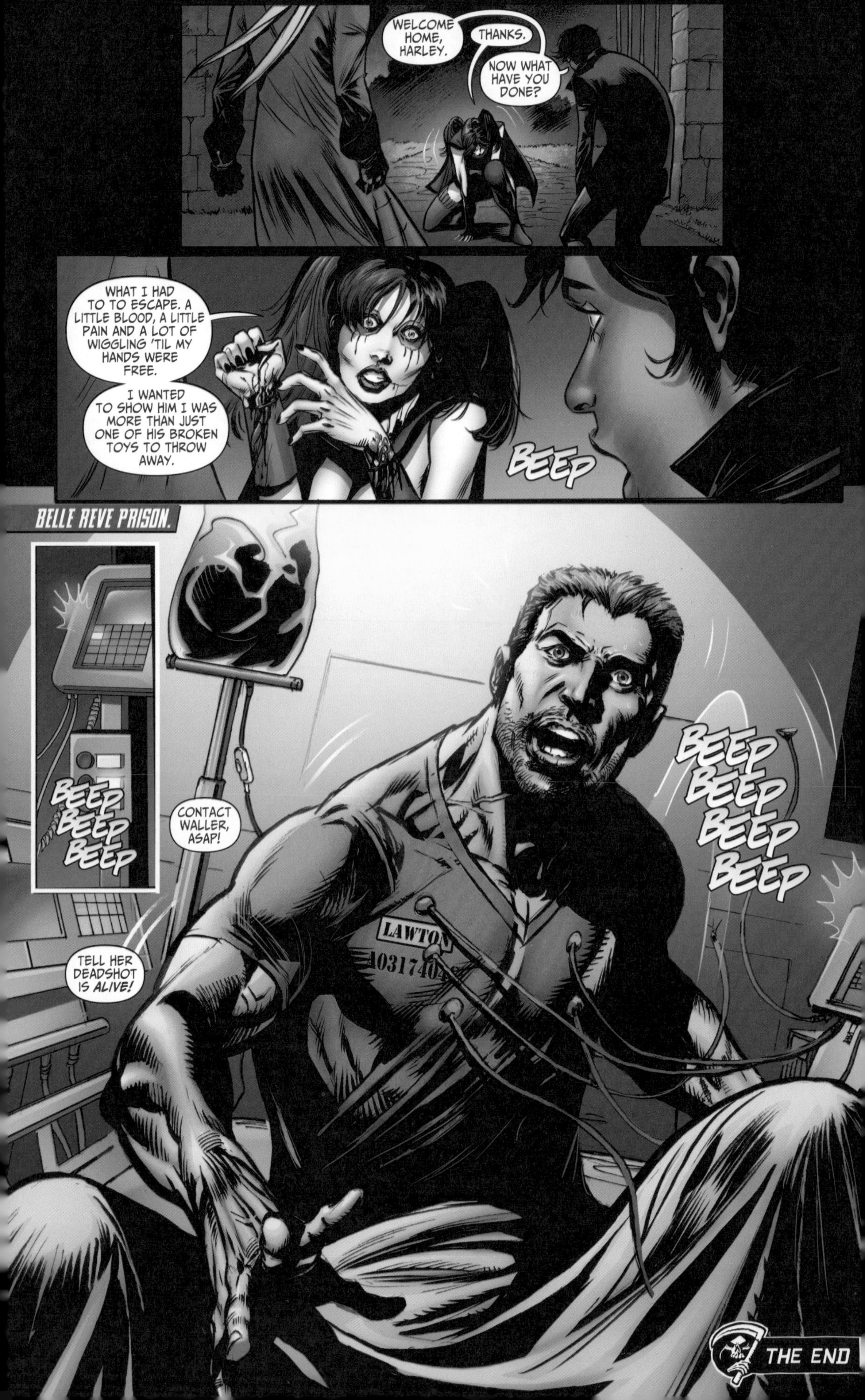
WELCOME HOME, HARLEY.
THANKS.
NOW WHAT HAVE YOU DONE?
WHAT I HAD TO TO ESCAPE. A LITTLE BLOOD, A LITTLE PAIN AND A LOT OF WIGGLING 'TIL MY HANDS WERE FREE.
I WANTED TO SHOW HIM I WAS MORE THAN JUST ONE OF HIS BROKEN TOYS TO THROW AWAY.
BEEP
BELLE REVE PRISON.
BEEP BEEP BEEP
CONTACT WALLER, ASAP!
TELL HER DEADSHOT IS ALIVE!
LAWTON
A0317404
BEEP BEEP BEEP BEEP
THE END

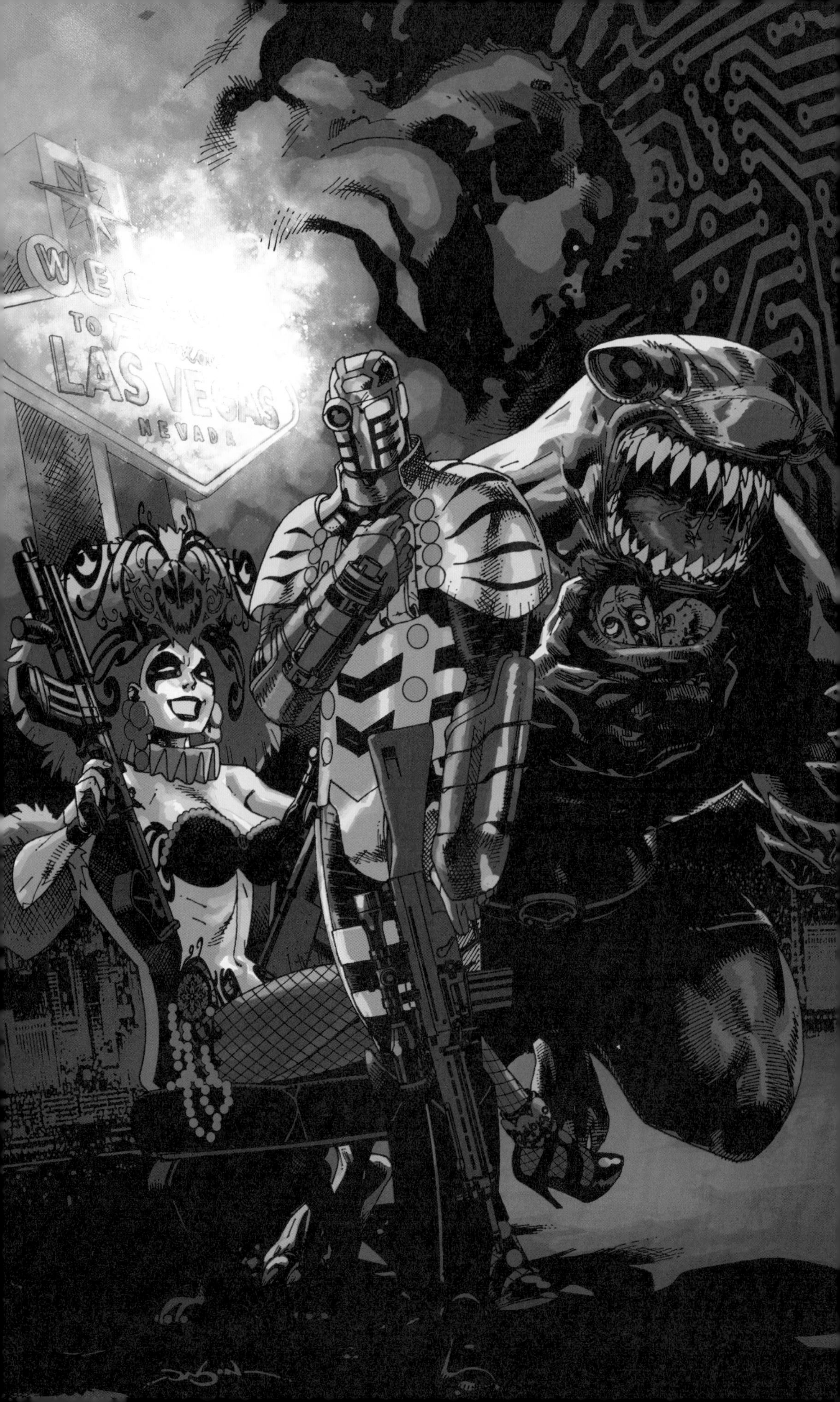
LAS VEGAS
NEVADA

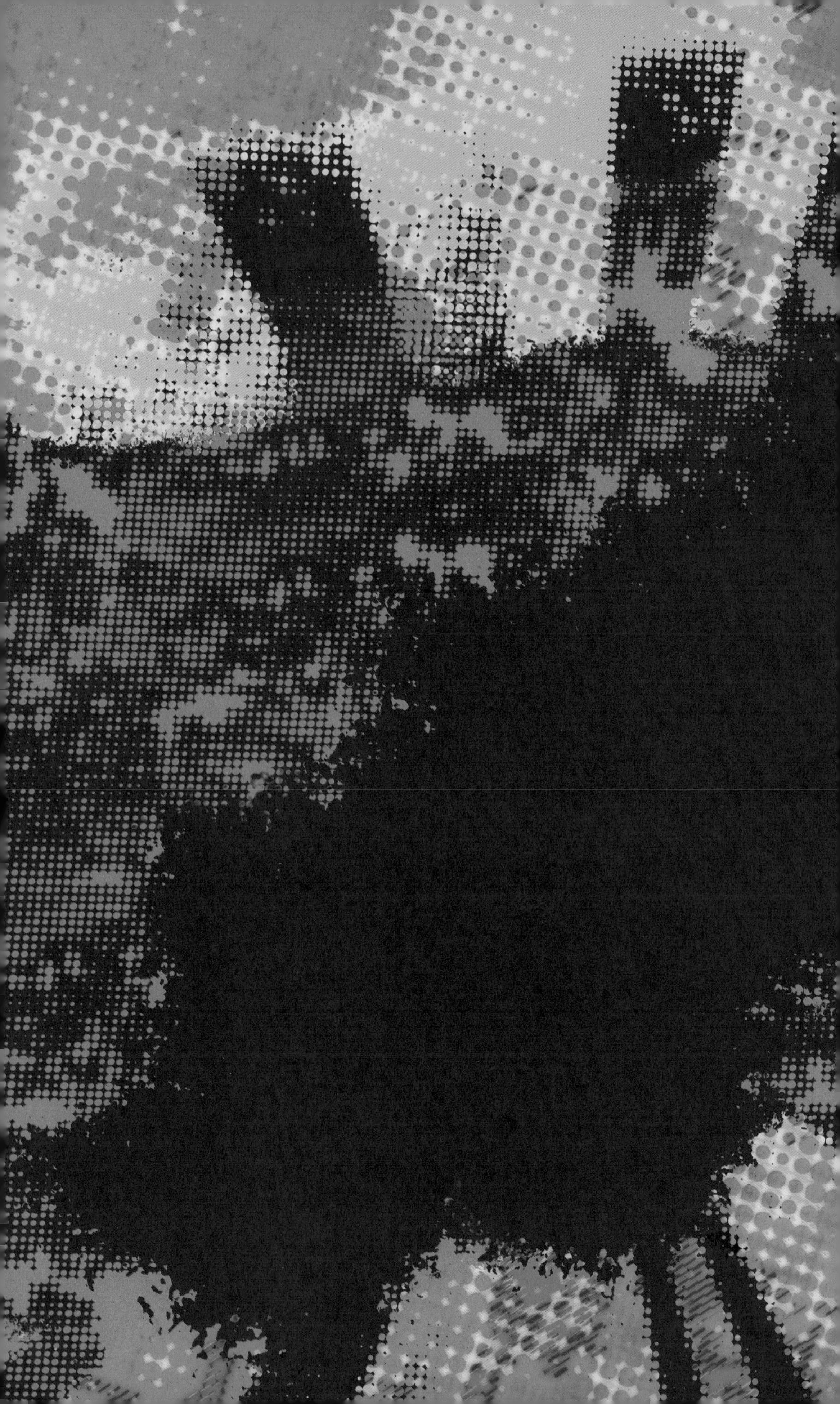

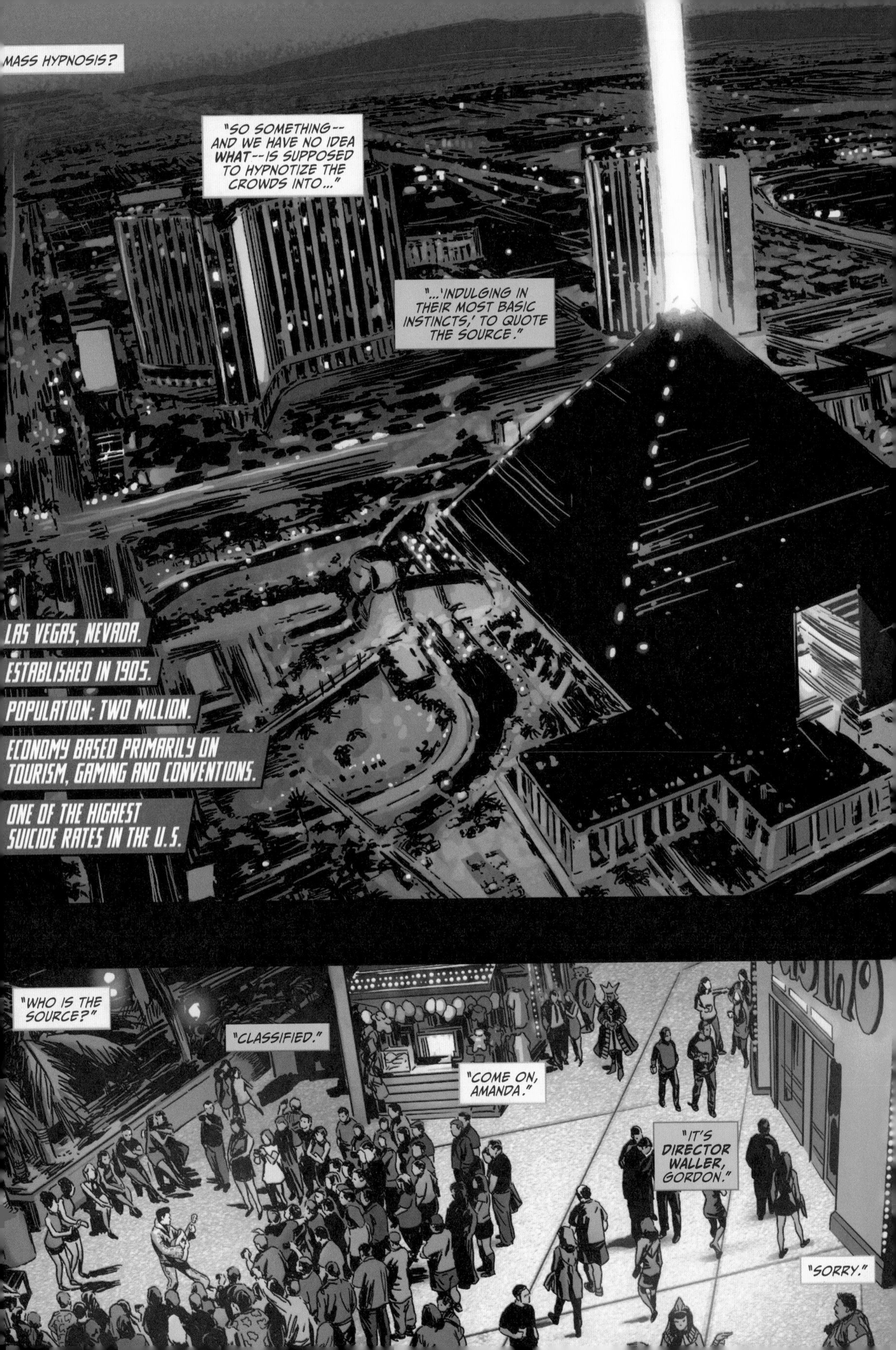
MASS HYPNOSIS?
"SO SOMETHING-- AND WE HAVE NO IDEA WHAT--IS SUPPOSED TO HYPNOTIZE THE CROWDS INTO..."
"...'INDULGING IN THEIR MOST BASIC INSTINCTS,' TO QUOTE THE SOURCE."
LAS VEGAS, NEVADA.
ESTABLISHED IN 1905.
POPULATION: TWO MILLION.
ECONOMY BASED PRIMARILY ON TOURISM, GAMING AND CONVENTIONS.
ONE OF THE HIGHEST SUICIDE RATES IN THE U.S.
"WHO IS THE SOURCE?"
"CLASSIFIED."
"COME ON, AMANDA."
"IT'S DIRECTOR WALLER, GORDON."
"SORRY."

HARVEY RICHARDS ASSOCIATE EDITOR WIL MOSS EDITOR BRIAN CUNNINGHAM SENIOR EDITOR

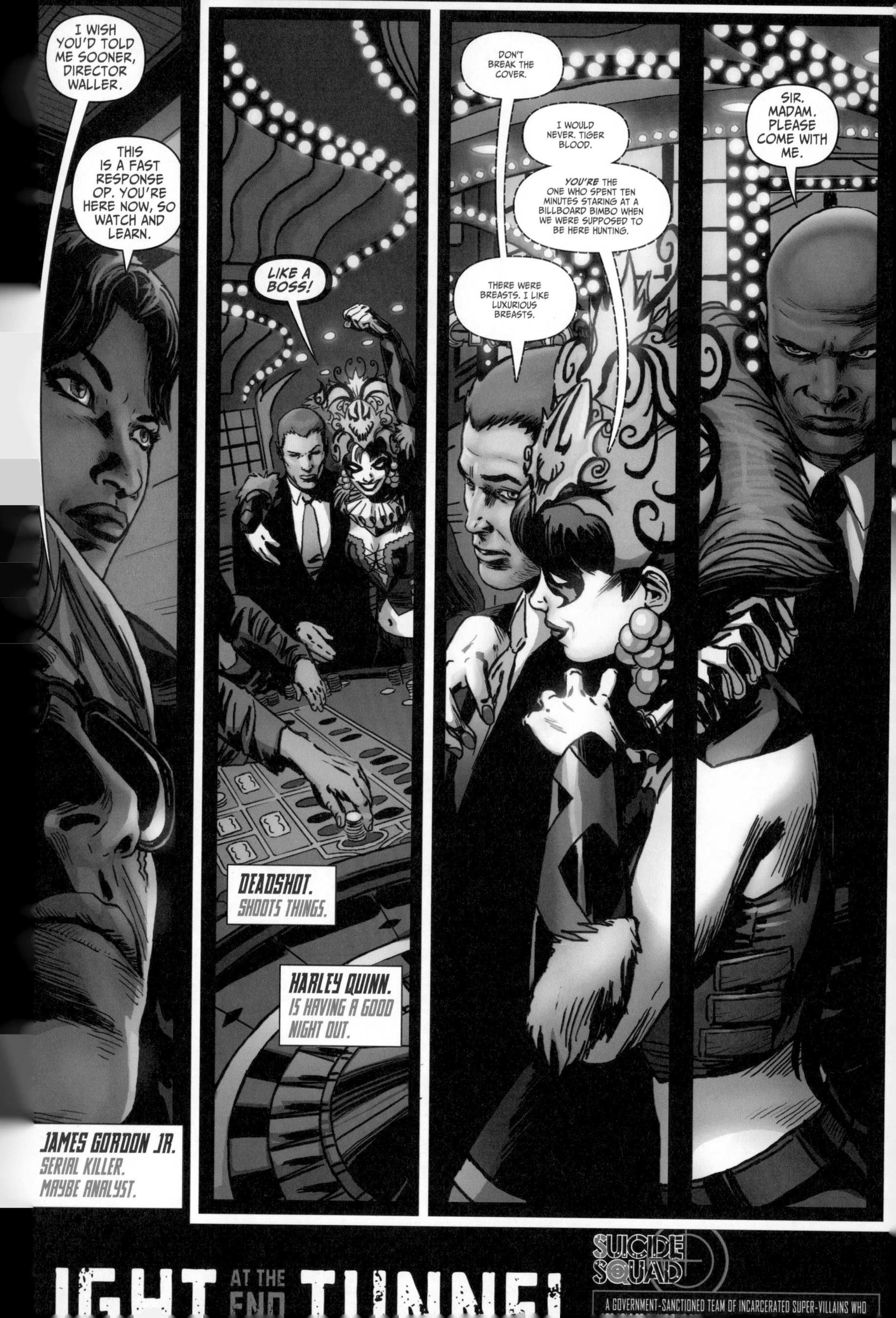
I WISH YOU'D TOLD ME SOONER, DIRECTOR WALLER.
THIS IS A FAST RESPONSE OP. YOU'RE HERE NOW, SO WATCH AND LEARN.
JAMES GORDON JR. SERIAL KILLER. MAYBE ANALYST.
LIKE A BOSS!
DEADSHOT. SHOOTS THINGS.
HARLEY QUINN. IS HAVING A GOOD NIGHT OUT.
DON'T BREAK THE COVER.
I WOULD NEVER. TIGER BLOOD.
YOU'RE THE ONE WHO SPENT TEN MINUTES STARING AT A BILLBOARD BIMBO WHEN WE WERE SUPPOSED TO BE HERE HUNTING.
THERE WERE BREASTS. I LIKE LUXURIOUS BREASTS.
SIR. MADAM. PLEASE COME WITH ME.

IGHT AT THE END TUNNEL

SUICIDE SQUAD

A GOVERNMENT-SANCTIONED TEAM OF INCARCERATED SUPER-VILLAINS WHO

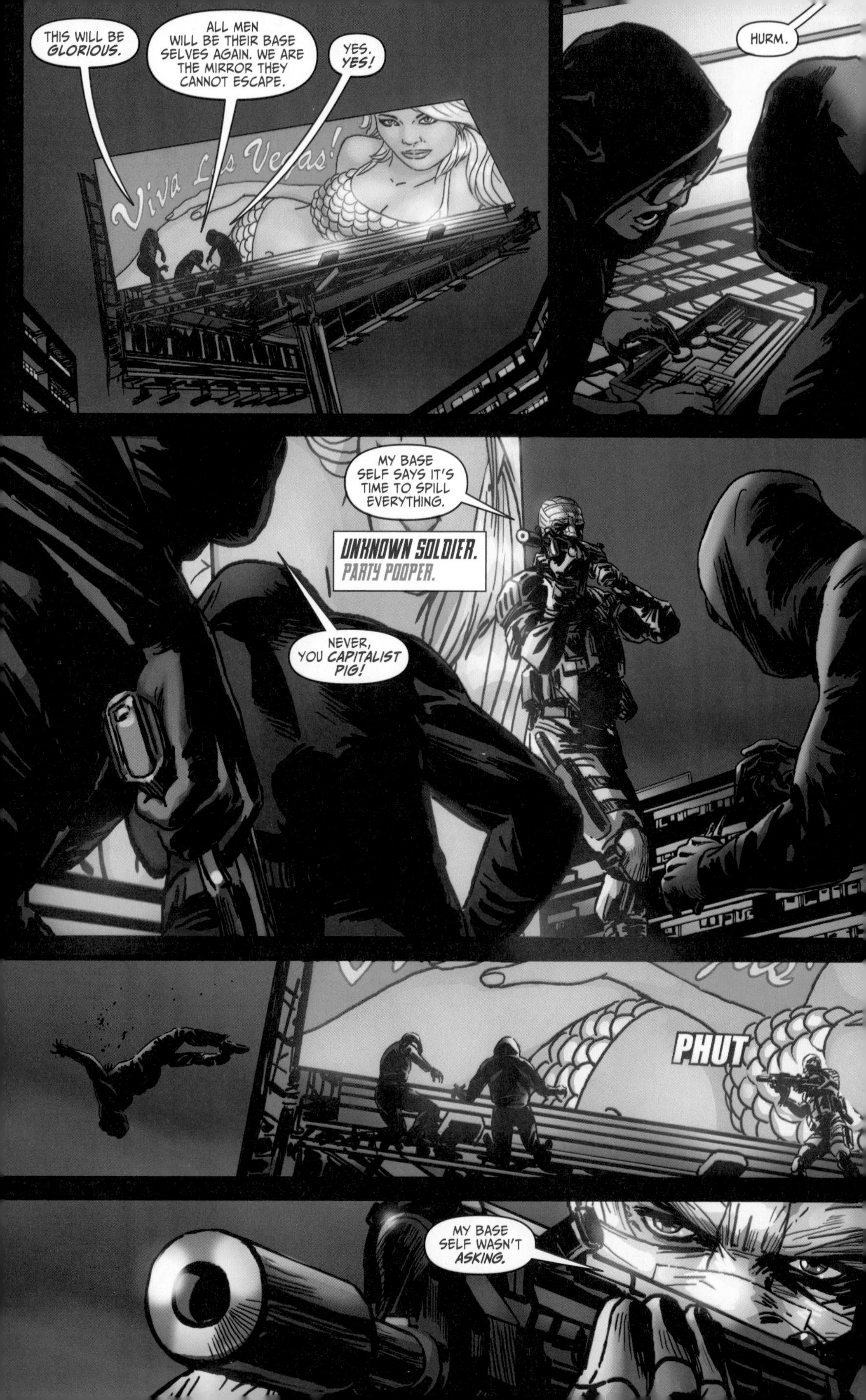
THIS WILL BE GLORIOUS.
ALL MEN WILL BE THEIR BASE SELVES AGAIN. WE ARE THE MIRROR THEY CANNOT ESCAPE.
YES. YES!
Viva Las Vegas!
HURM.
MY BASE SELF SAYS IT'S TIME TO SPILL EVERYTHING.
UNKNOWN SOLDIER.
PARTY POOPER.
NEVER, YOU CAPITALIST PIG!
PHUT
MY BASE SELF WASN'T ASKING.

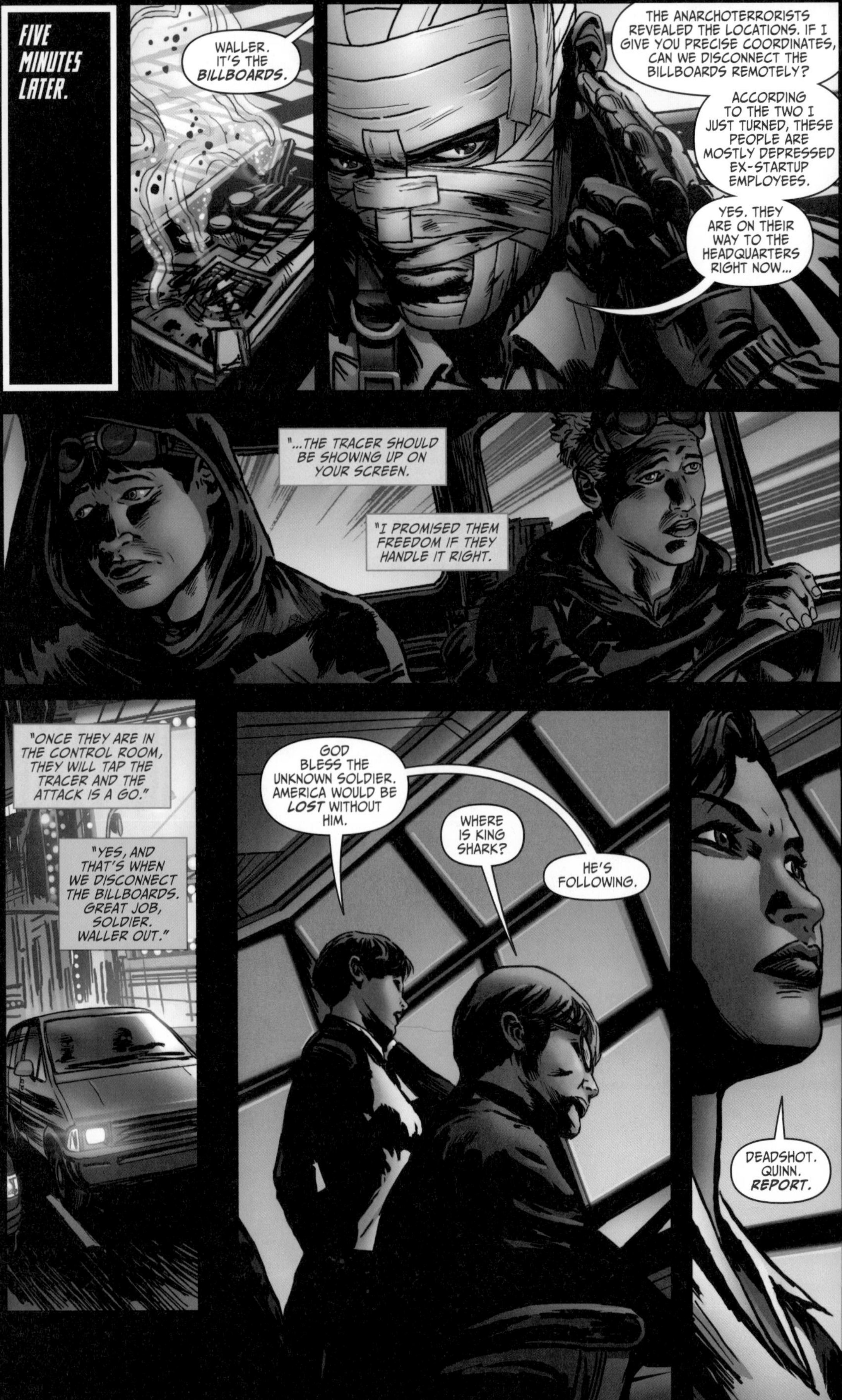
FIVE MINUTES LATER.
WALLER. IT'S THE BILLBOARDS.
THE ANARCHOTERRORISTS REVEALED THE LOCATIONS. IF I GIVE YOU PRECISE COORDINATES, CAN WE DISCONNECT THE BILLBOARDS REMOTELY?
ACCORDING TO THE TWO I JUST TURNED, THESE PEOPLE ARE MOSTLY DEPRESSED EX-STARTUP EMPLOYEES.
YES. THEY ARE ON THEIR WAY TO THE HEADQUARTERS RIGHT NOW...
"...THE TRACER SHOULD BE SHOWING UP ON YOUR SCREEN.
"I PROMISED THEM FREEDOM IF THEY HANDLE IT RIGHT.
"ONCE THEY ARE IN THE CONTROL ROOM, THEY WILL TAP THE TRACER AND THE ATTACK IS A GO."
"YES, AND THAT'S WHEN WE DISCONNECT THE BILLBOARDS. GREAT JOB, SOLDIER. WALLER OUT."
GOD BLESS THE UNKNOWN SOLDIER. AMERICA WOULD BE LOST WITHOUT HIM.
WHERE IS KING SHARK?
HE'S FOLLOWING.
DEADSHOT. QUINN. REPORT.

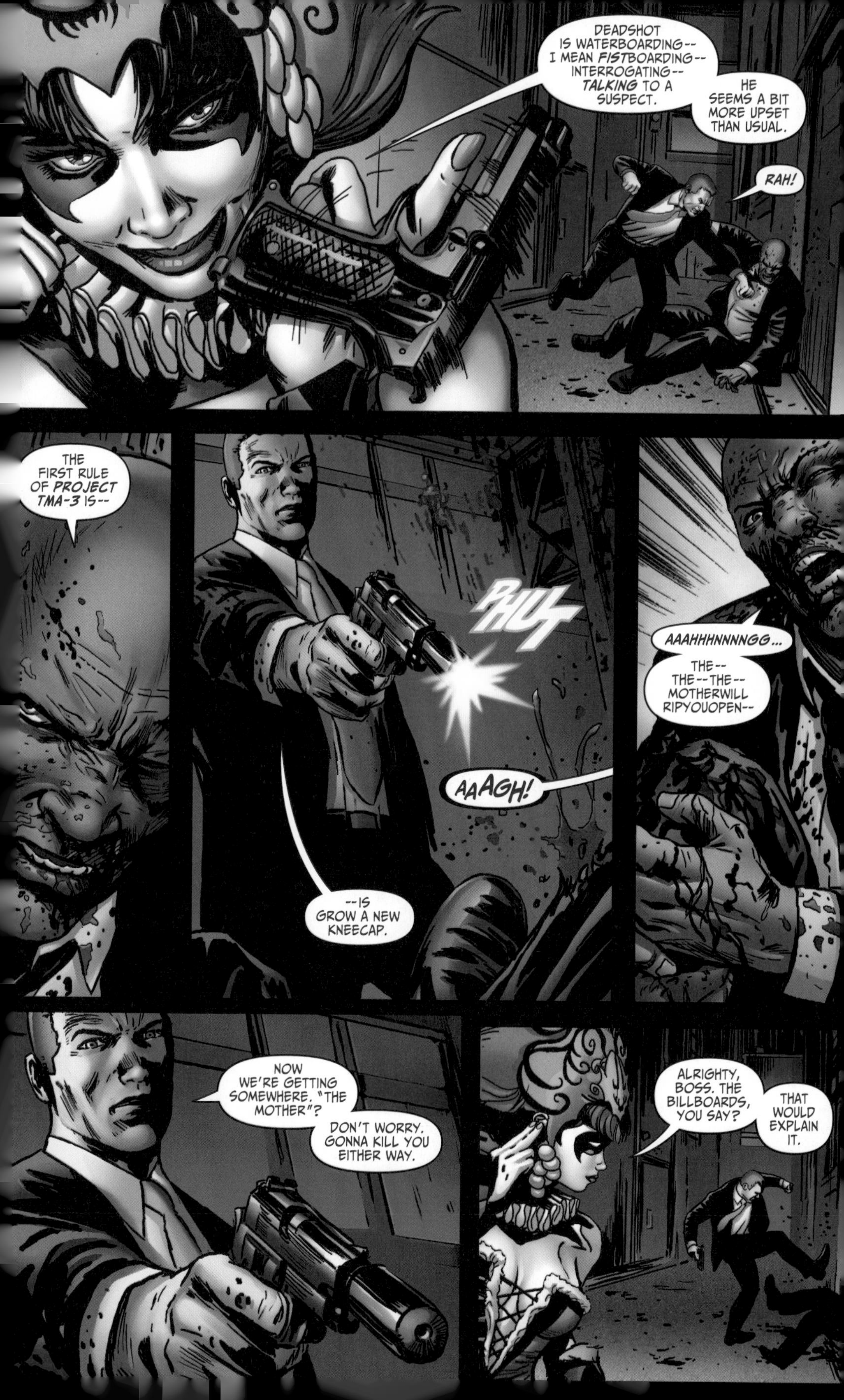
DEADSHOT IS WATERBOARDING-- I MEAN FISTBOARDING-- INTERROGATING-- TALKING TO A SUSPECT.
HE SEEMS A BIT MORE UPSET THAN USUAL.
RAH!
THE FIRST RULE OF PROJECT TMA-3 IS--
PHUT
--IS GROW A NEW KNEECAP.
AAAGH!
AAAHHHNNNNGG...
THE-- THE--THE-- MOTHERWILL RIPYOUOPEN--
NOW WE'RE GETTING SOMEWHERE. "THE MOTHER"?
DON'T WORRY. GONNA KILL YOU EITHER WAY.
ALRIGHTY, BOSS. THE BILLBOARDS, YOU SAY?
THAT WOULD EXPLAIN IT.

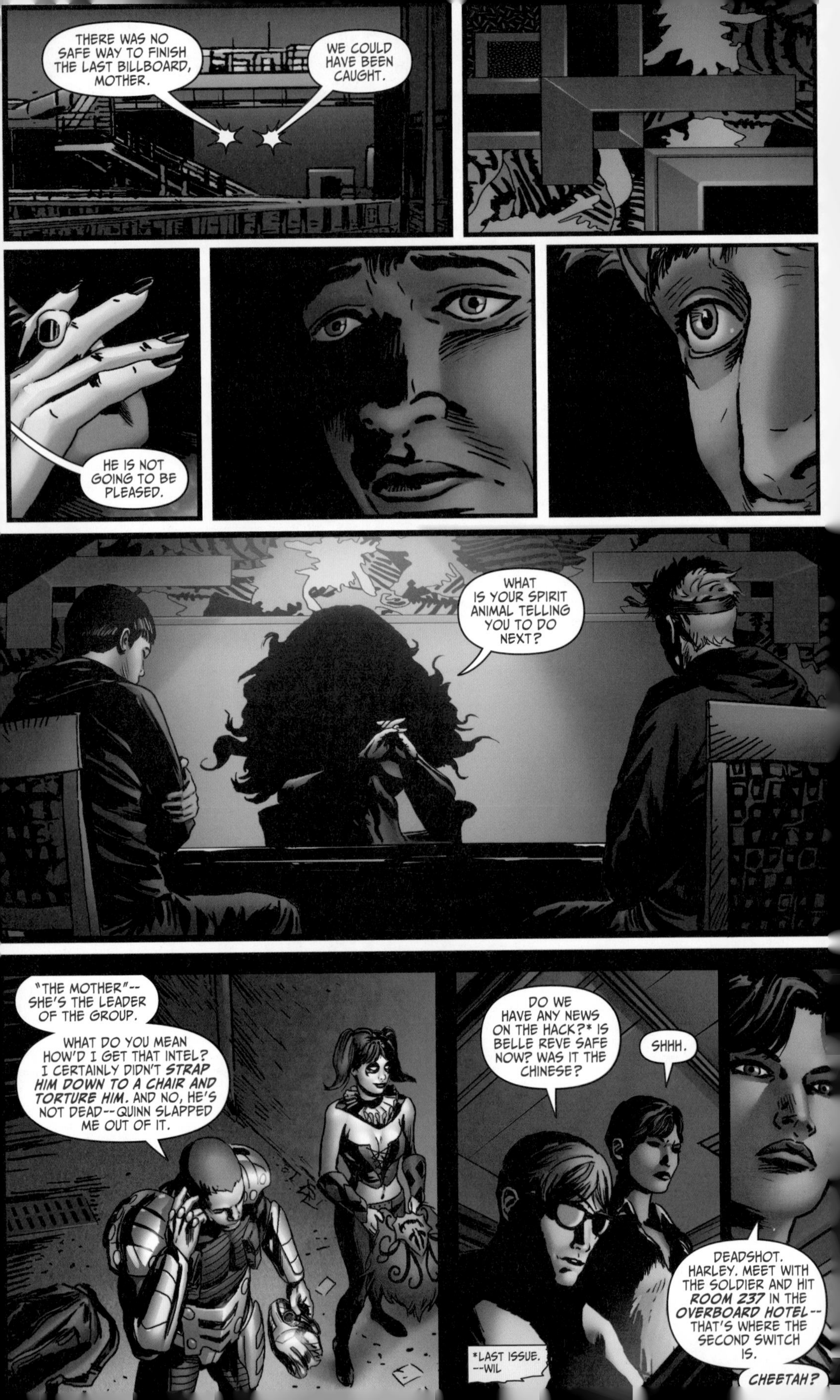
THERE WAS NO SAFE WAY TO FINISH THE LAST BILLBOARD, MOTHER.
WE COULD HAVE BEEN CAUGHT.
HE IS NOT GOING TO BE PLEASED.
WHAT IS YOUR SPIRIT ANIMAL TELLING YOU TO DO NEXT?
"THE MOTHER"-- SHE'S THE LEADER OF THE GROUP.
WHAT DO YOU MEAN HOW'D I GET THAT INTEL? I CERTAINLY DIDN'T STRAP HIM DOWN TO A CHAIR AND TORTURE HIM. AND NO, HE'S NOT DEAD--QUINN SLAPPED ME OUT OF IT.
DO WE HAVE ANY NEWS ON THE HACK?* IS BELLE REVE SAFE NOW? WAS IT THE CHINESE?
SHHH.
*LAST ISSUE. --WIL
DEADSHOT. HARLEY. MEET WITH THE SOLDIER AND HIT ROOM 237 IN THE OVERBOARD HOTEL-- THAT'S WHERE THE SECOND SWITCH IS.
CHEETAH?

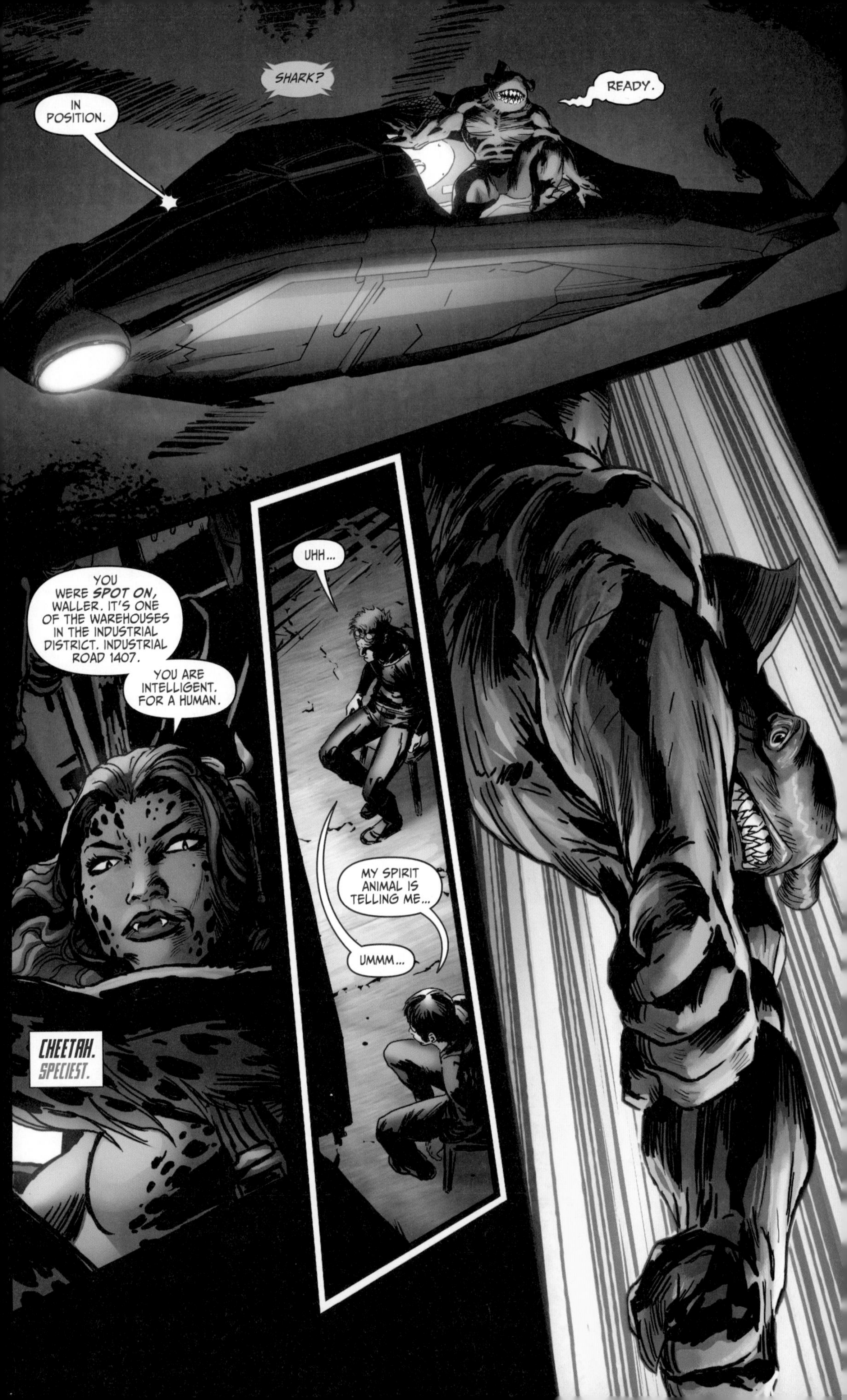
IN POSITION.
SHARK?
READY.
UHH...
YOU WERE SPOT ON, WALLER. IT'S ONE OF THE WAREHOUSES IN THE INDUSTRIAL DISTRICT. INDUSTRIAL ROAD 1407.
YOU ARE INTELLIGENT. FOR A HUMAN.
CHEETAH. SPECIEST.
MY SPIRIT ANIMAL IS TELLING ME...
UMMM...

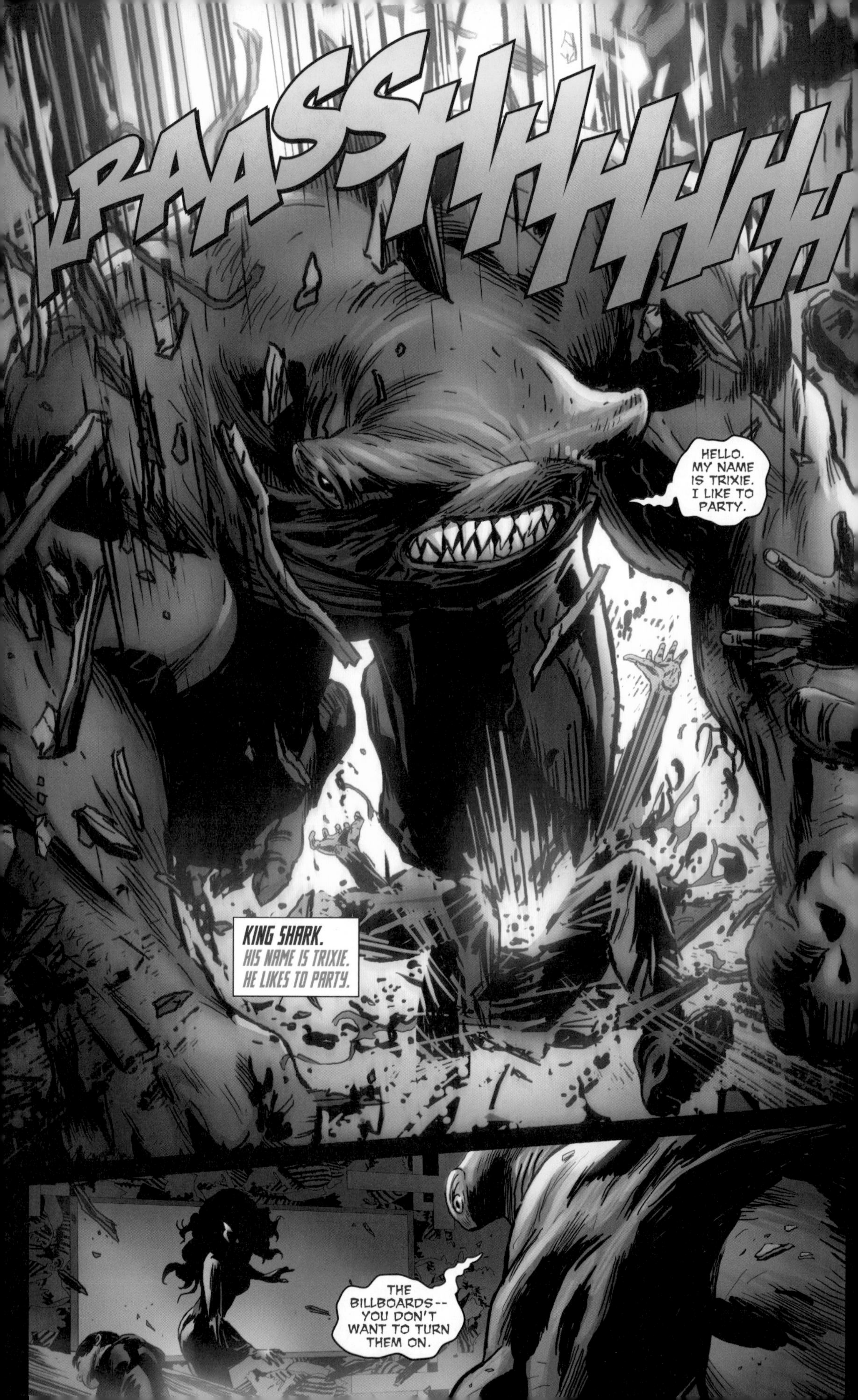
KRAASHHHHH
HELLO. MY NAME IS TRIXIE. I LIKE TO PARTY.
KING SHARK.
HIS NAME IS TRIXIE. HE LIKES TO PARTY.
THE BILLBOARDS-- YOU DON'T WANT TO TURN THEM ON.

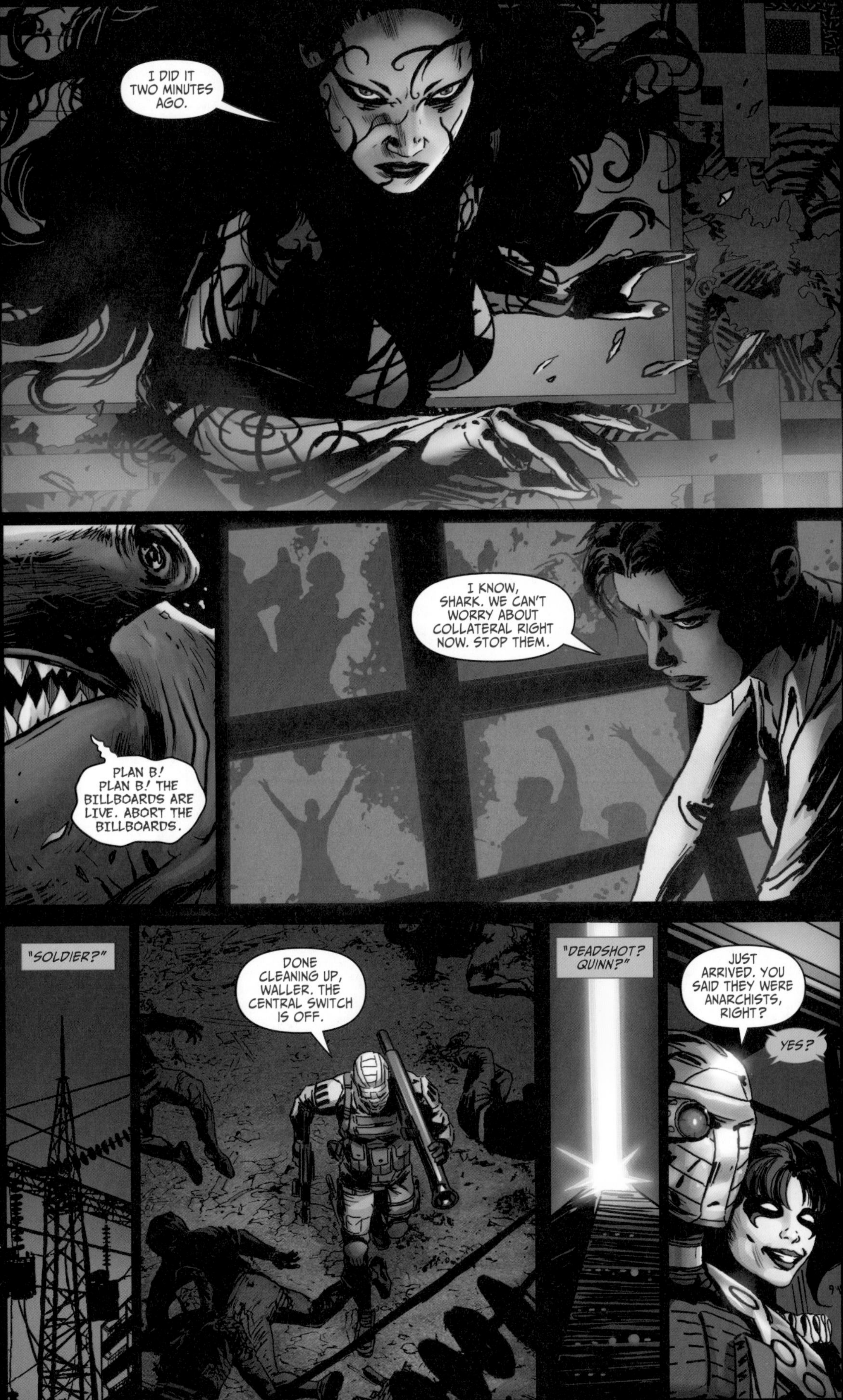
I DID IT TWO MINUTES AGO.
PLAN B! PLAN B! THE BILLBOARDS ARE LIVE. ABORT THE BILLBOARDS.
I KNOW, SHARK. WE CAN'T WORRY ABOUT COLLATERAL RIGHT NOW. STOP THEM.
"SOLDIER?"
DONE CLEANING UP, WALLER. THE CENTRAL SWITCH IS OFF.
"DEADSHOT? QUINN?"
JUST ARRIVED. YOU SAID THEY WERE ANARCHISTS, RIGHT?
YES?

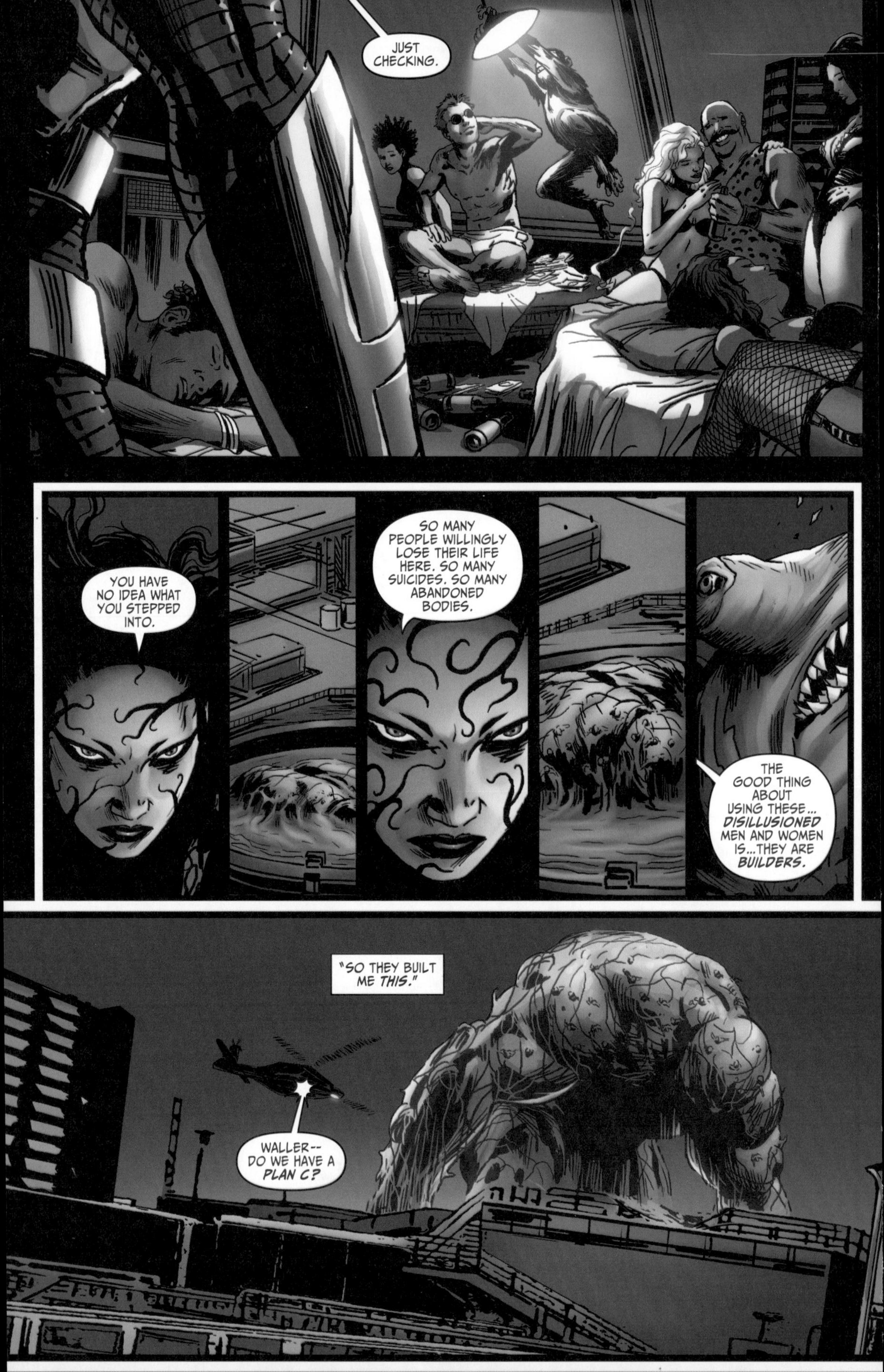
JUST CHECKING.
YOU HAVE NO IDEA WHAT YOU STEPPED INTO.
SO MANY PEOPLE WILLINGLY LOSE THEIR LIFE HERE. SO MANY SUICIDES. SO MANY ABANDONED BODIES.
THE GOOD THING ABOUT USING THESE... DISILLUSIONED MEN AND WOMEN IS...THEY ARE BUILDERS.
"SO THEY BUILT ME THIS."
WALLER-- DO WE HAVE A PLAN C?

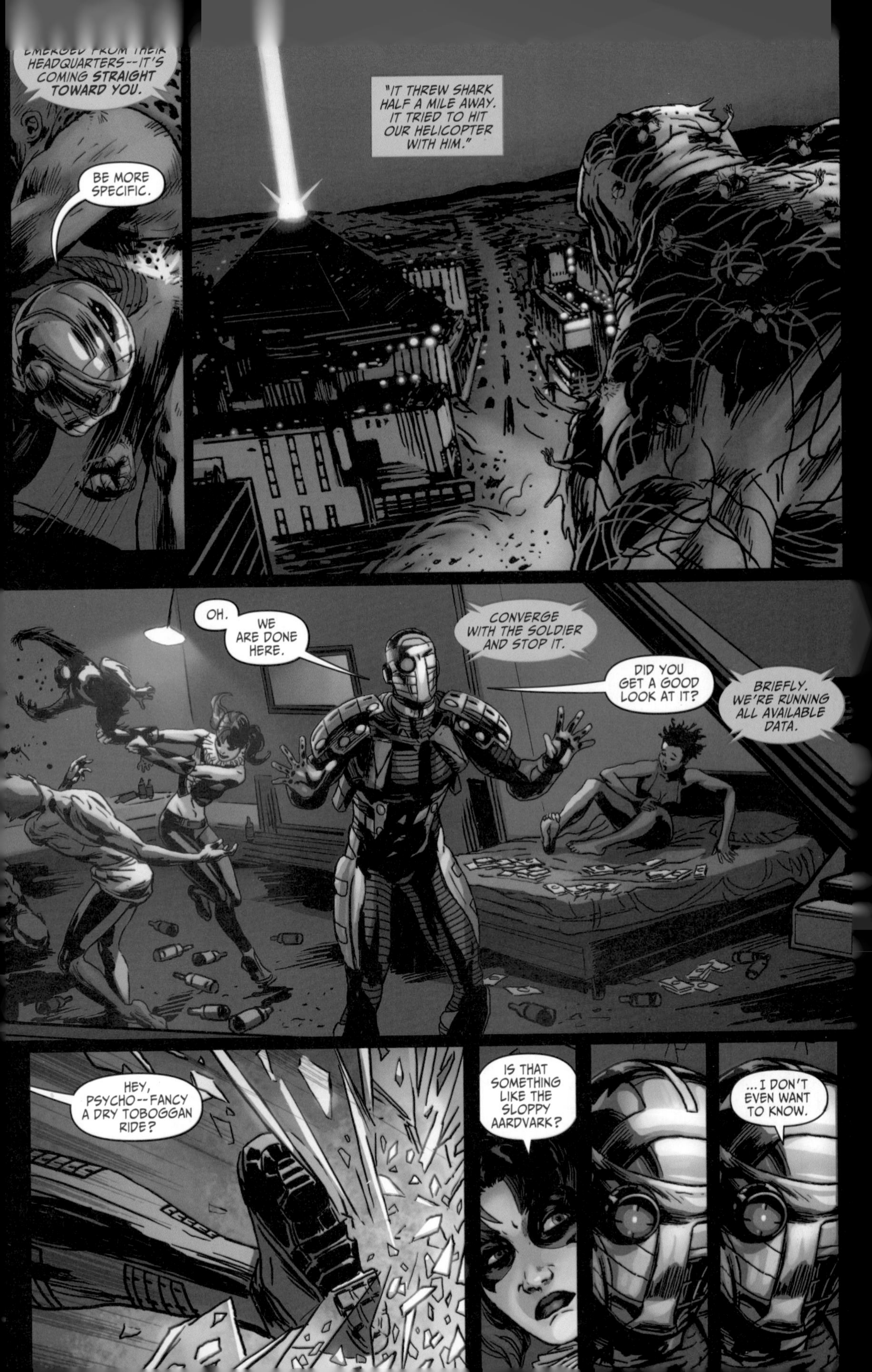
EMERGED FROM THEIR HEADQUARTERS--IT'S COMING STRAIGHT TOWARD YOU.
BE MORE SPECIFIC.
"IT THREW SHARK HALF A MILE AWAY. IT TRIED TO HIT OUR HELICOPTER WITH HIM."
OH.
WE ARE DONE HERE.
CONVERGE WITH THE SOLDIER AND STOP IT.
DID YOU GET A GOOD LOOK AT IT?
BRIEFLY. WE'RE RUNNING ALL AVAILABLE DATA.
HEY, PSYCHO--FANCY A DRY TOBOGGAN RIDE?
IS THAT SOMETHING LIKE THE SLOPPY AARDVARK?
...I DON'T EVEN WANT TO KNOW.

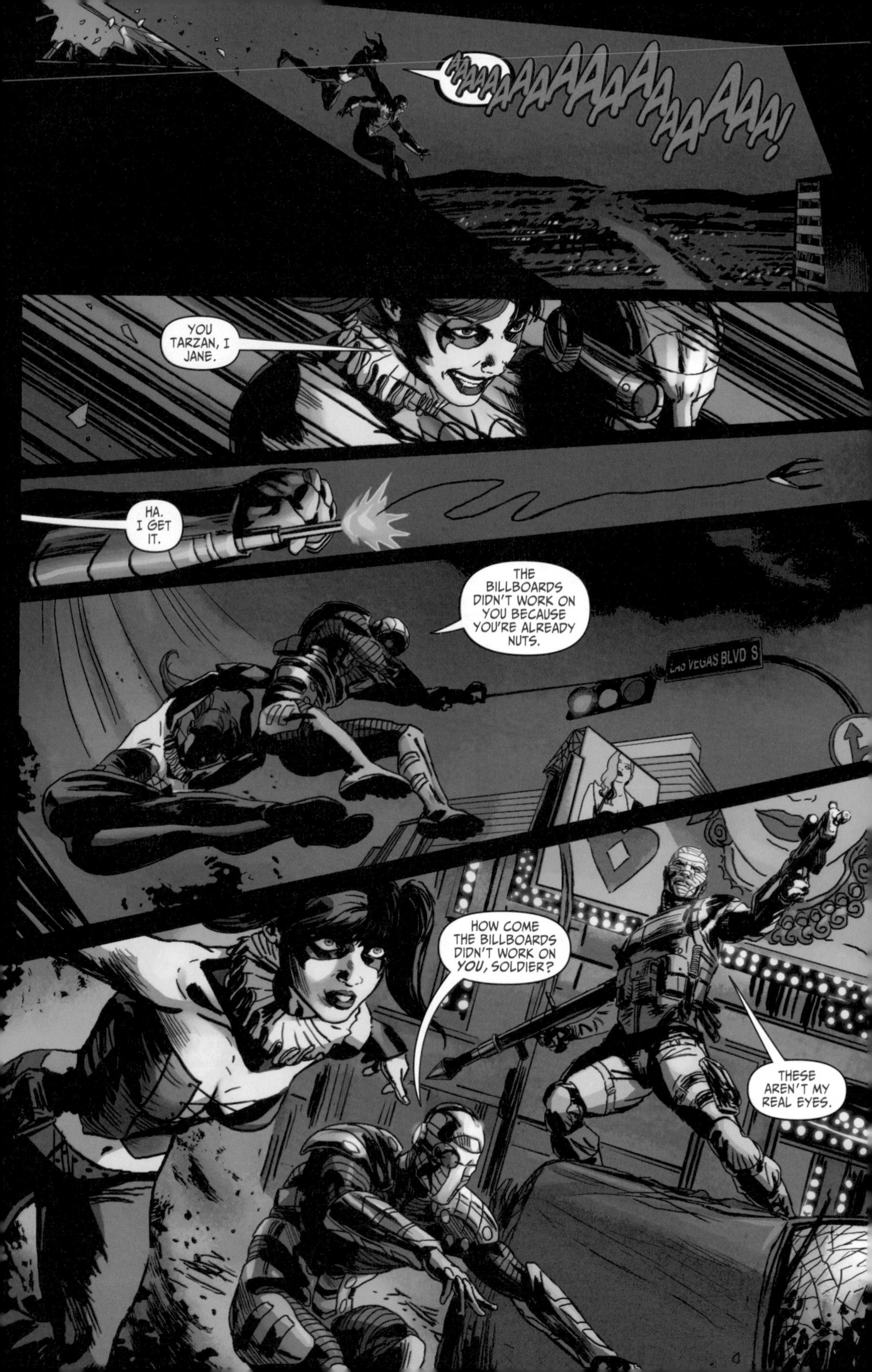
AAAAAAAAAAAAAAAAAA!
YOU TARZAN, I JANE.
HA. I GET IT.
THE BILLBOARDS DIDN'T WORK ON YOU BECAUSE YOU'RE ALREADY NUTS.
LAS VEGAS BLVD S
HOW COME THE BILLBOARDS DIDN'T WORK ON *YOU*, SOLDIER?
THESE AREN'T MY REAL EYES.

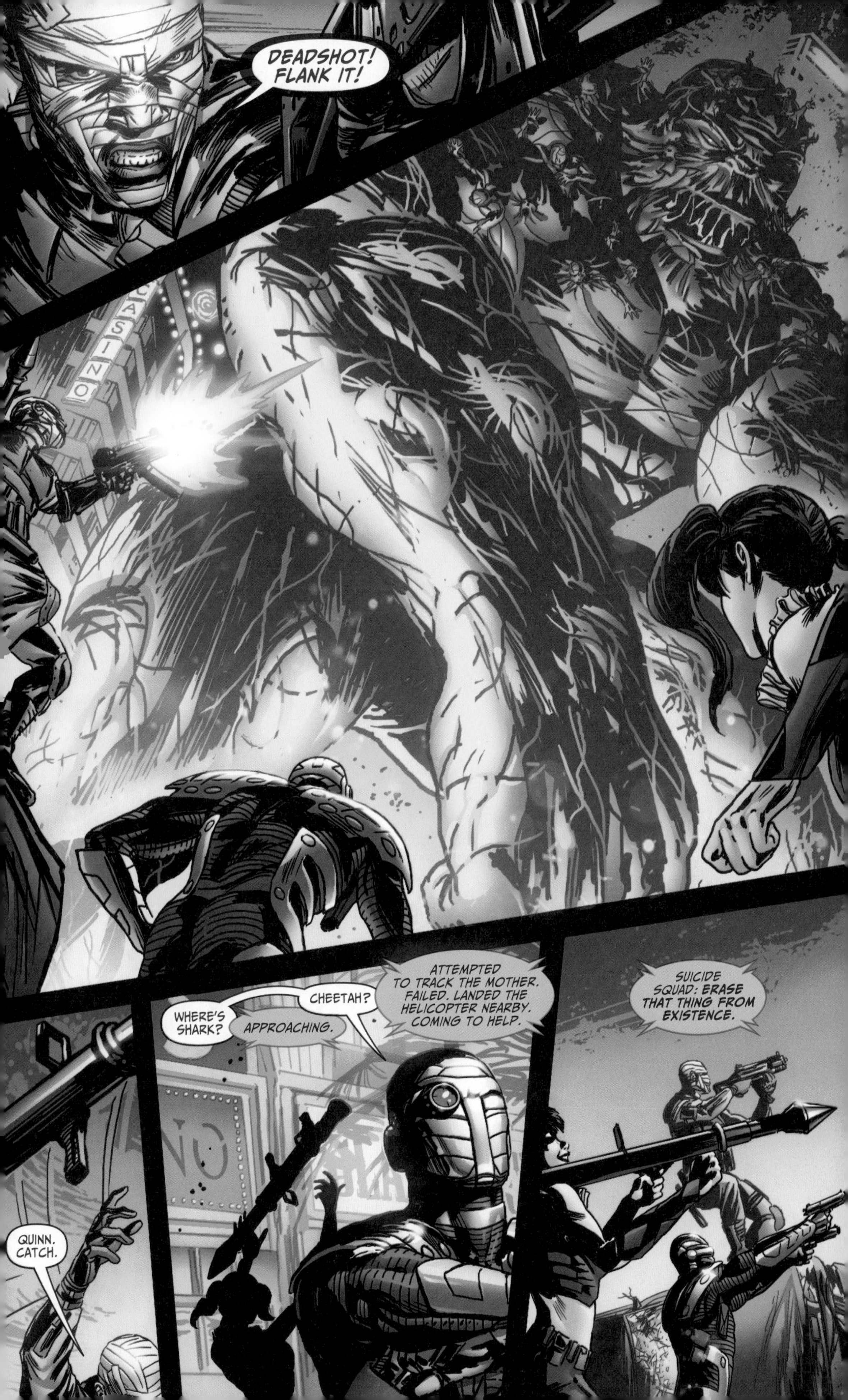
DEADSHOT! FLANK IT!
CASINO
WHERE'S SHARK?
CHEETAH?
APPROACHING.
ATTEMPTED TO TRACK THE MOTHER. FAILED. LANDED THE HELICOPTER NEARBY. COMING TO HELP.
SUICIDE SQUAD: ERASE THAT THING FROM EXISTENCE.
QUINN. CATCH.

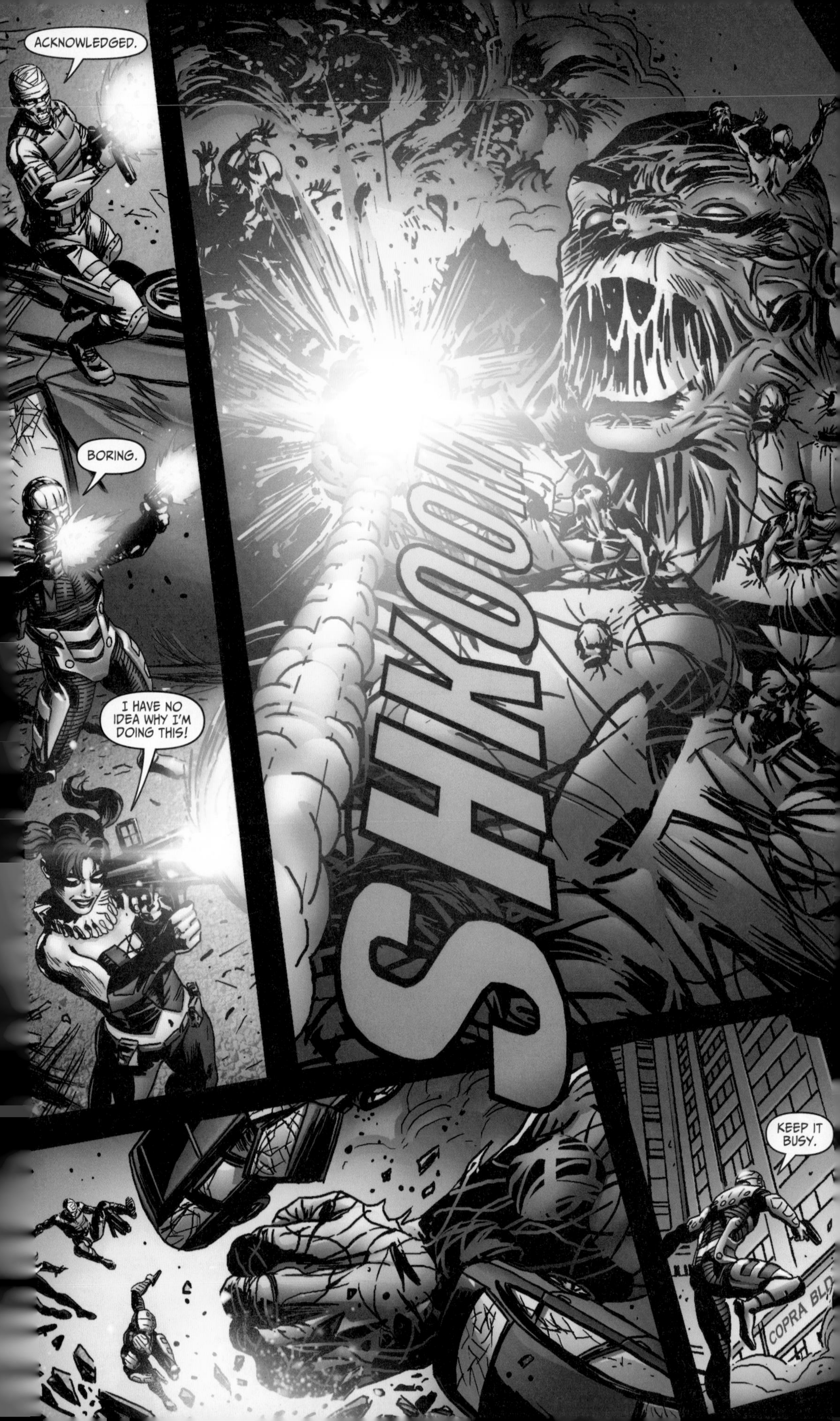
ACKNOWLEDGED.
BORING.
I HAVE NO IDEA WHY I'M DOING THIS!
SHHOOM
KEEP IT BUSY.
COPRA BLD

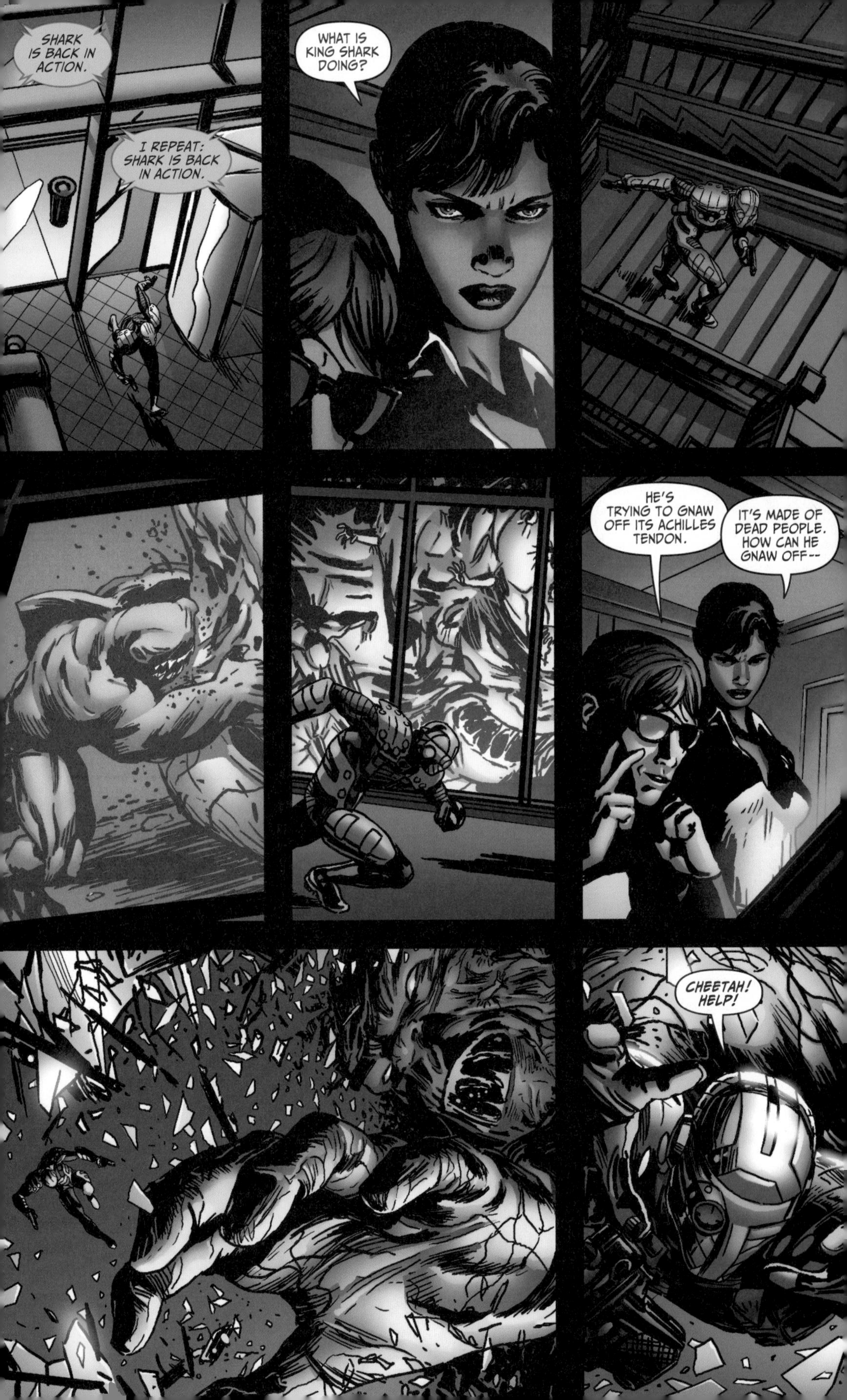
SHARK IS BACK IN ACTION.
I REPEAT: SHARK IS BACK IN ACTION.
WHAT IS KING SHARK DOING?
HE'S TRYING TO GNAW OFF ITS ACHILLES TENDON.
IT'S MADE OF DEAD PEOPLE. HOW CAN HE GNAW OFF--
CHEETAH! HELP!

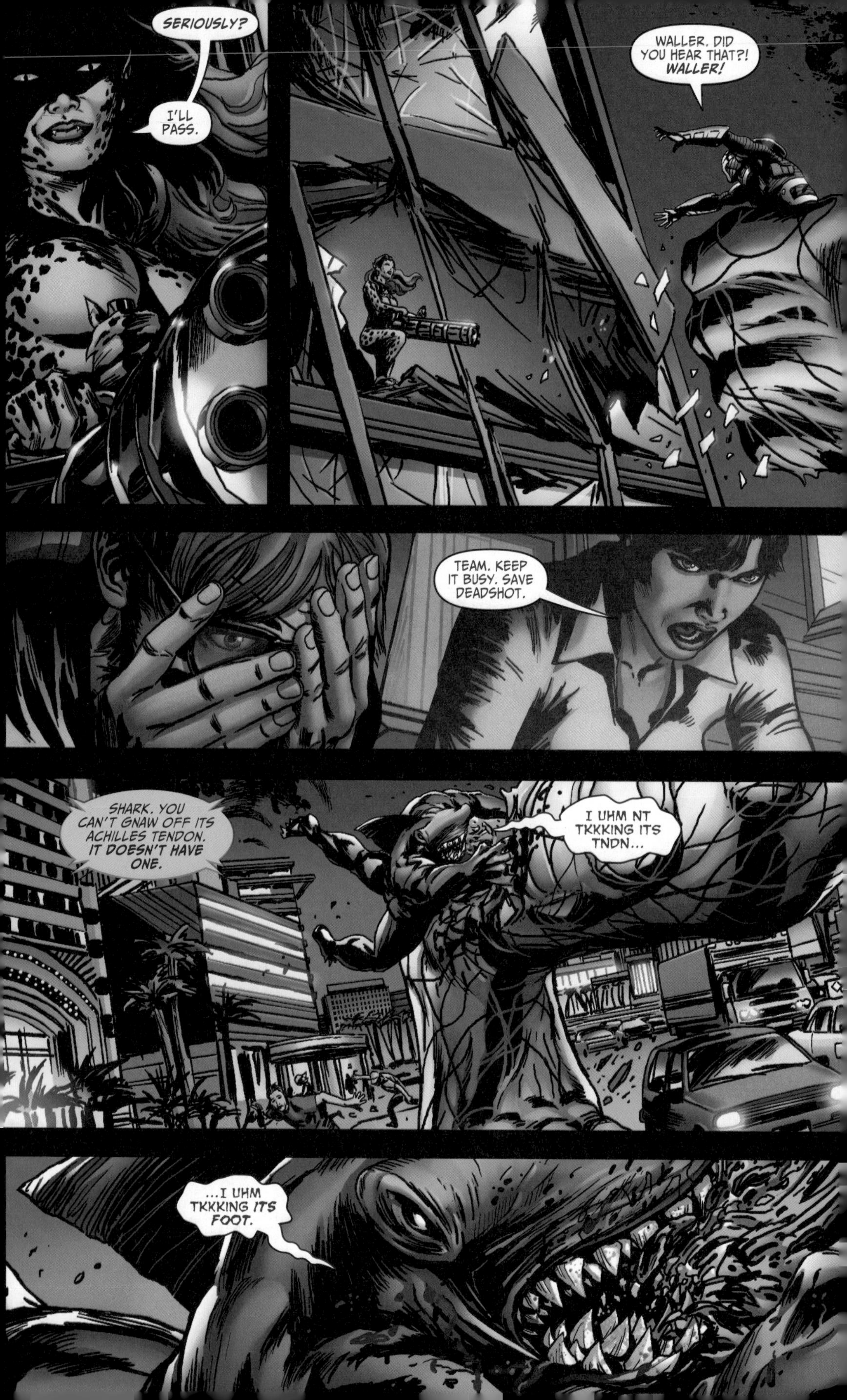
SERIOUSLY?
I'LL PASS.
WALLER. DID YOU HEAR THAT?! WALLER!
TEAM. KEEP IT BUSY. SAVE DEADSHOT.
SHARK. YOU CAN'T GNAW OFF ITS ACHILLES TENDON. IT DOESN'T HAVE ONE.
I UHM NT TKKKING ITS TNDN...
...I UHM TKKKING ITS FOOT.

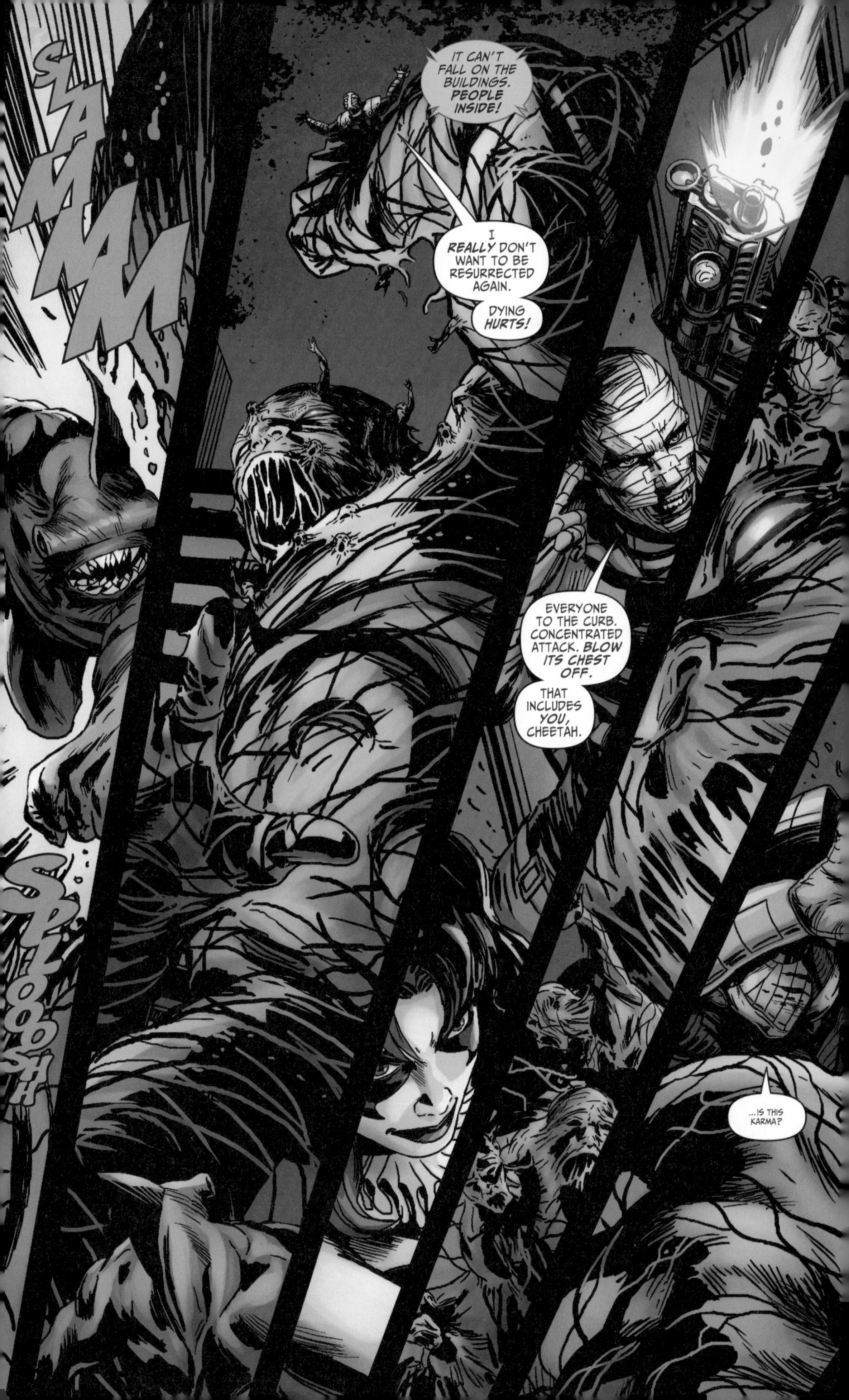
SLAMM
IT CAN'T FALL ON THE BUILDINGS. PEOPLE INSIDE!
I REALLY DON'T WANT TO BE RESURRECTED AGAIN.
DYING HURTS!
EVERYONE TO THE CURB. CONCENTRATED ATTACK. BLOW ITS CHEST OFF.
THAT INCLUDES YOU, CHEETAH.
SPLOOOSH
...IS THIS KARMA?

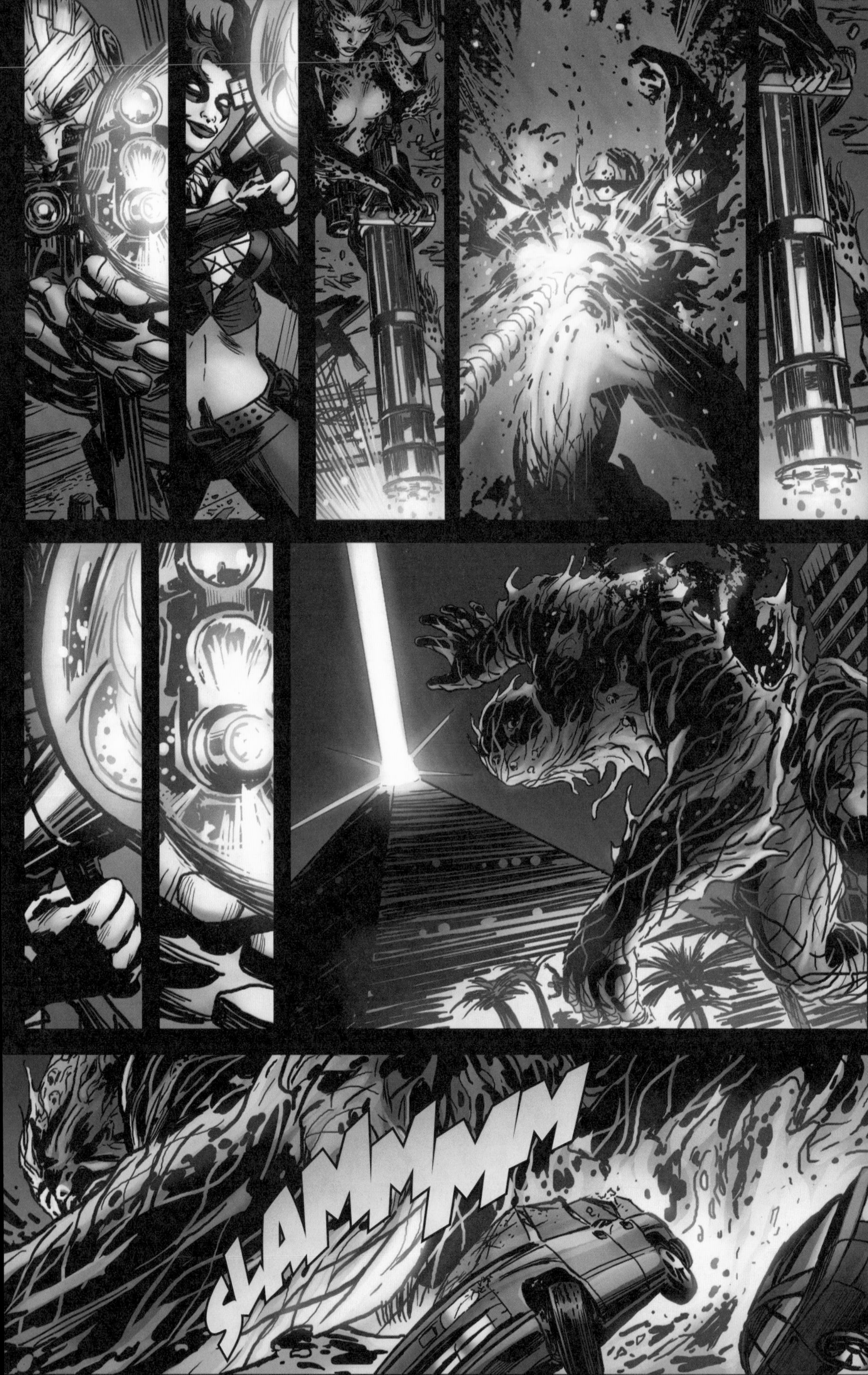
SLAMMMMM

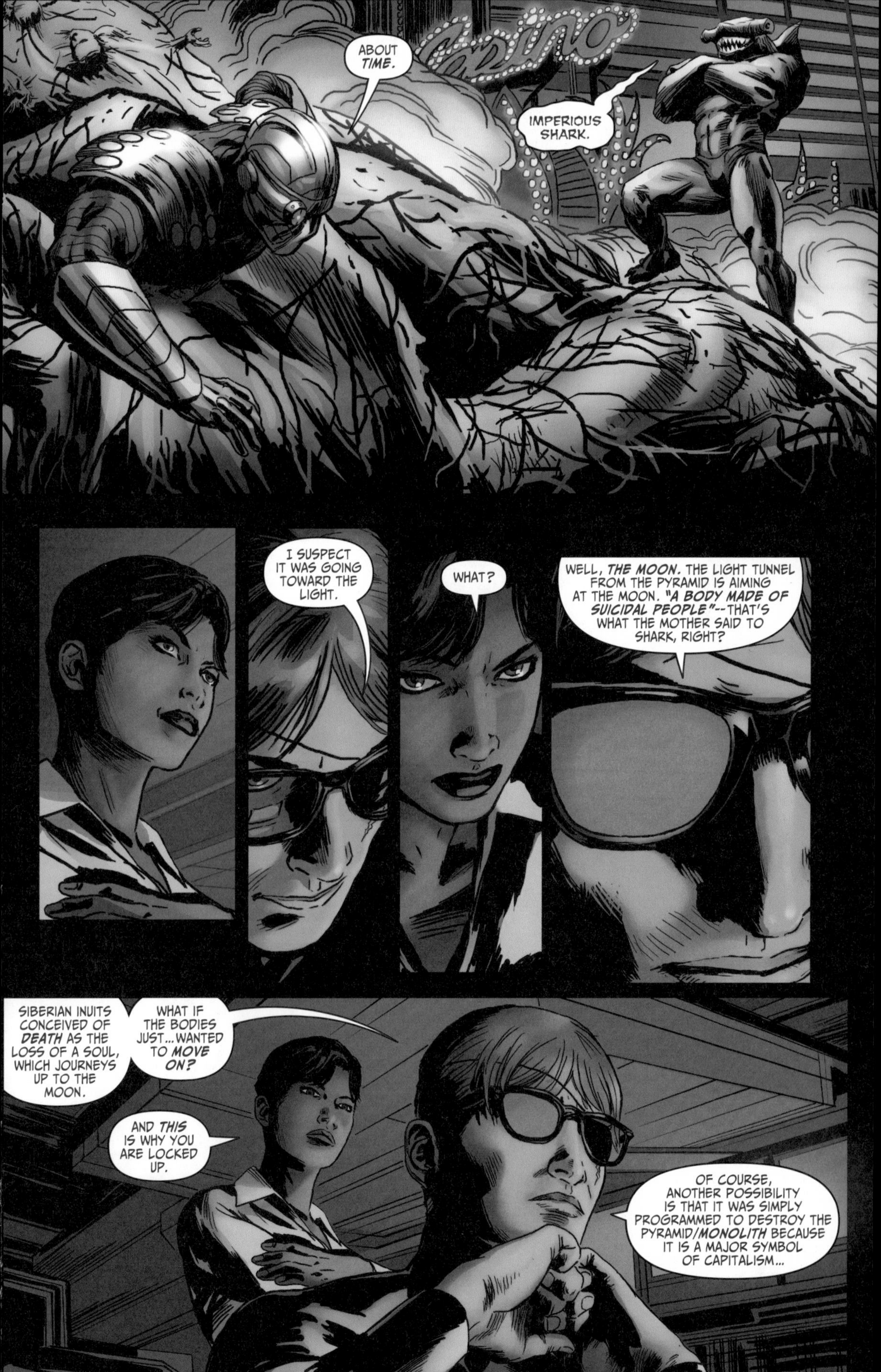
ABOUT TIME.
IMPERIOUS SHARK.
I SUSPECT IT WAS GOING TOWARD THE LIGHT.
WHAT?
WELL, THE MOON. THE LIGHT TUNNEL FROM THE PYRAMID IS AIMING AT THE MOON. "A BODY MADE OF SUICIDAL PEOPLE"--THAT'S WHAT THE MOTHER SAID TO SHARK, RIGHT?
WHAT IF THE BODIES JUST...WANTED TO MOVE ON?
SIBERIAN INUITS CONCEIVED OF DEATH AS THE LOSS OF A SOUL, WHICH JOURNEYS UP TO THE MOON.
AND THIS IS WHY YOU ARE LOCKED UP.
OF COURSE, ANOTHER POSSIBILITY IS THAT IT WAS SIMPLY PROGRAMMED TO DESTROY THE PYRAMID/MONOLITH BECAUSE IT IS A MAJOR SYMBOL OF CAPITALISM...

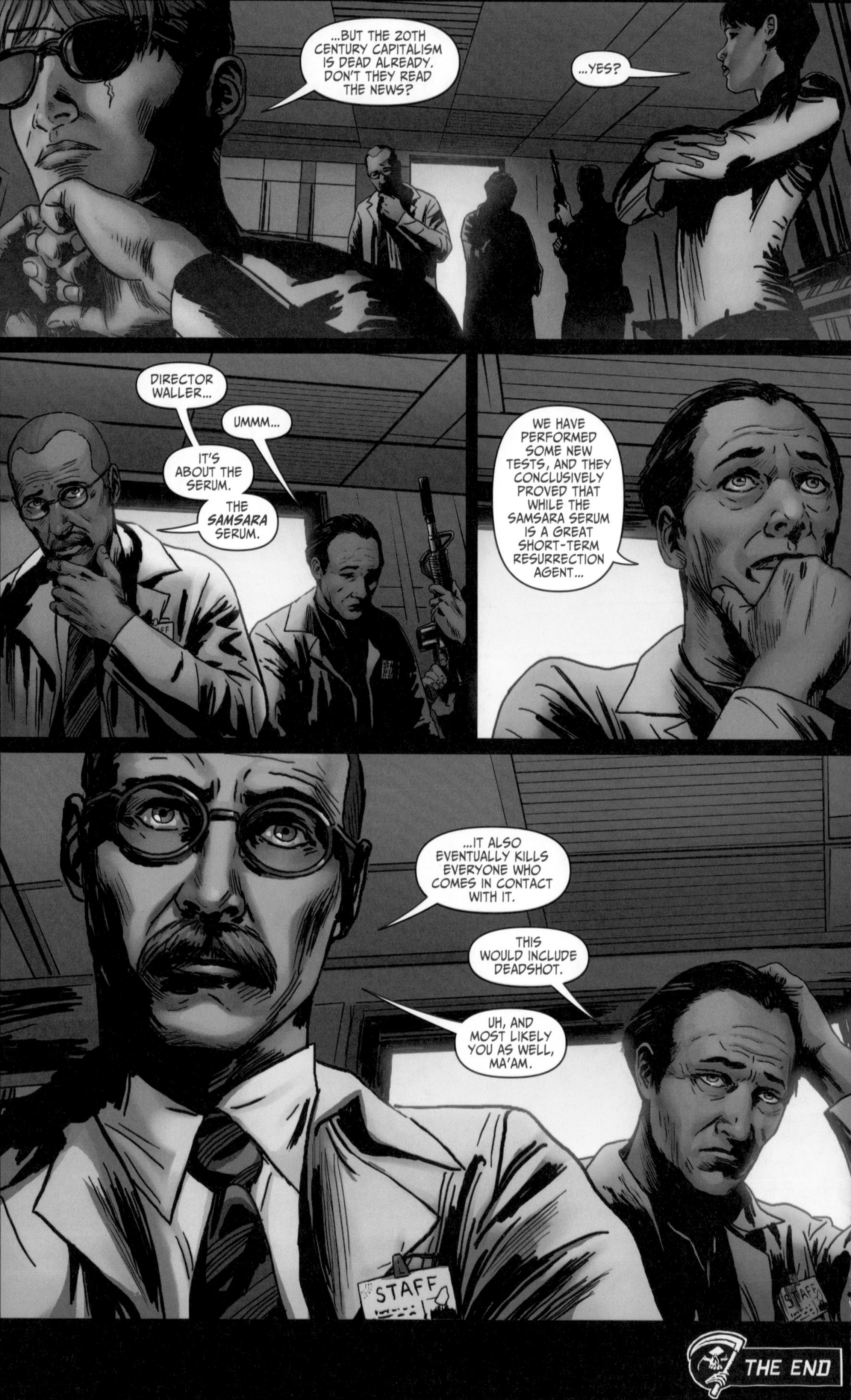
...BUT THE 20TH CENTURY CAPITALISM IS DEAD ALREADY. DON'T THEY READ THE NEWS?
...YES?
DIRECTOR WALLER...
UMMM...
IT'S ABOUT THE SERUM.
THE SAMSARA SERUM.
WE HAVE PERFORMED SOME NEW TESTS, AND THEY CONCLUSIVELY PROVED THAT WHILE THE SAMSARA SERUM IS A GREAT SHORT-TERM RESURRECTION AGENT...
...IT ALSO EVENTUALLY KILLS EVERYONE WHO COMES IN CONTACT WITH IT.
THIS WOULD INCLUDE DEADSHOT.
UH, AND MOST LIKELY YOU AS WELL, MA'AM.
STAFF
THE END

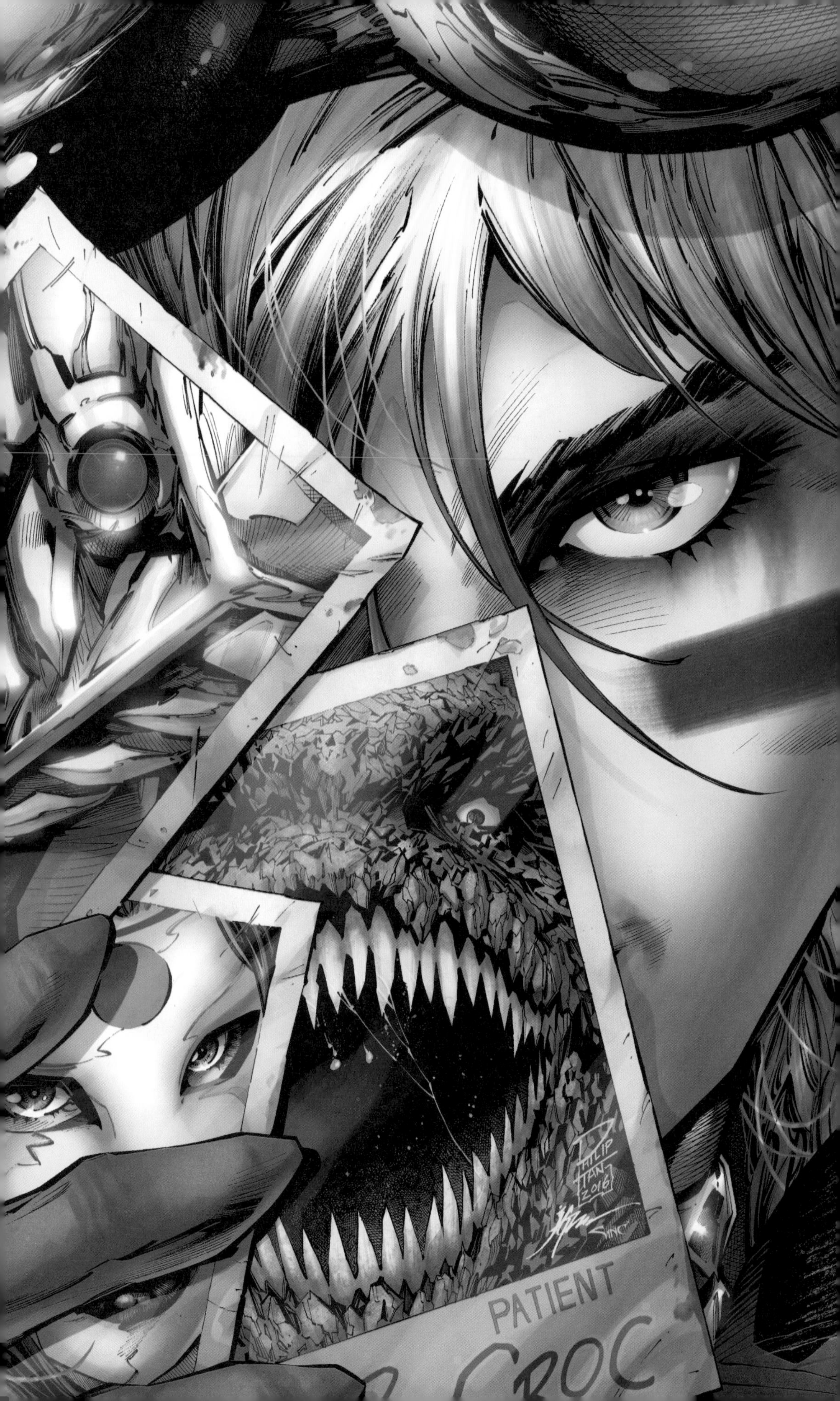
PHILIP TAN 2016
PATIENT
CROC

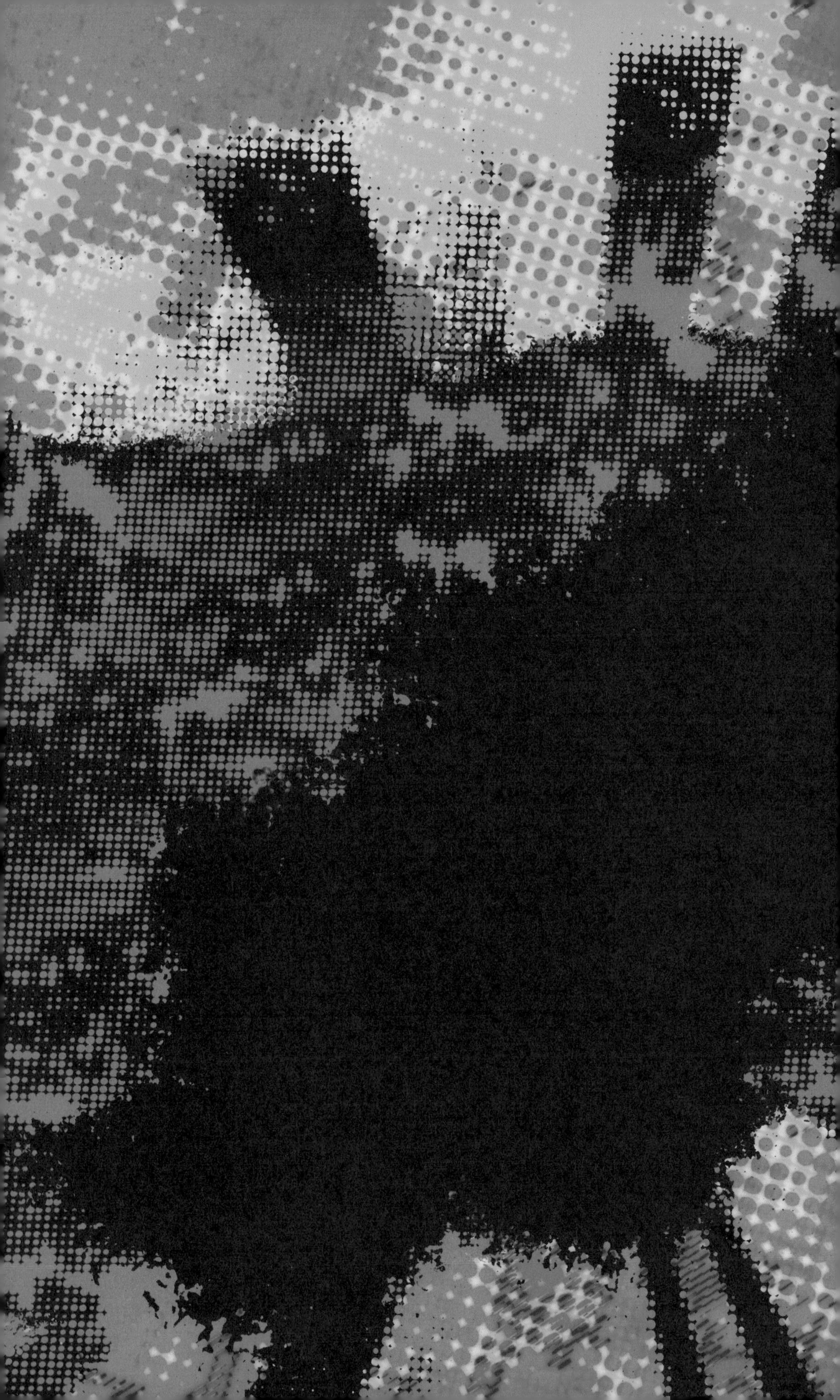

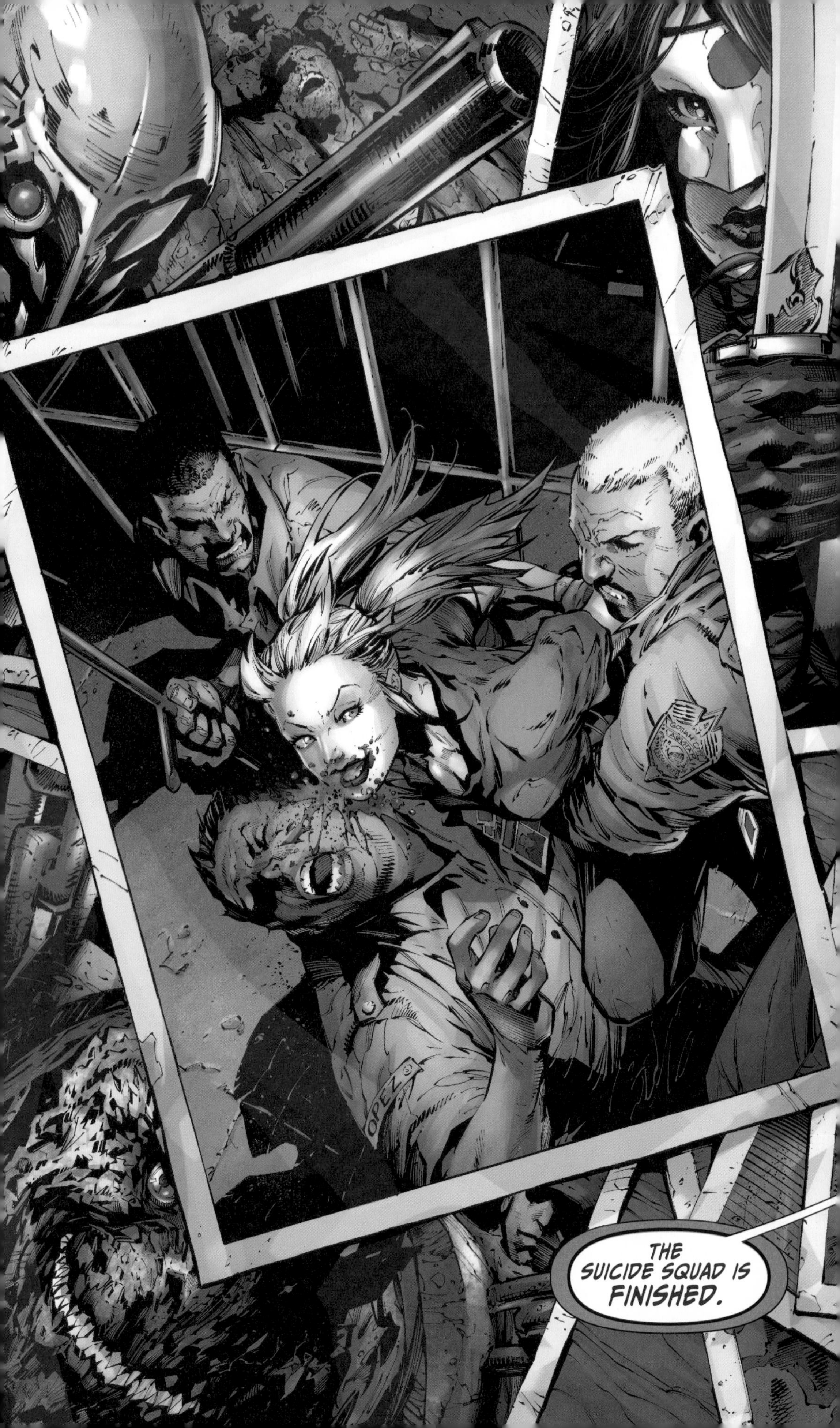
THE SUICIDE SQUAD IS FINISHED.

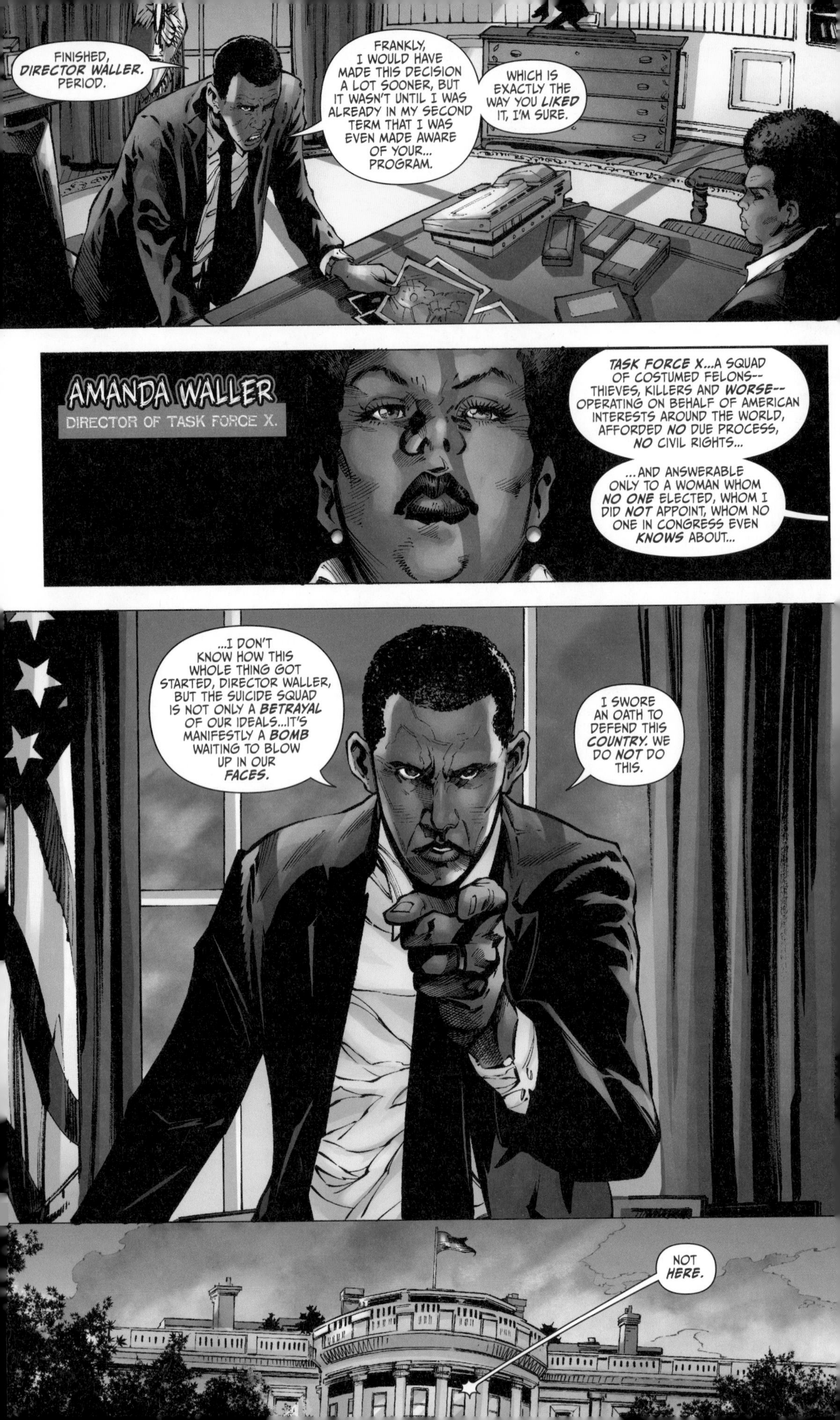
FINISHED, DIRECTOR WALLER. PERIOD.
FRANKLY, I WOULD HAVE MADE THIS DECISION A LOT SOONER, BUT IT WASN'T UNTIL I WAS ALREADY IN MY SECOND TERM THAT I WAS EVEN MADE AWARE OF YOUR... PROGRAM.
WHICH IS EXACTLY THE WAY YOU LIKED IT, I'M SURE.
AMANDA WALLER
DIRECTOR OF TASK FORCE X.
TASK FORCE X...A SQUAD OF COSTUMED FELONS--THIEVES, KILLERS AND WORSE--OPERATING ON BEHALF OF AMERICAN INTERESTS AROUND THE WORLD, AFFORDED NO DUE PROCESS, NO CIVIL RIGHTS...
...AND ANSWERABLE ONLY TO A WOMAN WHOM NO ONE ELECTED, WHOM I DID NOT APPOINT, WHOM NO ONE IN CONGRESS EVEN KNOWS ABOUT...
...I DON'T KNOW HOW THIS WHOLE THING GOT STARTED, DIRECTOR WALLER, BUT THE SUICIDE SQUAD IS NOT ONLY A BETRAYAL OF OUR IDEALS...IT'S MANIFESTLY A BOMB WAITING TO BLOW UP IN OUR FACES.
I SWORE AN OATH TO DEFEND THIS COUNTRY. WE DO NOT DO THIS.
NOT HERE.

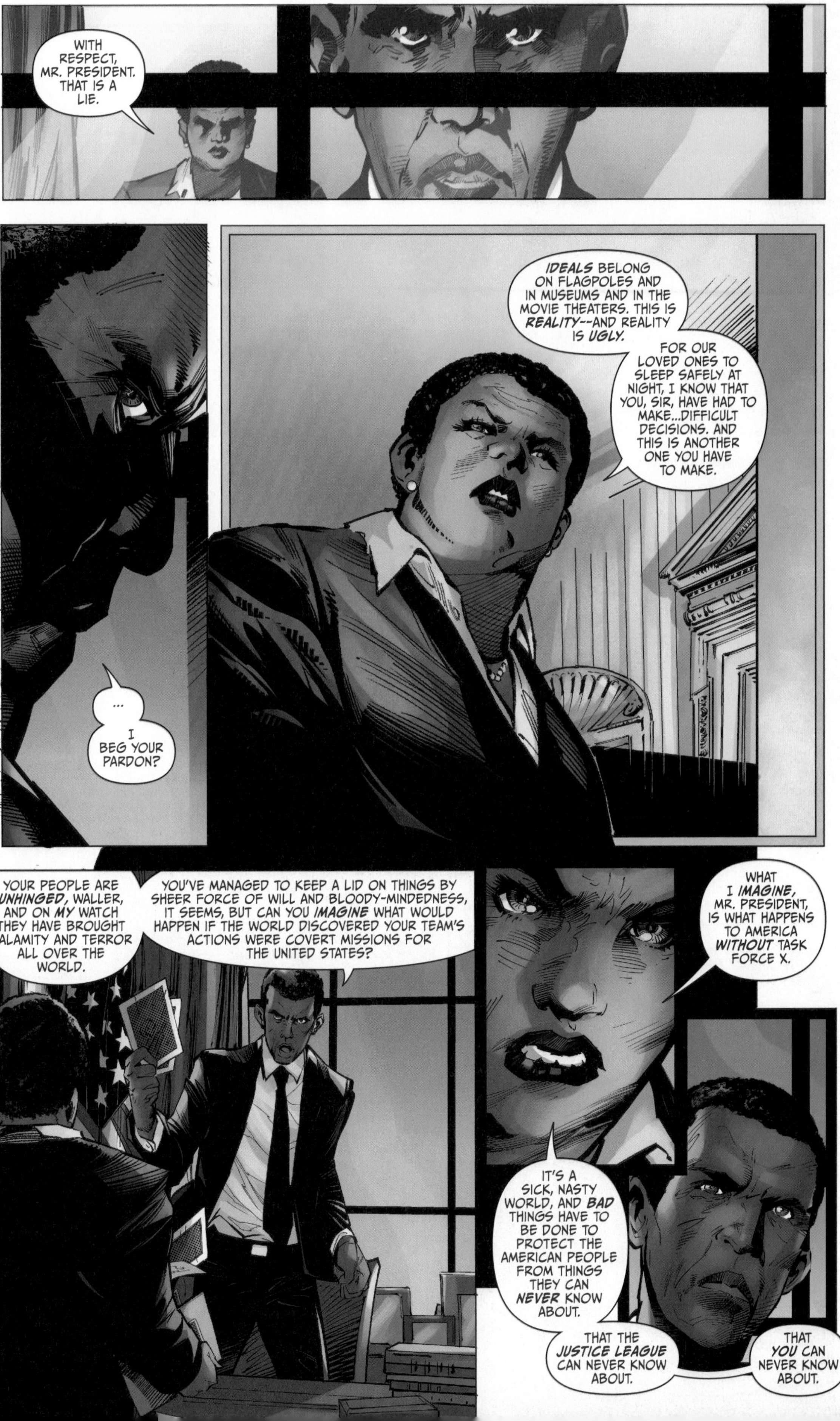
WITH RESPECT, MR. PRESIDENT. THAT IS A LIE.
IDEALS BELONG ON FLAGPOLES AND IN MUSEUMS AND IN THE MOVIE THEATERS. THIS IS REALITY--AND REALITY IS UGLY.
FOR OUR LOVED ONES TO SLEEP SAFELY AT NIGHT, I KNOW THAT YOU, SIR, HAVE HAD TO MAKE...DIFFICULT DECISIONS. AND THIS IS ANOTHER ONE YOU HAVE TO MAKE.
...
I BEG YOUR PARDON?
YOUR PEOPLE ARE UNHINGED, WALLER, AND ON MY WATCH THEY HAVE BROUGHT CALAMITY AND TERROR ALL OVER THE WORLD.
YOU'VE MANAGED TO KEEP A LID ON THINGS BY SHEER FORCE OF WILL AND BLOODY-MINDEDNESS, IT SEEMS, BUT CAN YOU IMAGINE WHAT WOULD HAPPEN IF THE WORLD DISCOVERED YOUR TEAM'S ACTIONS WERE COVERT MISSIONS FOR THE UNITED STATES?
WHAT I IMAGINE, MR. PRESIDENT, IS WHAT HAPPENS TO AMERICA WITHOUT TASK FORCE X.
IT'S A SICK, NASTY WORLD, AND BAD THINGS HAVE TO BE DONE TO PROTECT THE AMERICAN PEOPLE FROM THINGS THEY CAN NEVER KNOW ABOUT.
THAT THE JUSTICE LEAGUE CAN NEVER KNOW ABOUT.
THAT YOU CAN NEVER KNOW ABOUT.

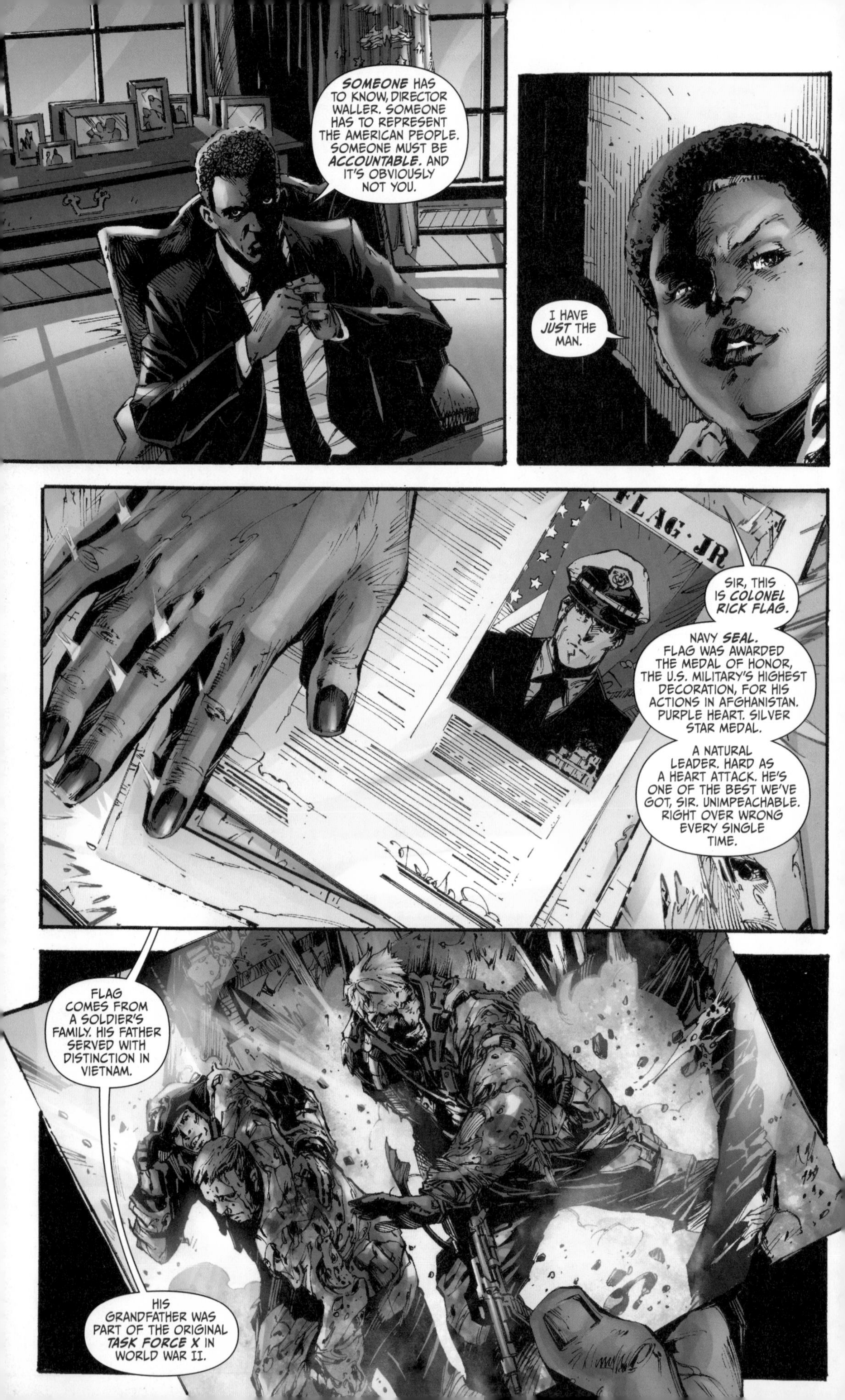
SOMEONE HAS TO KNOW, DIRECTOR WALLER. SOMEONE HAS TO REPRESENT THE AMERICAN PEOPLE. SOMEONE MUST BE ACCOUNTABLE. AND IT'S OBVIOUSLY NOT YOU.
I HAVE JUST THE MAN.
FLAG · JR
SIR, THIS IS COLONEL RICK FLAG.
NAVY SEAL. FLAG WAS AWARDED THE MEDAL OF HONOR, THE U.S. MILITARY'S HIGHEST DECORATION, FOR HIS ACTIONS IN AFGHANISTAN. PURPLE HEART. SILVER STAR MEDAL.
A NATURAL LEADER. HARD AS A HEART ATTACK. HE'S ONE OF THE BEST WE'VE GOT, SIR. UNIMPEACHABLE. RIGHT OVER WRONG EVERY SINGLE TIME.
FLAG COMES FROM A SOLDIER'S FAMILY. HIS FATHER SERVED WITH DISTINCTION IN VIETNAM.
HIS GRANDFATHER WAS PART OF THE ORIGINAL TASK FORCE X IN WORLD WAR II.

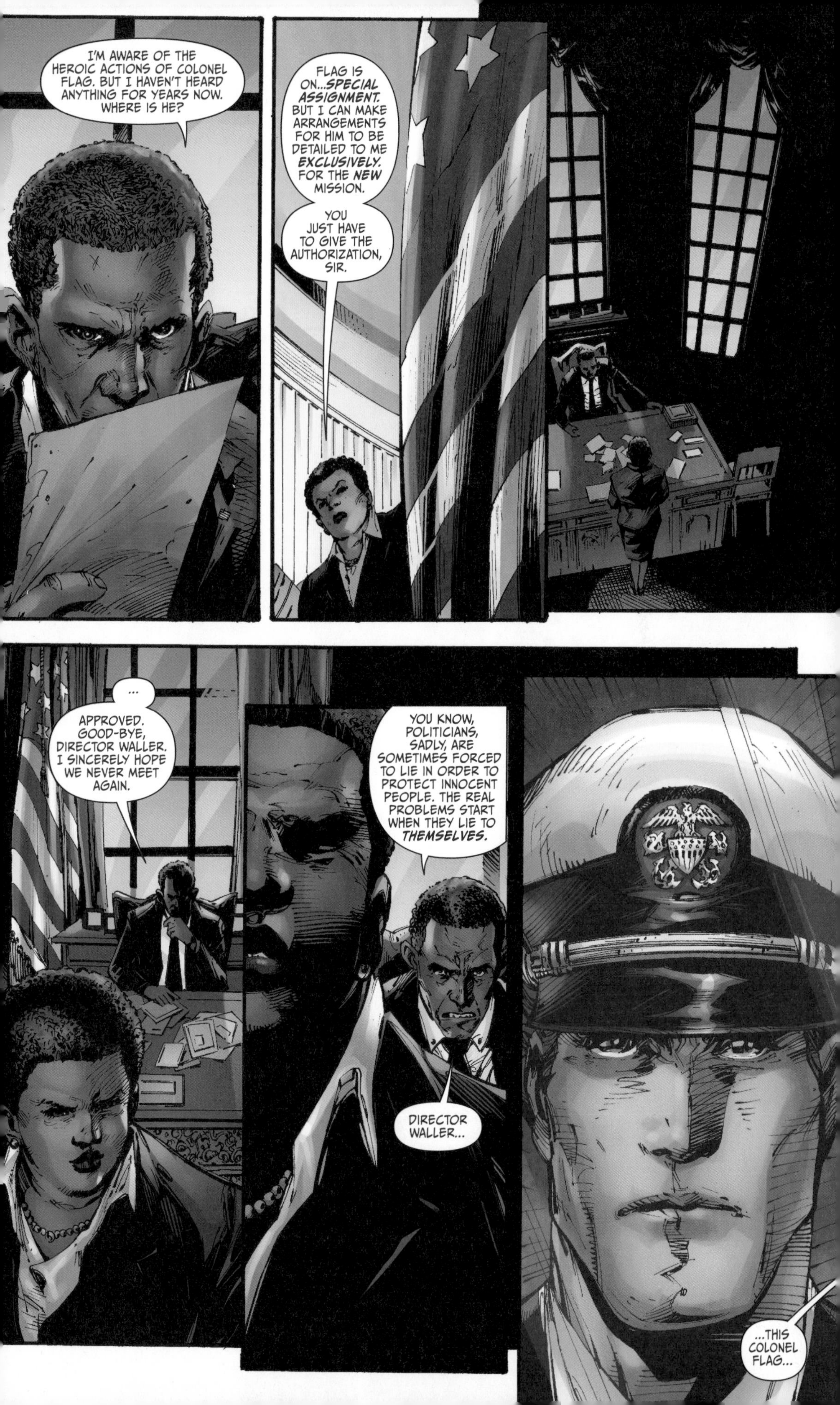
I'M AWARE OF THE HEROIC ACTIONS OF COLONEL FLAG. BUT I HAVEN'T HEARD ANYTHING FOR YEARS NOW. WHERE IS HE?
FLAG IS ON...SPECIAL ASSIGNMENT. BUT I CAN MAKE ARRANGEMENTS FOR HIM TO BE DETAILED TO ME EXCLUSIVELY. FOR THE NEW MISSION.
YOU JUST HAVE TO GIVE THE AUTHORIZATION, SIR.
...
APPROVED. GOOD-BYE, DIRECTOR WALLER. I SINCERELY HOPE WE NEVER MEET AGAIN.
YOU KNOW, POLITICIANS, SADLY, ARE SOMETIMES FORCED TO LIE IN ORDER TO PROTECT INNOCENT PEOPLE. THE REAL PROBLEMS START WHEN THEY LIE TO THEMSELVES.
DIRECTOR WALLER...
...THIS COLONEL FLAG...

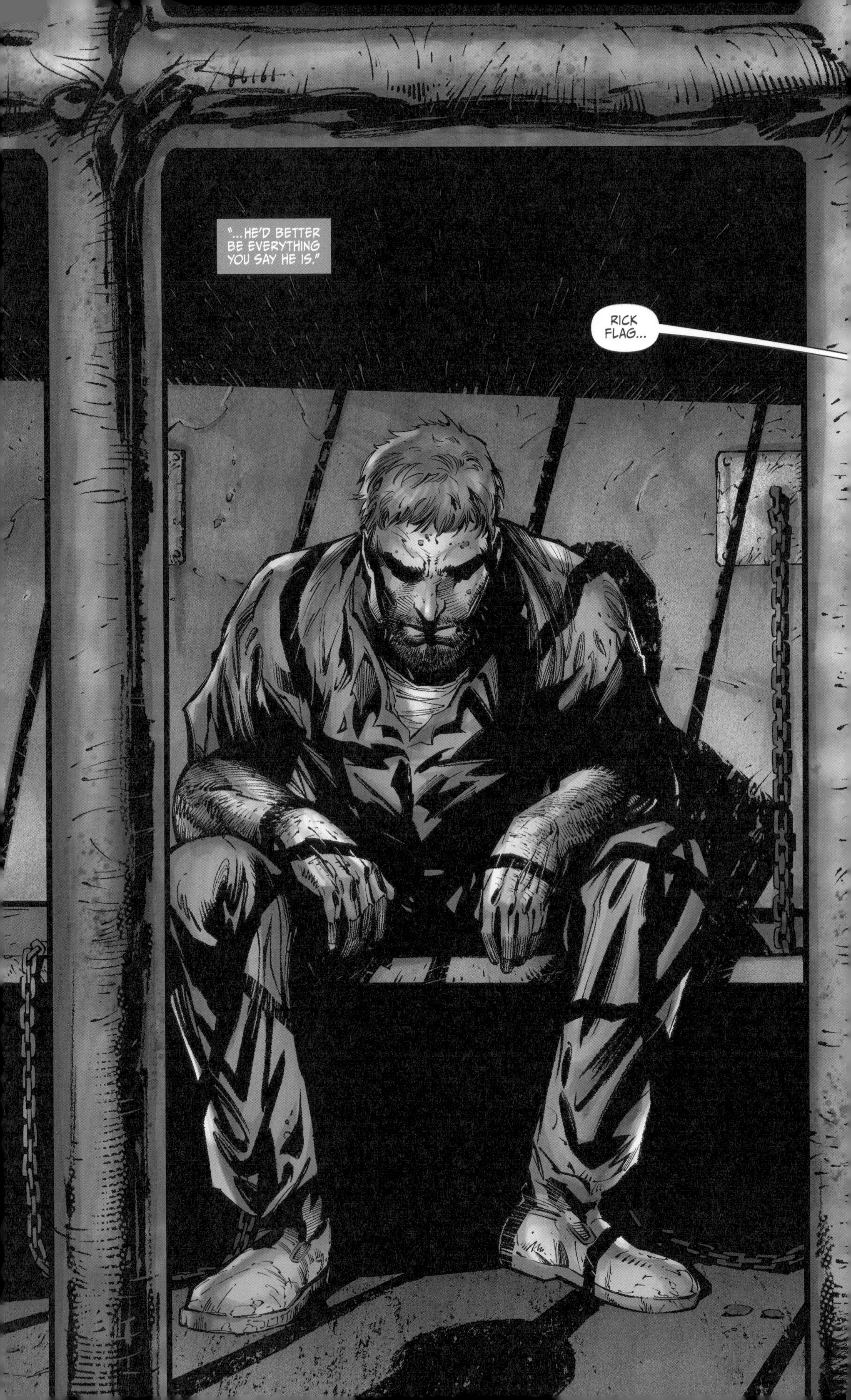
"...HE'D BETTER BE EVERYTHING YOU SAY HE IS."
RICK FLAG...

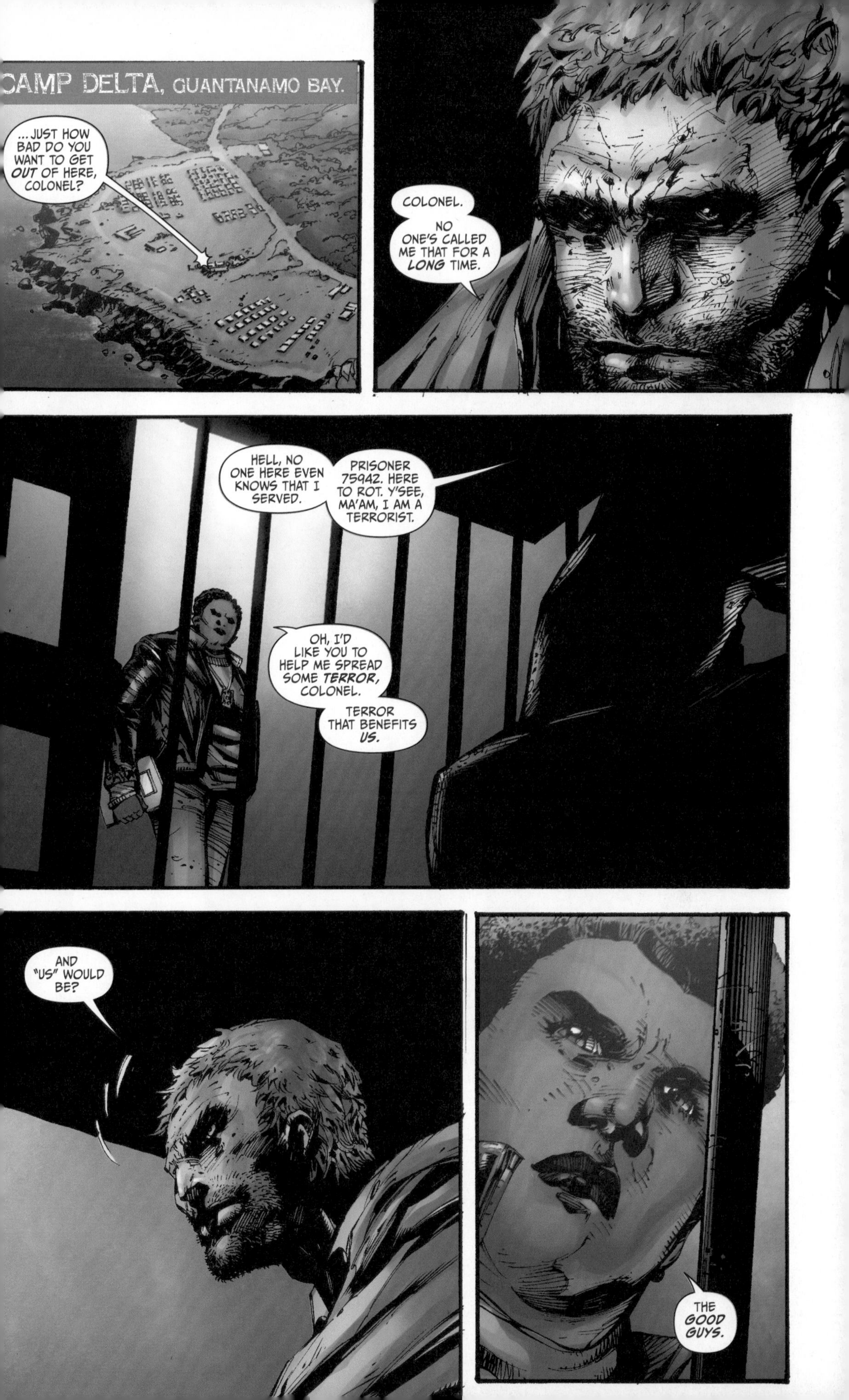
CAMP DELTA, GUANTANAMO BAY.
...JUST HOW BAD DO YOU WANT TO GET OUT OF HERE, COLONEL?
COLONEL.
NO ONE'S CALLED ME THAT FOR A LONG TIME.
HELL, NO ONE HERE EVEN KNOWS THAT I SERVED.
PRISONER 75942. HERE TO ROT. Y'SEE, MA'AM, I AM A TERRORIST.
OH, I'D LIKE YOU TO HELP ME SPREAD SOME TERROR, COLONEL.
TERROR THAT BENEFITS US.
AND "US" WOULD BE?
THE GOOD GUYS.

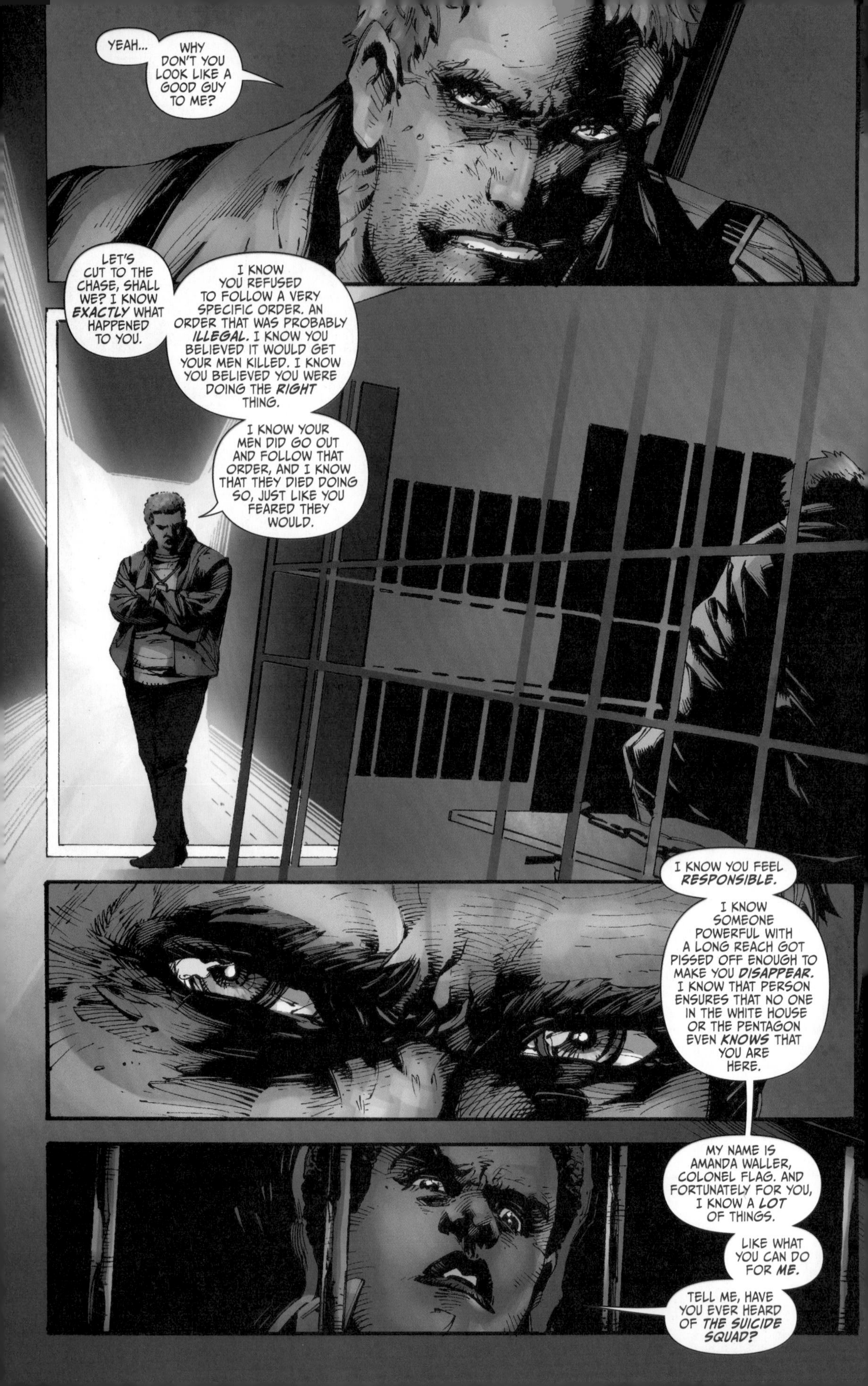
YEAH...
WHY DON'T YOU LOOK LIKE A GOOD GUY TO ME?
LET'S CUT TO THE CHASE, SHALL WE? I KNOW *EXACTLY* WHAT HAPPENED TO YOU.
I KNOW YOU REFUSED TO FOLLOW A VERY SPECIFIC ORDER. AN ORDER THAT WAS PROBABLY *ILLEGAL.* I KNOW YOU BELIEVED IT WOULD GET YOUR MEN KILLED. I KNOW YOU BELIEVED YOU WERE DOING THE *RIGHT* THING.
I KNOW YOUR MEN DID GO OUT AND FOLLOW THAT ORDER, AND I KNOW THAT THEY DIED DOING SO, JUST LIKE YOU FEARED THEY WOULD.
I KNOW YOU FEEL *RESPONSIBLE.*
I KNOW SOMEONE POWERFUL WITH A LONG REACH GOT PISSED OFF ENOUGH TO MAKE YOU *DISAPPEAR.* I KNOW THAT PERSON ENSURES THAT NO ONE IN THE WHITE HOUSE OR THE PENTAGON EVEN *KNOWS* THAT YOU ARE HERE.
MY NAME IS AMANDA WALLER, COLONEL FLAG. AND FORTUNATELY FOR YOU, I KNOW A *LOT* OF THINGS.
LIKE WHAT YOU CAN DO FOR *ME.*
TELL ME, HAVE YOU EVER HEARD OF *THE SUICIDE SQUAD?*

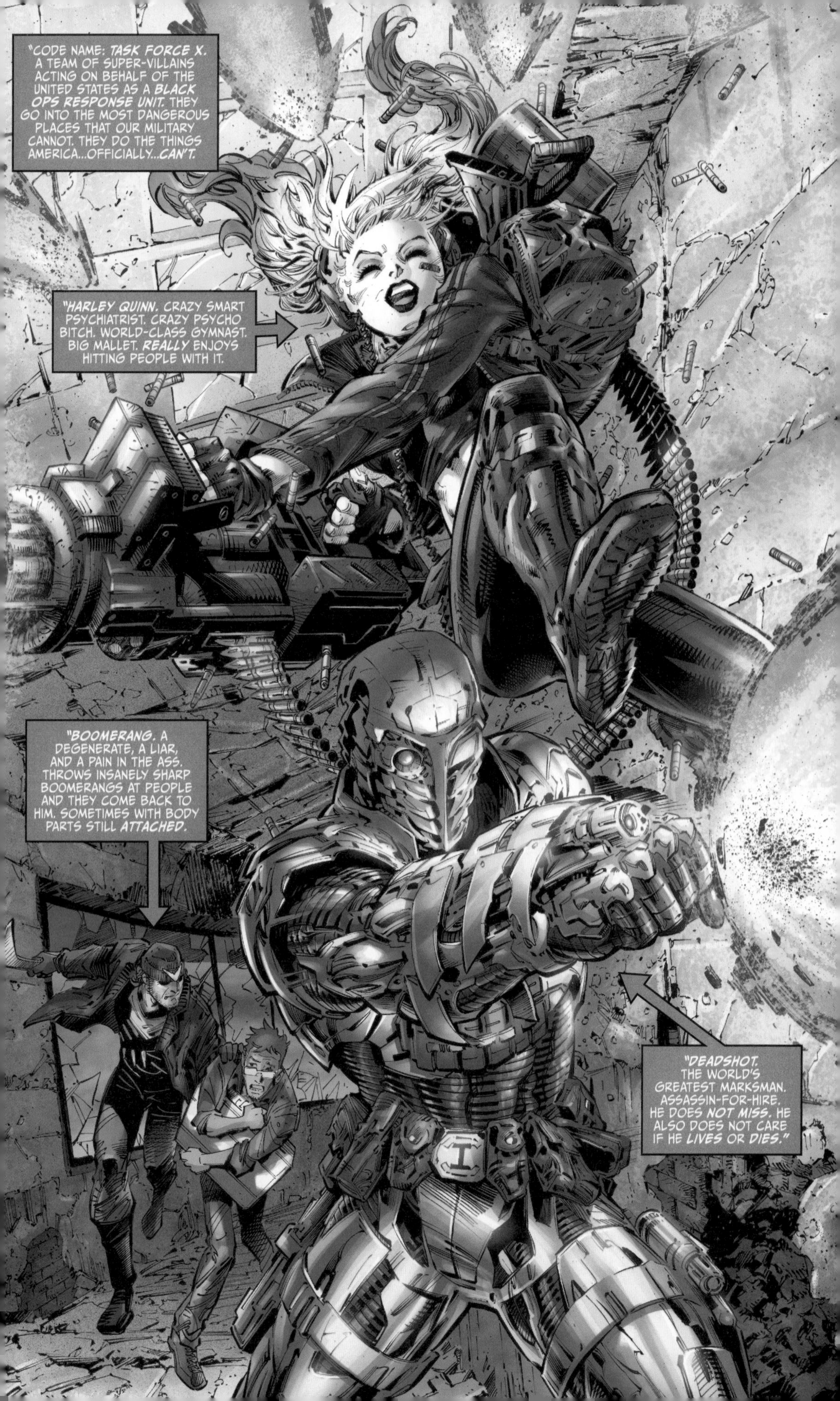
"CODE NAME: TASK FORCE X. A TEAM OF SUPER-VILLAINS ACTING ON BEHALF OF THE UNITED STATES AS A BLACK OPS RESPONSE UNIT. THEY GO INTO THE MOST DANGEROUS PLACES THAT OUR MILITARY CANNOT. THEY DO THE THINGS AMERICA...OFFICIALLY...CAN'T.
"HARLEY QUINN. CRAZY SMART PSYCHIATRIST. CRAZY PSYCHO BITCH. WORLD-CLASS GYMNAST. BIG MALLET. REALLY ENJOYS HITTING PEOPLE WITH IT.
"BOOMERANG. A DEGENERATE, A LIAR, AND A PAIN IN THE ASS. THROWS INSANELY SHARP BOOMERANGS AT PEOPLE AND THEY COME BACK TO HIM. SOMETIMES WITH BODY PARTS STILL ATTACHED.
"DEADSHOT. THE WORLD'S GREATEST MARKSMAN. ASSASSIN-FOR-HIRE. HE DOES NOT MISS. HE ALSO DOES NOT CARE IF HE LIVES OR DIES."

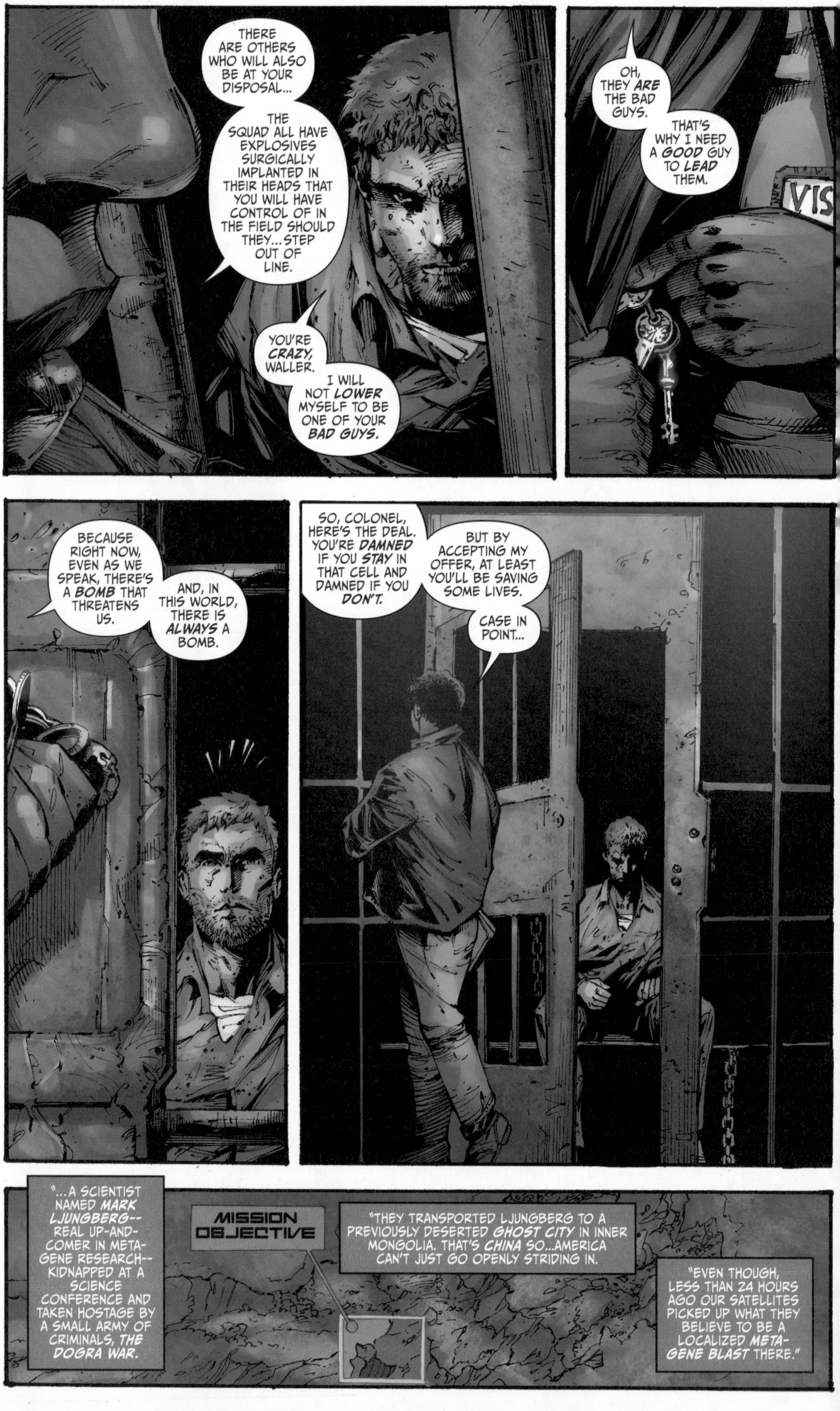

THERE ARE OTHERS WHO WILL ALSO BE AT YOUR DISPOSAL...
THE SQUAD ALL HAVE EXPLOSIVES SURGICALLY IMPLANTED IN THEIR HEADS THAT YOU WILL HAVE CONTROL OF IN THE FIELD SHOULD THEY...STEP OUT OF LINE.
YOU'RE CRAZY, WALLER.
I WILL NOT LOWER MYSELF TO BE ONE OF YOUR BAD GUYS.
OH, THEY ARE THE BAD GUYS.
THAT'S WHY I NEED A GOOD GUY TO LEAD THEM.
VIS
BECAUSE RIGHT NOW, EVEN AS WE SPEAK, THERE'S A BOMB THAT THREATENS US.
AND, IN THIS WORLD, THERE IS ALWAYS A BOMB.
SO, COLONEL, HERE'S THE DEAL. YOU'RE DAMNED IF YOU STAY IN THAT CELL AND DAMNED IF YOU DON'T.
BUT BY ACCEPTING MY OFFER, AT LEAST YOU'LL BE SAVING SOME LIVES.
CASE IN POINT...
"...A SCIENTIST NAMED MARK LJUNGBERG--REAL UP-AND-COMER IN META-GENE RESEARCH--KIDNAPPED AT A SCIENCE CONFERENCE AND TAKEN HOSTAGE BY A SMALL ARMY OF CRIMINALS, THE DOGRA WAR.
MISSION OBJECTIVE
"THEY TRANSPORTED LJUNGBERG TO A PREVIOUSLY DESERTED GHOST CITY IN INNER MONGOLIA. THAT'S CHINA SO...AMERICA CAN'T JUST GO OPENLY STRIDING IN.
"EVEN THOUGH, LESS THAN 24 HOURS AGO OUR SATELLITES PICKED UP WHAT THEY BELIEVE TO BE A LOCALIZED META-GENE BLAST THERE."

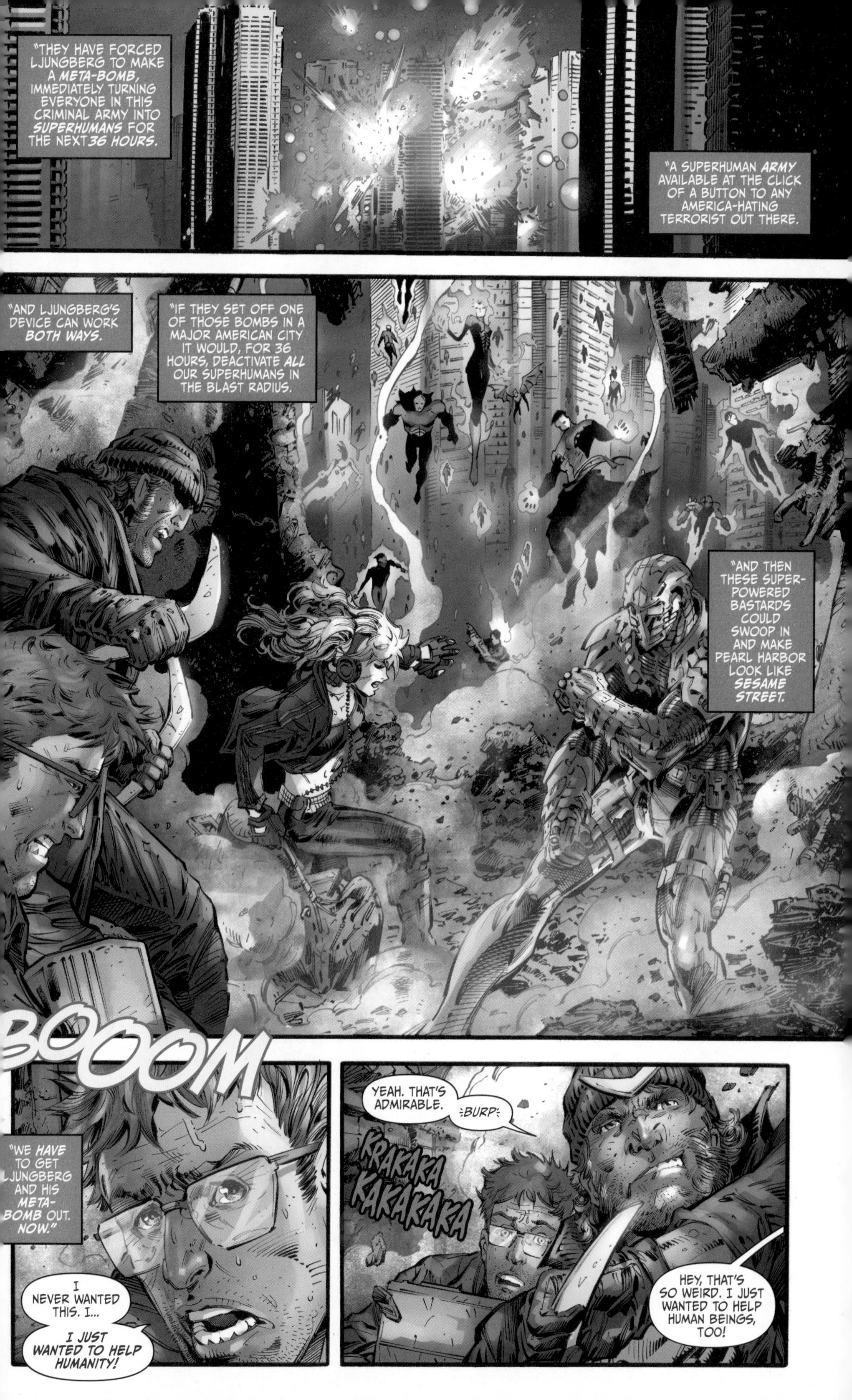

"THEY HAVE FORCED LJUNGBERG TO MAKE A *META-BOMB*, IMMEDIATELY TURNING EVERYONE IN THIS CRIMINAL ARMY INTO *SUPERHUMANS* FOR THE NEXT *36 HOURS*.
"A SUPERHUMAN *ARMY* AVAILABLE AT THE CLICK OF A BUTTON TO ANY AMERICA-HATING TERRORIST OUT THERE.
"AND LJUNGBERG'S DEVICE CAN WORK *BOTH WAYS*.
"IF THEY SET OFF ONE OF THOSE BOMBS IN A MAJOR AMERICAN CITY IT WOULD, FOR 36 HOURS, DEACTIVATE *ALL* OUR SUPERHUMANS IN THE BLAST RADIUS.
"AND THEN THESE SUPER-POWERED BASTARDS COULD SWOOP IN AND MAKE PEARL HARBOR LOOK LIKE *SESAME STREET*.
BOOOM
"WE *HAVE* TO GET LJUNGBERG AND HIS *META-BOMB* OUT. *NOW*."
I NEVER WANTED THIS. I... *I JUST WANTED TO HELP HUMANITY!*
YEAH. THAT'S ADMIRABLE.
:BURP:
KRAKAKA KAKAKAKA
HEY, THAT'S SO WEIRD. I JUST WANTED TO HELP HUMAN BEINGS, TOO!

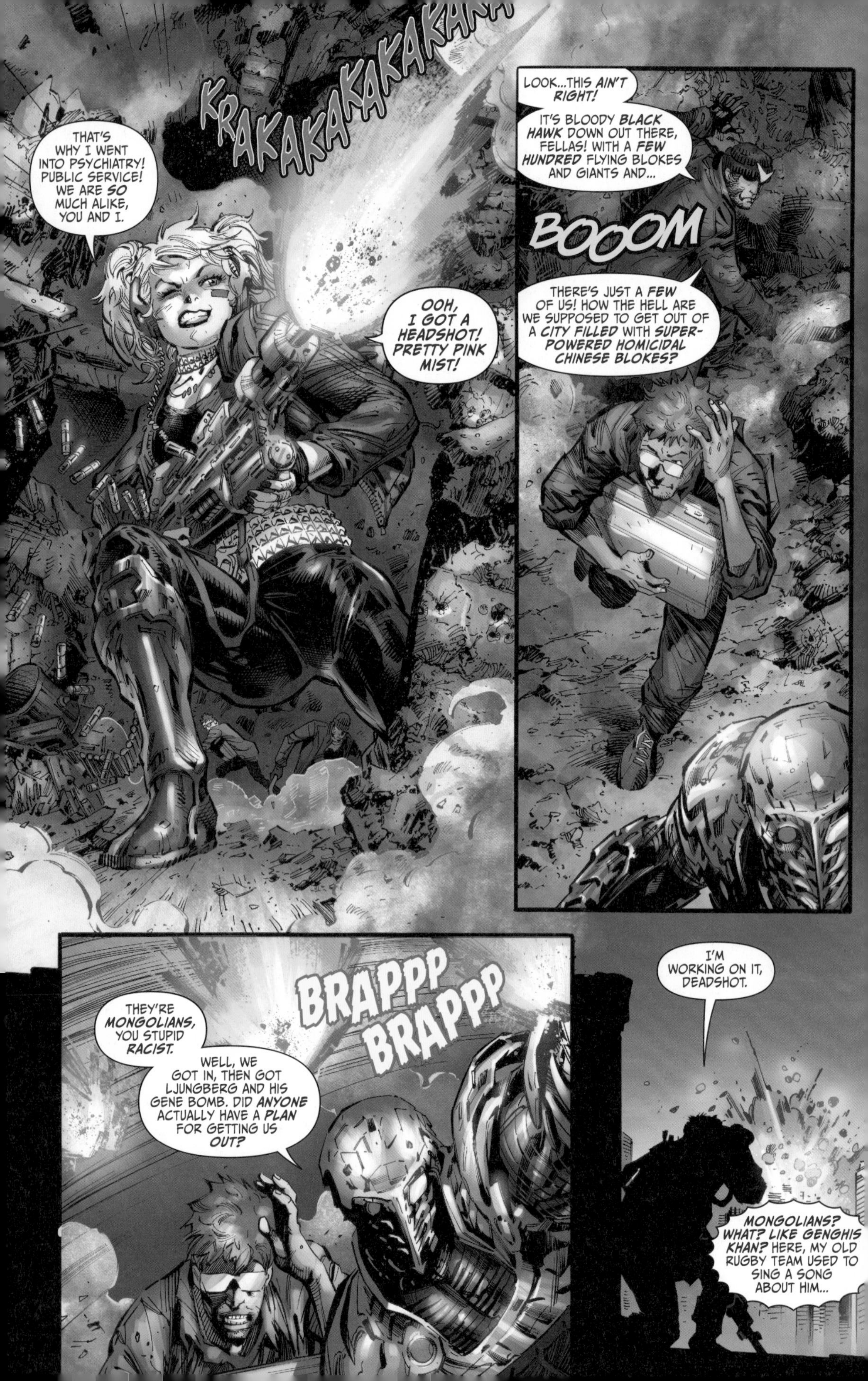

KRAKAKAKAKAKAKAKAKA
THAT'S WHY I WENT INTO PSYCHIATRY! PUBLIC SERVICE! WE ARE SO MUCH ALIKE, YOU AND I.
OOH, I GOT A HEADSHOT! PRETTY PINK MIST!
LOOK...THIS AIN'T RIGHT!
IT'S BLOODY BLACK HAWK DOWN OUT THERE, FELLAS! WITH A FEW HUNDRED FLYING BLOKES AND GIANTS AND...
BOOOM
THERE'S JUST A FEW OF US! HOW THE HELL ARE WE SUPPOSED TO GET OUT OF A CITY FILLED WITH SUPER-POWERED HOMICIDAL CHINESE BLOKES?
BRAPPP BRAPPP
THEY'RE MONGOLIANS, YOU STUPID RACIST.
WELL, WE GOT IN, THEN GOT LJUNGBERG AND HIS GENE BOMB. DID ANYONE ACTUALLY HAVE A PLAN FOR GETTING US OUT?
I'M WORKING ON IT, DEADSHOT.
MONGOLIANS? WHAT? LIKE GENGHIS KHAN? HERE, MY OLD RUGBY TEAM USED TO SING A SONG ABOUT HIM...

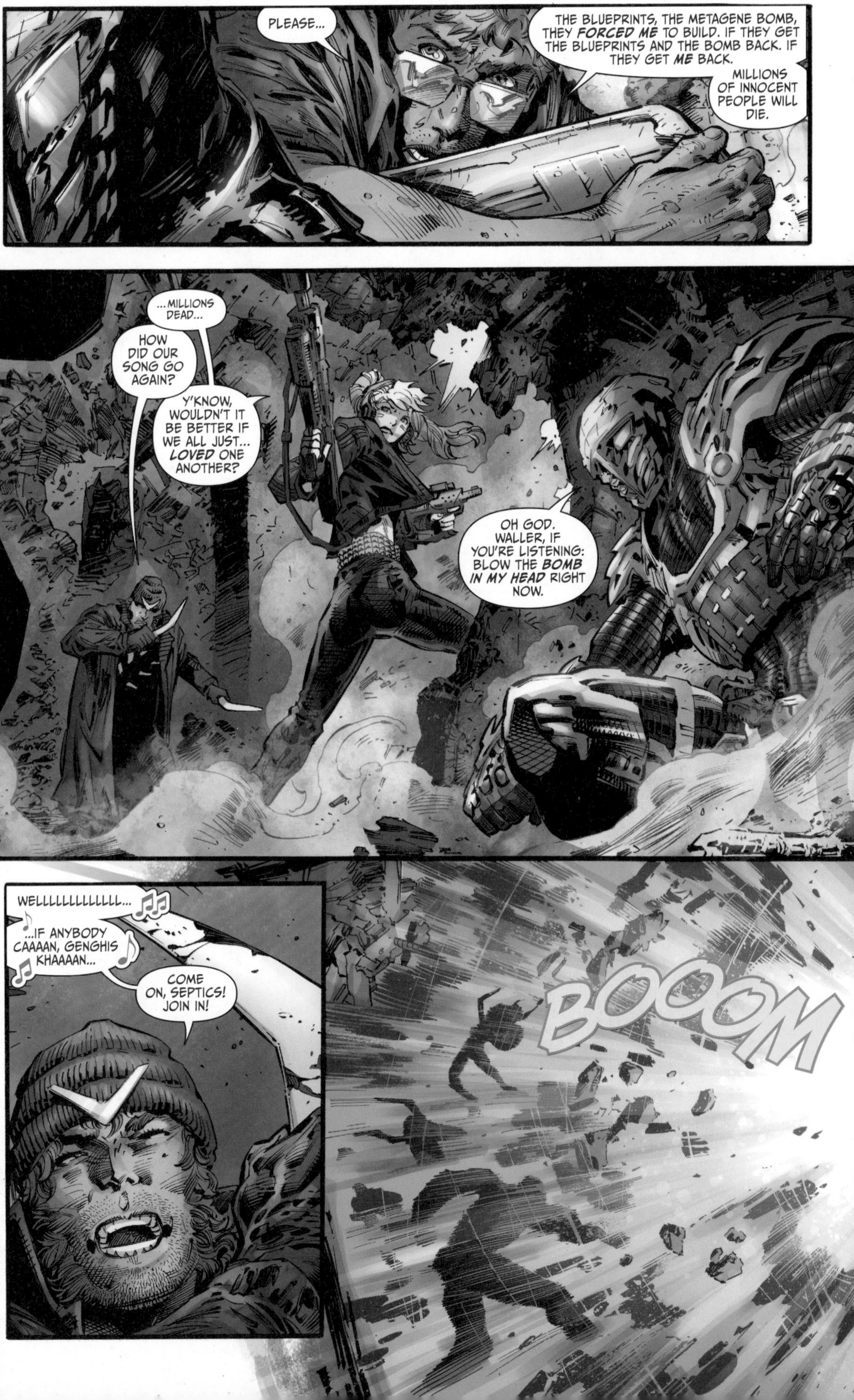
PLEASE...
THE BLUEPRINTS, THE METAGENE BOMB, THEY FORCED ME TO BUILD. IF THEY GET THE BLUEPRINTS AND THE BOMB BACK. IF THEY GET ME BACK.
MILLIONS OF INNOCENT PEOPLE WILL DIE.
...MILLIONS DEAD...
HOW DID OUR SONG GO AGAIN?
Y'KNOW, WOULDN'T IT BE BETTER IF WE ALL JUST... LOVED ONE ANOTHER?
OH GOD. WALLER, IF YOU'RE LISTENING: BLOW THE BOMB IN MY HEAD RIGHT NOW.
WELLLLLLLLLLLLLL...
...IF ANYBODY CAAAAN, GENGHIS KHAAAAN...
COME ON, SEPTICS! JOIN IN!
BOOOM

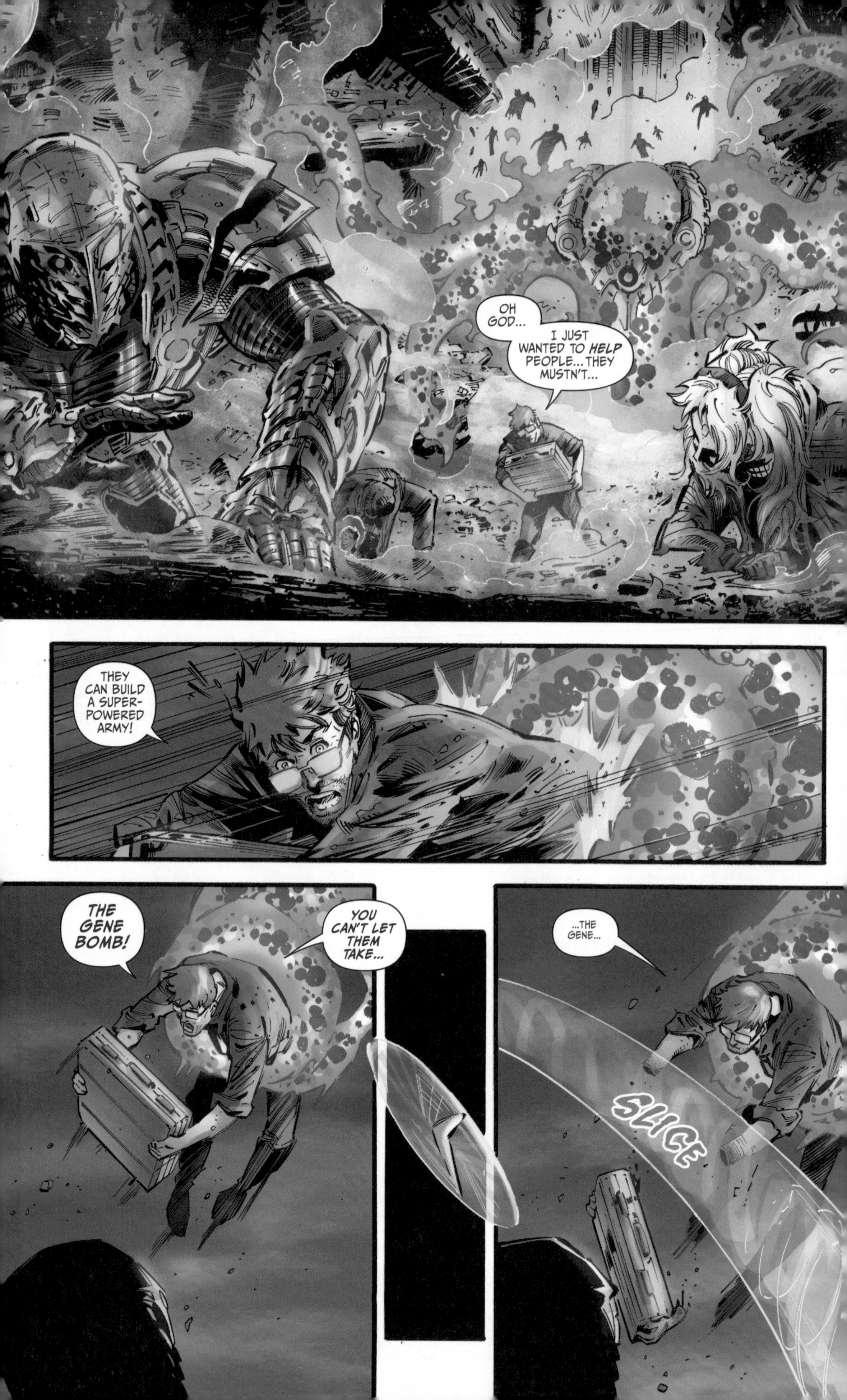
OH GOD...
I JUST WANTED TO HELP PEOPLE... THEY MUSTN'T...
THEY CAN BUILD A SUPER-POWERED ARMY!
THE GENE BOMB!
YOU CAN'T LET THEM TAKE...
...THE GENE...
SLICE

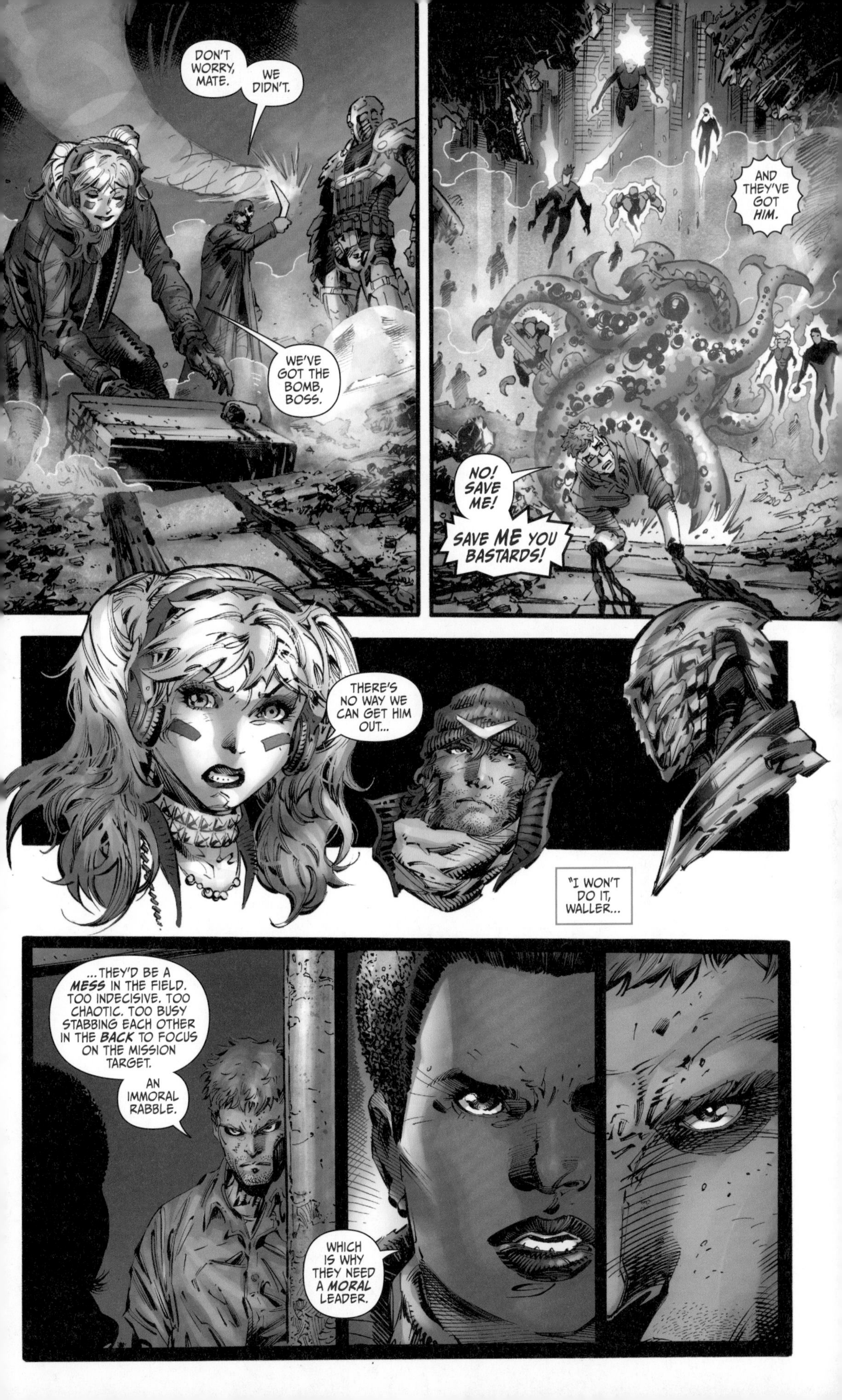

DON'T WORRY, MATE.
WE DIDN'T.
WE'VE GOT THE BOMB, BOSS.
AND THEY'VE GOT HIM.
NO! SAVE ME!
SAVE ME YOU BASTARDS!
THERE'S NO WAY WE CAN GET HIM OUT...
"I WON'T DO IT, WALLER...
...THEY'D BE A MESS IN THE FIELD. TOO INDECISIVE. TOO CHAOTIC. TOO BUSY STABBING EACH OTHER IN THE BACK TO FOCUS ON THE MISSION TARGET.
AN IMMORAL RABBLE.
WHICH IS WHY THEY NEED A MORAL LEADER.

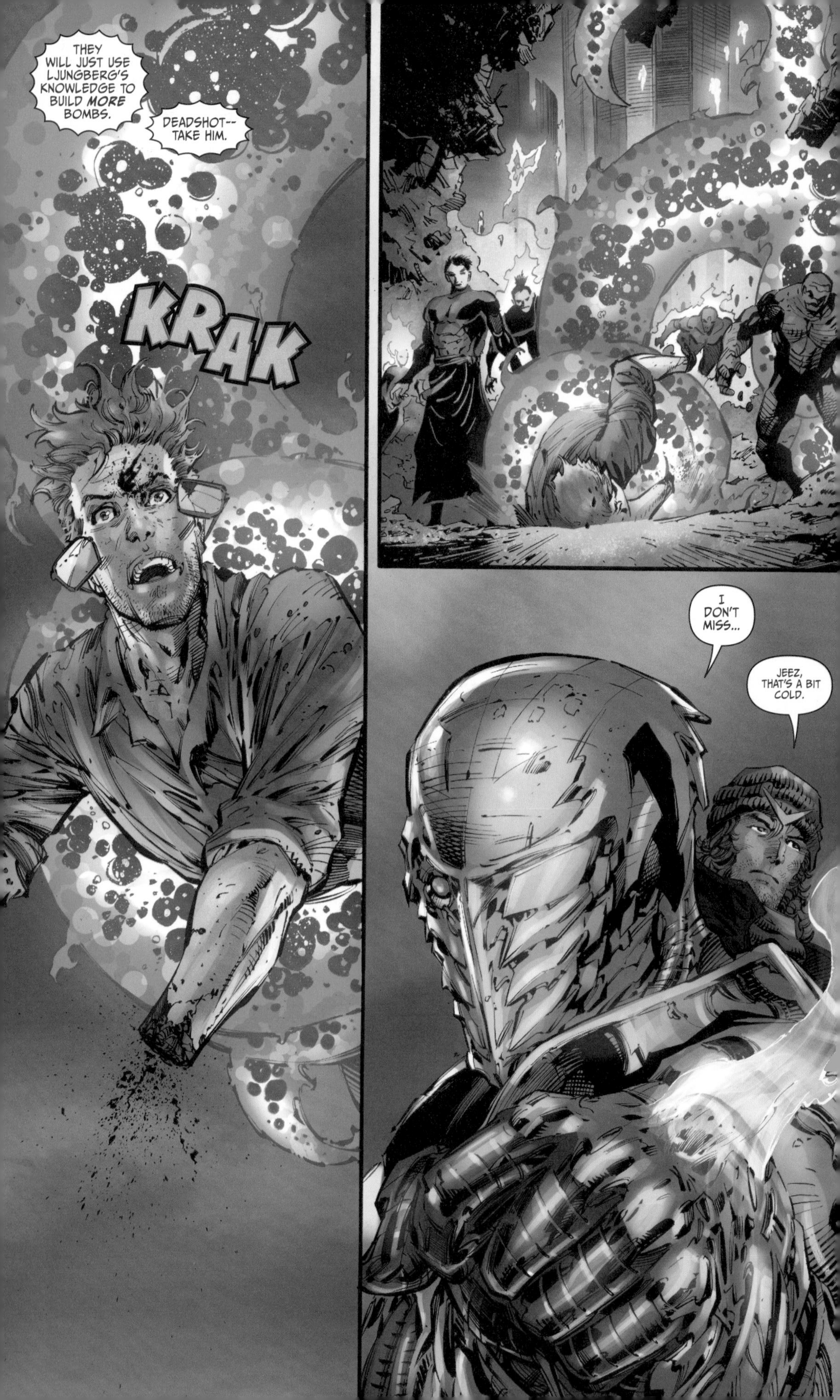
THEY WILL JUST USE LJUNGBERG'S KNOWLEDGE TO BUILD *MORE* BOMBS.
DEADSHOT-- TAKE HIM.
KRAK
I DON'T MISS...
JEEZ, THAT'S A BIT COLD.

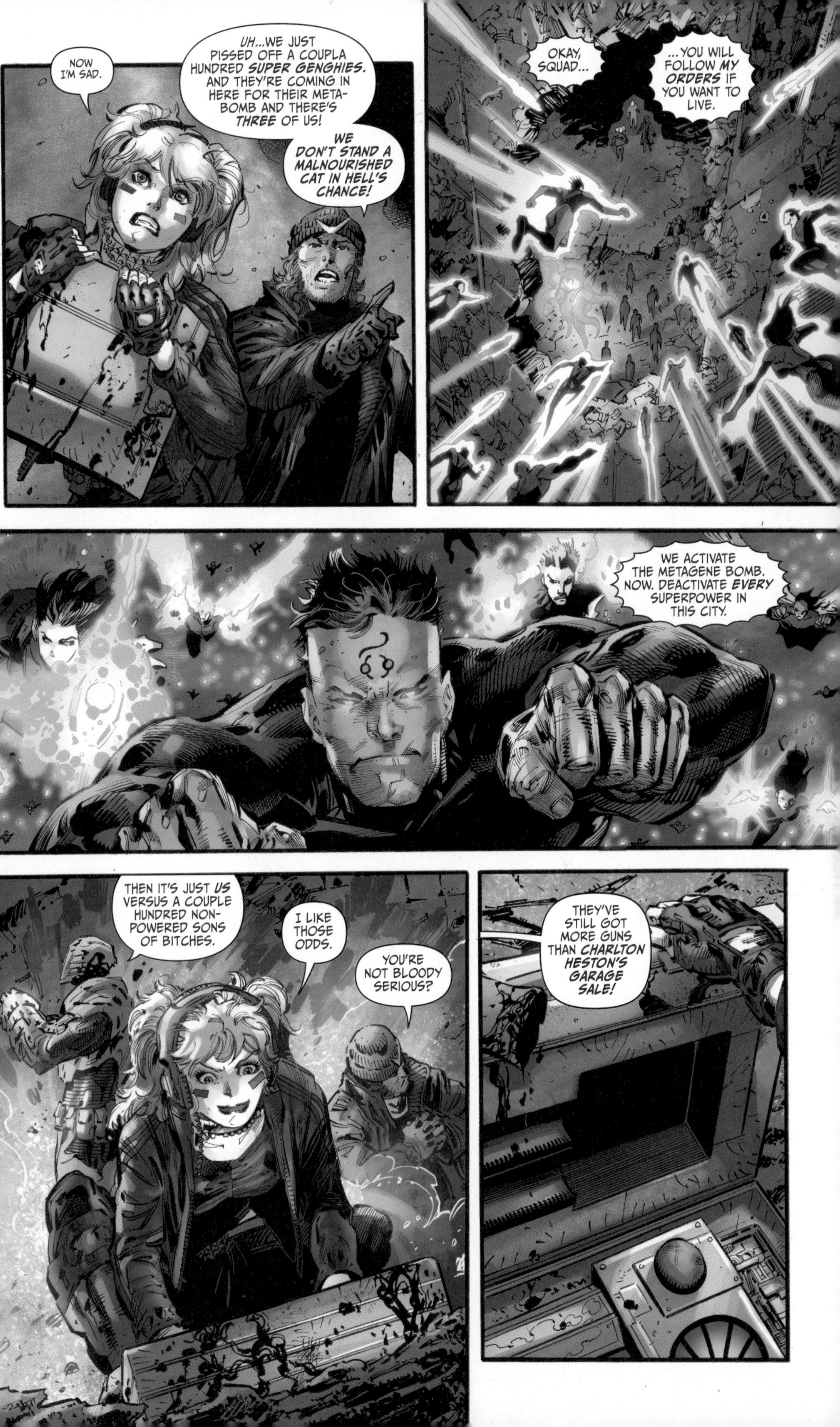

NOW I'M SAD.
UH...WE JUST PISSED OFF A COUPLA HUNDRED SUPER GENGHIES. AND THEY'RE COMING IN HERE FOR THEIR META-BOMB AND THERE'S THREE OF US!
WE DON'T STAND A MALNOURISHED CAT IN HELL'S CHANCE!
OKAY, SQUAD...
...YOU WILL FOLLOW MY ORDERS IF YOU WANT TO LIVE.
WE ACTIVATE THE METAGENE BOMB. NOW. DEACTIVATE EVERY SUPERPOWER IN THIS CITY.
THEN IT'S JUST US VERSUS A COUPLE HUNDRED NON-POWERED SONS OF BITCHES.
I LIKE THOSE ODDS.
YOU'RE NOT BLOODY SERIOUS?
THEY'VE STILL GOT MORE GUNS THAN CHARLTON HESTON'S GARAGE SALE!

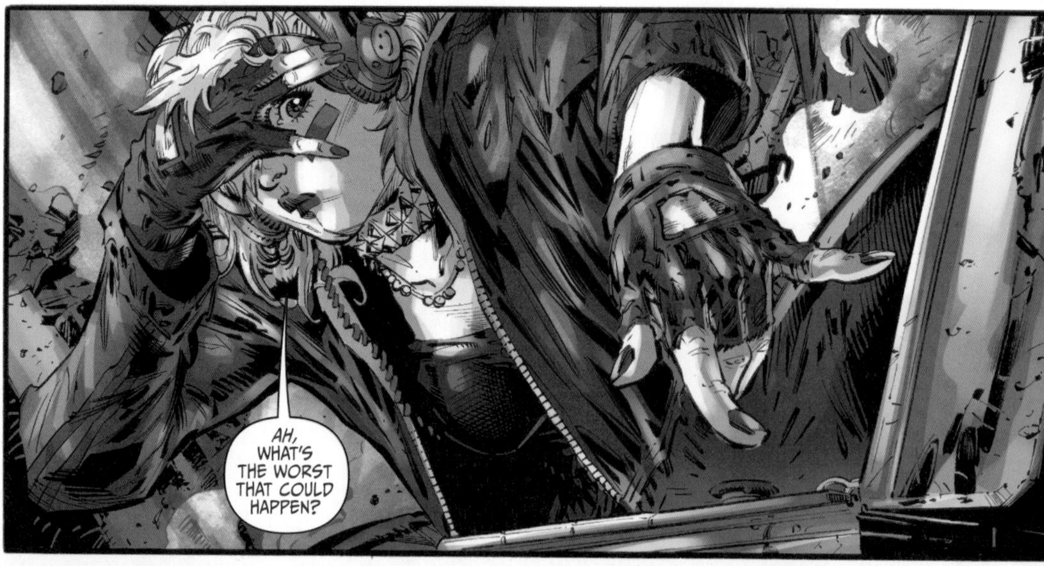
AH, WHAT'S THE WORST THAT COULD HAPPEN?

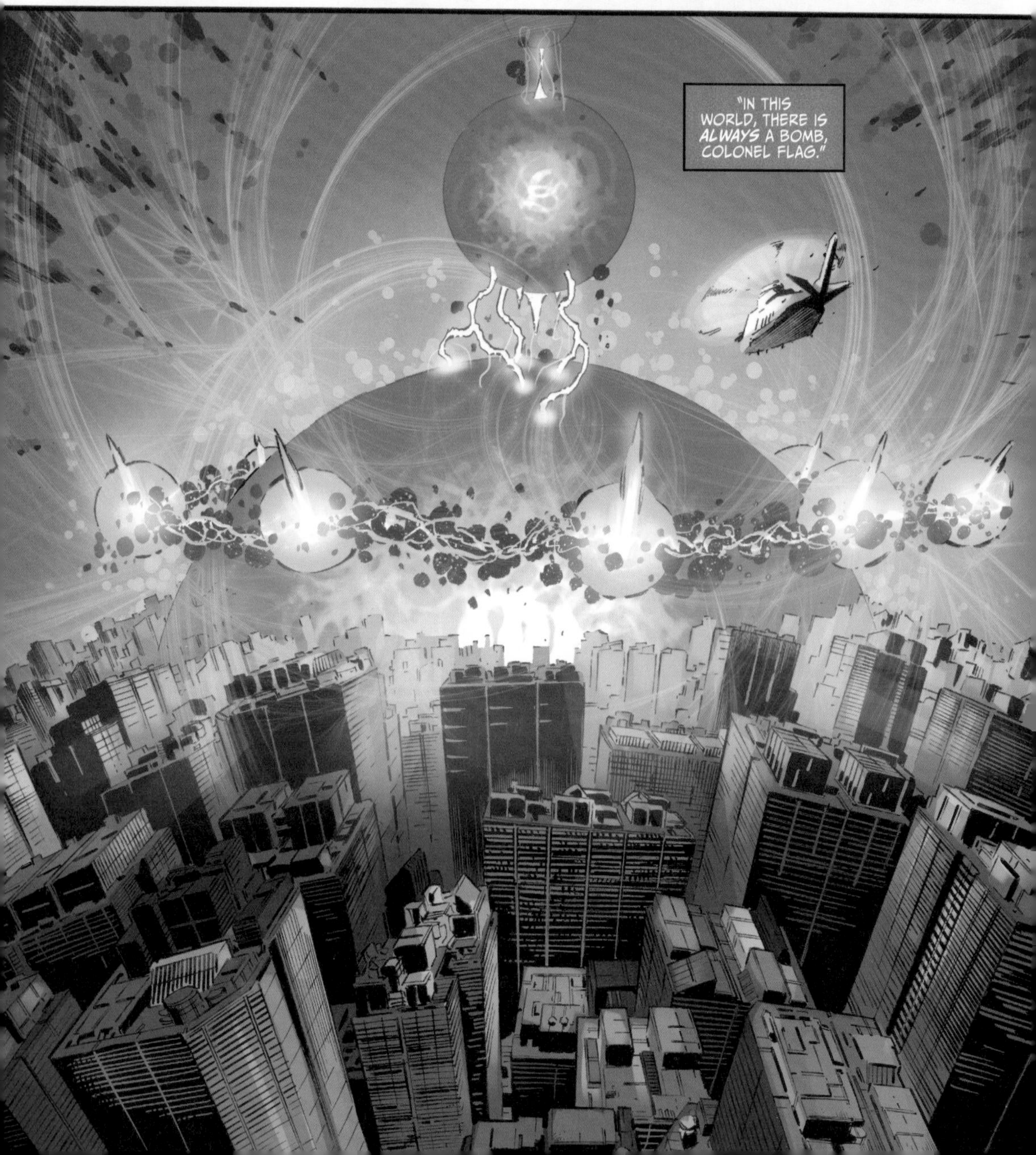
"IN THIS WORLD, THERE IS *ALWAYS* A BOMB, COLONEL FLAG."

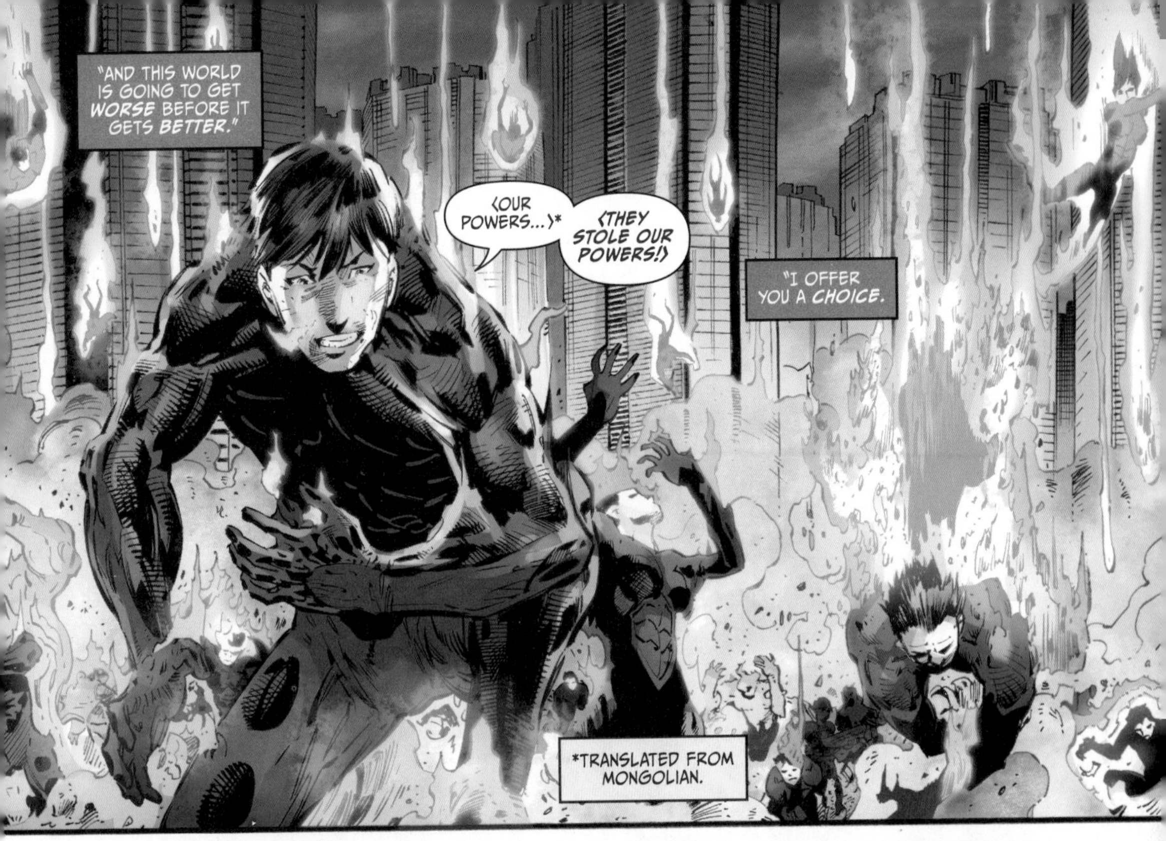
"AND THIS WORLD IS GOING TO GET WORSE BEFORE IT GETS BETTER."
‹OUR POWERS...›*
‹THEY STOLE OUR POWERS!›
"I OFFER YOU A CHOICE.
*TRANSLATED FROM MONGOLIAN.

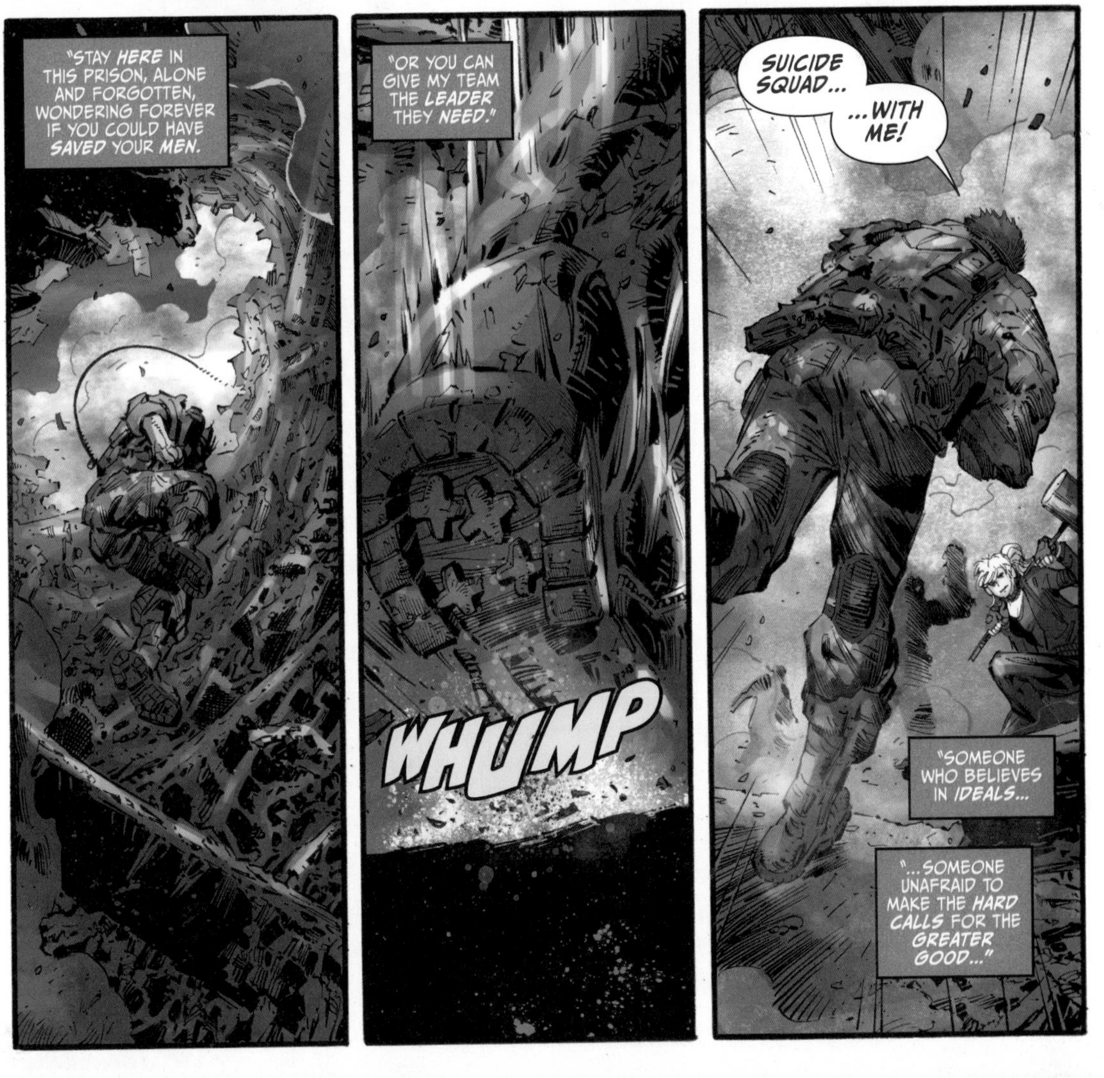
"STAY HERE IN THIS PRISON, ALONE AND FORGOTTEN, WONDERING FOREVER IF YOU COULD HAVE SAVED YOUR MEN.
"OR YOU CAN GIVE MY TEAM THE LEADER THEY NEED."
WHUMP
SUICIDE SQUAD...
...WITH ME!
"SOMEONE WHO BELIEVES IN IDEALS...
"...SOMEONE UNAFRAID TO MAKE THE HARD CALLS FOR THE GREATER GOOD..."

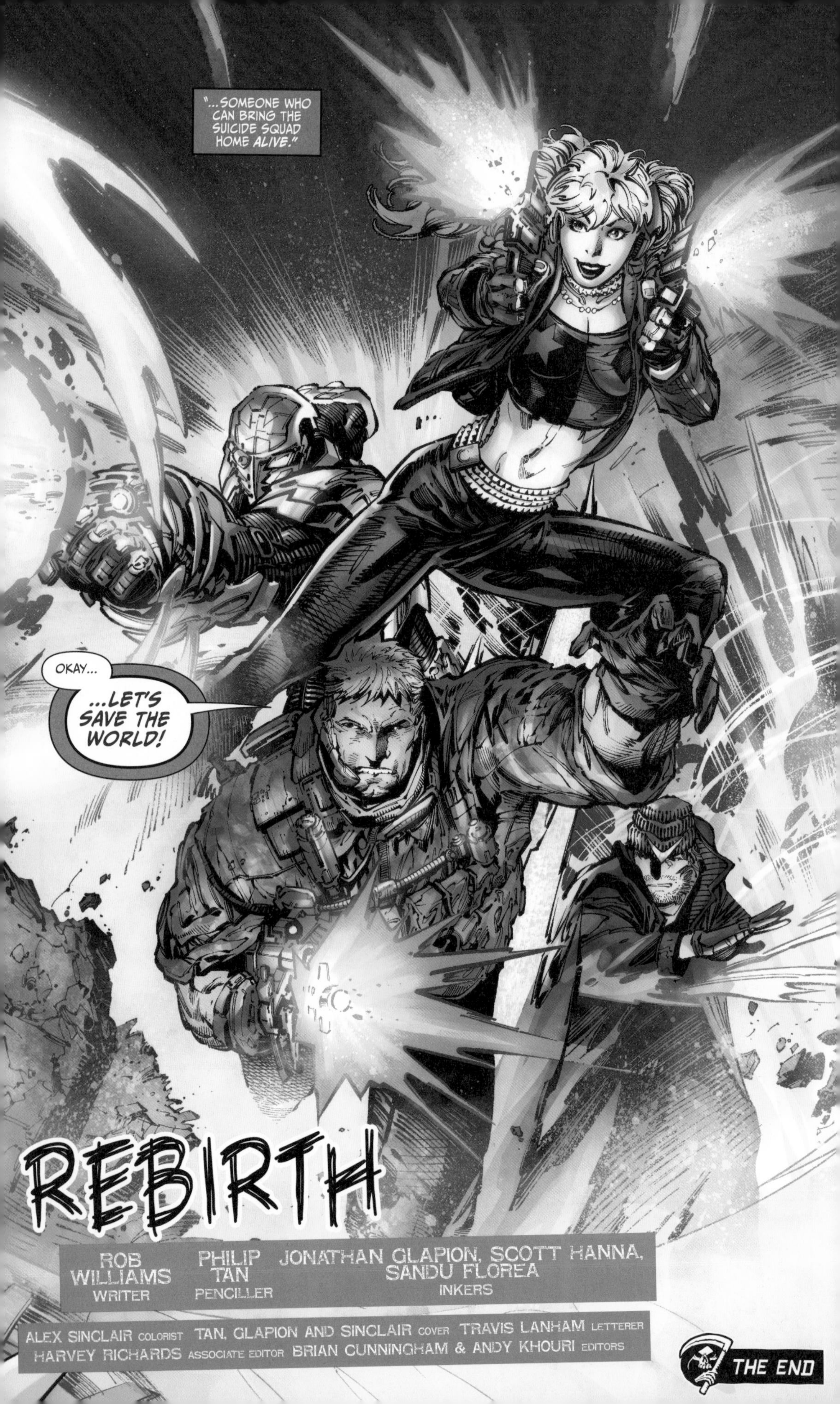

"...SOMEONE WHO CAN BRING THE SUICIDE SQUAD HOME ALIVE."
OKAY...
...LET'S SAVE THE WORLD!
REBIRTH
ROB WILLIAMS WRITER
PHILIP TAN PENCILLER
JONATHAN GLAPION, SCOTT HANNA, SANDU FLOREA INKERS
ALEX SINCLAIR COLORIST TAN, GLAPION AND SINCLAIR COVER TRAVIS LANHAM LETTERER
HARVEY RICHARDS ASSOCIATE EDITOR BRIAN CUNNINGHAM & ANDY KHOURI EDITORS
THE END

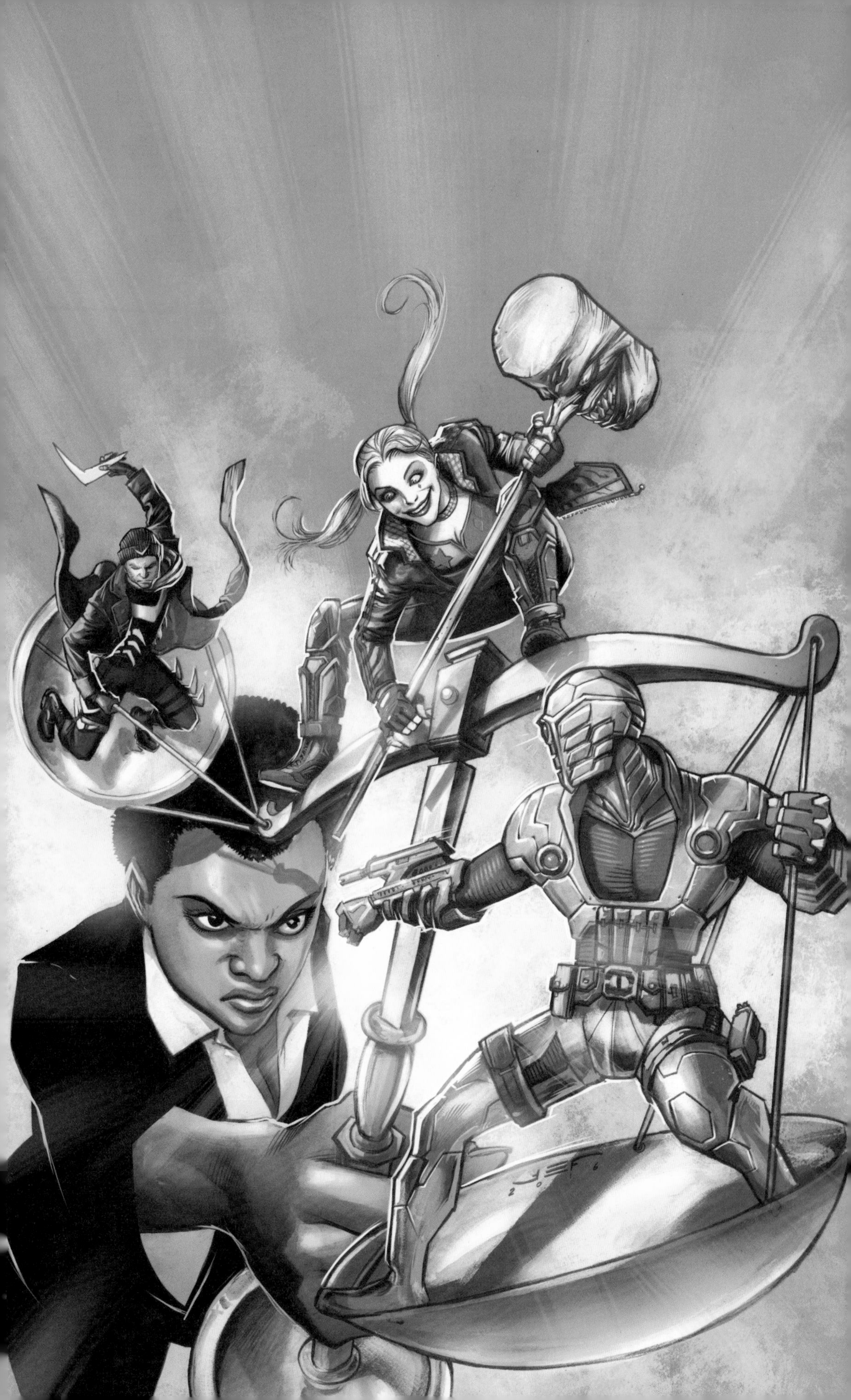

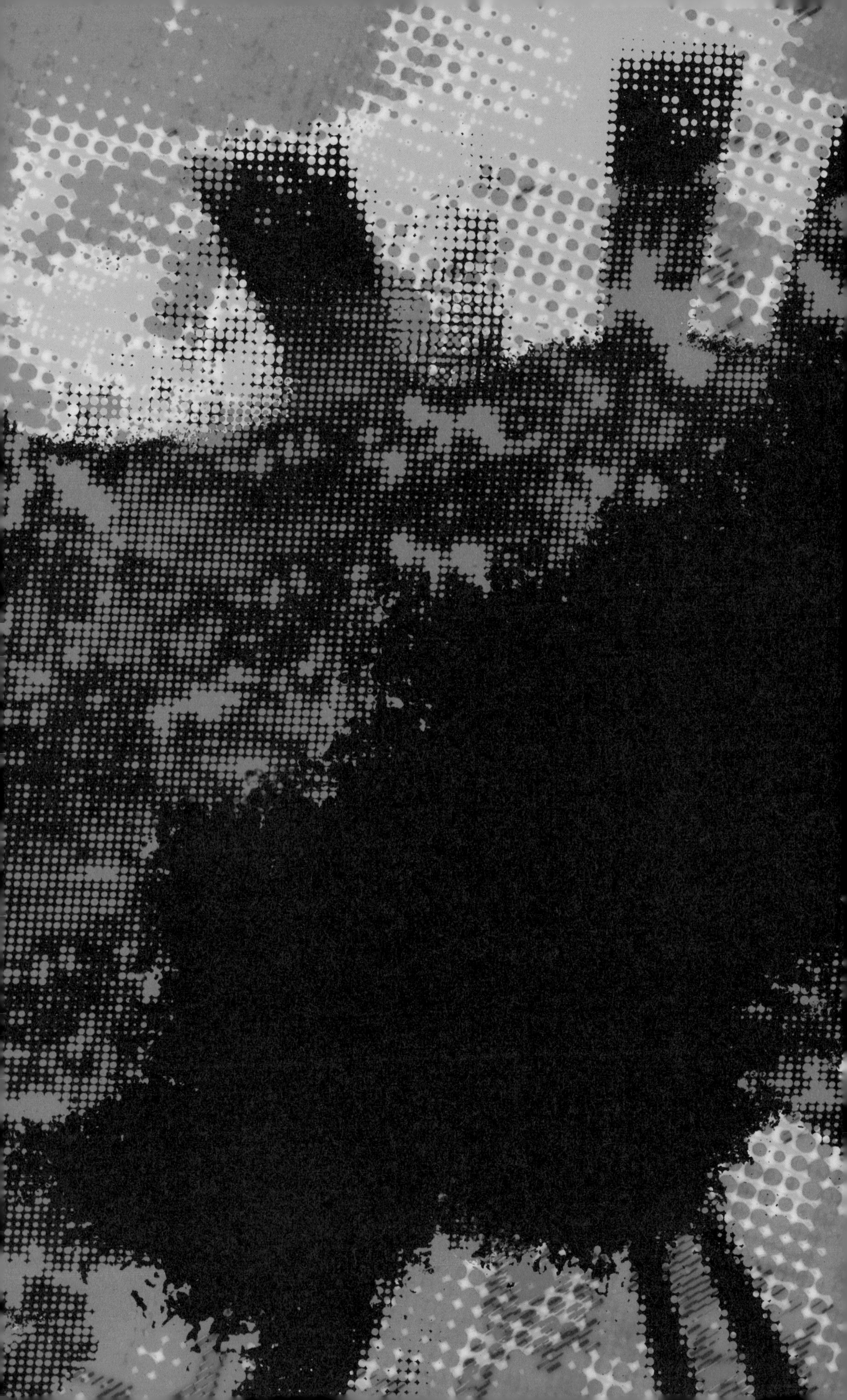

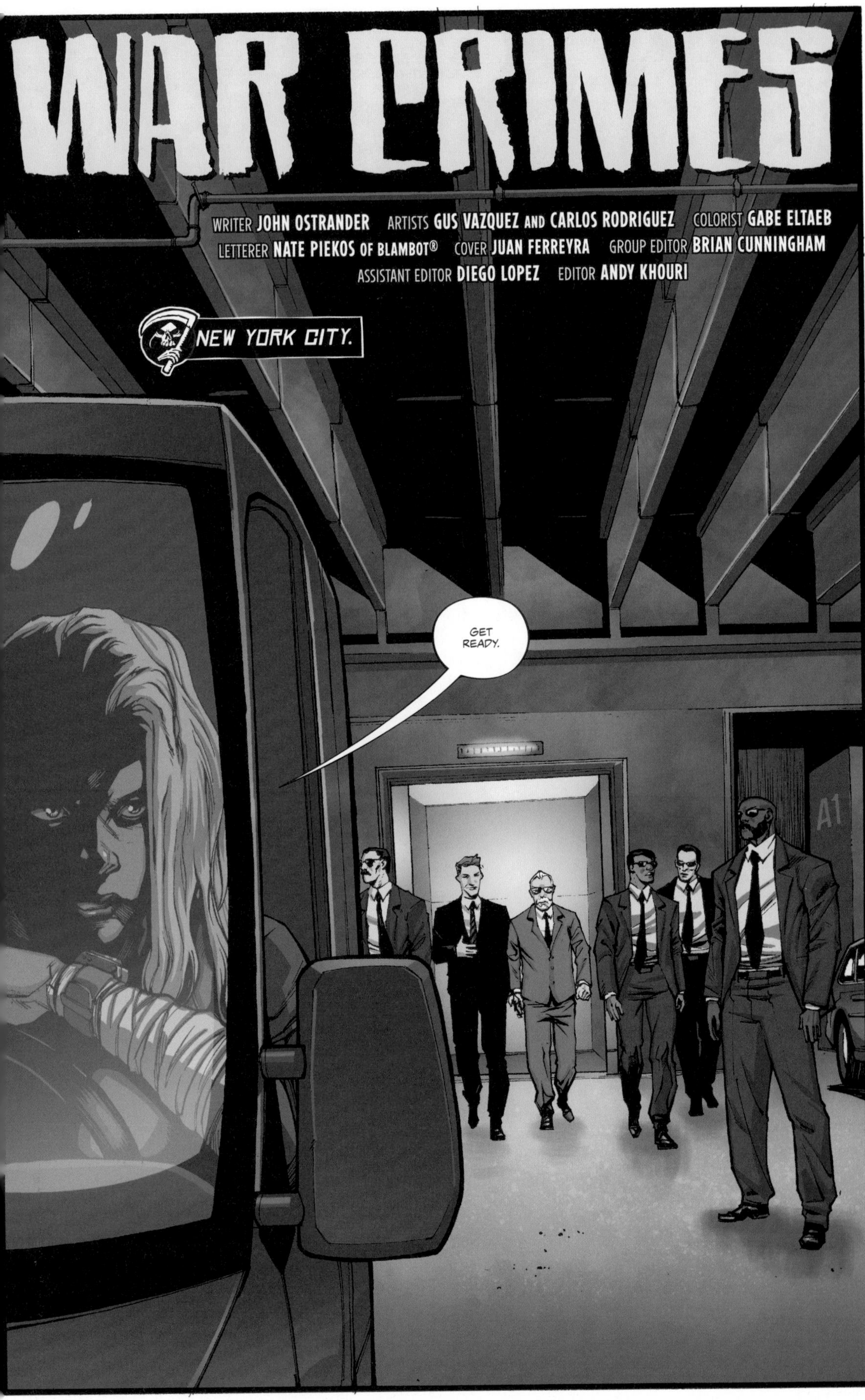
WAR CRIMES
WRITER JOHN OSTRANDER ARTISTS GUS VAZQUEZ AND CARLOS RODRIGUEZ COLORIST GABE ELTAEB
LETTERER NATE PIEKOS OF BLAMBOT® COVER JUAN FERREYRA GROUP EDITOR BRIAN CUNNINGHAM
ASSISTANT EDITOR DIEGO LOPEZ EDITOR ANDY KHOURI
NEW YORK CITY.
GET READY.
A1

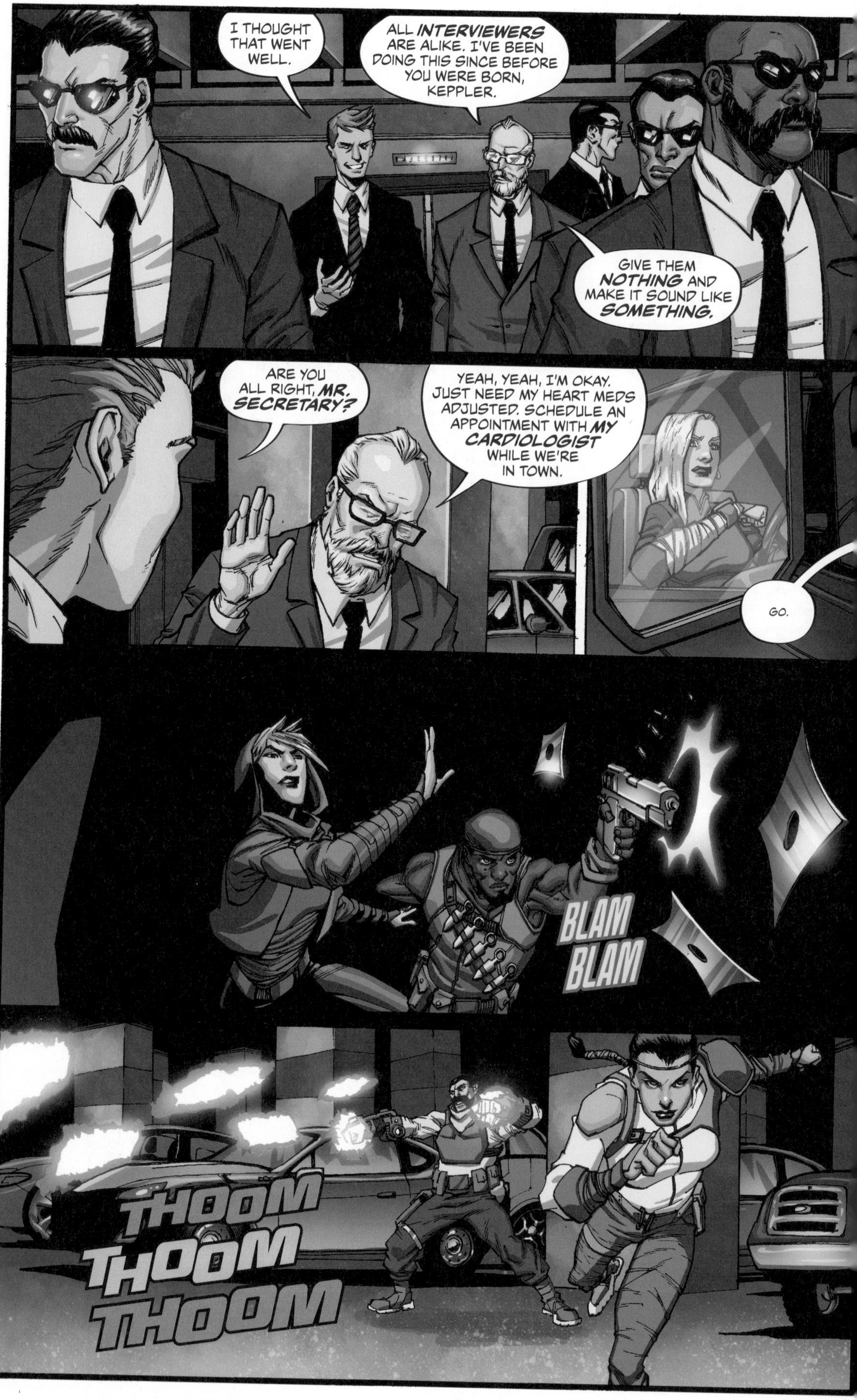
I THOUGHT THAT WENT WELL.
ALL INTERVIEWERS ARE ALIKE. I'VE BEEN DOING THIS SINCE BEFORE YOU WERE BORN, KEPPLER.
GIVE THEM NOTHING AND MAKE IT SOUND LIKE SOMETHING.
ARE YOU ALL RIGHT, MR. SECRETARY?
YEAH, YEAH, I'M OKAY. JUST NEED MY HEART MEDS ADJUSTED. SCHEDULE AN APPOINTMENT WITH MY CARDIOLOGIST WHILE WE'RE IN TOWN.
GO.
BLAM BLAM
THOOM THOOM THOOM

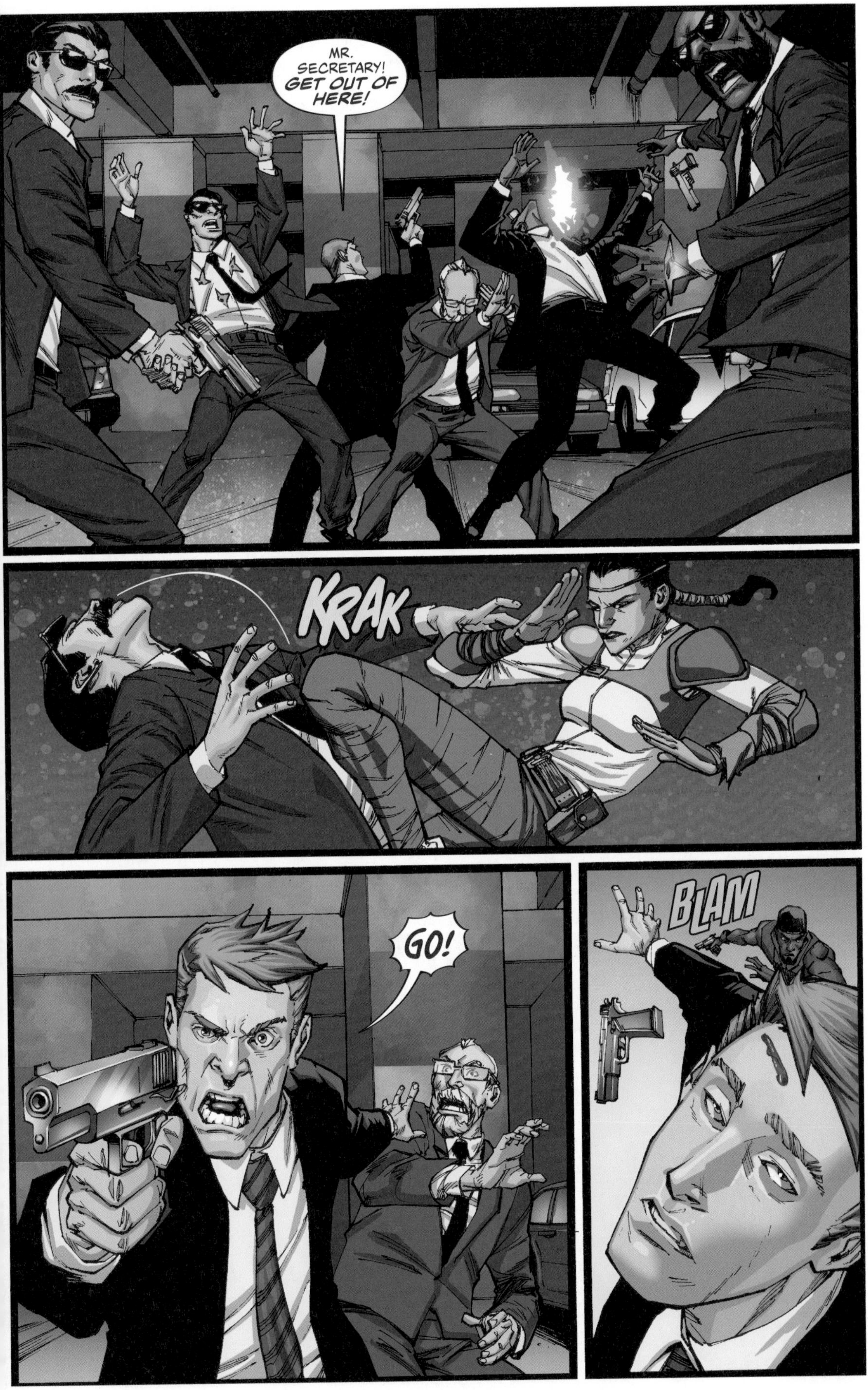
MR. SECRETARY! GET OUT OF HERE!
KRAK
GO!
BLAM

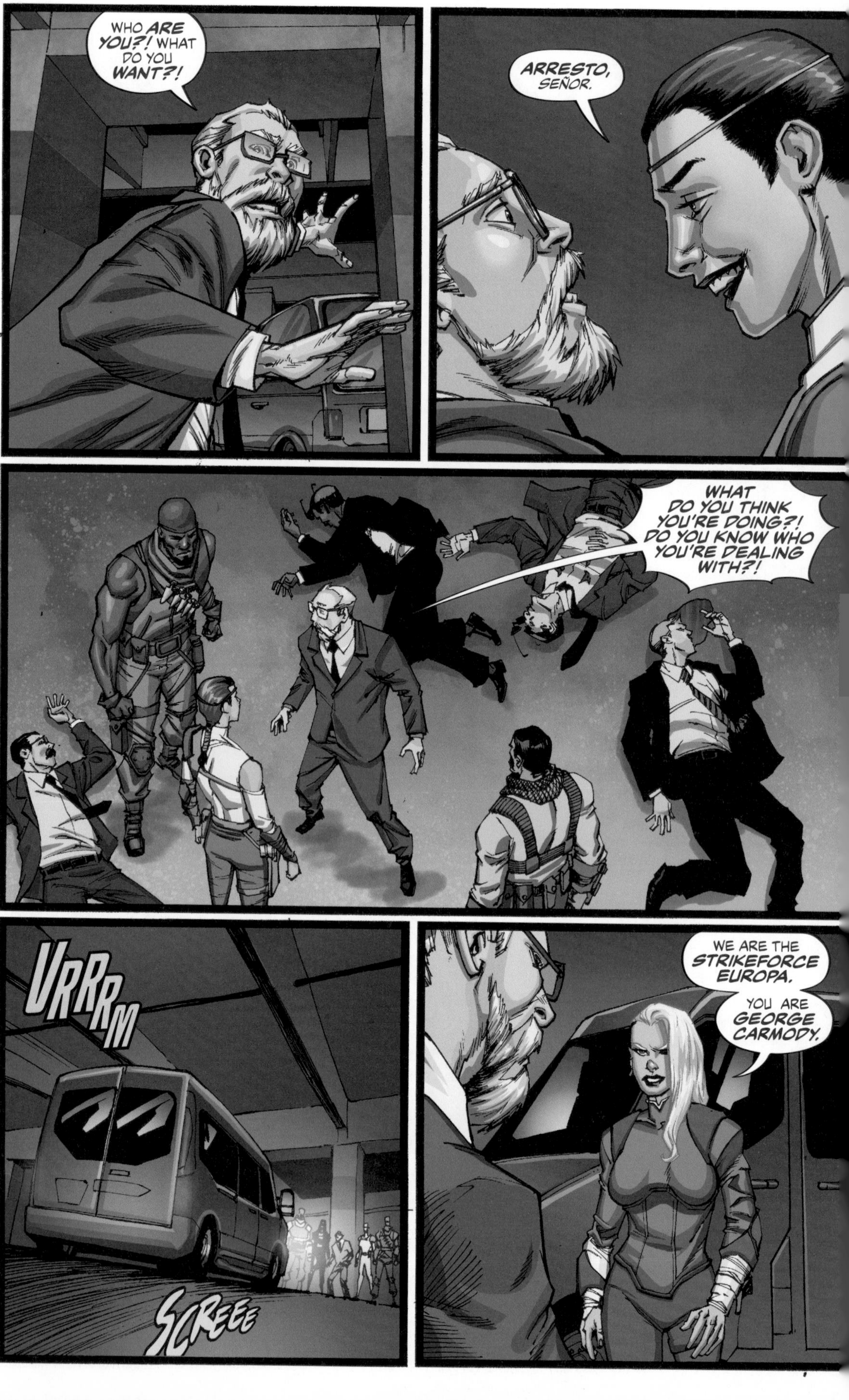
WHO ARE YOU?! WHAT DO YOU WANT?!
ARRESTO, SEÑOR.
WHAT DO YOU THINK YOU'RE DOING?! DO YOU KNOW WHO YOU'RE DEALING WITH?!
URRRM
SCREEE
WE ARE THE STRIKEFORCE EUROPA.
YOU ARE GEORGE CARMODY.

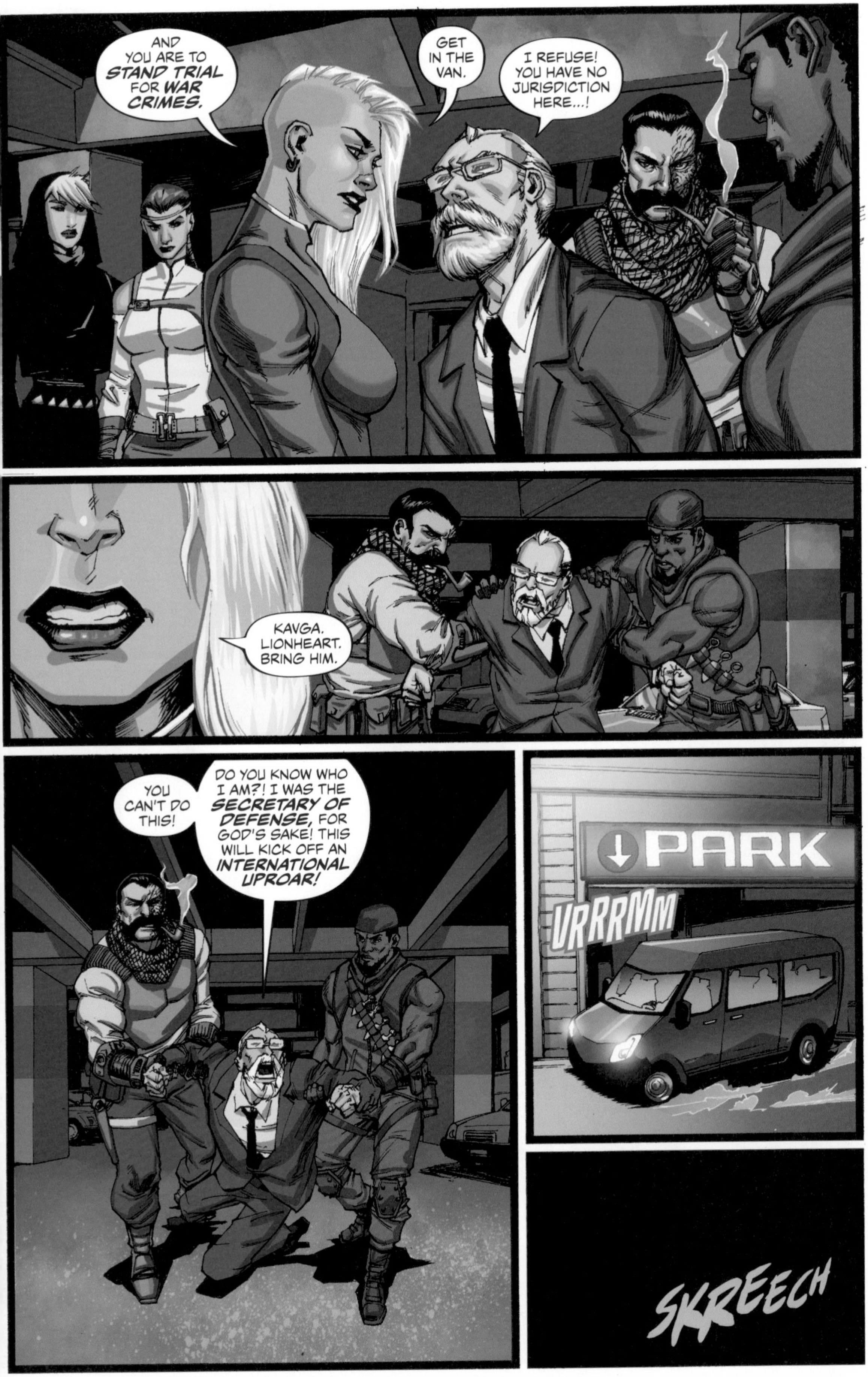
AND YOU ARE TO STAND TRIAL FOR WAR CRIMES.
GET IN THE VAN.
I REFUSE! YOU HAVE NO JURISDICTION HERE...!
KAVGA. LIONHEART. BRING HIM.
YOU CAN'T DO THIS!
DO YOU KNOW WHO I AM?! I WAS THE SECRETARY OF DEFENSE, FOR GOD'S SAKE! THIS WILL KICK OFF AN INTERNATIONAL UPROAR!
PARK
VRRRMM
SKREECH

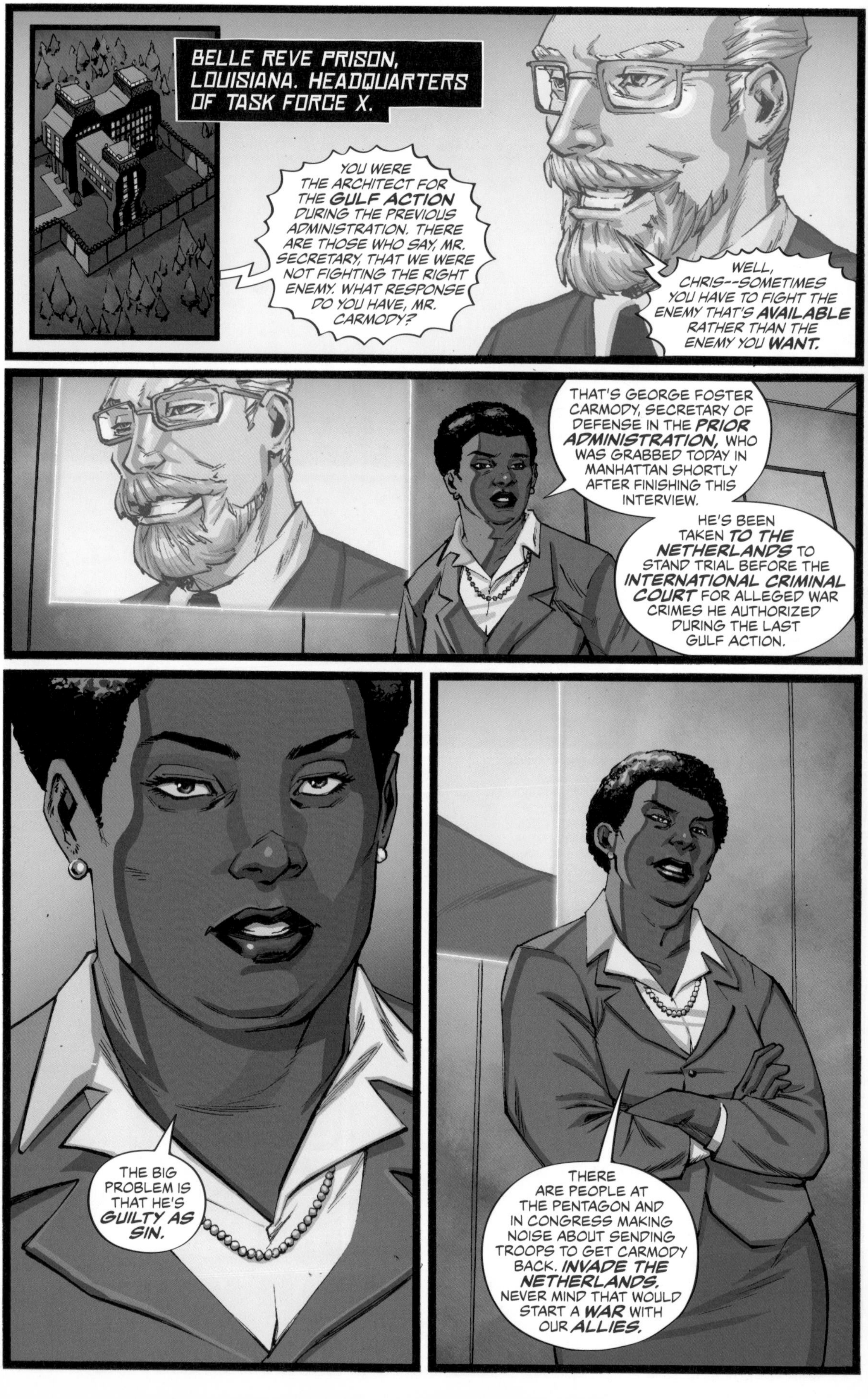
BELLE REVE PRISON, LOUISIANA. HEADQUARTERS OF TASK FORCE X.
YOU WERE THE ARCHITECT FOR THE GULF ACTION DURING THE PREVIOUS ADMINISTRATION. THERE ARE THOSE WHO SAY, MR. SECRETARY, THAT WE WERE NOT FIGHTING THE RIGHT ENEMY. WHAT RESPONSE DO YOU HAVE, MR. CARMODY?
WELL, CHRIS--SOMETIMES YOU HAVE TO FIGHT THE ENEMY THAT'S AVAILABLE RATHER THAN THE ENEMY YOU WANT.
THAT'S GEORGE FOSTER CARMODY, SECRETARY OF DEFENSE IN THE PRIOR ADMINISTRATION, WHO WAS GRABBED TODAY IN MANHATTAN SHORTLY AFTER FINISHING THIS INTERVIEW.
HE'S BEEN TAKEN TO THE NETHERLANDS TO STAND TRIAL BEFORE THE INTERNATIONAL CRIMINAL COURT FOR ALLEGED WAR CRIMES HE AUTHORIZED DURING THE LAST GULF ACTION.
THE BIG PROBLEM IS THAT HE'S GUILTY AS SIN.
THERE ARE PEOPLE AT THE PENTAGON AND IN CONGRESS MAKING NOISE ABOUT SENDING TROOPS TO GET CARMODY BACK. INVADE THE NETHERLANDS. NEVER MIND THAT WOULD START A WAR WITH OUR ALLIES.

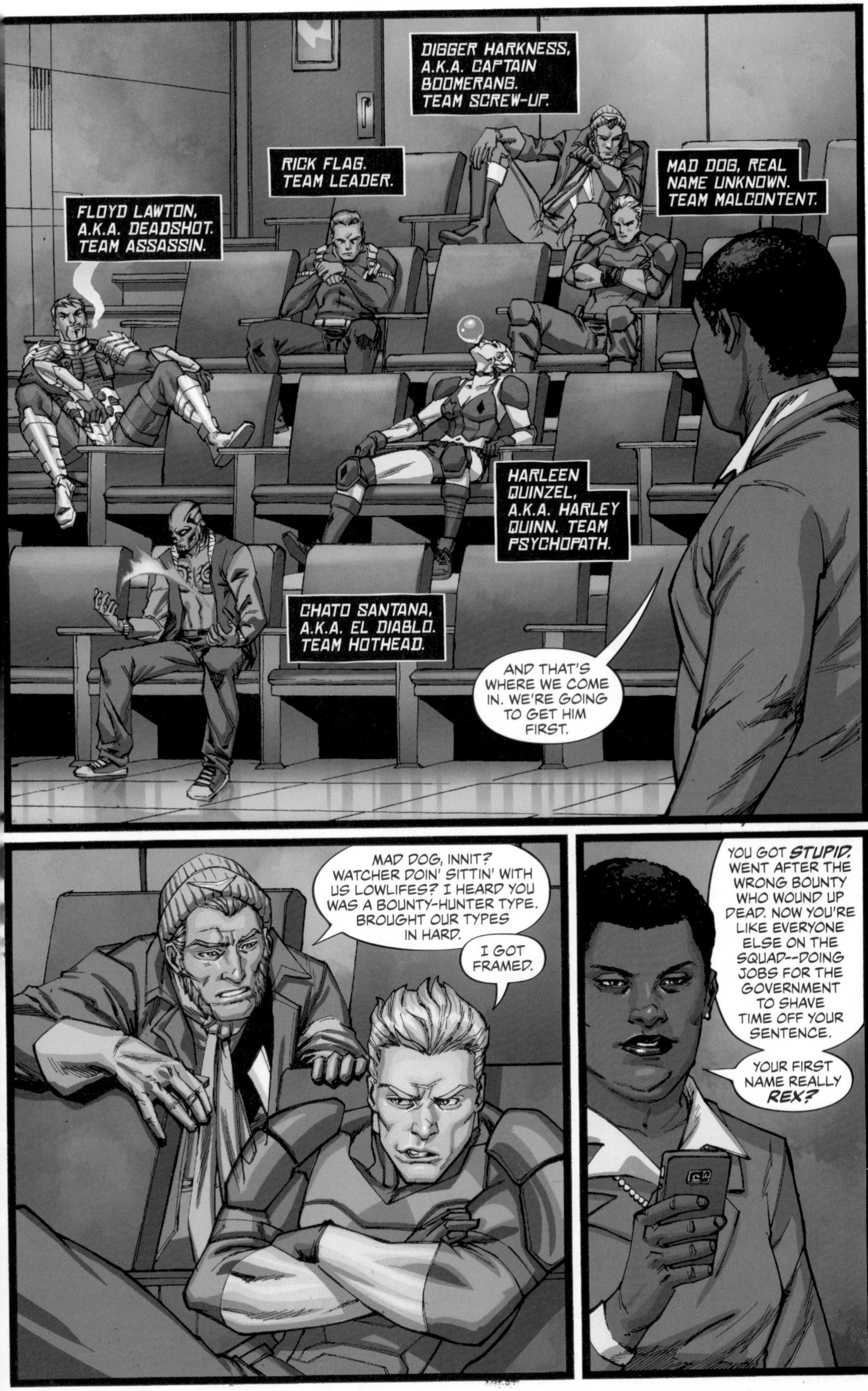

DIGGER HARKNESS, A.K.A. CAPTAIN BOOMERANG. TEAM SCREW-UP.
RICK FLAG. TEAM LEADER.
MAD DOG, REAL NAME UNKNOWN. TEAM MALCONTENT.
FLOYD LAWTON, A.K.A. DEADSHOT. TEAM ASSASSIN.
HARLEEN QUINZEL, A.K.A. HARLEY QUINN. TEAM PSYCHOPATH.
CHATO SANTANA, A.K.A. EL DIABLO. TEAM HOTHEAD.
AND THAT'S WHERE WE COME IN. WE'RE GOING TO GET HIM FIRST.
MAD DOG, INNIT? WATCHER DOIN' SITTIN' WITH US LOWLIFES? I HEARD YOU WAS A BOUNTY-HUNTER TYPE. BROUGHT OUR TYPES IN HARD.
I GOT FRAMED.
YOU GOT STUPID. WENT AFTER THE WRONG BOUNTY WHO WOUND UP DEAD. NOW YOU'RE LIKE EVERYONE ELSE ON THE SQUAD--DOING JOBS FOR THE GOVERNMENT TO SHAVE TIME OFF YOUR SENTENCE.
YOUR FIRST NAME REALLY REX?

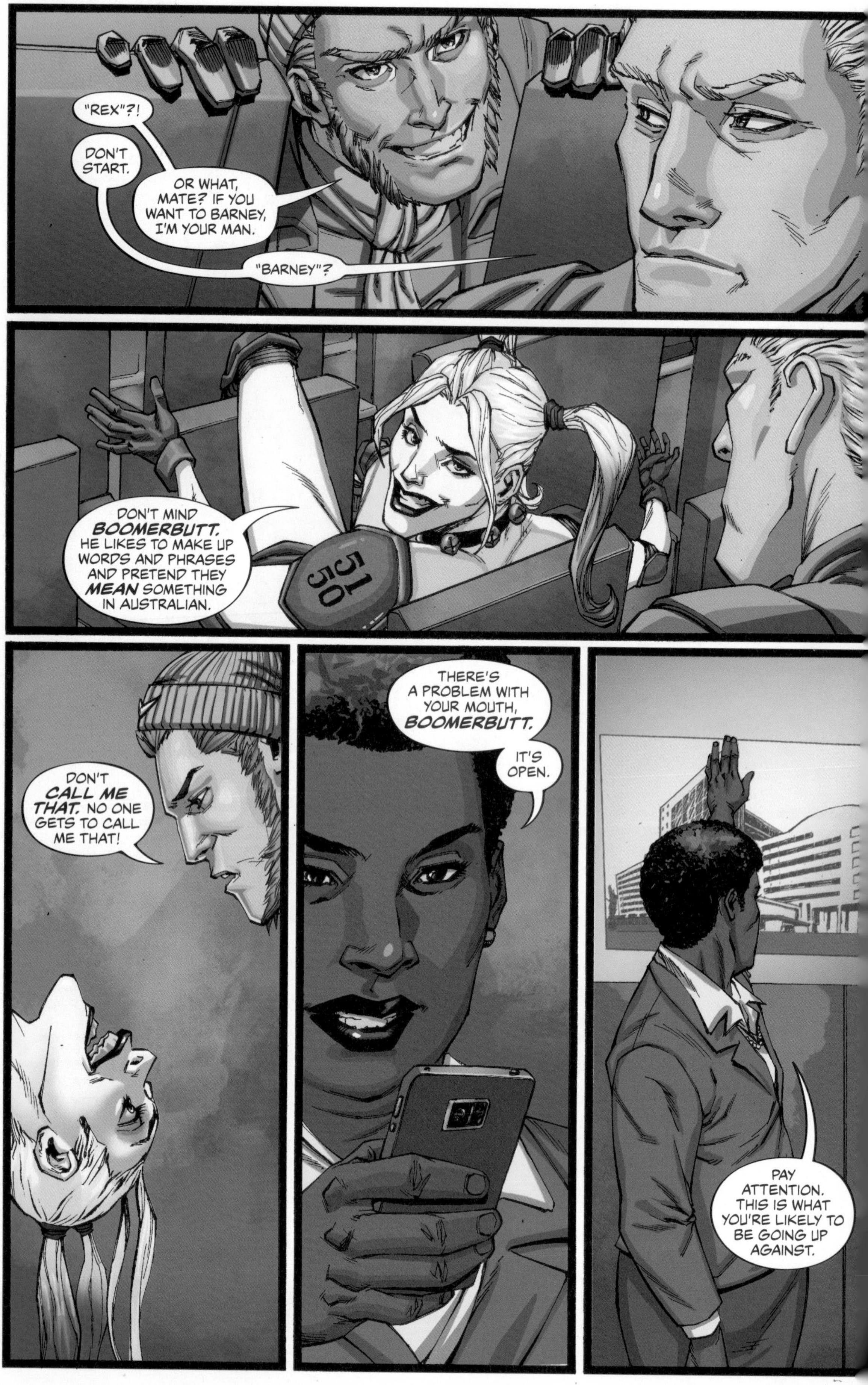
"REX"?!
DON'T START.
OR WHAT, MATE? IF YOU WANT TO BARNEY, I'M YOUR MAN.
"BARNEY"?
DON'T MIND BOOMERBUTT. HE LIKES TO MAKE UP WORDS AND PHRASES AND PRETEND THEY MEAN SOMETHING IN AUSTRALIAN.
51 50
DON'T CALL ME THAT. NO ONE GETS TO CALL ME THAT!
THERE'S A PROBLEM WITH YOUR MOUTH, BOOMERBUTT.
IT'S OPEN.
PAY ATTENTION. THIS IS WHAT YOU'RE LIKELY TO BE GOING UP AGAINST.

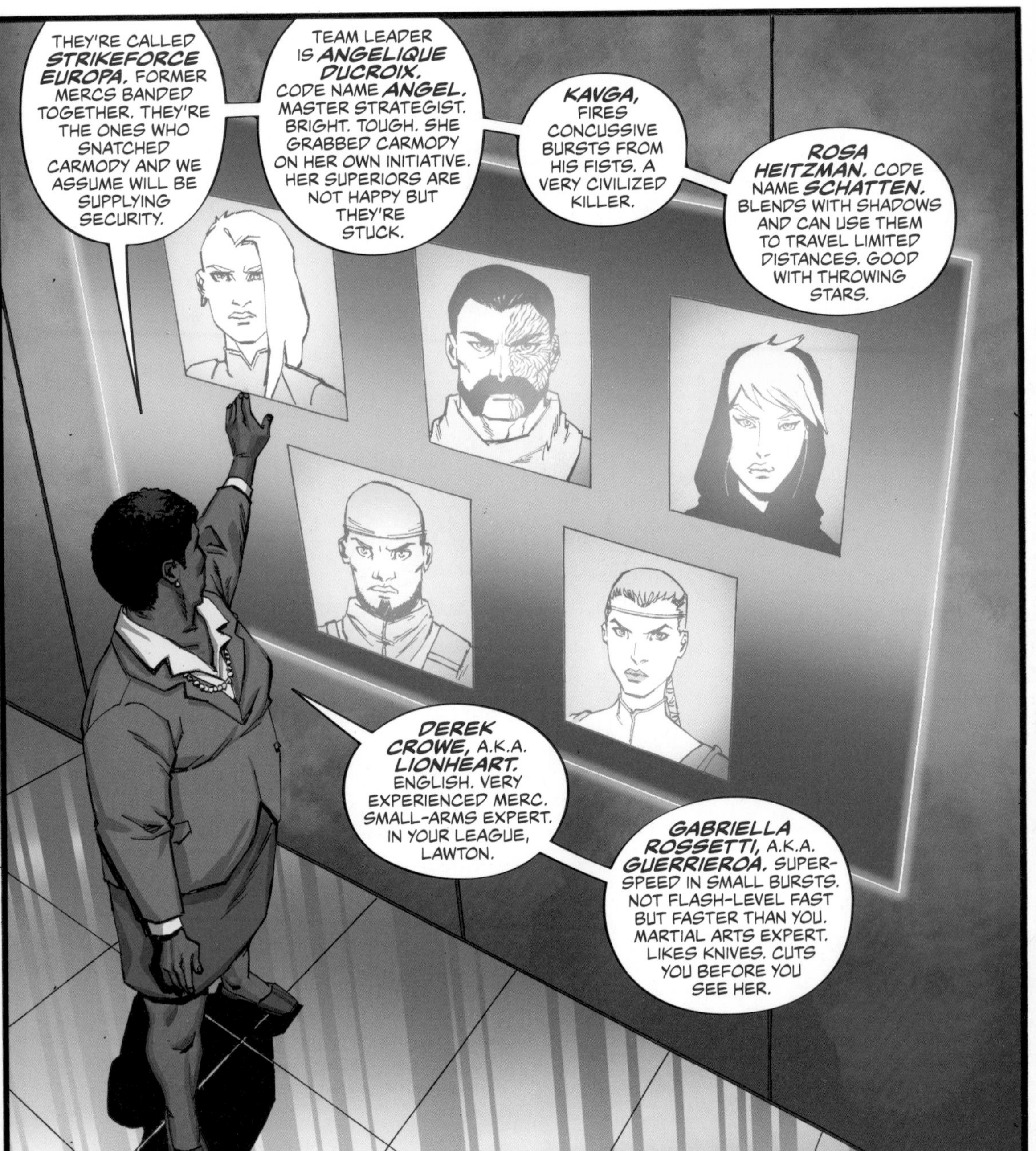
THEY'RE CALLED STRIKEFORCE EUROPA. FORMER MERCS BANDED TOGETHER. THEY'RE THE ONES WHO SNATCHED CARMODY AND WE ASSUME WILL BE SUPPLYING SECURITY.
TEAM LEADER IS ANGELIQUE DUCROIX. CODE NAME ANGEL. MASTER STRATEGIST. BRIGHT. TOUGH. SHE GRABBED CARMODY ON HER OWN INITIATIVE. HER SUPERIORS ARE NOT HAPPY BUT THEY'RE STUCK.
KAVGA, FIRES CONCUSSIVE BURSTS FROM HIS FISTS. A VERY CIVILIZED KILLER.
ROSA HEITZMAN. CODE NAME SCHATTEN. BLENDS WITH SHADOWS AND CAN USE THEM TO TRAVEL LIMITED DISTANCES. GOOD WITH THROWING STARS.
DEREK CROWE, A.K.A. LIONHEART. ENGLISH. VERY EXPERIENCED MERC. SMALL-ARMS EXPERT. IN YOUR LEAGUE, LAWTON.
GABRIELLA ROSSETTI, A.K.A. GUERRIEROA. SUPER-SPEED IN SMALL BURSTS. NOT FLASH-LEVEL FAST BUT FASTER THAN YOU. MARTIAL ARTS EXPERT. LIKES KNIVES. CUTS YOU BEFORE YOU SEE HER.

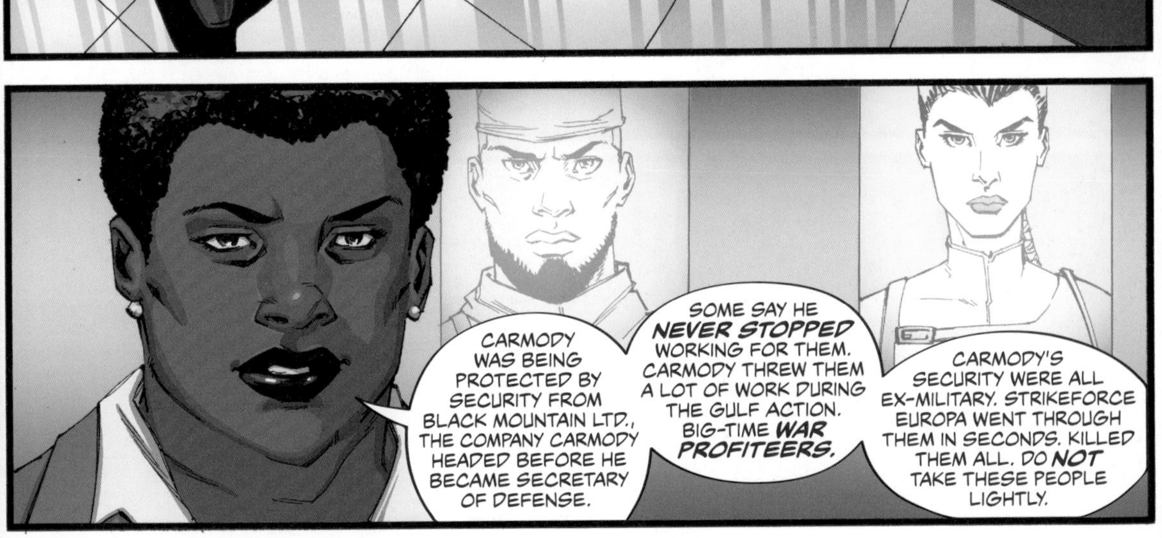
CARMODY WAS BEING PROTECTED BY SECURITY FROM BLACK MOUNTAIN LTD., THE COMPANY CARMODY HEADED BEFORE HE BECAME SECRETARY OF DEFENSE.
SOME SAY HE NEVER STOPPED WORKING FOR THEM. CARMODY THREW THEM A LOT OF WORK DURING THE GULF ACTION. BIG-TIME WAR PROFITEERS.
CARMODY'S SECURITY WERE ALL EX-MILITARY. STRIKEFORCE EUROPA WENT THROUGH THEM IN SECONDS. KILLED THEM ALL. DO NOT TAKE THESE PEOPLE LIGHTLY.

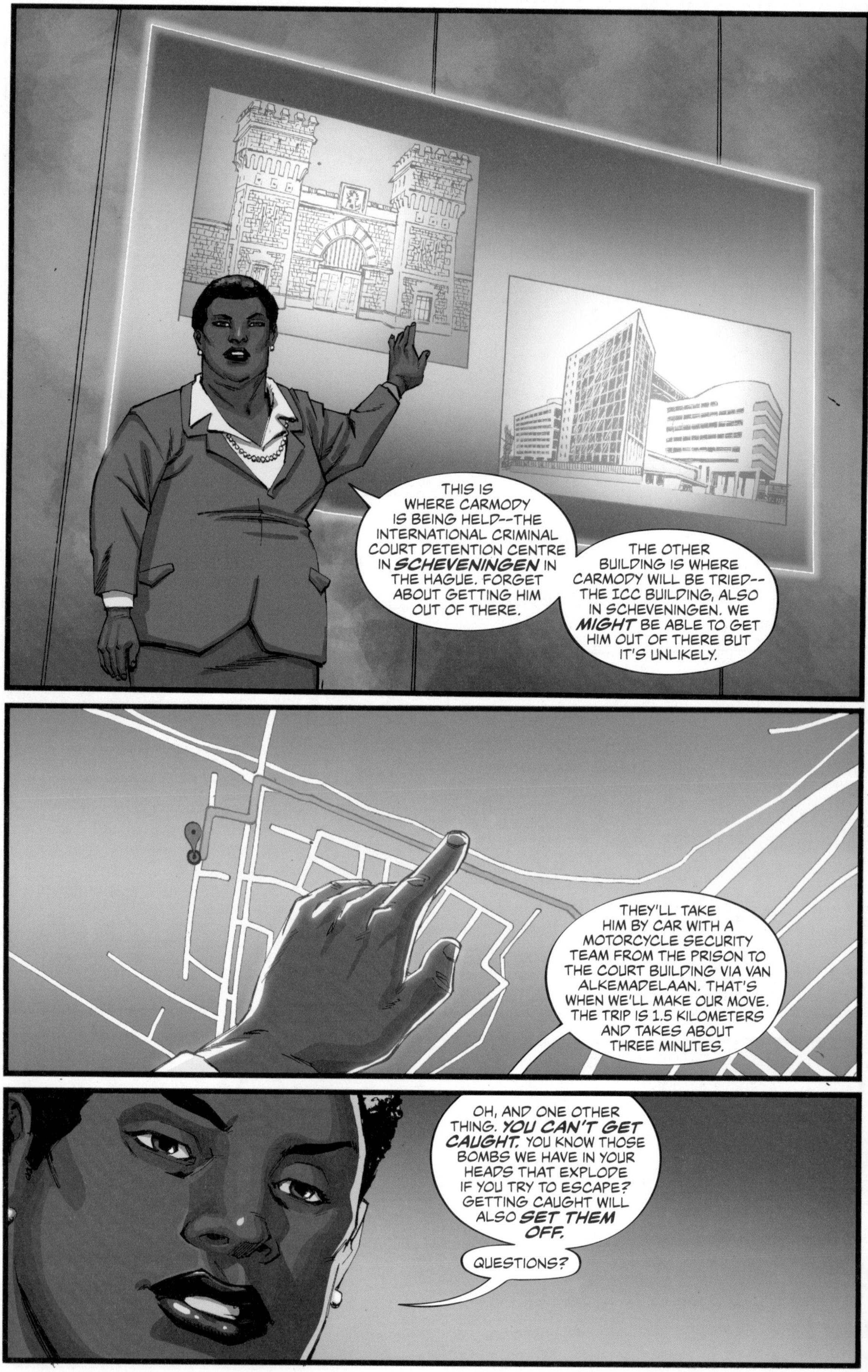
THIS IS WHERE CARMODY IS BEING HELD--THE INTERNATIONAL CRIMINAL COURT DETENTION CENTRE IN SCHEVENINGEN IN THE HAGUE. FORGET ABOUT GETTING HIM OUT OF THERE.
THE OTHER BUILDING IS WHERE CARMODY WILL BE TRIED--THE ICC BUILDING, ALSO IN SCHEVENINGEN. WE MIGHT BE ABLE TO GET HIM OUT OF THERE BUT IT'S UNLIKELY.
THEY'LL TAKE HIM BY CAR WITH A MOTORCYCLE SECURITY TEAM FROM THE PRISON TO THE COURT BUILDING VIA VAN ALKEMADELAAN. THAT'S WHEN WE'LL MAKE OUR MOVE. THE TRIP IS 1.5 KILOMETERS AND TAKES ABOUT THREE MINUTES.
OH, AND ONE OTHER THING. YOU CAN'T GET CAUGHT. YOU KNOW THOSE BOMBS WE HAVE IN YOUR HEADS THAT EXPLODE IF YOU TRY TO ESCAPE? GETTING CAUGHT WILL ALSO SET THEM OFF.
QUESTIONS?

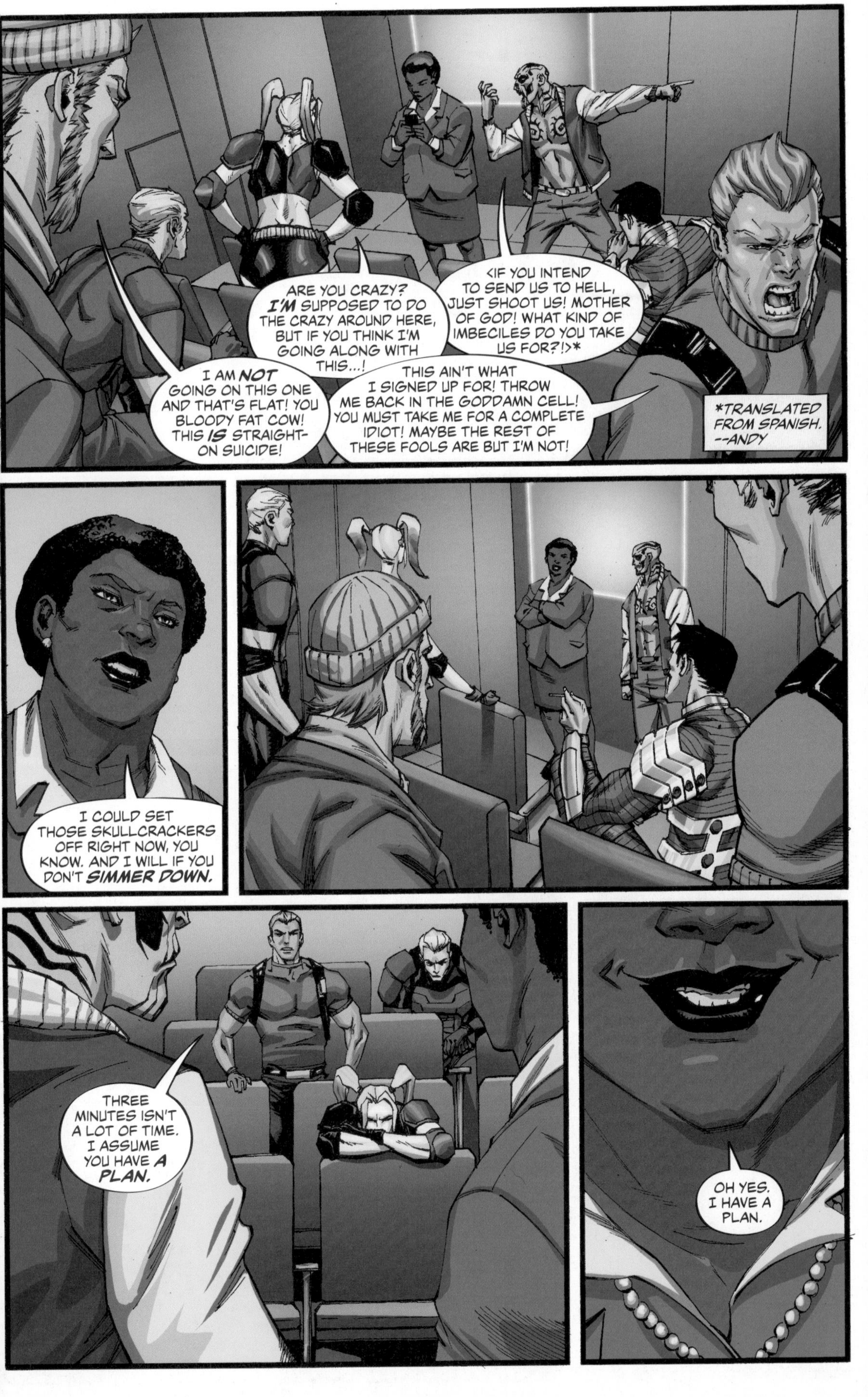

ARE YOU CRAZY? I'M SUPPOSED TO DO THE CRAZY AROUND HERE, BUT IF YOU THINK I'M GOING ALONG WITH THIS...!
<IF YOU INTEND TO SEND US TO HELL, JUST SHOOT US! MOTHER OF GOD! WHAT KIND OF IMBECILES DO YOU TAKE US FOR?!>*
I AM NOT GOING ON THIS ONE AND THAT'S FLAT! YOU BLOODY FAT COW! THIS IS STRAIGHT-ON SUICIDE!
THIS AIN'T WHAT I SIGNED UP FOR! THROW ME BACK IN THE GODDAMN CELL! YOU MUST TAKE ME FOR A COMPLETE IDIOT! MAYBE THE REST OF THESE FOOLS ARE BUT I'M NOT!
*TRANSLATED FROM SPANISH. --ANDY
I COULD SET THOSE SKULLCRACKERS OFF RIGHT NOW, YOU KNOW. AND I WILL IF YOU DON'T SIMMER DOWN.
THREE MINUTES ISN'T A LOT OF TIME. I ASSUME YOU HAVE A PLAN.
OH YES. I HAVE A PLAN.

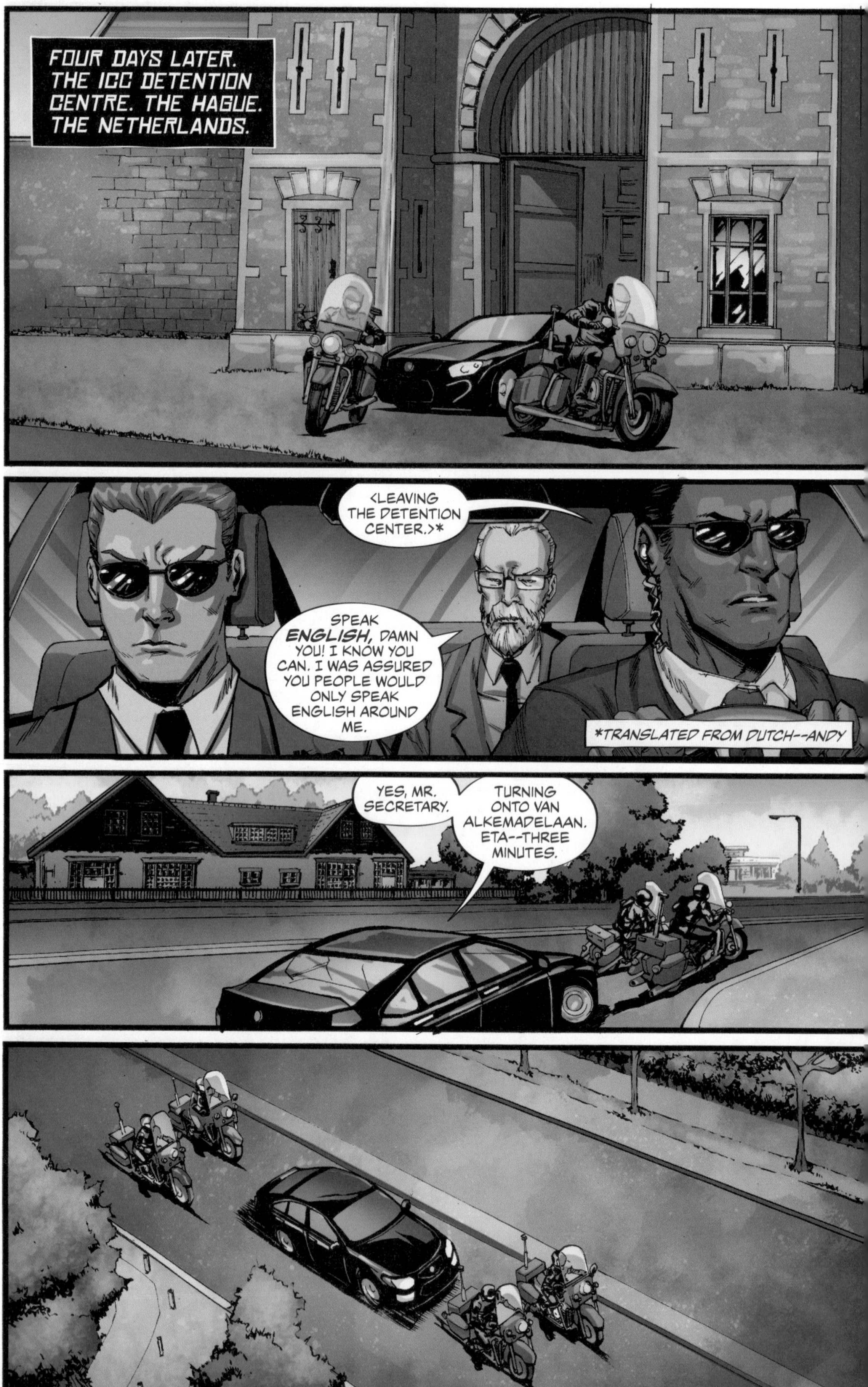

FOUR DAYS LATER. THE ICC DETENTION CENTRE. THE HAGUE. THE NETHERLANDS.
<LEAVING THE DETENTION CENTER.>*
SPEAK ENGLISH, DAMN YOU! I KNOW YOU CAN. I WAS ASSURED YOU PEOPLE WOULD ONLY SPEAK ENGLISH AROUND ME.
*TRANSLATED FROM DUTCH--ANDY
YES, MR. SECRETARY.
TURNING ONTO VAN ALKEMADELAAN. ETA--THREE MINUTES.

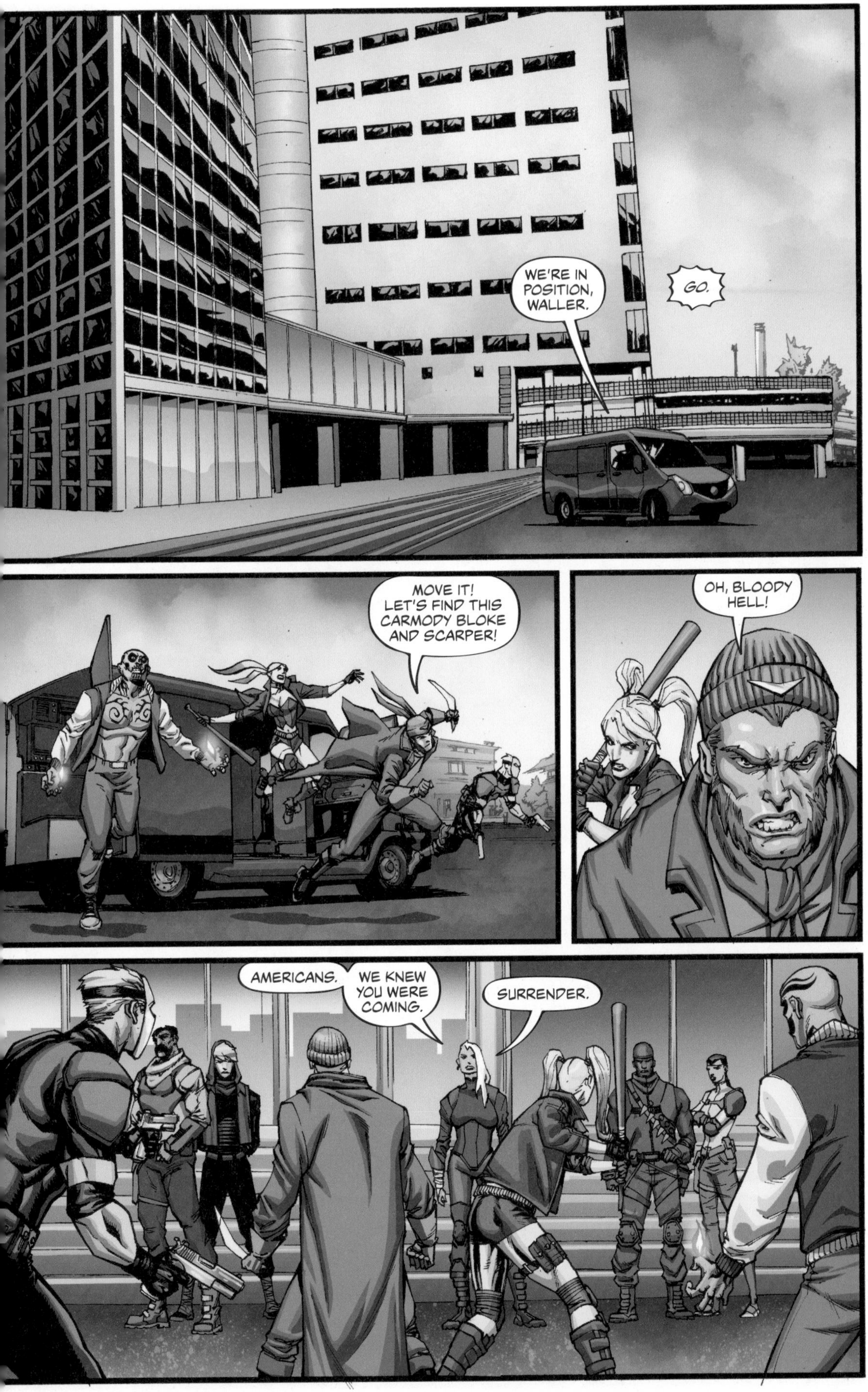
WE'RE IN POSITION, WALLER.
GO.
MOVE IT! LET'S FIND THIS CARMODY BLOKE AND SCARPER!
OH, BLOODY HELL!
AMERICANS.
WE KNEW YOU WERE COMING.
SURRENDER.

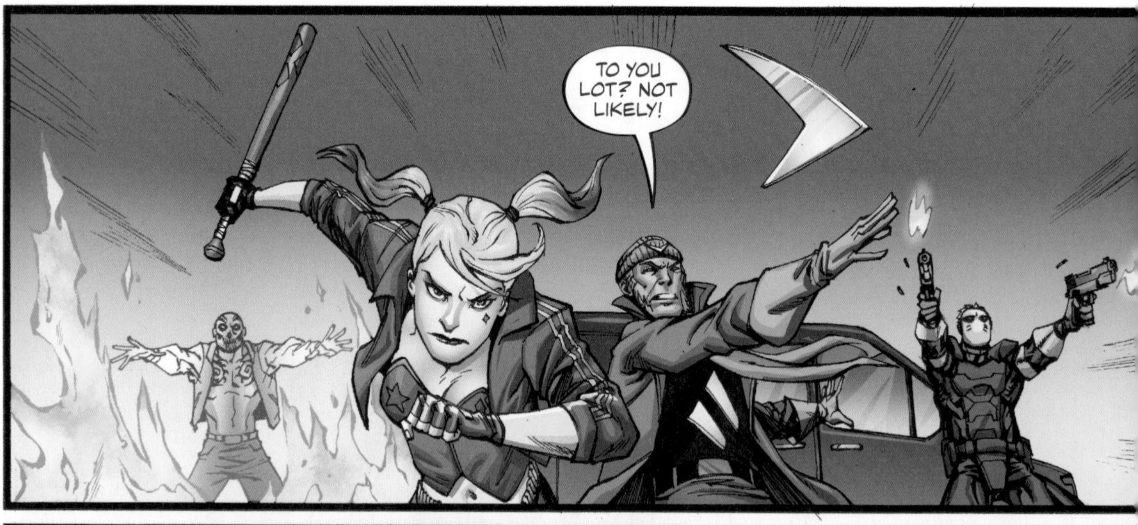
TO YOU LOT? NOT LIKELY!

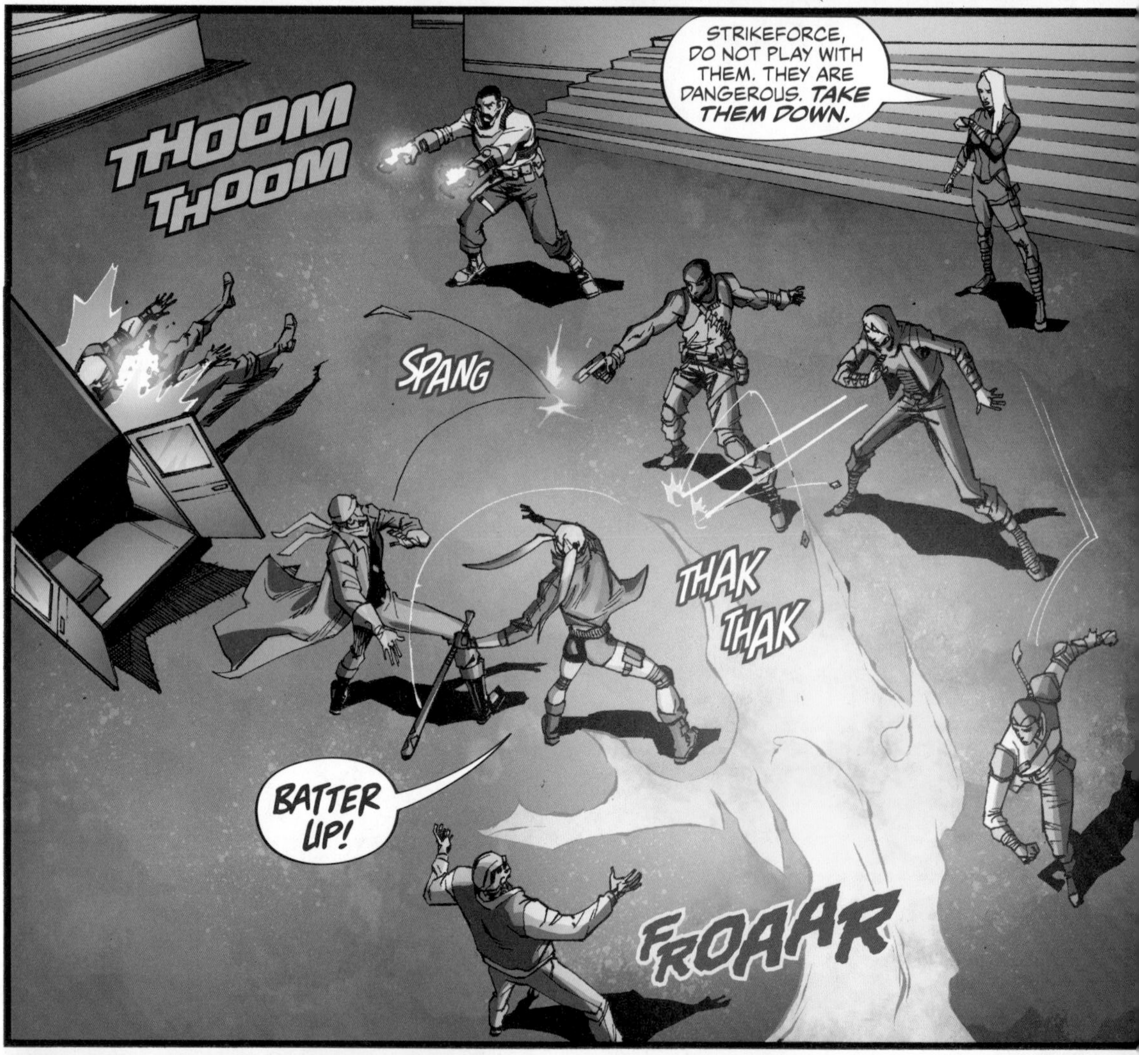
STRIKEFORCE, DO NOT PLAY WITH THEM. THEY ARE DANGEROUS. TAKE THEM DOWN.
THOOM THOOM
SPANG
THAK THAK
BATTER UP!
FROAAR

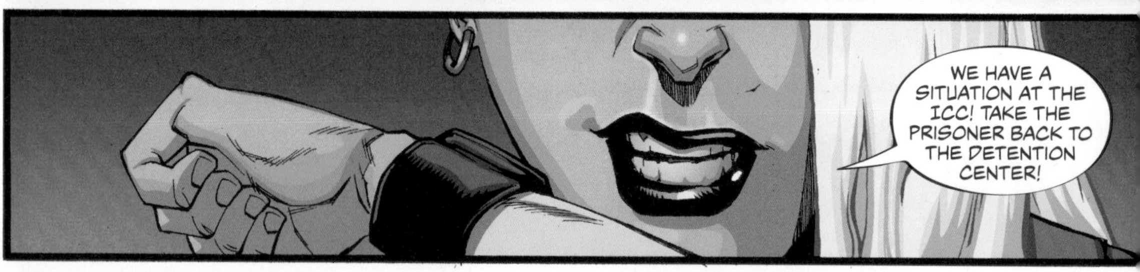
WE HAVE A SITUATION AT THE ICC! TAKE THE PRISONER BACK TO THE DETENTION CENTER!

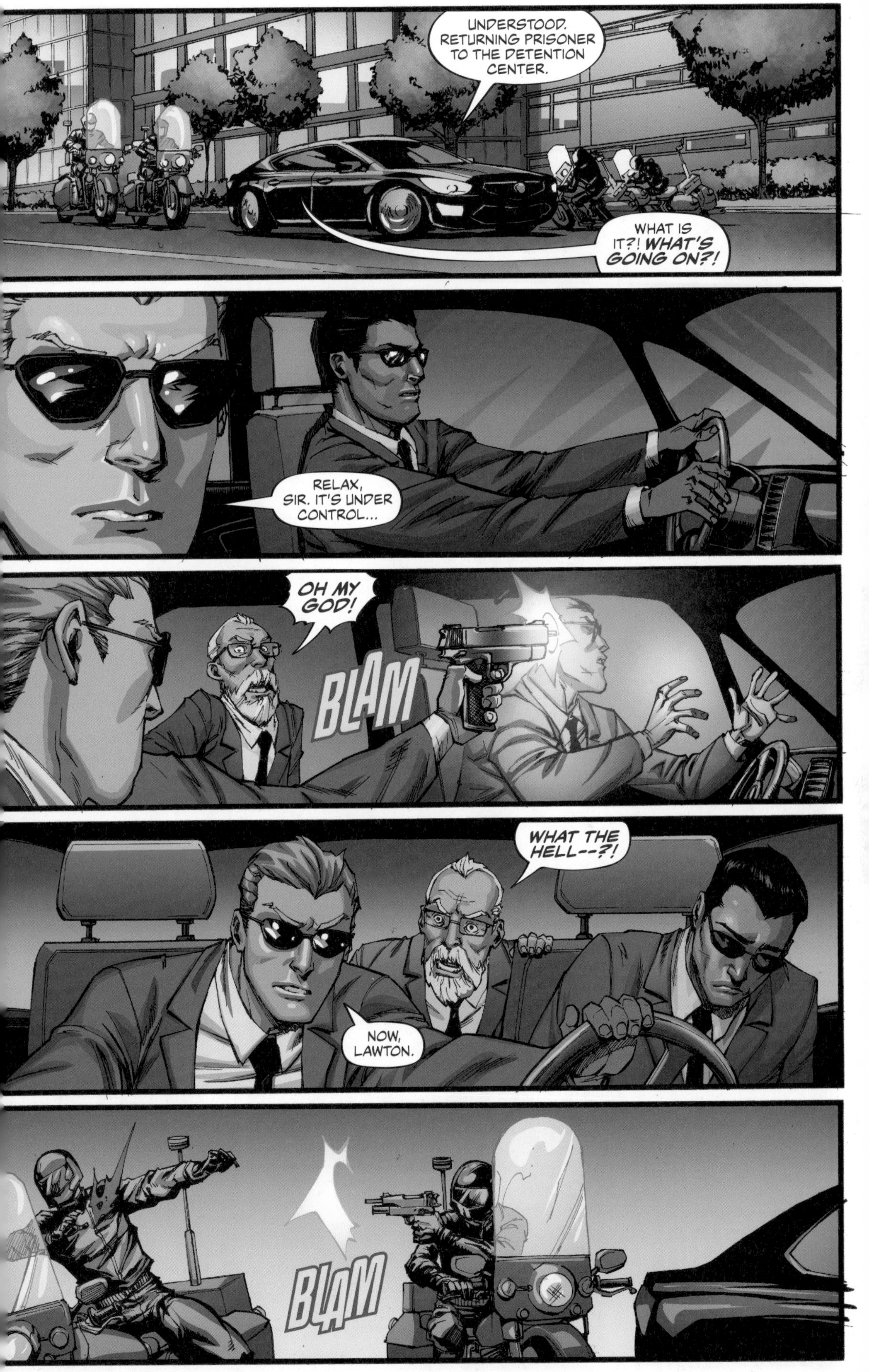
UNDERSTOOD. RETURNING PRISONER TO THE DETENTION CENTER.
WHAT IS IT?! WHAT'S GOING ON?!
RELAX, SIR. IT'S UNDER CONTROL...
OH MY GOD!
BLAM
WHAT THE HELL--?!
NOW, LAWTON.
BLAM

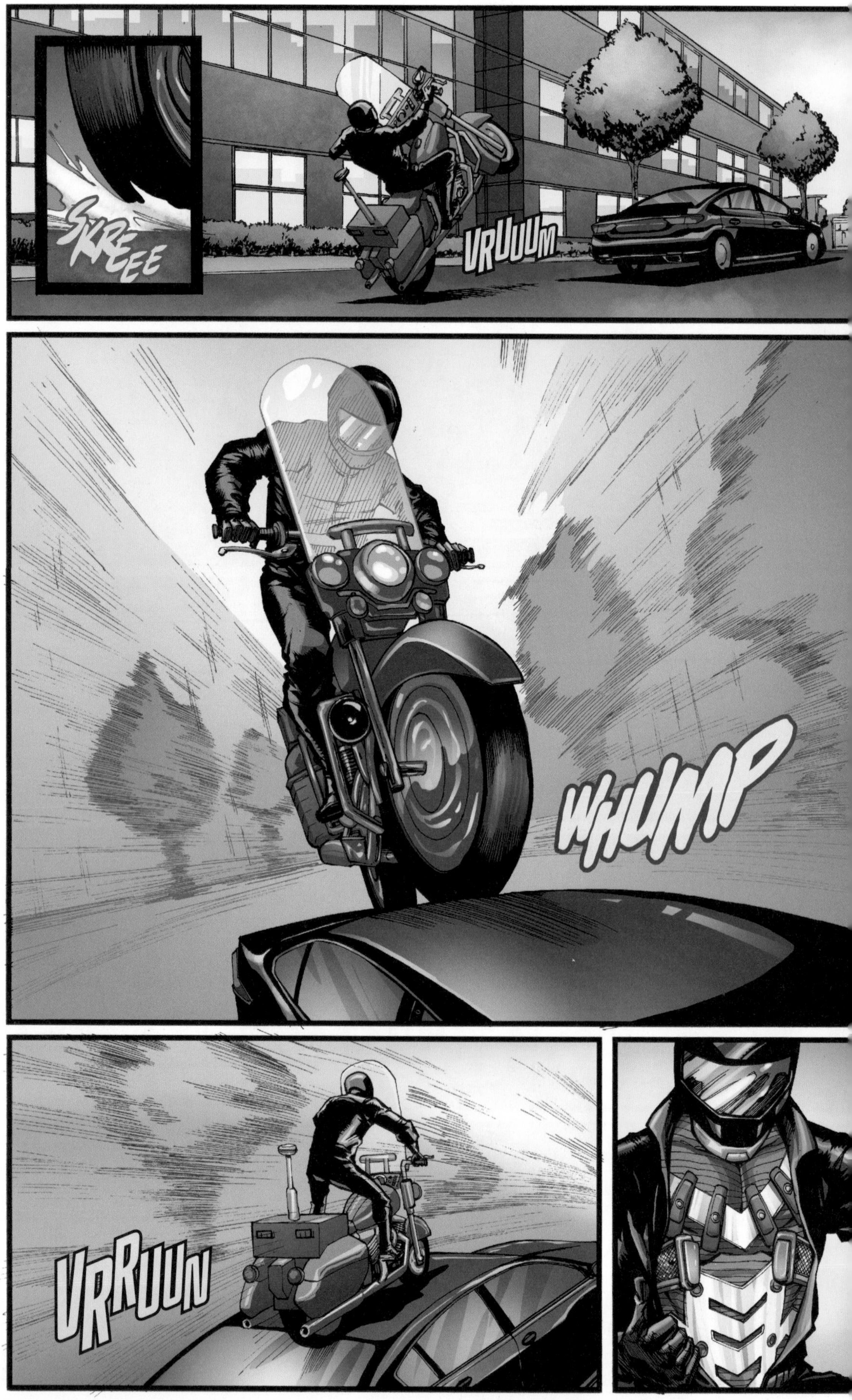
SKREEEE
VRUUUM
WHUMP
VRRUUN

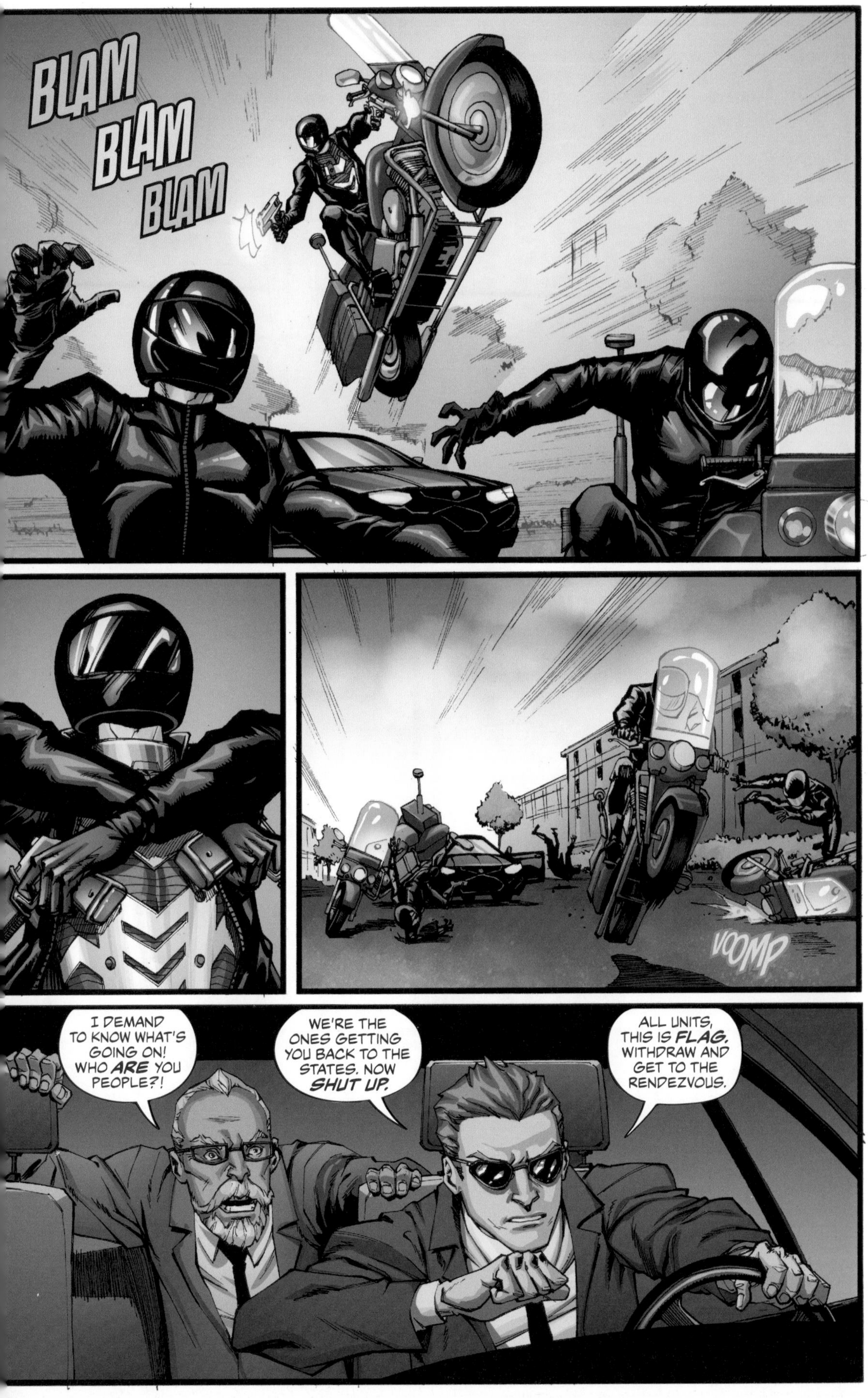
BLAM
BLAM
BLAM
VOOMP
I DEMAND TO KNOW WHAT'S GOING ON! WHO ARE YOU PEOPLE?!
WE'RE THE ONES GETTING YOU BACK TO THE STATES. NOW SHUT UP.
ALL UNITS, THIS IS FLAG. WITHDRAW AND GET TO THE RENDEZVOUS.

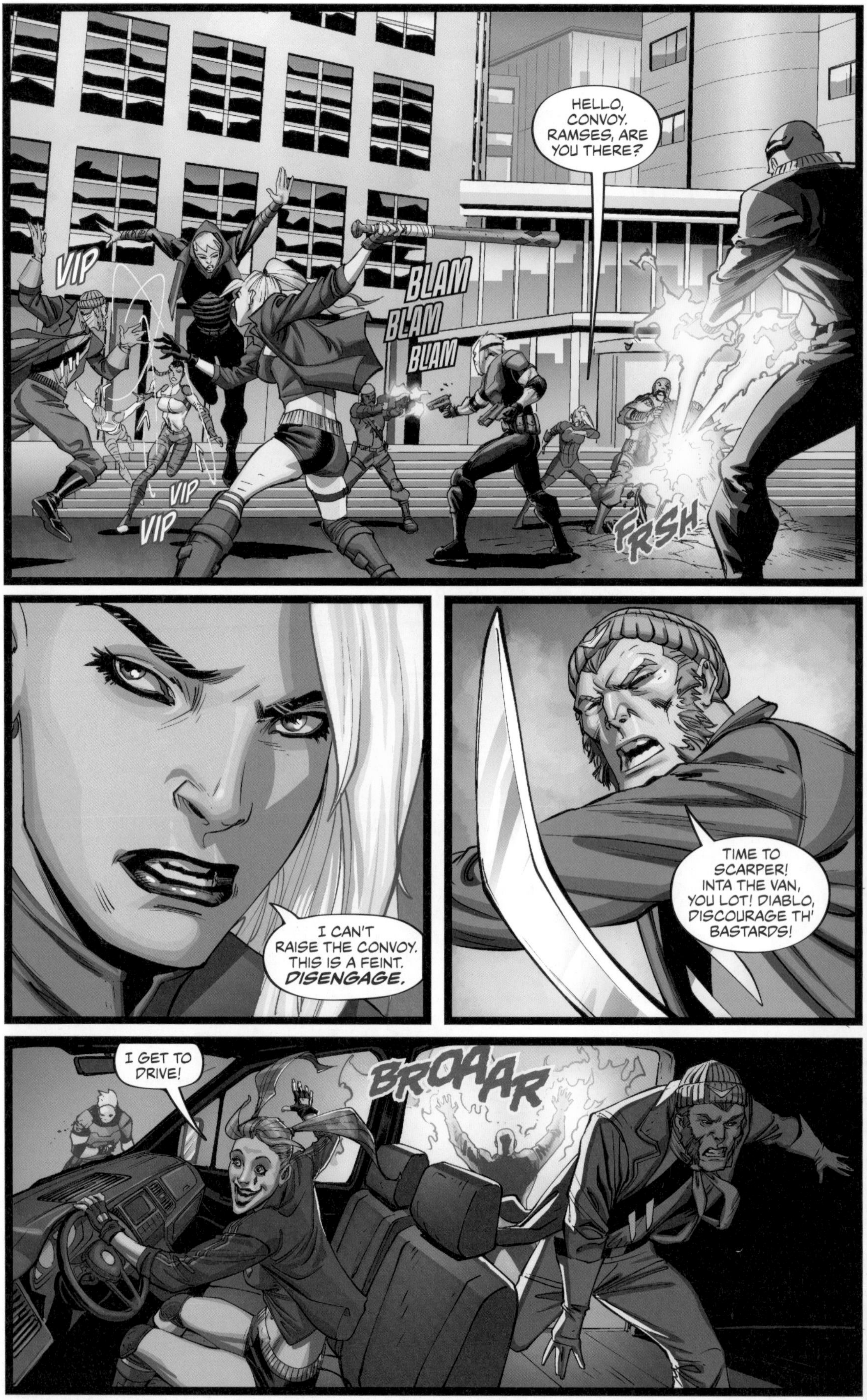
HELLO, CONVOY. RAMSES, ARE YOU THERE?
VIP
BLAM
BLAM
BLAM
VIP
VIP
FRSH
I CAN'T RAISE THE CONVOY. THIS IS A FEINT. *DISENGAGE.*
TIME TO SCARPER! INTA THE VAN, YOU LOT! DIABLO, DISCOURAGE TH' BASTARDS!
I GET TO DRIVE!
BROAAAR

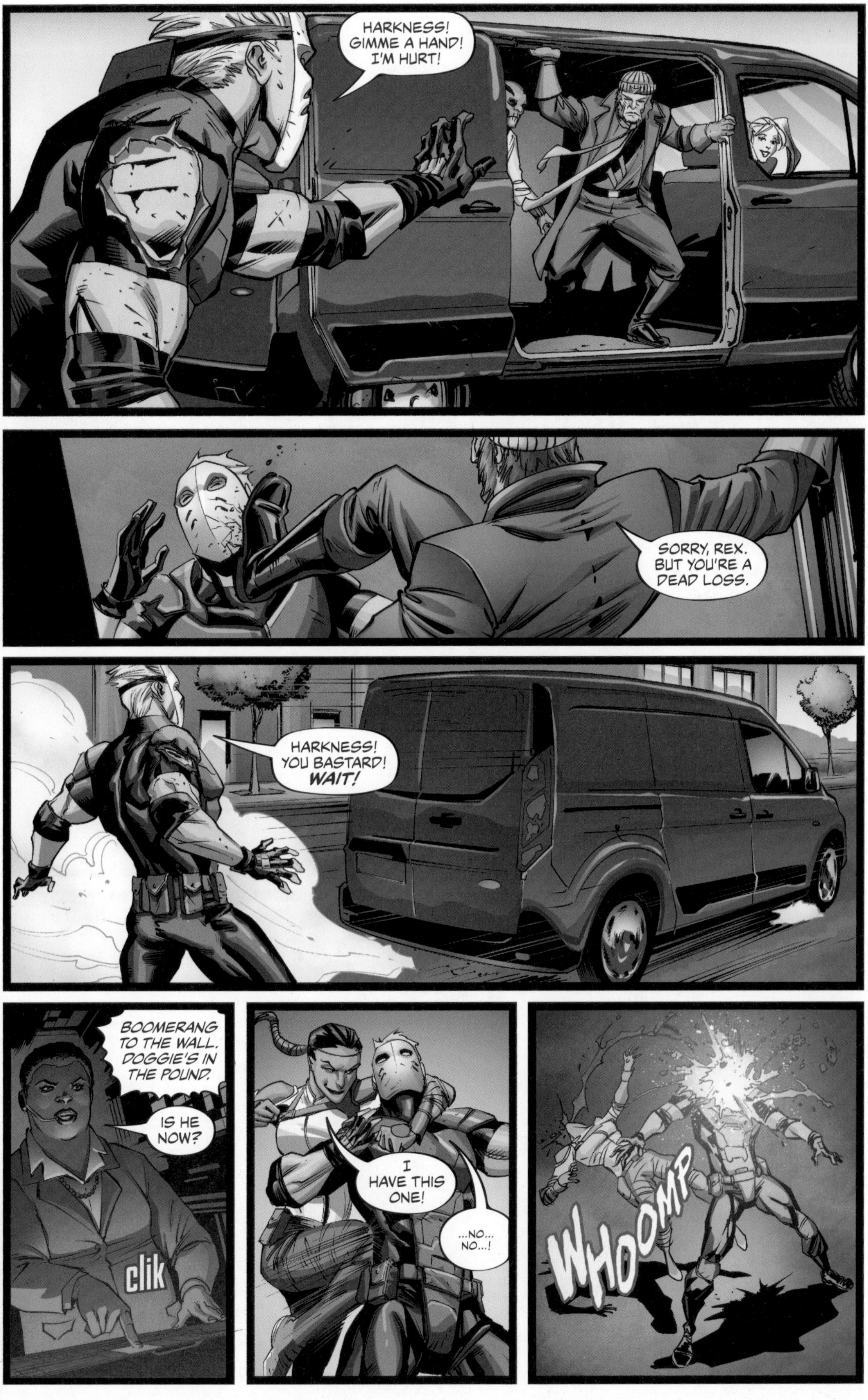
HARKNESS! GIMME A HAND! I'M HURT!
SORRY, REX. BUT YOU'RE A DEAD LOSS.
HARKNESS! YOU BASTARD! WAIT!
BOOMERANG TO THE WALL. DOGGIE'S IN THE POUND.
IS HE NOW?
clik
I HAVE THIS ONE!
...NO... NO...!
WHOOMP

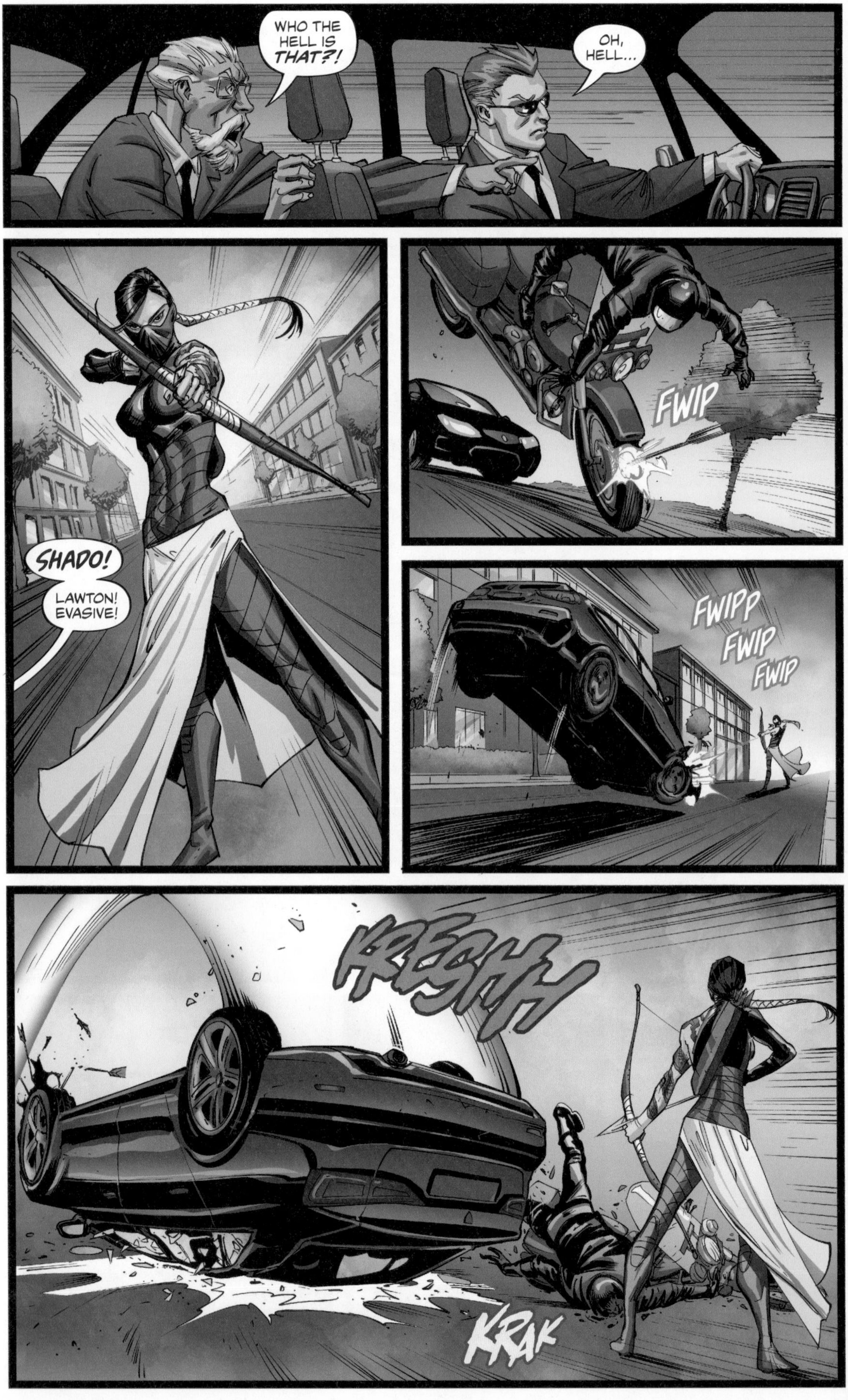
WHO THE HELL IS THAT?!
OH, HELL...
SHADO!
LAWTON! EVASIVE!
FWIP
FWIPP
FWIP
FWIP
KRESHH
KRAK

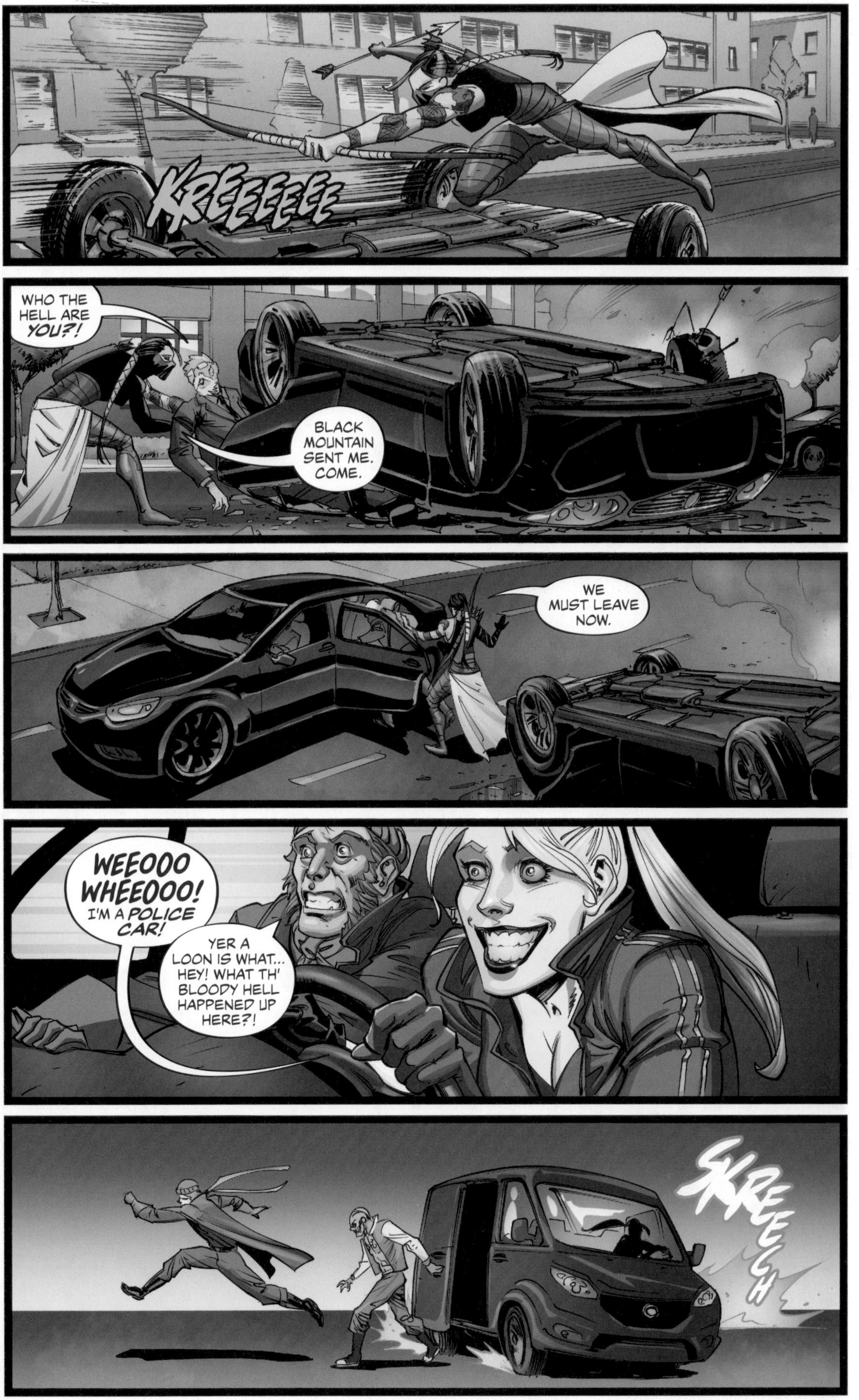
KREEEEEEE
WHO THE HELL ARE YOU?!
BLACK MOUNTAIN SENT ME. COME.
WE MUST LEAVE NOW.
WEEOOO WHEEOOO! I'M A POLICE CAR!
YER A LOON IS WHAT... HEY! WHAT TH' BLOODY HELL HAPPENED UP HERE?!
SKREECH

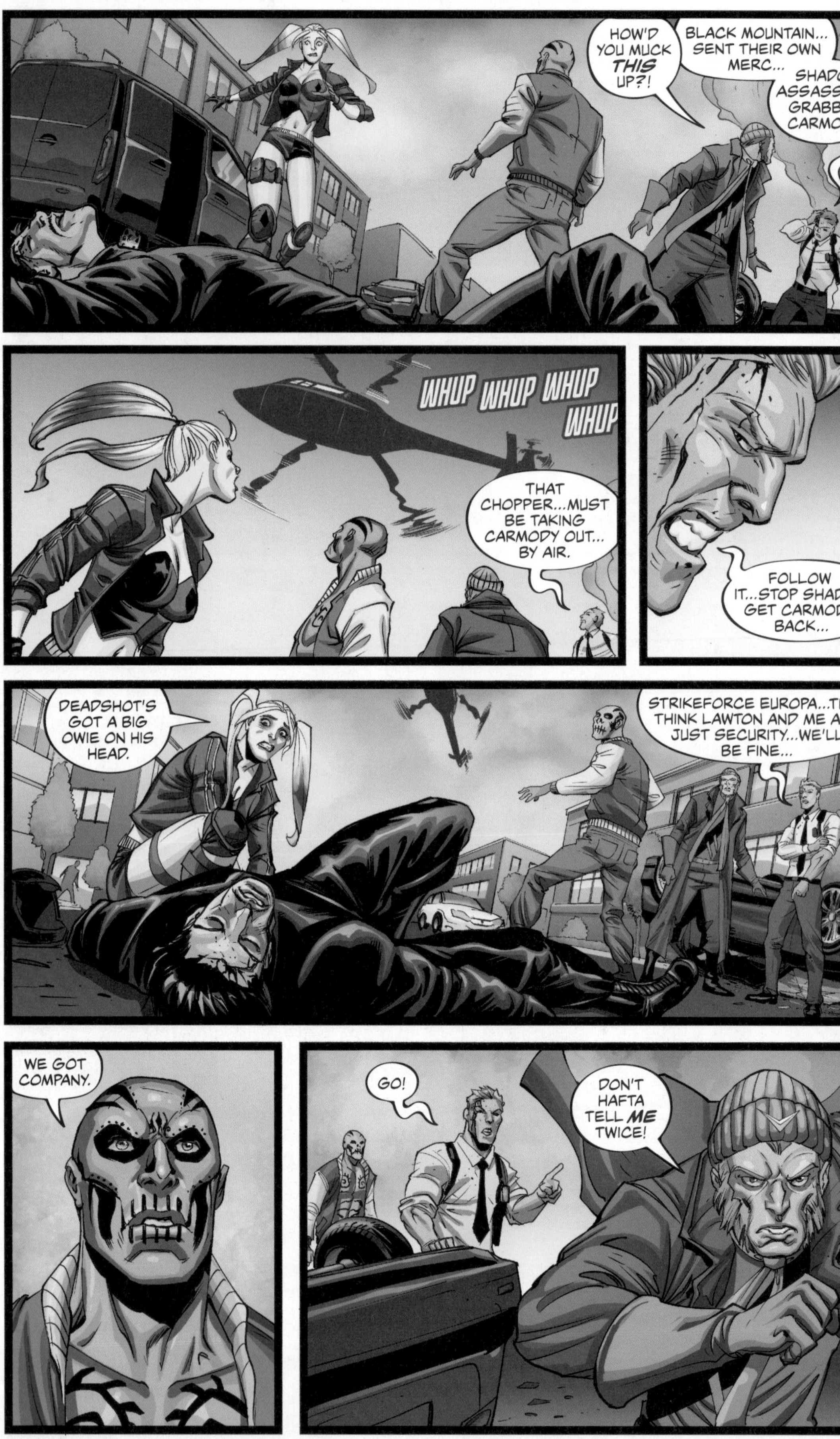
HOW'D YOU MUCK THIS UP?!
BLACK MOUNTAIN... SENT THEIR OWN MERC...
SHADO. ASSASSIN... GRABBED CARMODY.
WHUP WHUP WHUP WHUP
THAT CHOPPER...MUST BE TAKING CARMODY OUT... BY AIR.
FOLLOW IT...STOP SHADO... GET CARMODY BACK...
DEADSHOT'S GOT A BIG OWIE ON HIS HEAD.
STRIKEFORCE EUROPA...THEY THINK LAWTON AND ME ARE JUST SECURITY...WE'LL BE FINE...
WE GOT COMPANY.
GO!
DON'T HAFTA TELL ME TWICE!

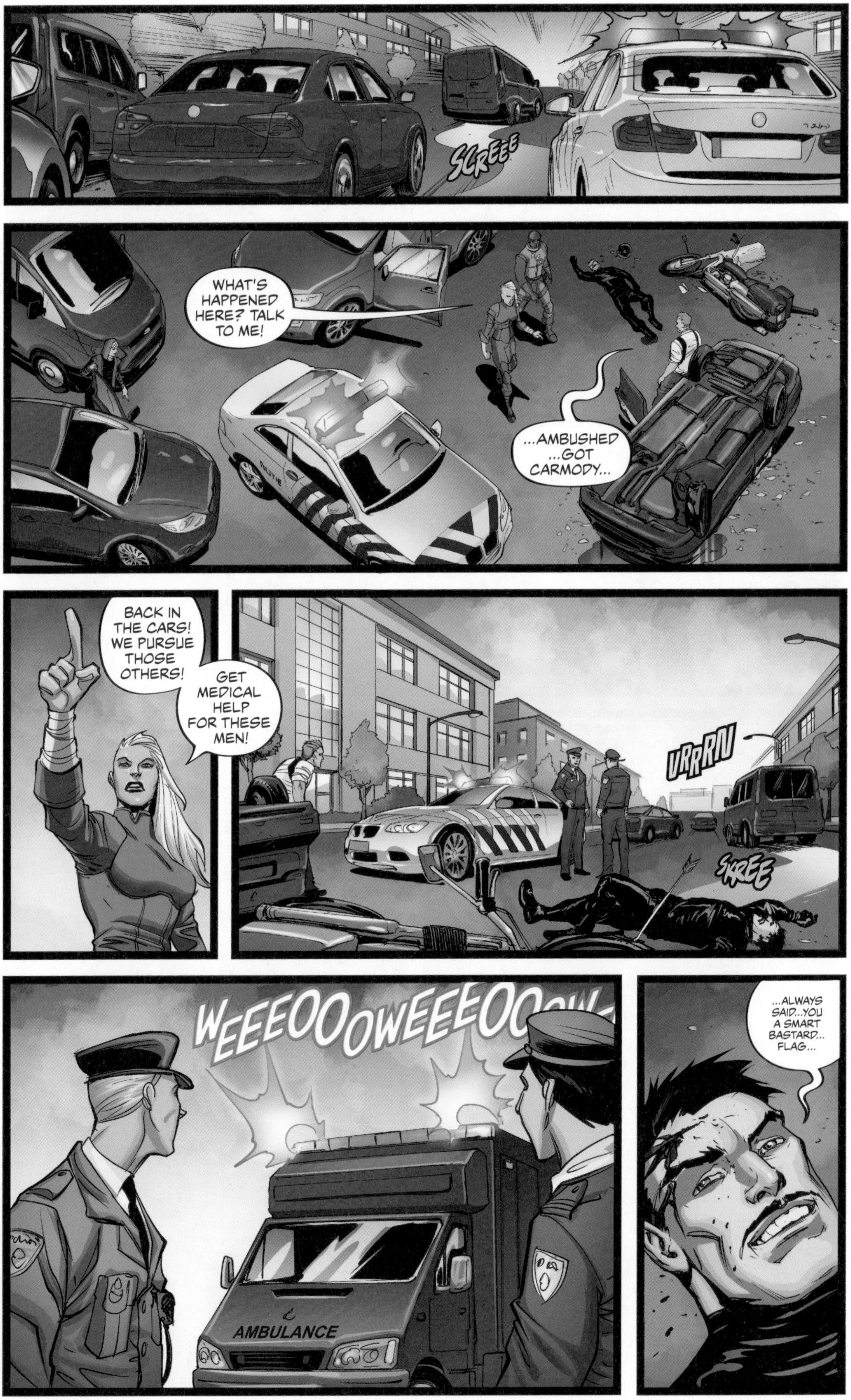
SCREEE
WHAT'S HAPPENED HERE? TALK TO ME!
...AMBUSHED ...GOT CARMODY...
BACK IN THE CARS! WE PURSUE THOSE OTHERS!
GET MEDICAL HELP FOR THESE MEN!
URRRN
SKREE
WEEEOOOWEEEOOOW-
AMBULANCE
...ALWAYS SAID...YOU A SMART BASTARD... FLAG...

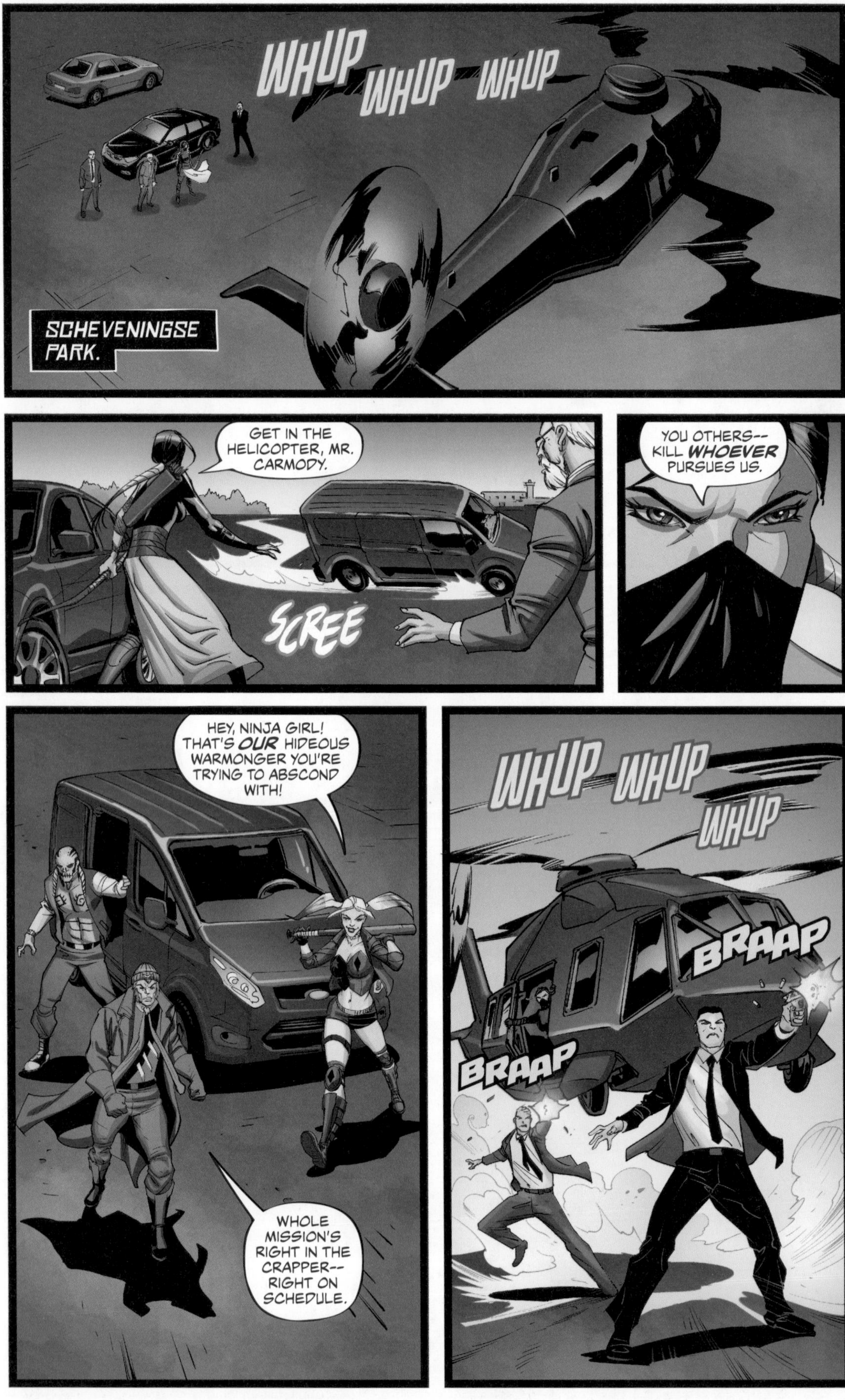
WHUP WHUP WHUP
SCHEVENINGSE PARK.
GET IN THE HELICOPTER, MR. CARMODY.
SCREE
YOU OTHERS-- KILL WHOEVER PURSUES US.
HEY, NINJA GIRL! THAT'S OUR HIDEOUS WARMONGER YOU'RE TRYING TO ABSCOND WITH!
WHOLE MISSION'S RIGHT IN THE CRAPPER-- RIGHT ON SCHEDULE.
WHUP WHUP WHUP
BRAAP
BRAAP

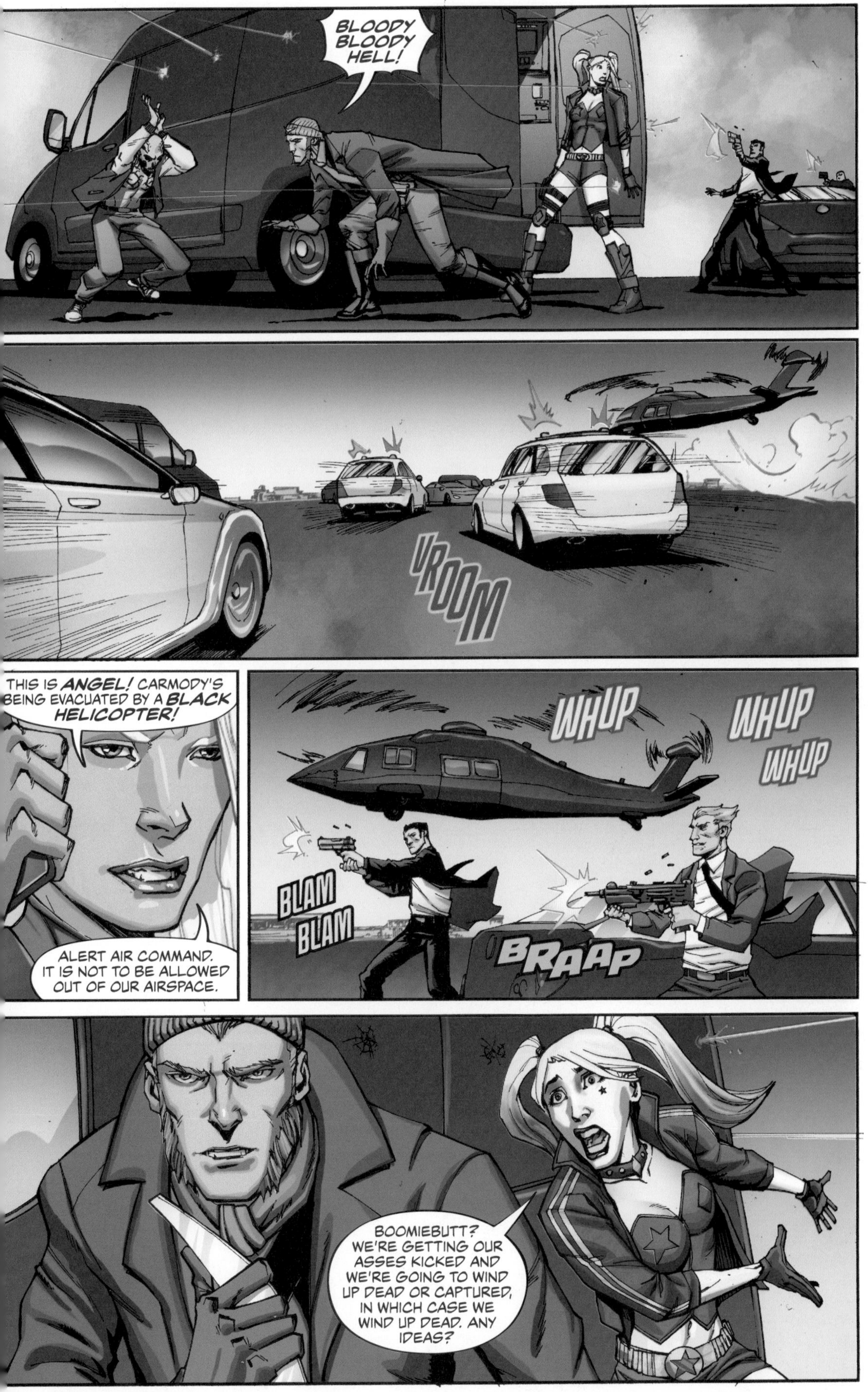
BLOODY BLOODY HELL!
UROOM
THIS IS ANGEL! CARMODY'S BEING EVACUATED BY A BLACK HELICOPTER!
ALERT AIR COMMAND. IT IS NOT TO BE ALLOWED OUT OF OUR AIRSPACE.
WHUP
WHUP
WHUP
BLAM
BLAM
BRAAP
BOOMIEBUTT? WE'RE GETTING OUR ASSES KICKED AND WE'RE GOING TO WIND UP DEAD OR CAPTURED, IN WHICH CASE WE WIND UP DEAD. ANY IDEAS?

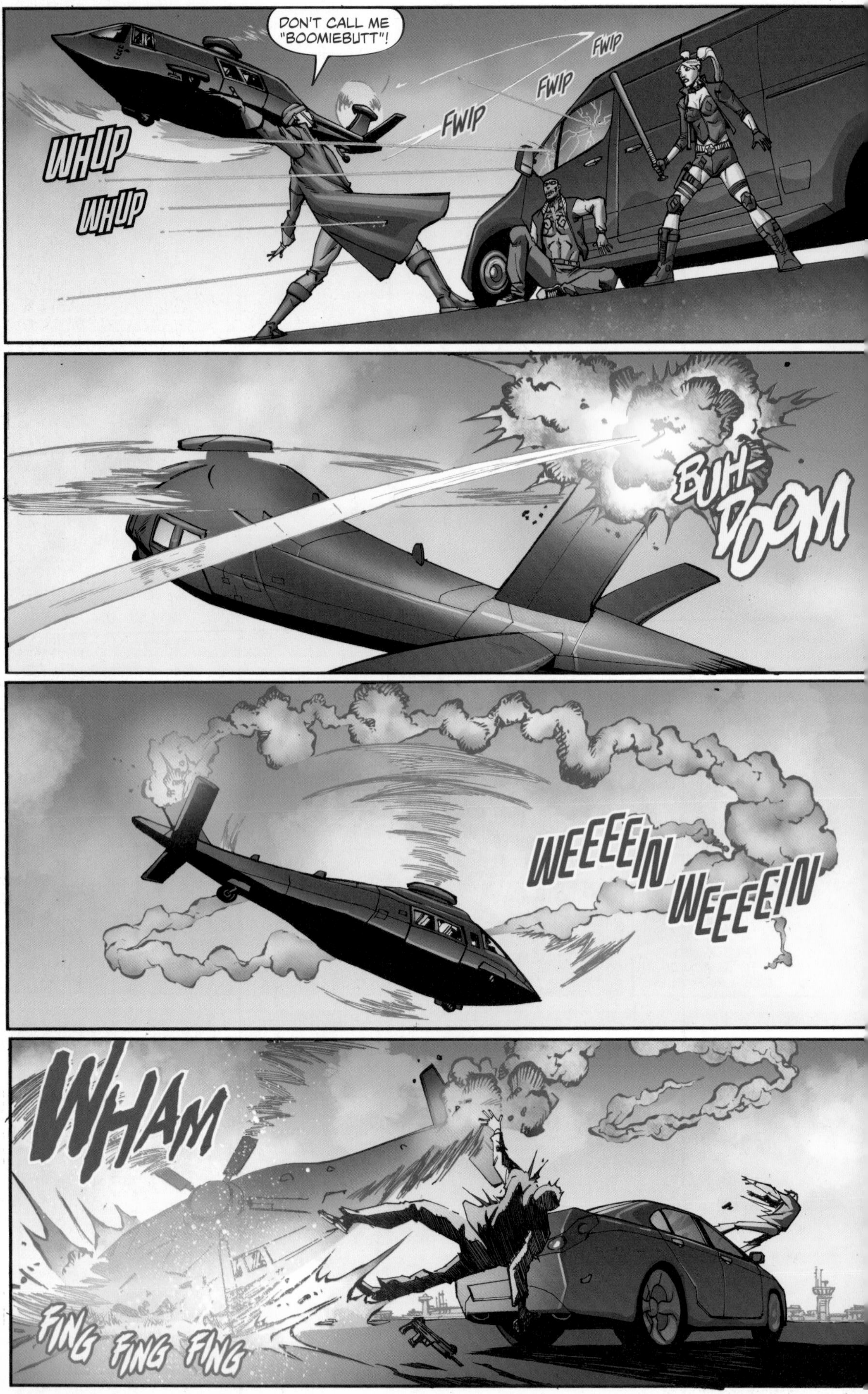
DON'T CALL ME "BOOMIEBUTT"!
FWIP
FWIP
FWIP
WHUP
WHUP
BUH-DOOM
WEEEEIN
WEEEEIN
WHAM
FING FING FING

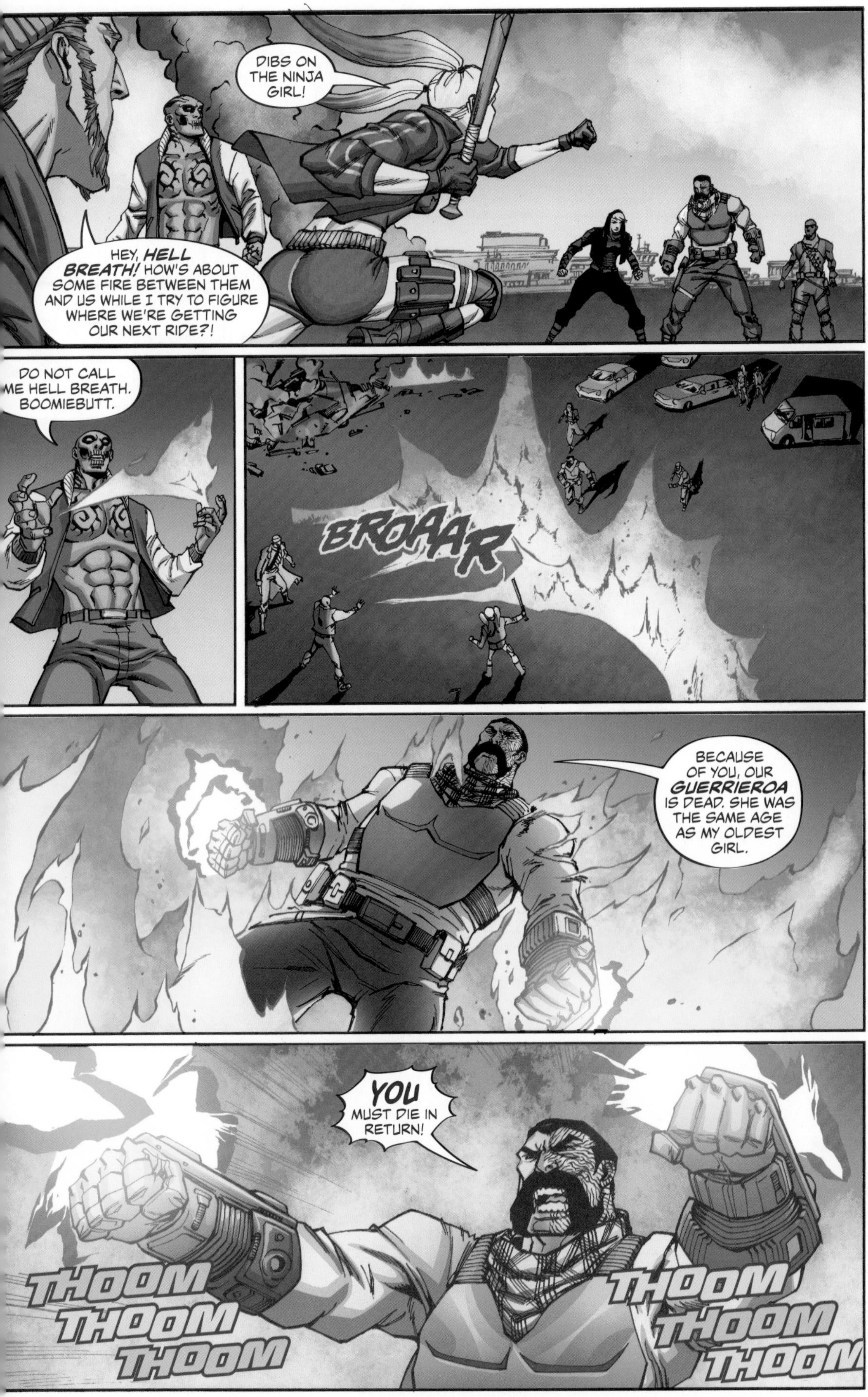

DIBS ON THE NINJA GIRL!
HEY, HELL BREATH! HOW'S ABOUT SOME FIRE BETWEEN THEM AND US WHILE I TRY TO FIGURE WHERE WE'RE GETTING OUR NEXT RIDE?!
DO NOT CALL ME HELL BREATH. BOOMIEBUTT.
BROAAR
BECAUSE OF YOU, OUR GUERRIEROA IS DEAD. SHE WAS THE SAME AGE AS MY OLDEST GIRL.
YOU MUST DIE IN RETURN!
THOOM THOOM THOOM
THOOM THOOM THOOM

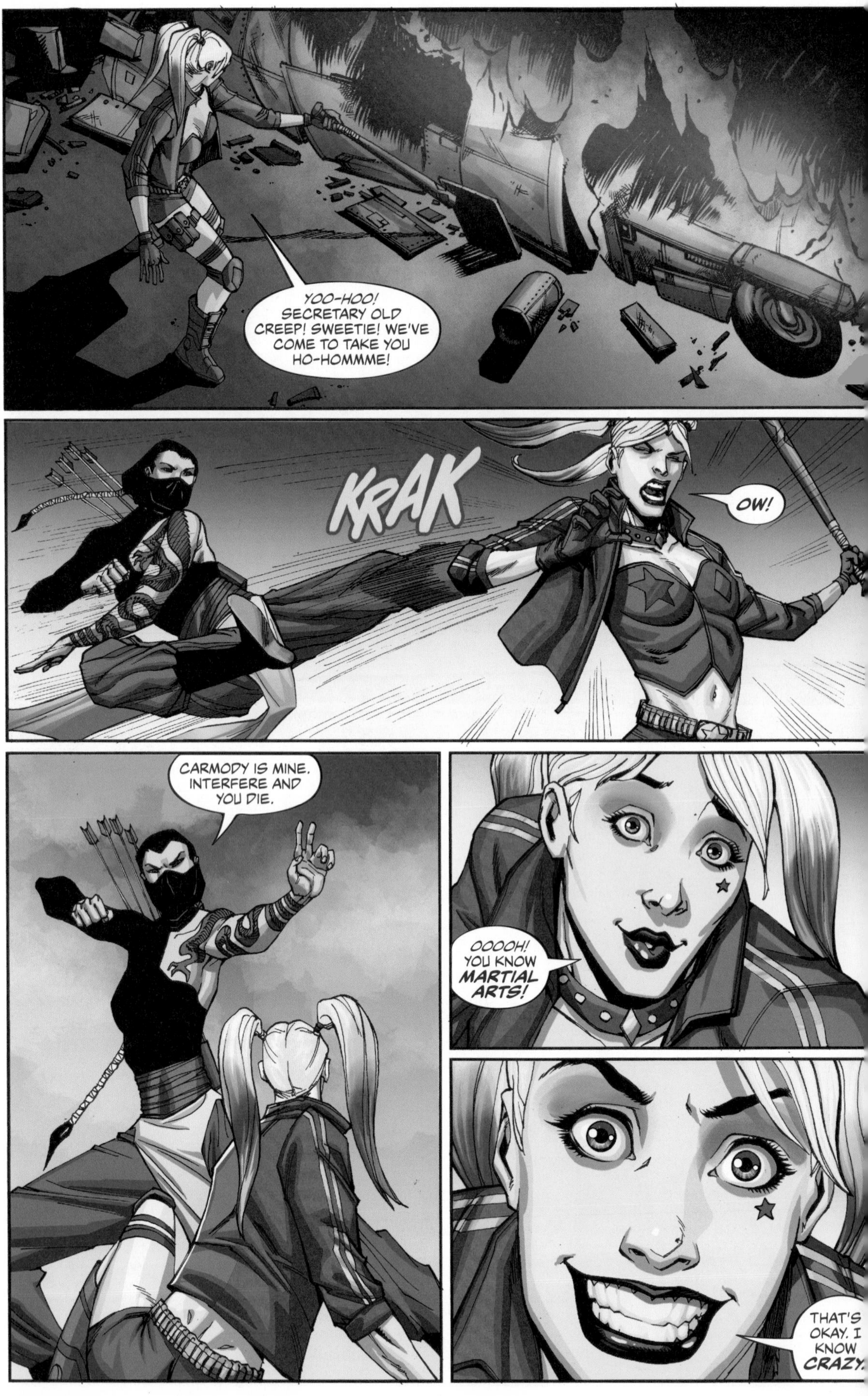
YOO-HOO! SECRETARY OLD CREEP! SWEETIE! WE'VE COME TO TAKE YOU HO-HOMMME!
KRAK
OW!
CARMODY IS MINE. INTERFERE AND YOU DIE.
OOOOH! YOU KNOW MARTIAL ARTS!
THAT'S OKAY. I KNOW CRAZY.

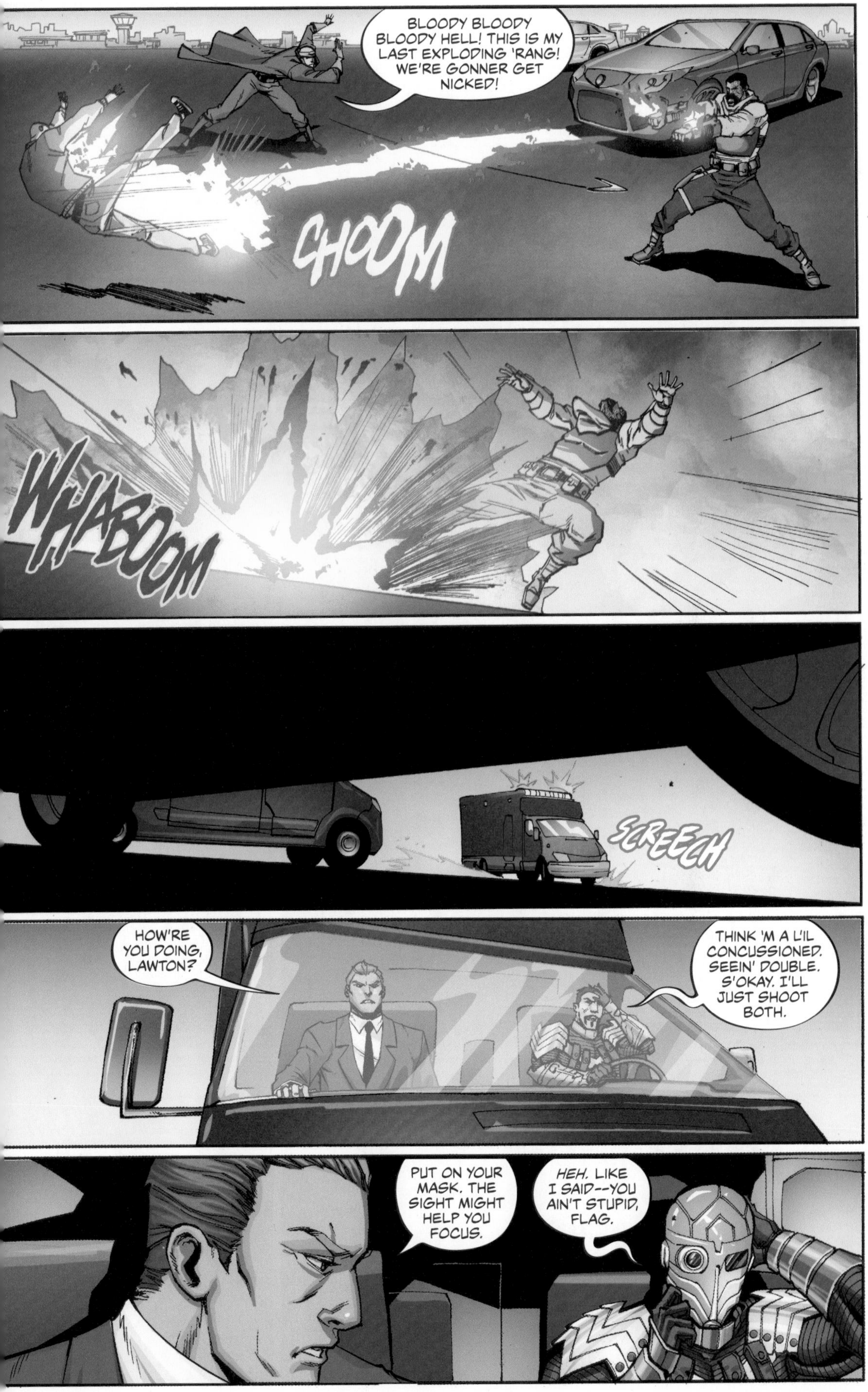
BLOODY BLOODY BLOODY HELL! THIS IS MY LAST EXPLODING 'RANG! WE'RE GONNER GET NICKED!
CHOOM
WHABOOM
SCREECH
HOW'RE YOU DOING, LAWTON?
THINK 'M A L'IL CONCUSSIONED. SEEIN' DOUBLE. S'OKAY. I'LL JUST SHOOT BOTH.
PUT ON YOUR MASK. THE SIGHT MIGHT HELP YOU FOCUS.
HEH. LIKE I SAID--YOU AIN'T STUPID, FLAG.

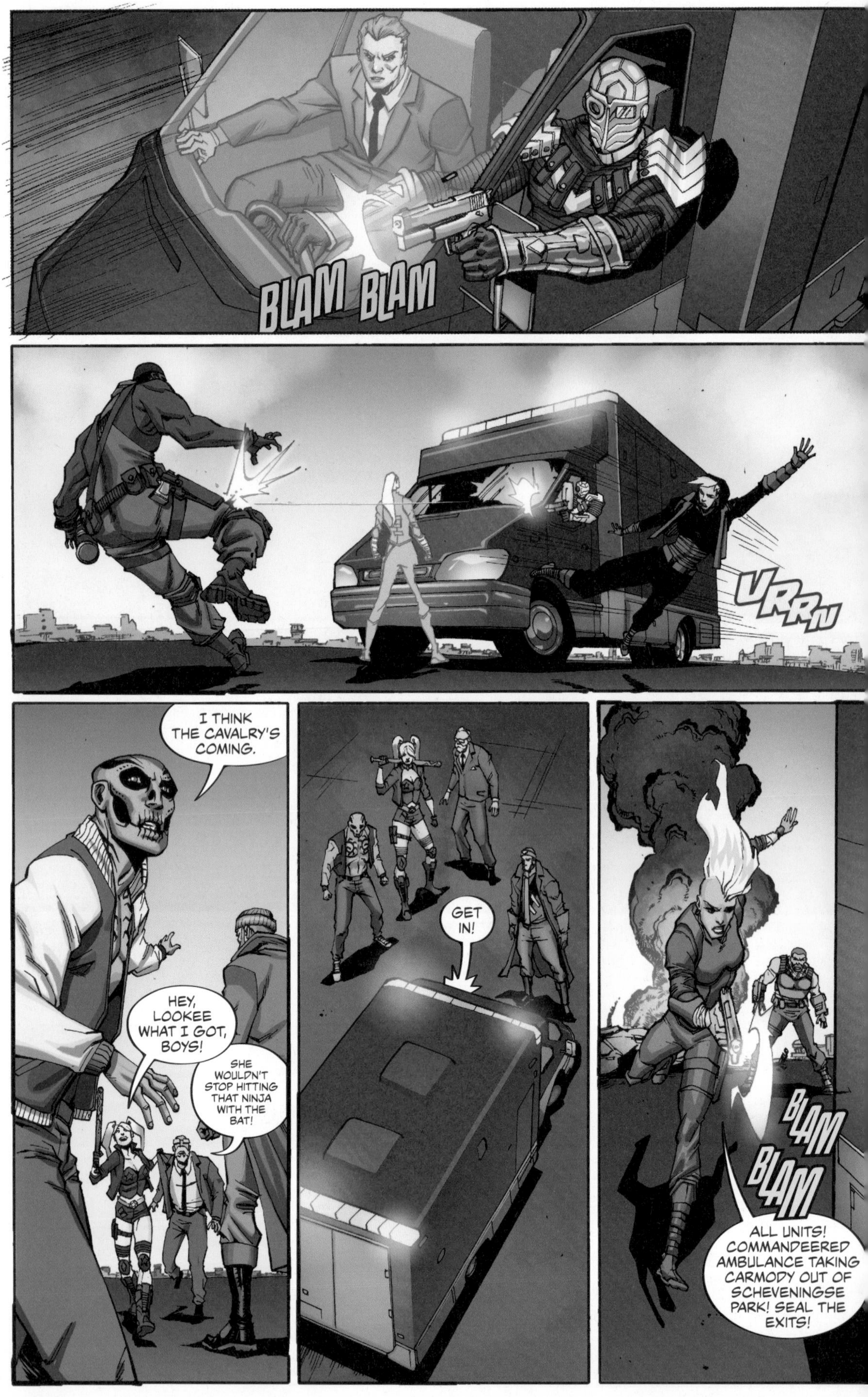
BLAM BLAM
URRN
I THINK THE CAVALRY'S COMING.
HEY, LOOKEE WHAT I GOT, BOYS!
SHE WOULDN'T STOP HITTING THAT NINJA WITH THE BAT!
GET IN!
BLAM BLAM
ALL UNITS! COMMANDEERED AMBULANCE TAKING CARMODY OUT OF SCHEVENINGSE PARK! SEAL THE EXITS!

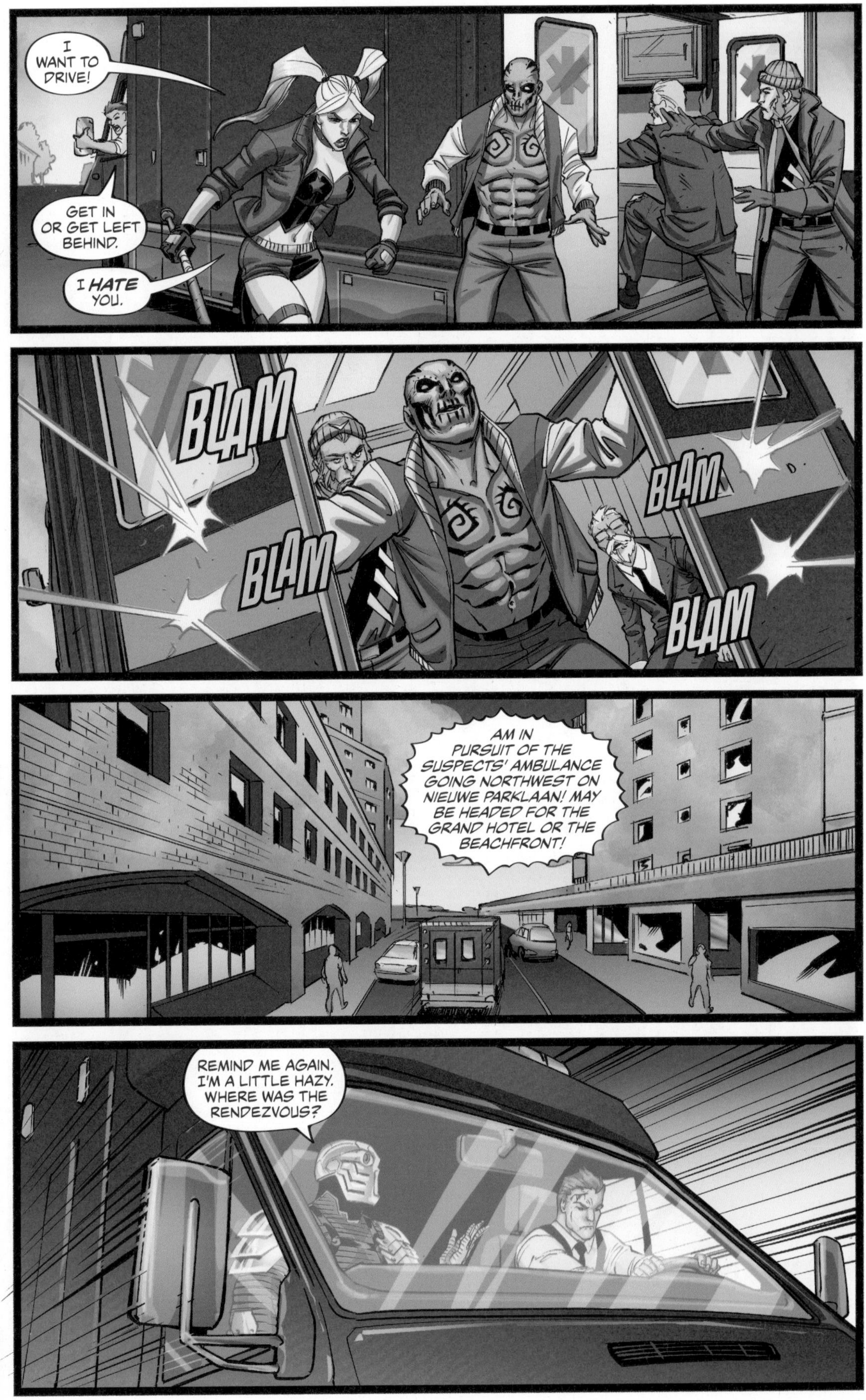
I WANT TO DRIVE!
GET IN OR GET LEFT BEHIND.
I HATE YOU.
BLAM
BLAM
BLAM
BLAM
AM IN PURSUIT OF THE SUSPECTS' AMBULANCE GOING NORTHWEST ON NIEUWE PARKLAAN! MAY BE HEADED FOR THE GRAND HOTEL OR THE BEACHFRONT!
REMIND ME AGAIN. I'M A LITTLE HAZY. WHERE WAS THE RENDEZVOUS?

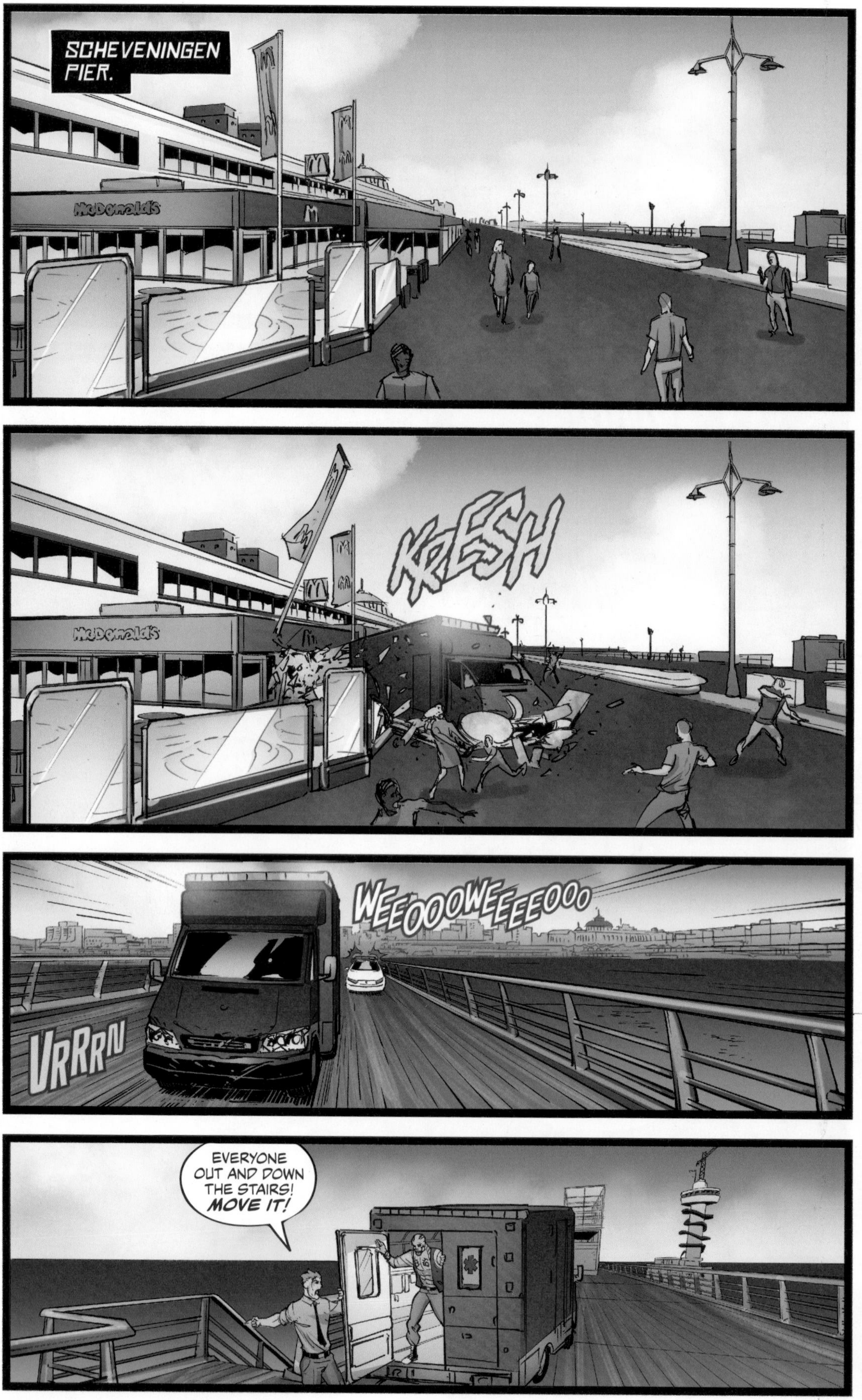
SCHEVENINGEN PIER.
McDonald's
KRESH
WEEOOOWEEEEOOO
VRRRN
EVERYONE OUT AND DOWN THE STAIRS! MOVE IT!

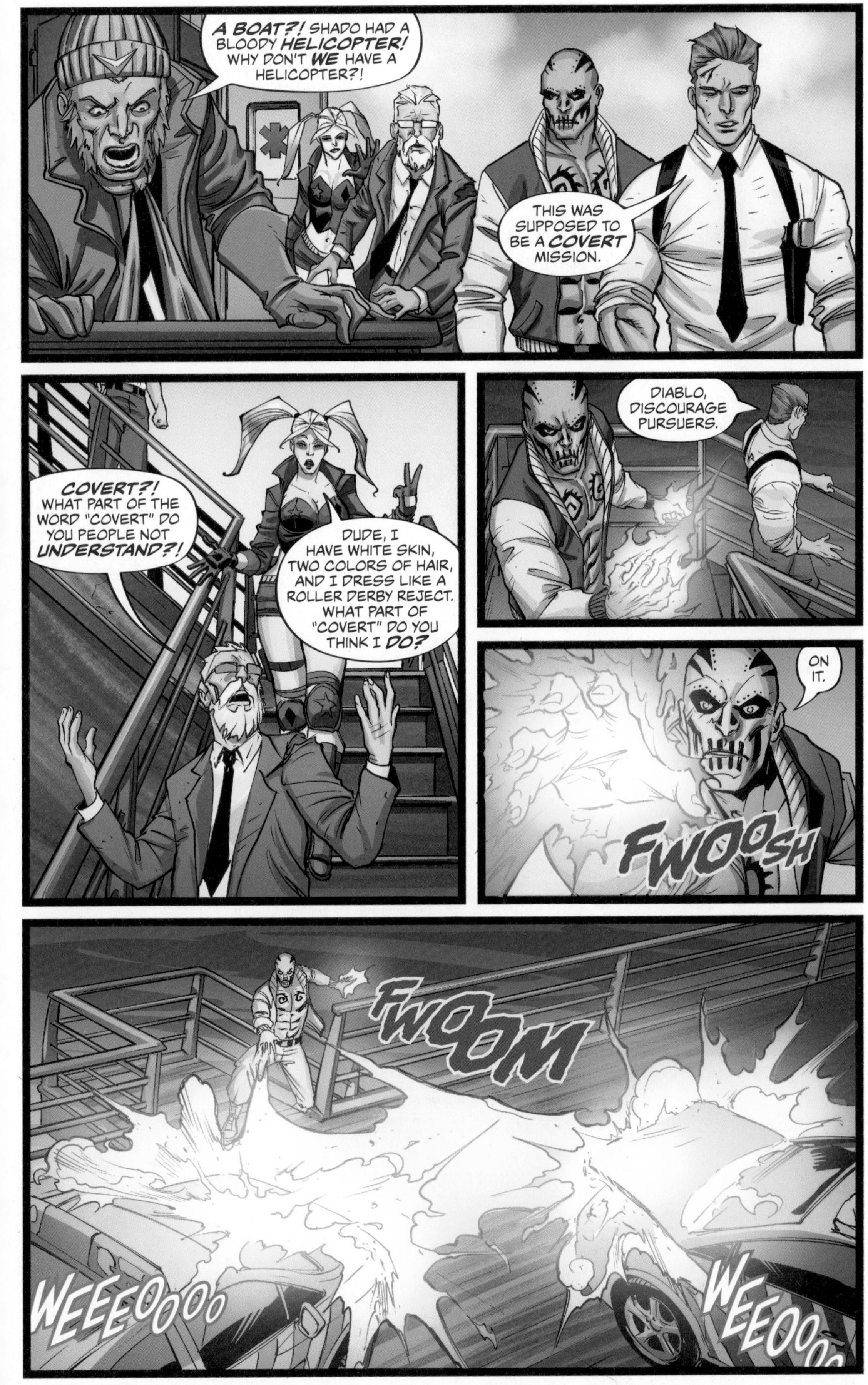
A BOAT?! SHADO HAD A BLOODY HELICOPTER! WHY DON'T WE HAVE A HELICOPTER?!
THIS WAS SUPPOSED TO BE A COVERT MISSION.
COVERT?! WHAT PART OF THE WORD "COVERT" DO YOU PEOPLE NOT UNDERSTAND?!
DUDE, I HAVE WHITE SKIN, TWO COLORS OF HAIR, AND I DRESS LIKE A ROLLER DERBY REJECT. WHAT PART OF "COVERT" DO YOU THINK I DO?
DIABLO, DISCOURAGE PURSUERS.
ON IT.
FWOOSH
FWOOM
WEEEOooo
WEEOooo

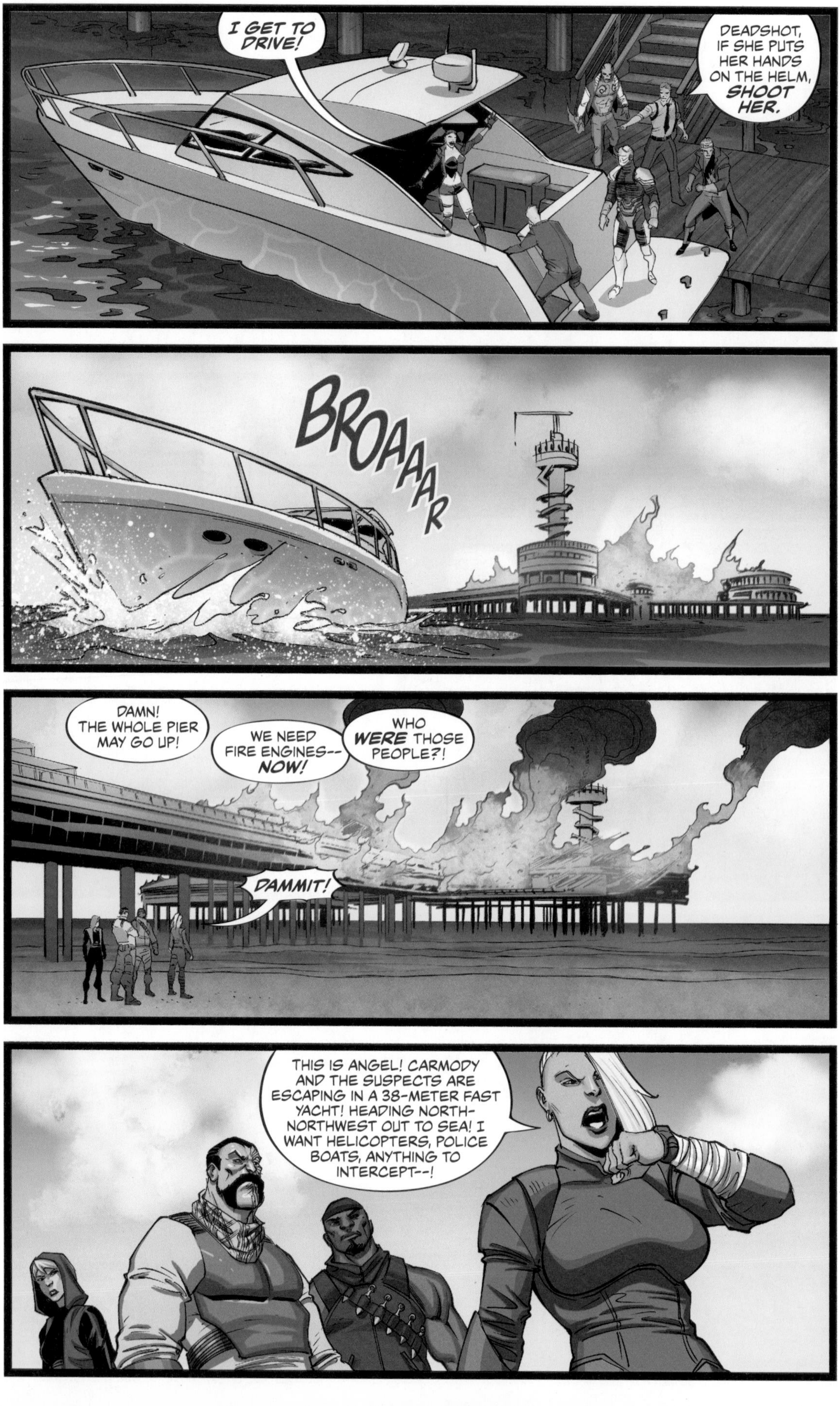
I GET TO DRIVE!
DEADSHOT, IF SHE PUTS HER HANDS ON THE HELM, SHOOT HER.
BROAAAAR
DAMN! THE WHOLE PIER MAY GO UP!
WE NEED FIRE ENGINES-- NOW!
WHO WERE THOSE PEOPLE?!
DAMMIT!
THIS IS ANGEL! CARMODY AND THE SUSPECTS ARE ESCAPING IN A 38-METER FAST YACHT! HEADING NORTH-NORTHWEST OUT TO SEA! I WANT HELICOPTERS, POLICE BOATS, ANYTHING TO INTERCEPT--!

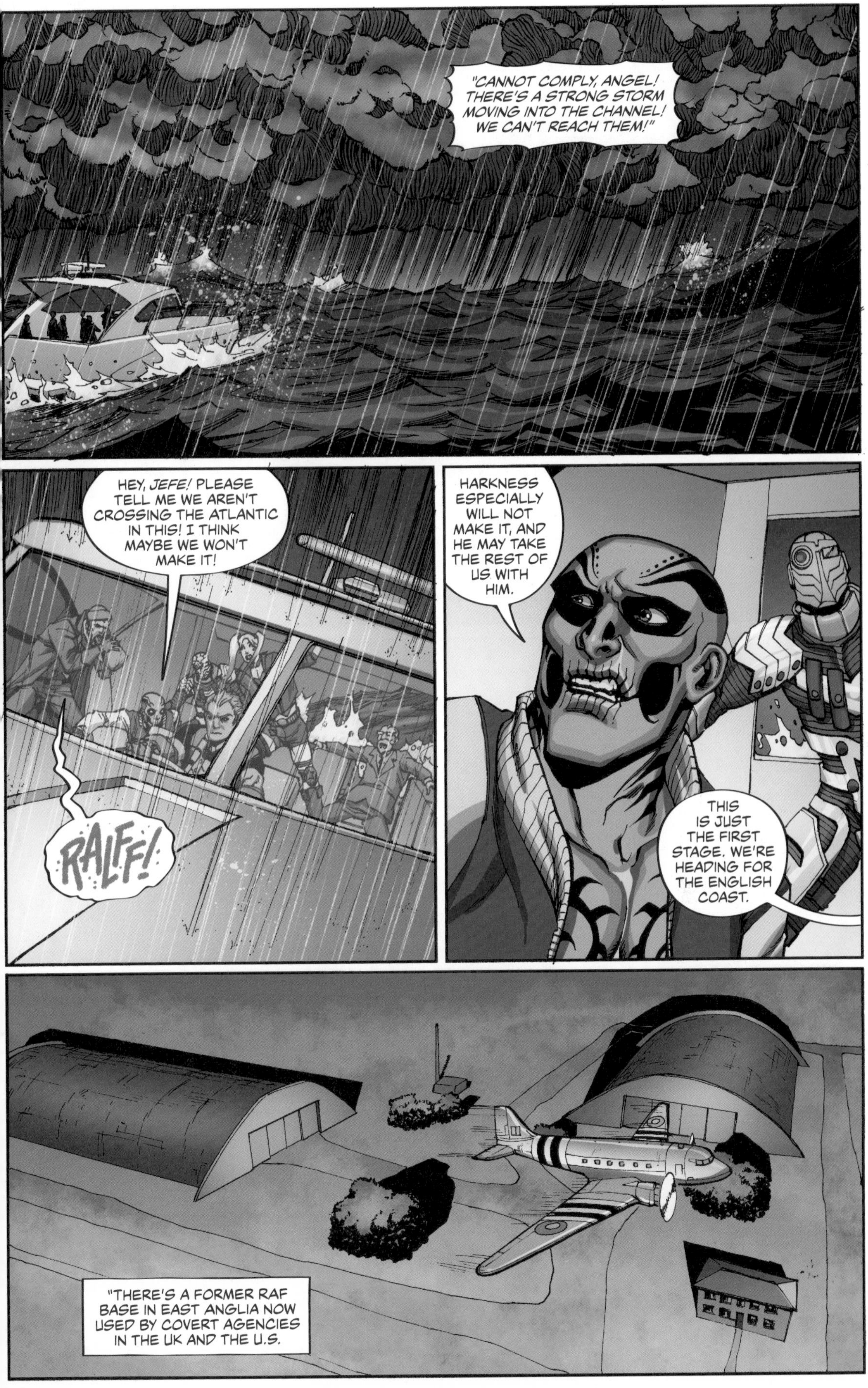
"CANNOT COMPLY, ANGEL! THERE'S A STRONG STORM MOVING INTO THE CHANNEL! WE CAN'T REACH THEM!"
HEY, *JEFE*! PLEASE TELL ME WE AREN'T CROSSING THE ATLANTIC IN THIS! I THINK MAYBE WE WON'T MAKE IT!
RALFF!
HARKNESS ESPECIALLY WILL NOT MAKE IT, AND HE MAY TAKE THE REST OF US WITH HIM.
THIS IS JUST THE FIRST STAGE. WE'RE HEADING FOR THE ENGLISH COAST.
"THERE'S A FORMER RAF BASE IN EAST ANGLIA NOW USED BY COVERT AGENCIES IN THE UK AND THE U.S.

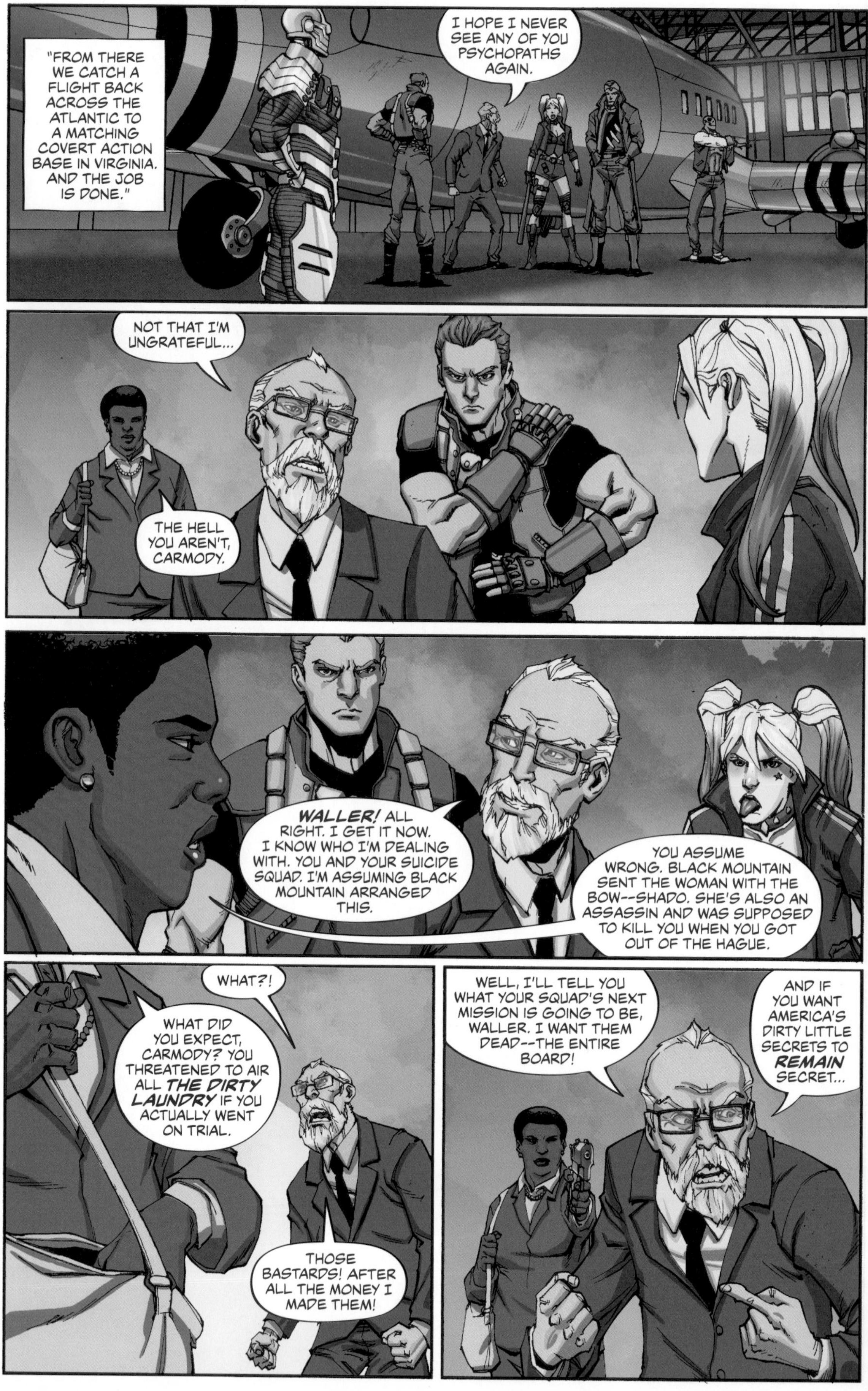
"FROM THERE WE CATCH A FLIGHT BACK ACROSS THE ATLANTIC TO A MATCHING COVERT ACTION BASE IN VIRGINIA. AND THE JOB IS DONE."
I HOPE I NEVER SEE ANY OF YOU PSYCHOPATHS AGAIN.
NOT THAT I'M UNGRATEFUL...
THE HELL YOU AREN'T, CARMODY.
WALLER! ALL RIGHT. I GET IT NOW. I KNOW WHO I'M DEALING WITH. YOU AND YOUR SUICIDE SQUAD. I'M ASSUMING BLACK MOUNTAIN ARRANGED THIS.
YOU ASSUME WRONG. BLACK MOUNTAIN SENT THE WOMAN WITH THE BOW--SHADO. SHE'S ALSO AN ASSASSIN AND WAS SUPPOSED TO KILL YOU WHEN YOU GOT OUT OF THE HAGUE.
WHAT?!
WHAT DID YOU EXPECT, CARMODY? YOU THREATENED TO AIR ALL THE DIRTY LAUNDRY IF YOU ACTUALLY WENT ON TRIAL.
THOSE BASTARDS! AFTER ALL THE MONEY I MADE THEM!
WELL, I'LL TELL YOU WHAT YOUR SQUAD'S NEXT MISSION IS GOING TO BE, WALLER. I WANT THEM DEAD--THE ENTIRE BOARD!
AND IF YOU WANT AMERICA'S DIRTY LITTLE SECRETS TO REMAIN SECRET...

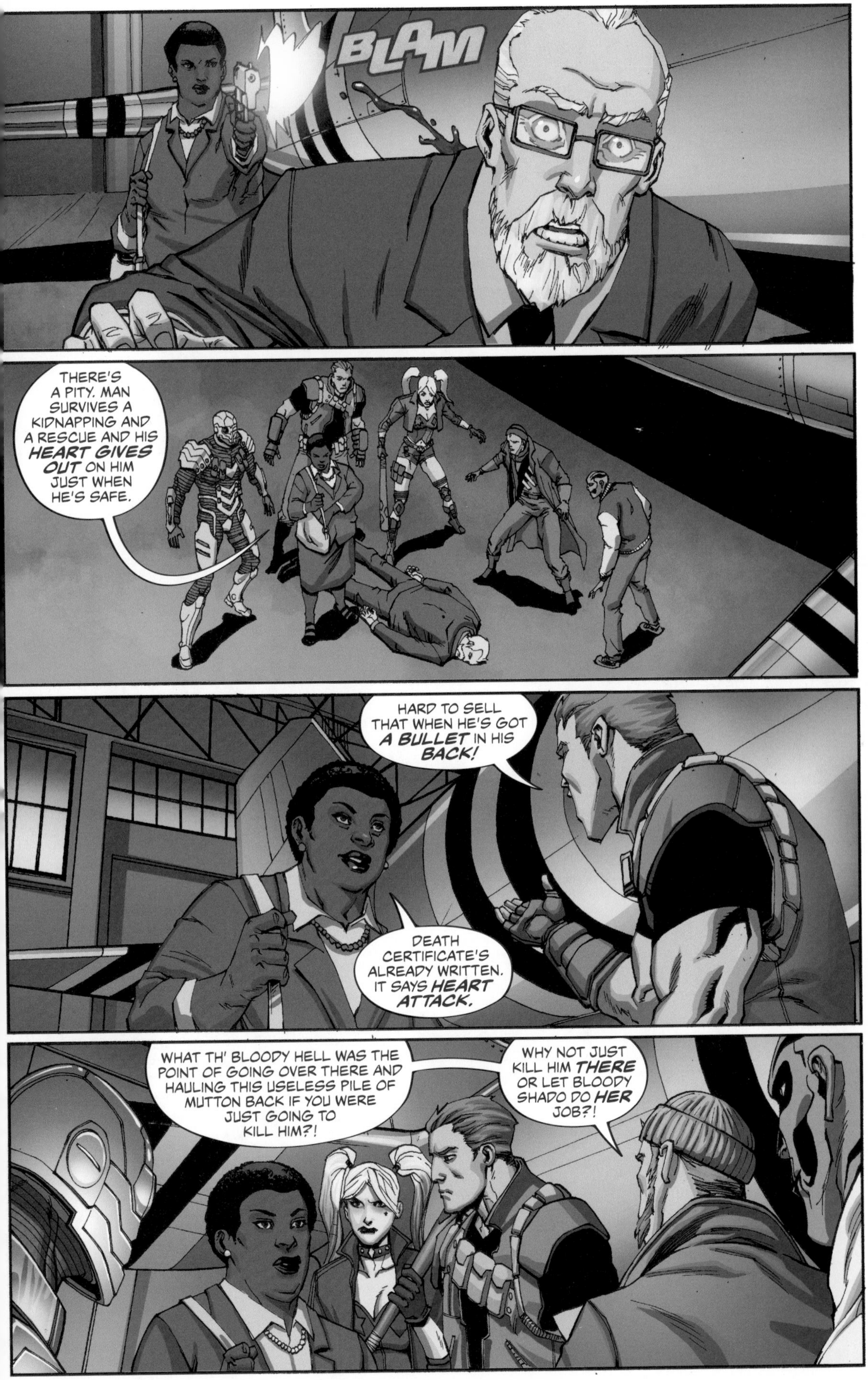
BLAM
THERE'S A PITY. MAN SURVIVES A KIDNAPPING AND A RESCUE AND HIS HEART GIVES OUT ON HIM JUST WHEN HE'S SAFE.
HARD TO SELL THAT WHEN HE'S GOT A BULLET IN HIS BACK!
DEATH CERTIFICATE'S ALREADY WRITTEN. IT SAYS HEART ATTACK.
WHAT TH' BLOODY HELL WAS THE POINT OF GOING OVER THERE AND HAULING THIS USELESS PILE OF MUTTON BACK IF YOU WERE JUST GOING TO KILL HIM?!
WHY NOT JUST KILL HIM THERE OR LET BLOODY SHADO DO HER JOB?!

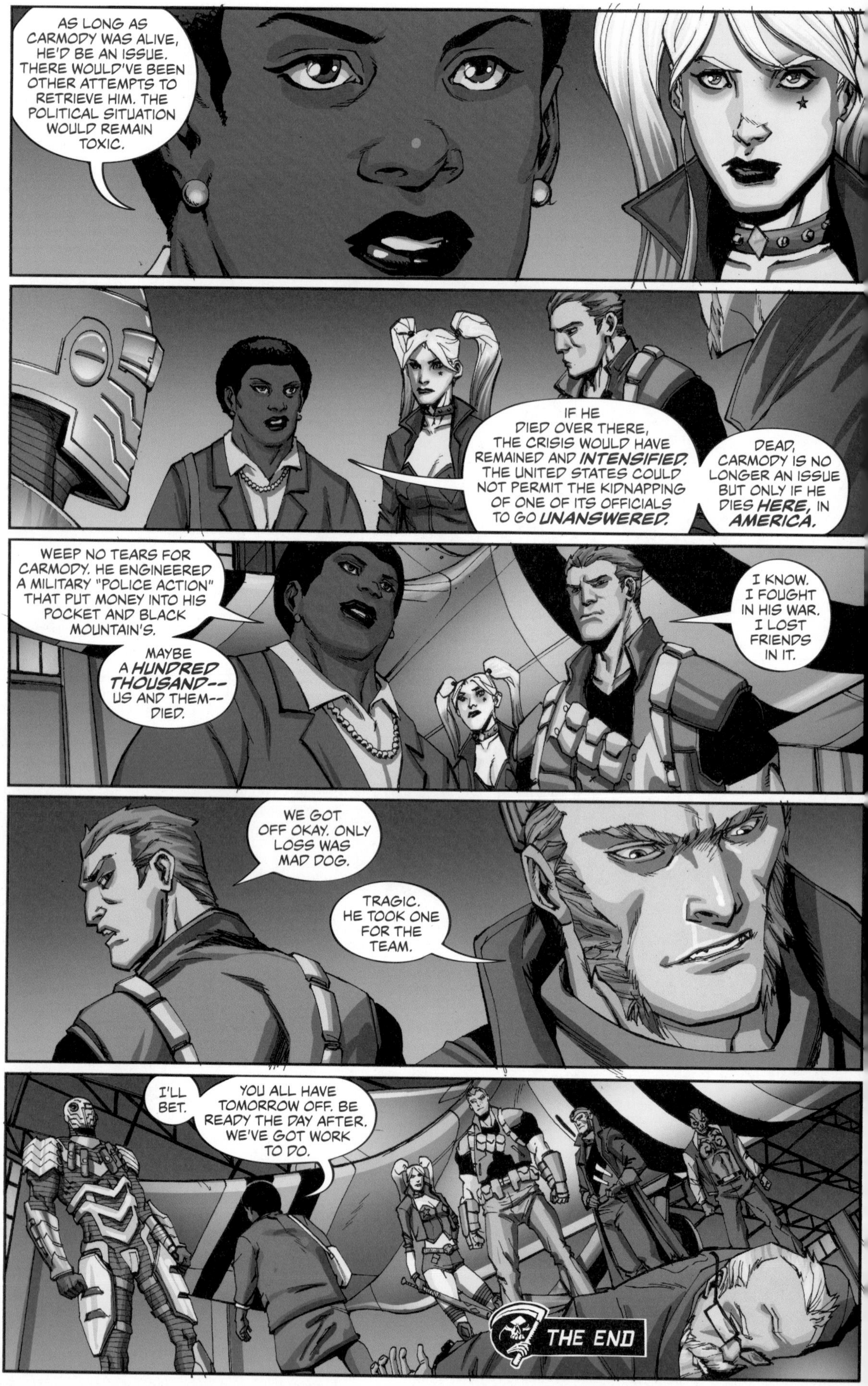
AS LONG AS CARMODY WAS ALIVE, HE'D BE AN ISSUE. THERE WOULD'VE BEEN OTHER ATTEMPTS TO RETRIEVE HIM. THE POLITICAL SITUATION WOULD REMAIN TOXIC.
IF HE DIED OVER THERE, THE CRISIS WOULD HAVE REMAINED AND INTENSIFIED. THE UNITED STATES COULD NOT PERMIT THE KIDNAPPING OF ONE OF ITS OFFICIALS TO GO UNANSWERED.
DEAD, CARMODY IS NO LONGER AN ISSUE BUT ONLY IF HE DIES HERE, IN AMERICA.
WEEP NO TEARS FOR CARMODY. HE ENGINEERED A MILITARY "POLICE ACTION" THAT PUT MONEY INTO HIS POCKET AND BLACK MOUNTAIN'S.
MAYBE A HUNDRED THOUSAND-- US AND THEM-- DIED.
I KNOW. I FOUGHT IN HIS WAR. I LOST FRIENDS IN IT.
WE GOT OFF OKAY. ONLY LOSS WAS MAD DOG.
TRAGIC. HE TOOK ONE FOR THE TEAM.
I'LL BET.
YOU ALL HAVE TOMORROW OFF. BE READY THE DAY AFTER. WE'VE GOT WORK TO DO.
THE END

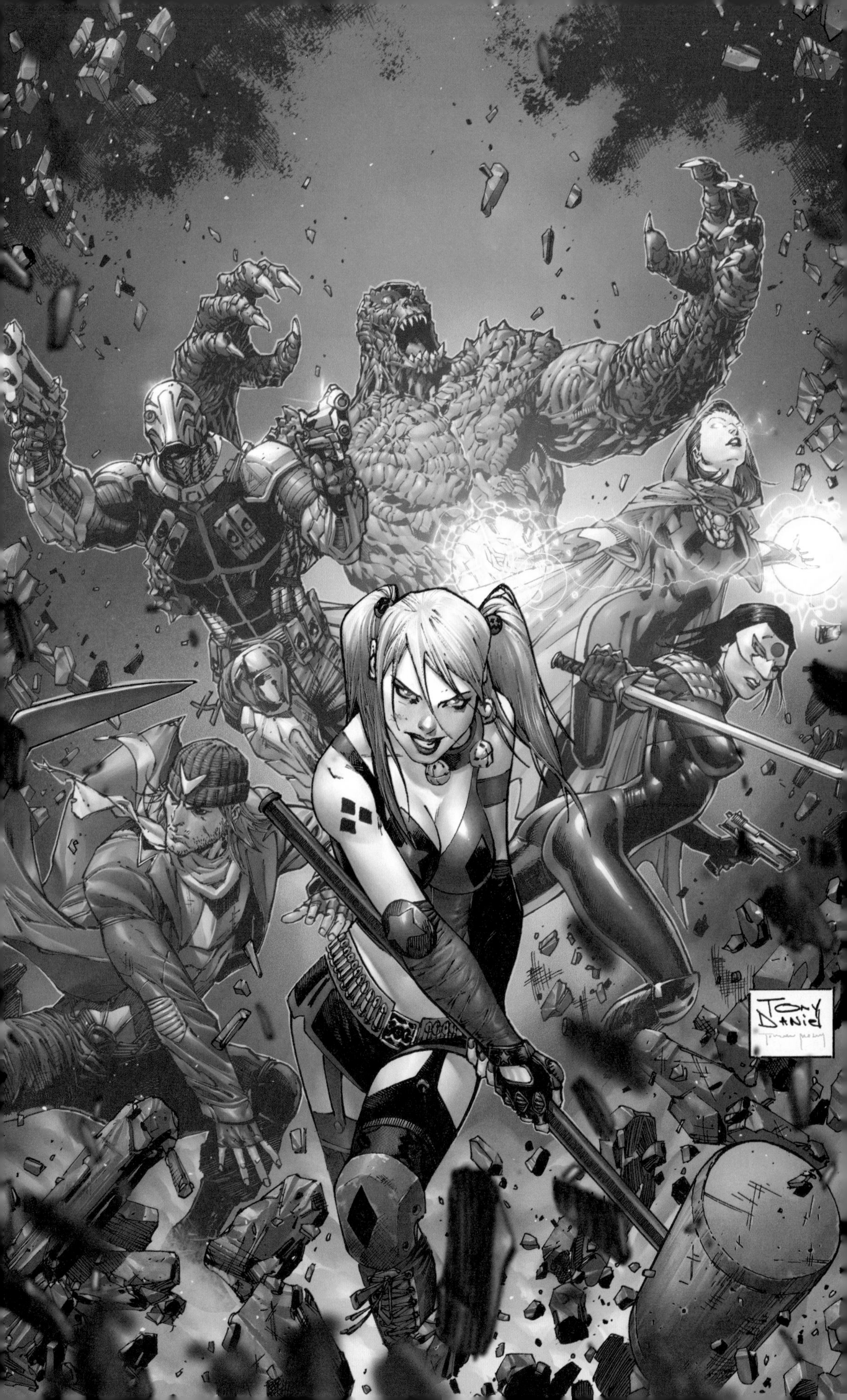
TONY DANIEL

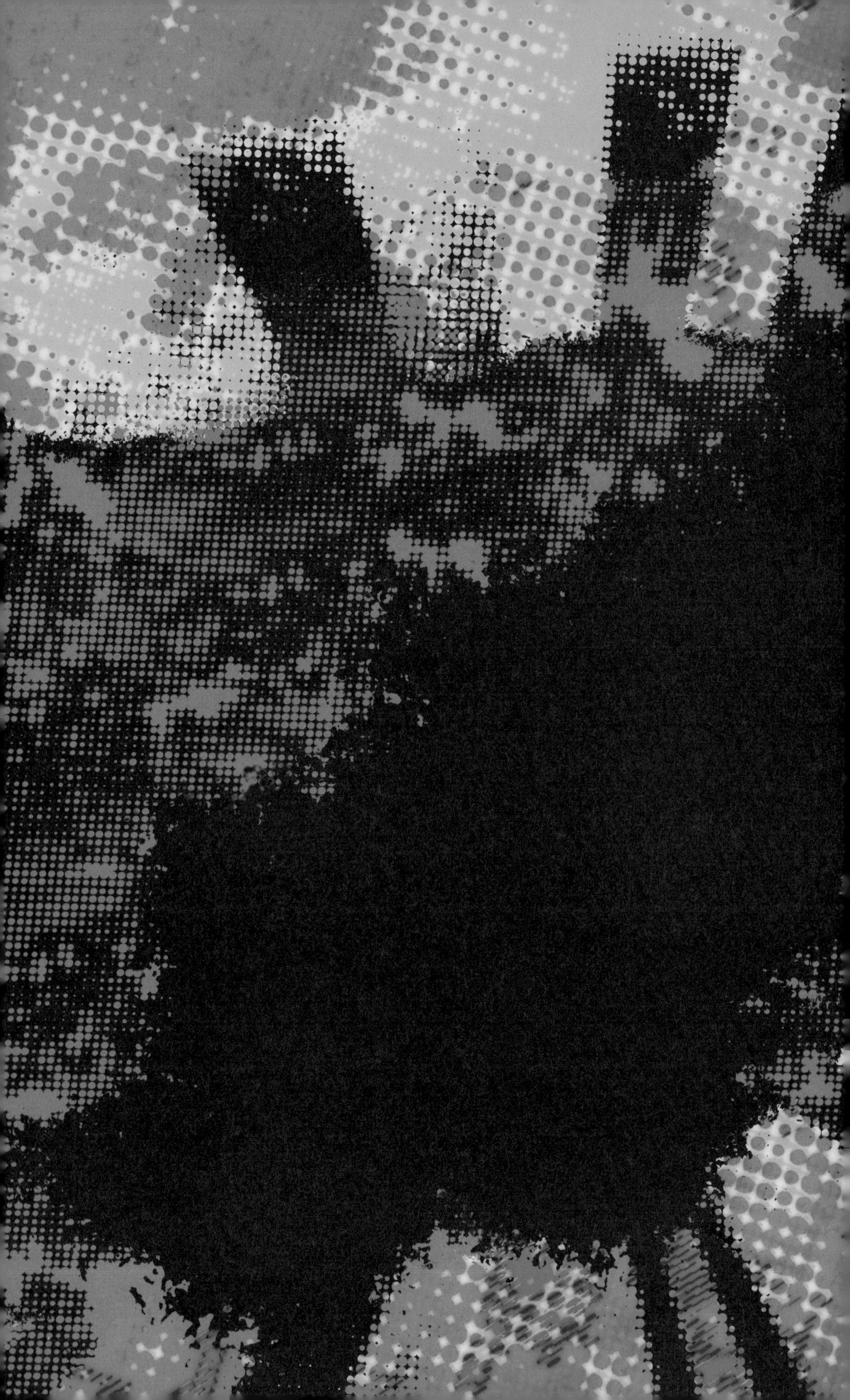

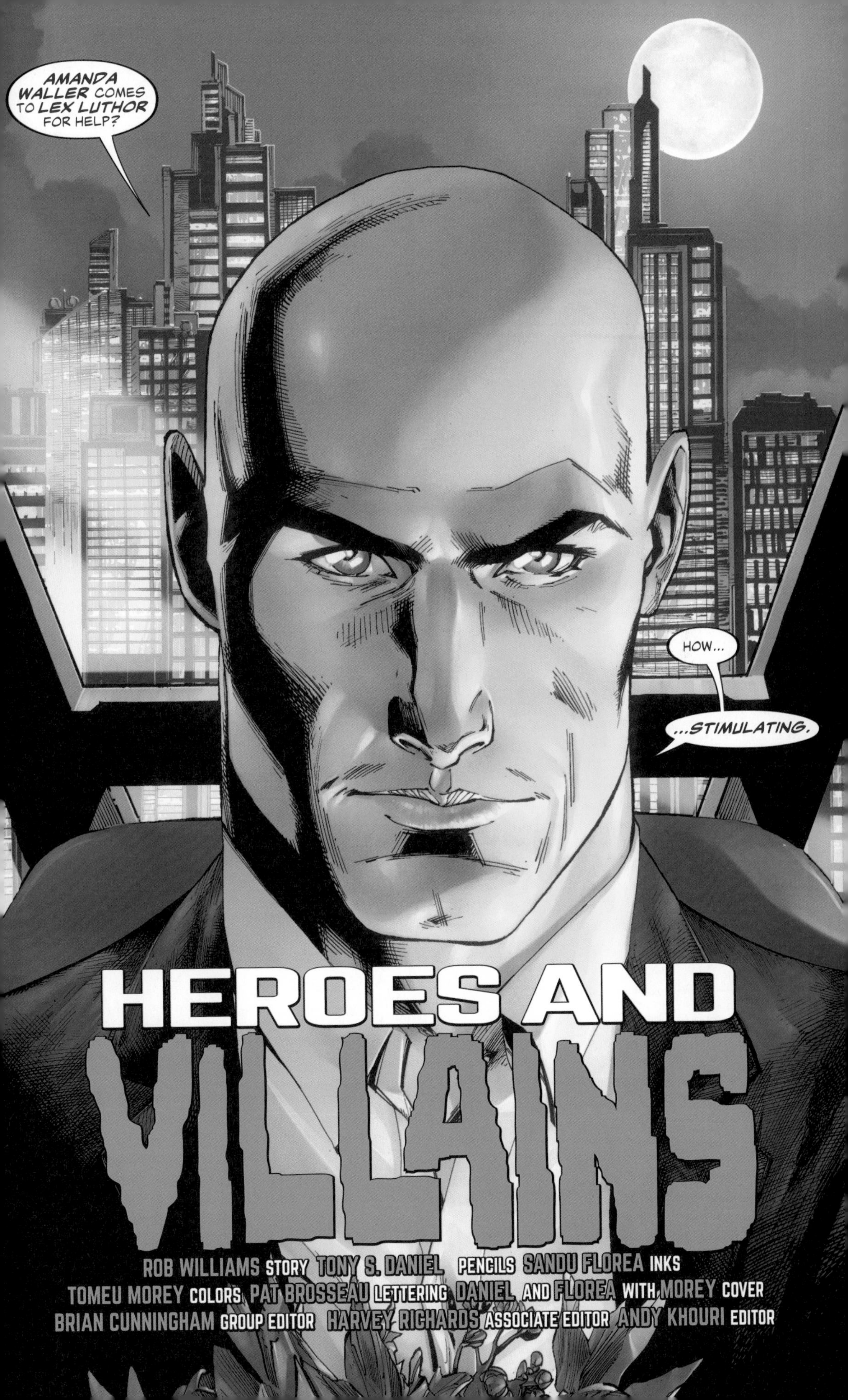

AMANDA WALLER COMES TO LEX LUTHOR FOR HELP?
HOW...
...STIMULATING.
HEROES AND VILLAINS
ROB WILLIAMS STORY TONY S. DANIEL PENCILS SANDU FLOREA INKS
TOMEU MOREY COLORS PAT BROSSEAU LETTERING DANIEL AND FLOREA WITH MOREY COVER
BRIAN CUNNINGHAM GROUP EDITOR HARVEY RICHARDS ASSOCIATE EDITOR ANDY KHOURI EDITOR

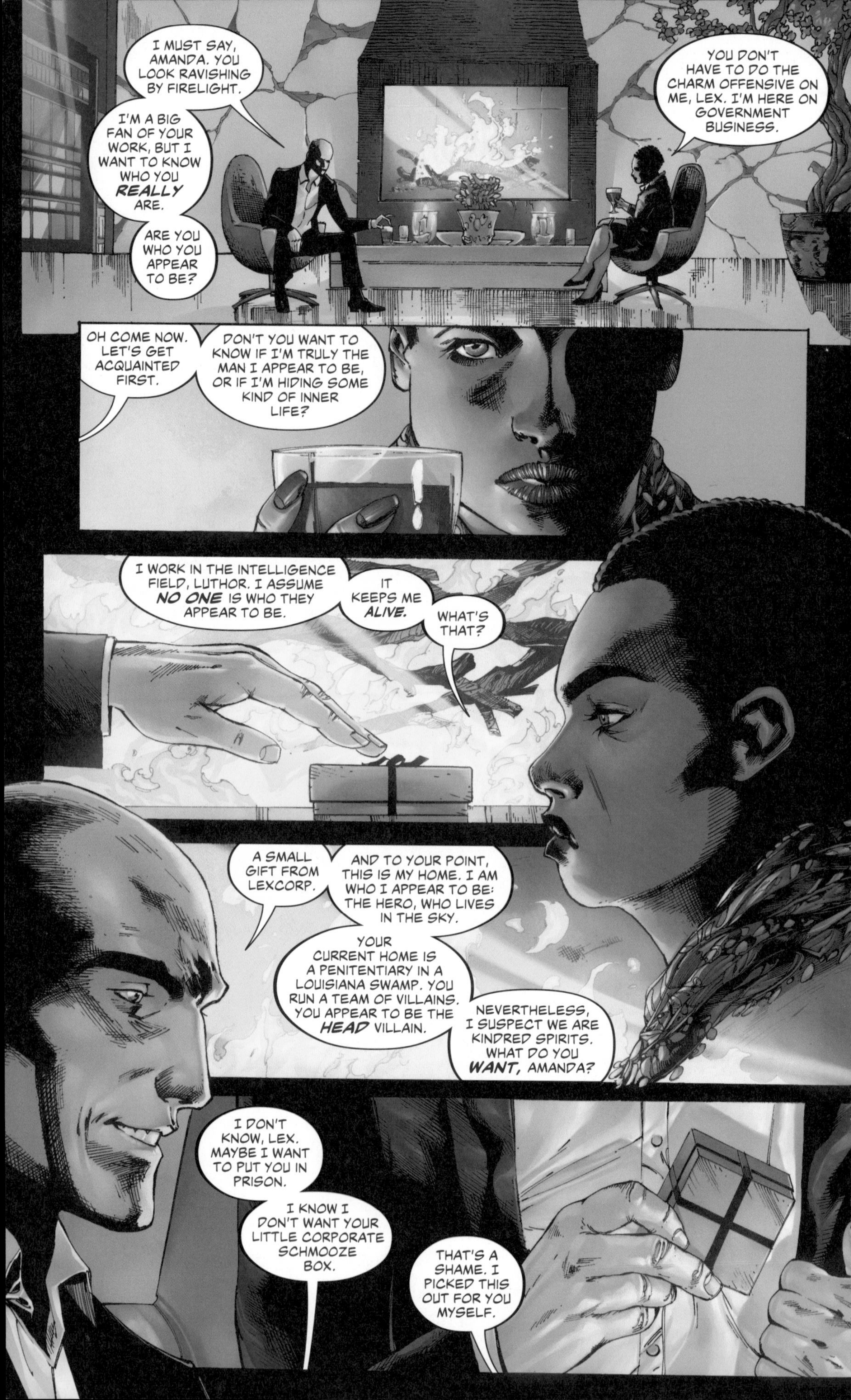
I MUST SAY, AMANDA. YOU LOOK RAVISHING BY FIRELIGHT.
I'M A BIG FAN OF YOUR WORK, BUT I WANT TO KNOW WHO YOU REALLY ARE.
ARE YOU WHO YOU APPEAR TO BE?
YOU DON'T HAVE TO DO THE CHARM OFFENSIVE ON ME, LEX. I'M HERE ON GOVERNMENT BUSINESS.
OH COME NOW. LET'S GET ACQUAINTED FIRST.
DON'T YOU WANT TO KNOW IF I'M TRULY THE MAN I APPEAR TO BE, OR IF I'M HIDING SOME KIND OF INNER LIFE?
I WORK IN THE INTELLIGENCE FIELD, LUTHOR. I ASSUME NO ONE IS WHO THEY APPEAR TO BE.
IT KEEPS ME ALIVE.
WHAT'S THAT?
A SMALL GIFT FROM LEXCORP.
AND TO YOUR POINT, THIS IS MY HOME. I AM WHO I APPEAR TO BE: THE HERO, WHO LIVES IN THE SKY.
YOUR CURRENT HOME IS A PENITENTIARY IN A LOUISIANA SWAMP. YOU RUN A TEAM OF VILLAINS. YOU APPEAR TO BE THE HEAD VILLAIN.
NEVERTHELESS, I SUSPECT WE ARE KINDRED SPIRITS. WHAT DO YOU WANT, AMANDA?
I DON'T KNOW, LEX. MAYBE I WANT TO PUT YOU IN PRISON.
I KNOW I DON'T WANT YOUR LITTLE CORPORATE SCHMOOZE BOX.
THAT'S A SHAME. I PICKED THIS OUT FOR YOU MYSELF.

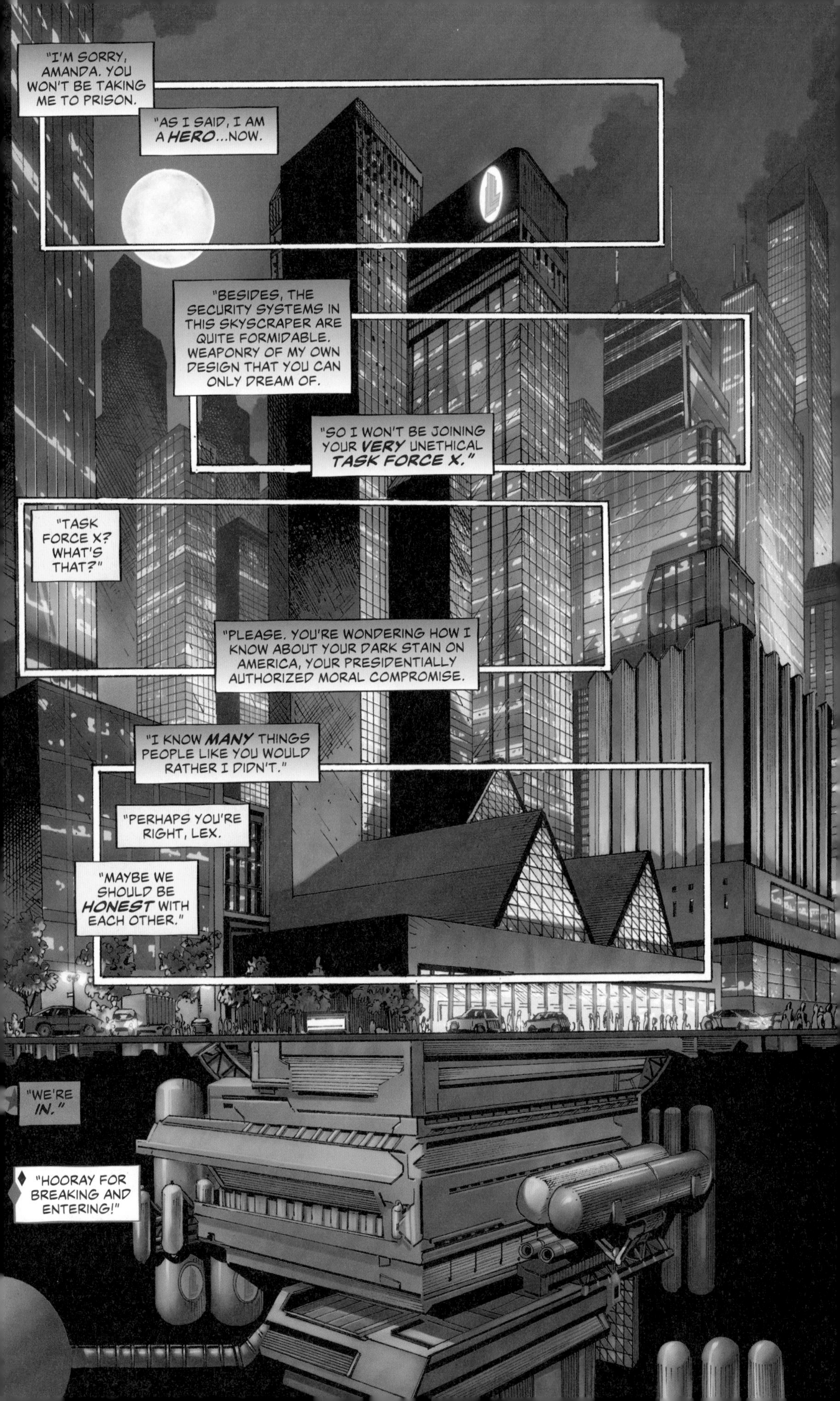

"I'M SORRY, AMANDA. YOU WON'T BE TAKING ME TO PRISON.
"AS I SAID, I AM A *HERO*...NOW.
"BESIDES, THE SECURITY SYSTEMS IN THIS SKYSCRAPER ARE QUITE FORMIDABLE. WEAPONRY OF MY OWN DESIGN THAT YOU CAN ONLY DREAM OF.
"SO I WON'T BE JOINING YOUR *VERY* UNETHICAL *TASK FORCE X.*"
"TASK FORCE X? WHAT'S THAT?"
"PLEASE. YOU'RE WONDERING HOW I KNOW ABOUT YOUR DARK STAIN ON AMERICA, YOUR PRESIDENTIALLY AUTHORIZED MORAL COMPROMISE.
"I KNOW *MANY* THINGS PEOPLE LIKE YOU WOULD RATHER I DIDN'T."
"PERHAPS YOU'RE RIGHT, LEX.
"MAYBE WE SHOULD BE *HONEST* WITH EACH OTHER."
"WE'RE *IN.*"
"HOORAY FOR BREAKING AND ENTERING!"

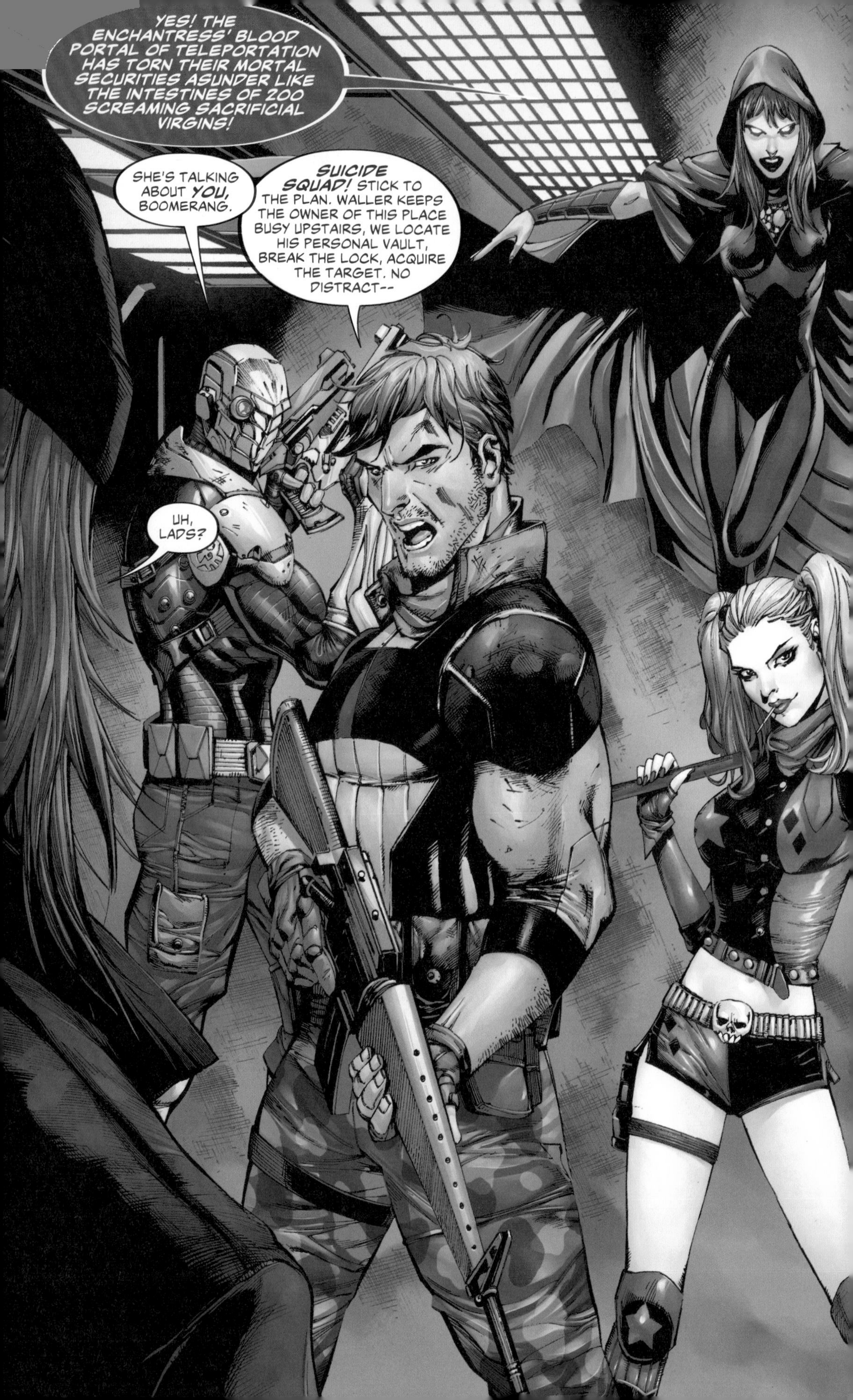
YES! THE ENCHANTRESS' BLOOD PORTAL OF TELEPORTATION HAS TORN THEIR MORTAL SECURITIES ASUNDER LIKE THE INTESTINES OF 200 SCREAMING SACRIFICIAL VIRGINS!
SHE'S TALKING ABOUT YOU, BOOMERANG.
SUICIDE SQUAD! STICK TO THE PLAN. WALLER KEEPS THE OWNER OF THIS PLACE BUSY UPSTAIRS, WE LOCATE HIS PERSONAL VAULT, BREAK THE LOCK, ACQUIRE THE TARGET. NO DISTRACT--
UH, LADS?

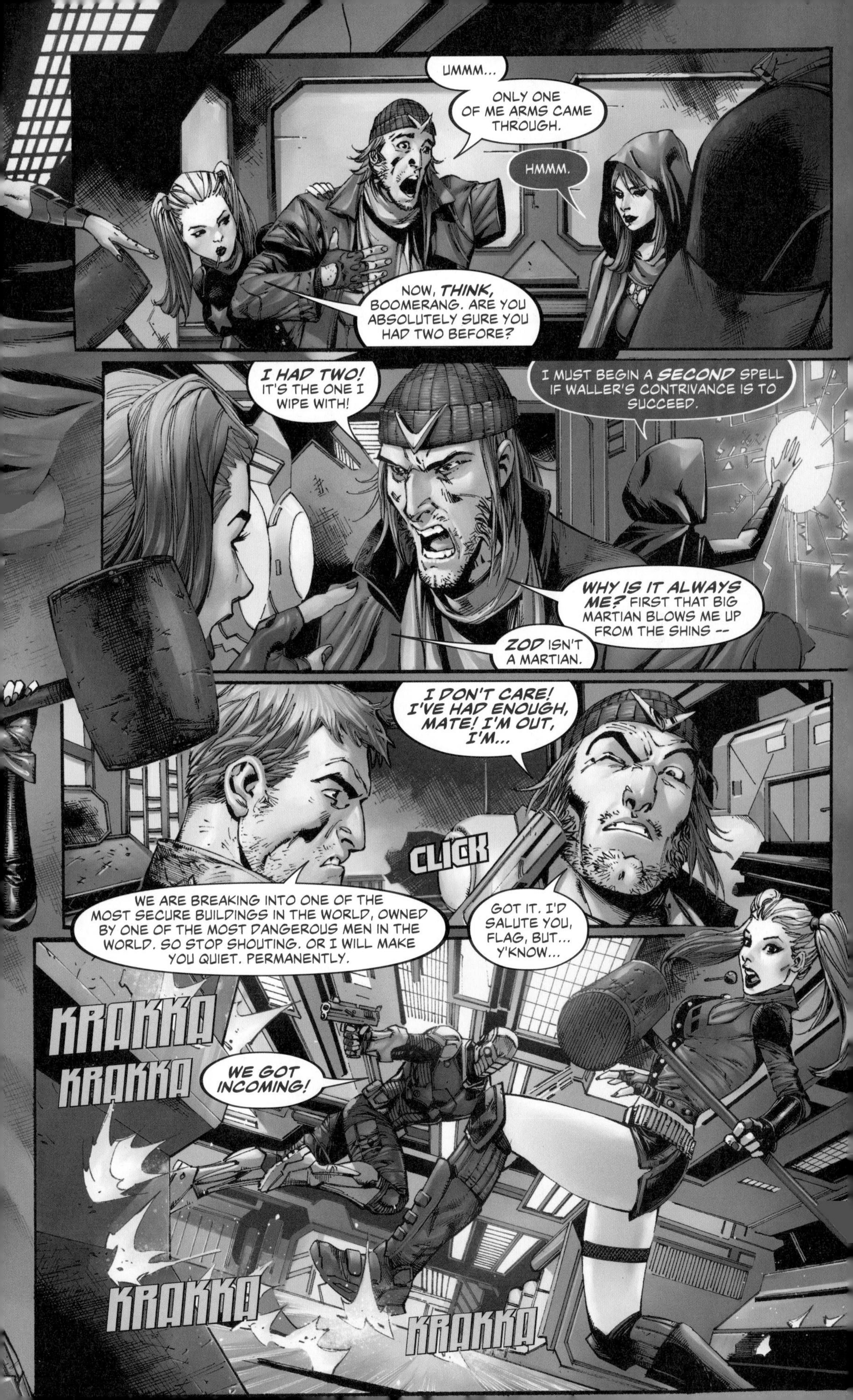
UMMM...
ONLY ONE OF ME ARMS CAME THROUGH.
HMMM.
NOW, THINK, BOOMERANG. ARE YOU ABSOLUTELY SURE YOU HAD TWO BEFORE?
I HAD TWO! IT'S THE ONE I WIPE WITH!
I MUST BEGIN A SECOND SPELL IF WALLER'S CONTRIVANCE IS TO SUCCEED.
WHY IS IT ALWAYS ME? FIRST THAT BIG MARTIAN BLOWS ME UP FROM THE SHINS --
ZOD ISN'T A MARTIAN.
I DON'T CARE! I'VE HAD ENOUGH, MATE! I'M OUT, I'M...
CLICK
WE ARE BREAKING INTO ONE OF THE MOST SECURE BUILDINGS IN THE WORLD, OWNED BY ONE OF THE MOST DANGEROUS MEN IN THE WORLD. SO STOP SHOUTING. OR I WILL MAKE YOU QUIET. PERMANENTLY.
GOT IT. I'D SALUTE YOU, FLAG, BUT... Y'KNOW...
KRAKKA
KRAKKA
WE GOT INCOMING!
KRAKKA
KRAKKA

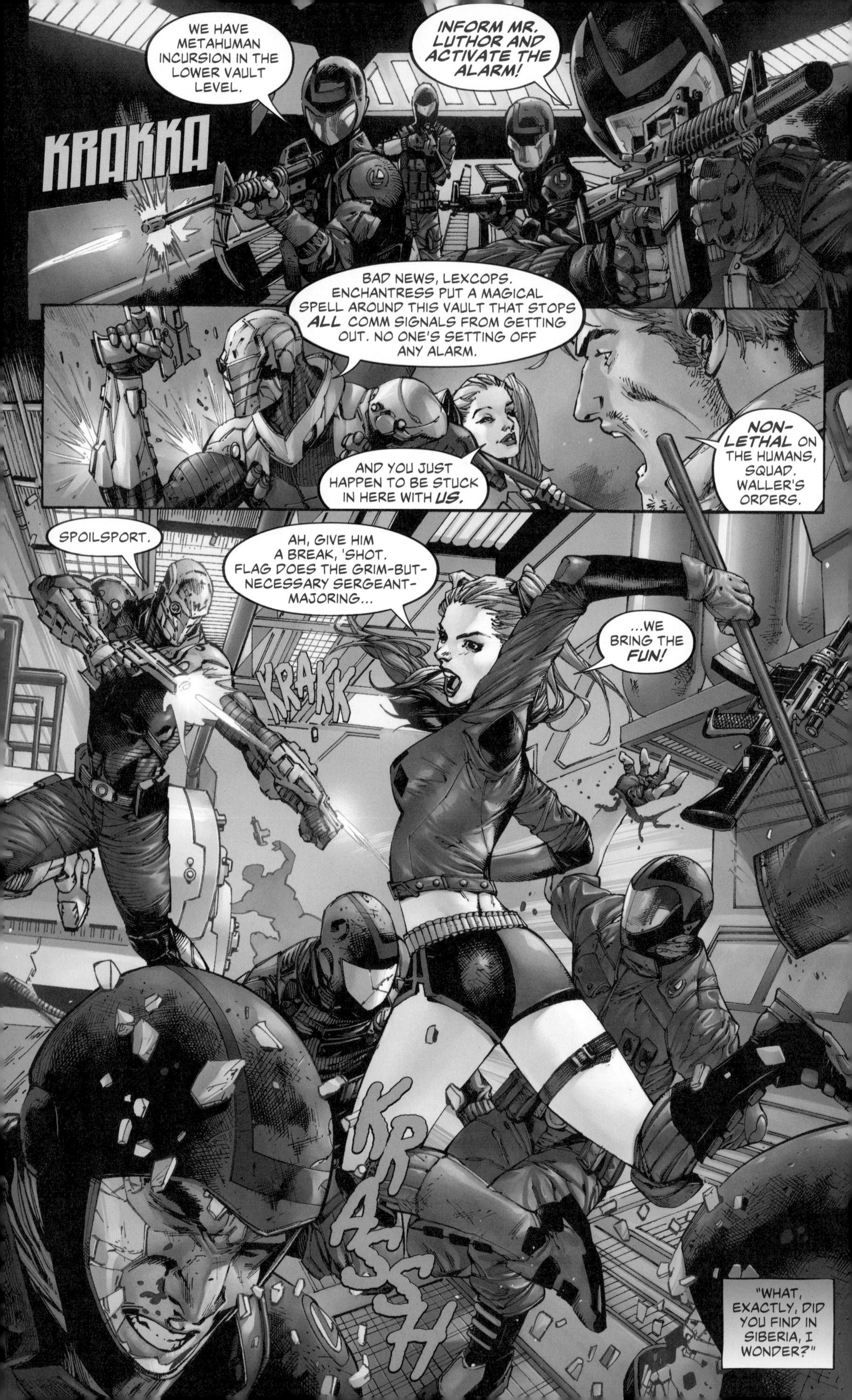

WE HAVE METAHUMAN INCURSION IN THE LOWER VAULT LEVEL.
INFORM MR. LUTHOR AND ACTIVATE THE ALARM!
KRAKKA
BAD NEWS, LEXCOPS. ENCHANTRESS PUT A MAGICAL SPELL AROUND THIS VAULT THAT STOPS ALL COMM SIGNALS FROM GETTING OUT. NO ONE'S SETTING OFF ANY ALARM.
AND YOU JUST HAPPEN TO BE STUCK IN HERE WITH US.
NON-LETHAL ON THE HUMANS, SQUAD. WALLER'S ORDERS.
SPOILSPORT.
AH, GIVE HIM A BREAK, 'SHOT. FLAG DOES THE GRIM-BUT-NECESSARY SERGEANT-MAJORING...
...WE BRING THE FUN!
KRAKK
KRRASSH
"WHAT, EXACTLY, DID YOU FIND IN SIBERIA, I WONDER?"

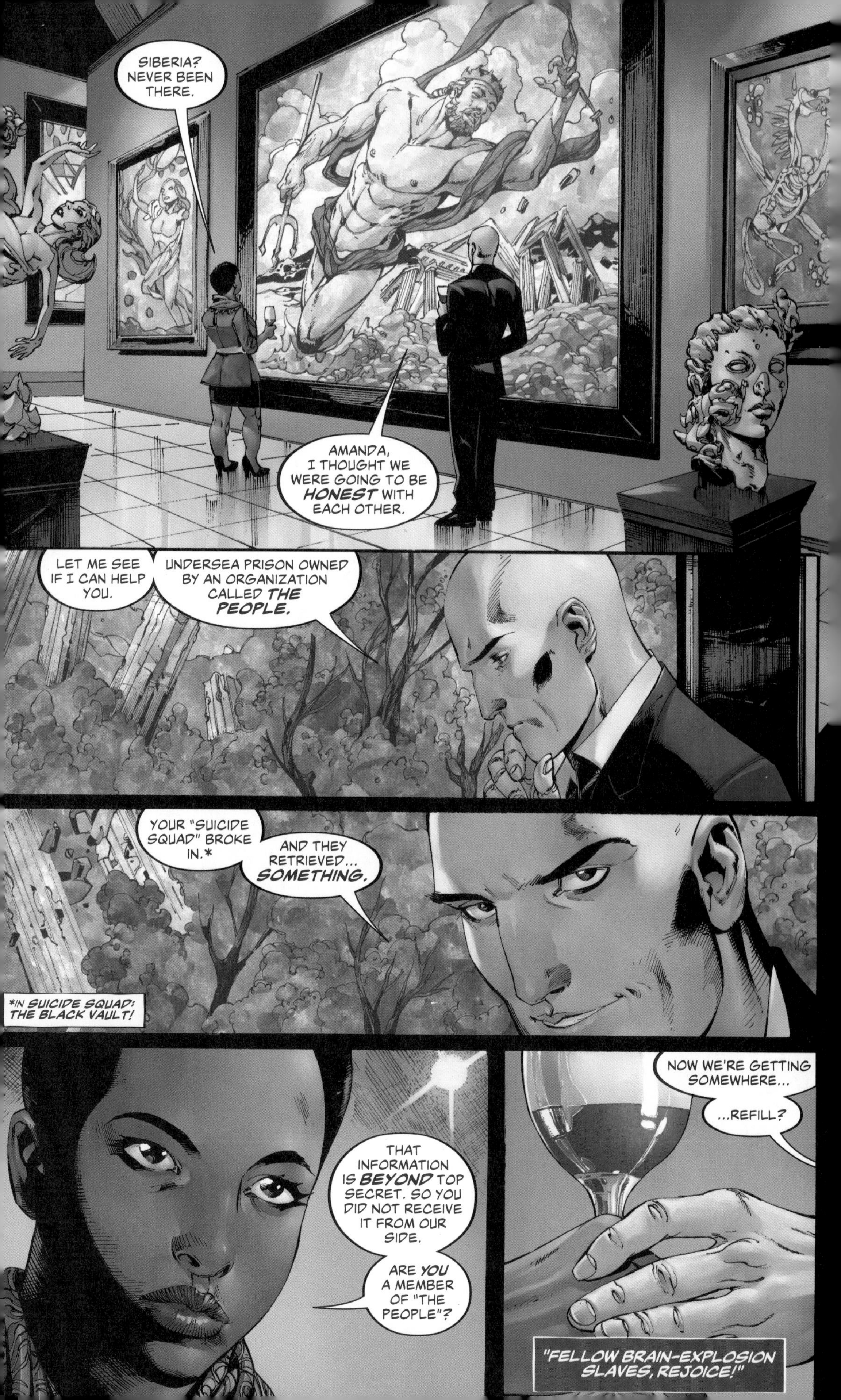

SIBERIA? NEVER BEEN THERE.
AMANDA, I THOUGHT WE WERE GOING TO BE HONEST WITH EACH OTHER.
LET ME SEE IF I CAN HELP YOU.
UNDERSEA PRISON OWNED BY AN ORGANIZATION CALLED THE PEOPLE.
YOUR "SUICIDE SQUAD" BROKE IN.*
AND THEY RETRIEVED... SOMETHING.
*IN SUICIDE SQUAD: THE BLACK VAULT!
THAT INFORMATION IS BEYOND TOP SECRET. SO YOU DID NOT RECEIVE IT FROM OUR SIDE.
ARE YOU A MEMBER OF "THE PEOPLE"?
NOW WE'RE GETTING SOMEWHERE...
...REFILL?
"FELLOW BRAIN-EXPLOSION SLAVES, REJOICE!"

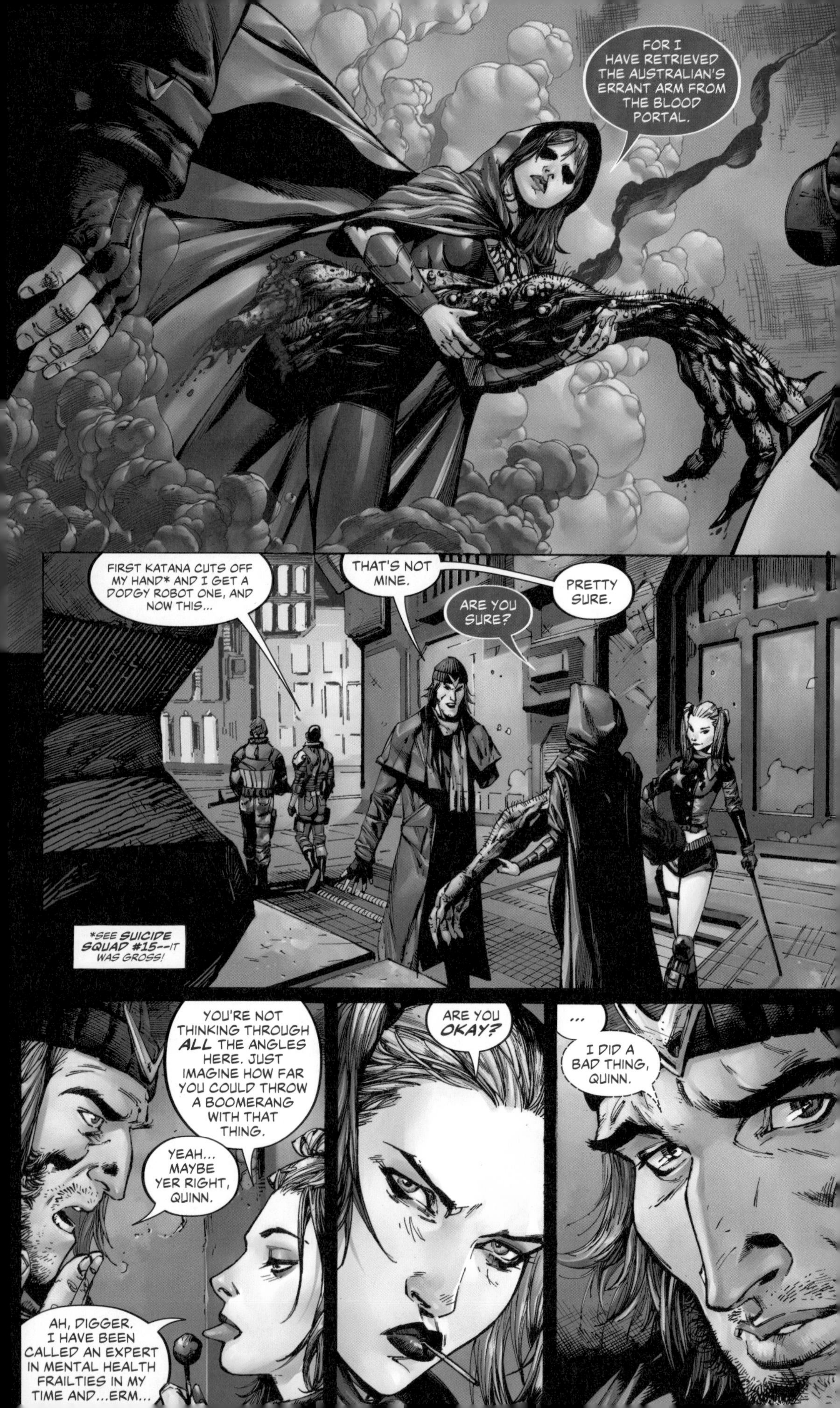
FOR I HAVE RETRIEVED THE AUSTRALIAN'S ERRANT ARM FROM THE BLOOD PORTAL.
FIRST KATANA CUTS OFF MY HAND* AND I GET A DODGY ROBOT ONE, AND NOW THIS...
THAT'S NOT MINE.
ARE YOU SURE?
PRETTY SURE.
*SEE SUICIDE SQUAD #15--IT WAS GROSS!
YOU'RE NOT THINKING THROUGH ALL THE ANGLES HERE. JUST IMAGINE HOW FAR YOU COULD THROW A BOOMERANG WITH THAT THING.
YEAH... MAYBE YER RIGHT, QUINN.
AH, DIGGER. I HAVE BEEN CALLED AN EXPERT IN MENTAL HEALTH FRAILTIES IN MY TIME AND...ERM...
ARE YOU OKAY?
...
I DID A BAD THING, QUINN.

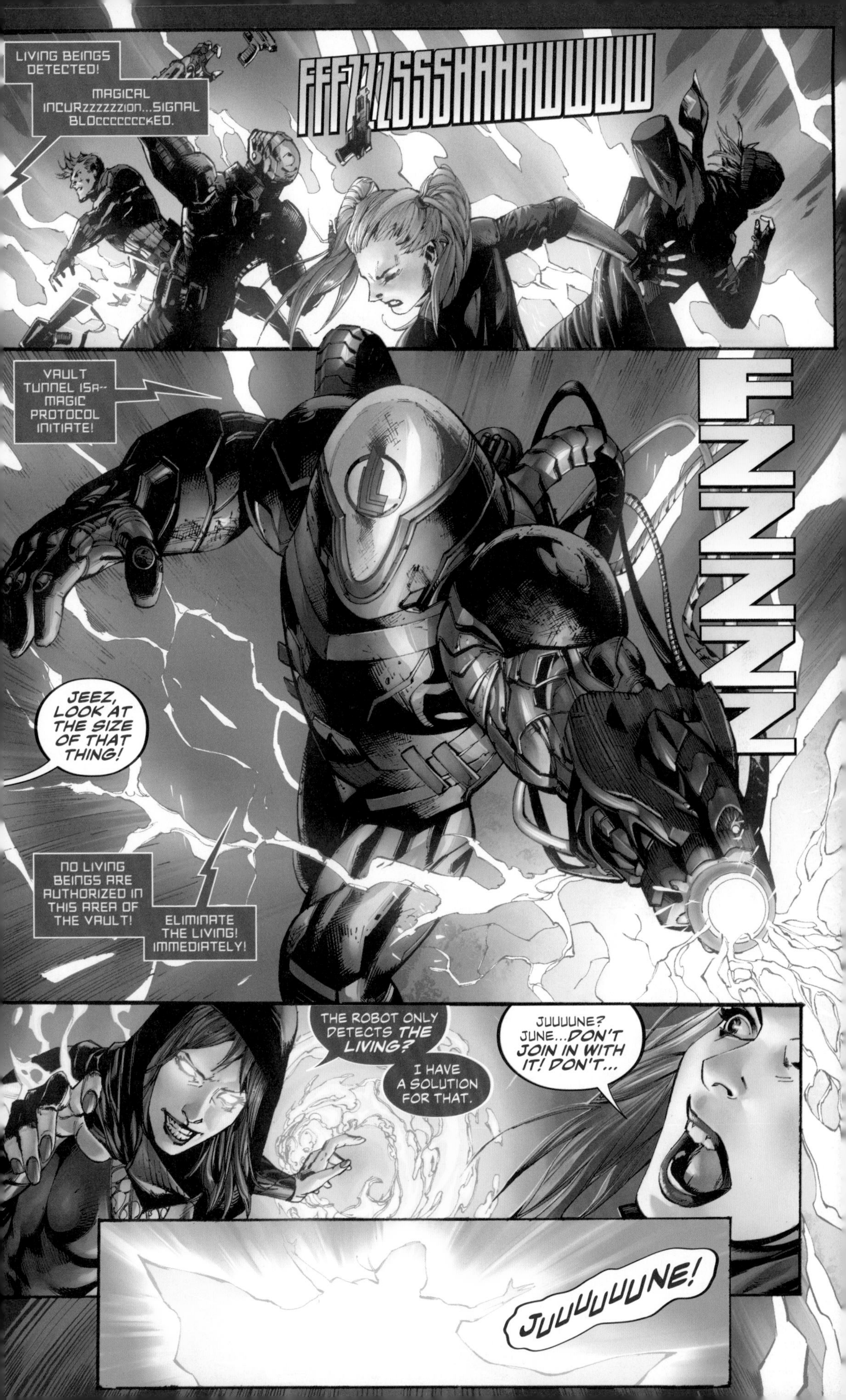
LIVING BEINGS DETECTED!
MAGICAL INCURzzzzzion...SIGNAL BLOccccccccKED.
FFFZZZSSSHHHHWWWW
VAULT TUNNEL ISa-- MAGIC PROTOCOL INITIATE!
FNNNN
JEEZ, LOOK AT THE SIZE OF THAT THING!
NO LIVING BEINGS ARE AUTHORIZED IN THIS AREA OF THE VAULT!
ELIMINATE THE LIVING! IMMEDIATELY!
THE ROBOT ONLY DETECTS THE LIVING?
I HAVE A SOLUTION FOR THAT.
JUUUUNE? JUNE...DON'T JOIN IN WITH IT! DON'T...
JUUUUUUNE!

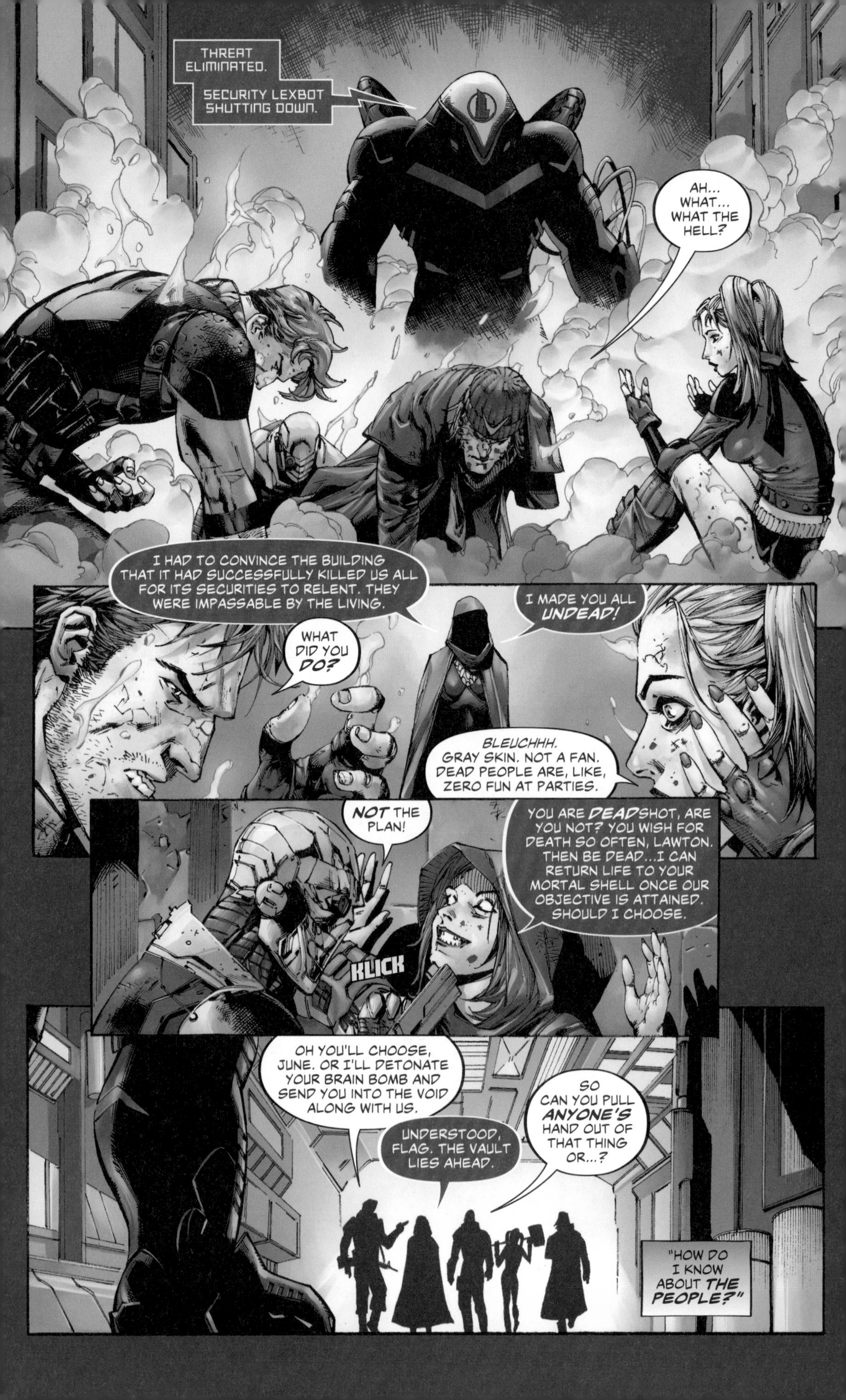
THREAT ELIMINATED.
SECURITY LEXBOT SHUTTING DOWN.
AH... WHAT... WHAT THE HELL?
I HAD TO CONVINCE THE BUILDING THAT IT HAD SUCCESSFULLY KILLED US ALL FOR ITS SECURITIES TO RELENT. THEY WERE IMPASSABLE BY THE LIVING.
WHAT DID YOU DO?
I MADE YOU ALL UNDEAD!
BLEUCHHH. GRAY SKIN. NOT A FAN. DEAD PEOPLE ARE, LIKE, ZERO FUN AT PARTIES.
NOT THE PLAN!
YOU ARE DEADSHOT, ARE YOU NOT? YOU WISH FOR DEATH SO OFTEN, LAWTON. THEN BE DEAD...I CAN RETURN LIFE TO YOUR MORTAL SHELL ONCE OUR OBJECTIVE IS ATTAINED. SHOULD I CHOOSE.
KLICK
OH YOU'LL CHOOSE, JUNE. OR I'LL DETONATE YOUR BRAIN BOMB AND SEND YOU INTO THE VOID ALONG WITH US.
UNDERSTOOD, FLAG. THE VAULT LIES AHEAD.
SO CAN YOU PULL ANYONE'S HAND OUT OF THAT THING OR...?
"HOW DO I KNOW ABOUT THE PEOPLE?"

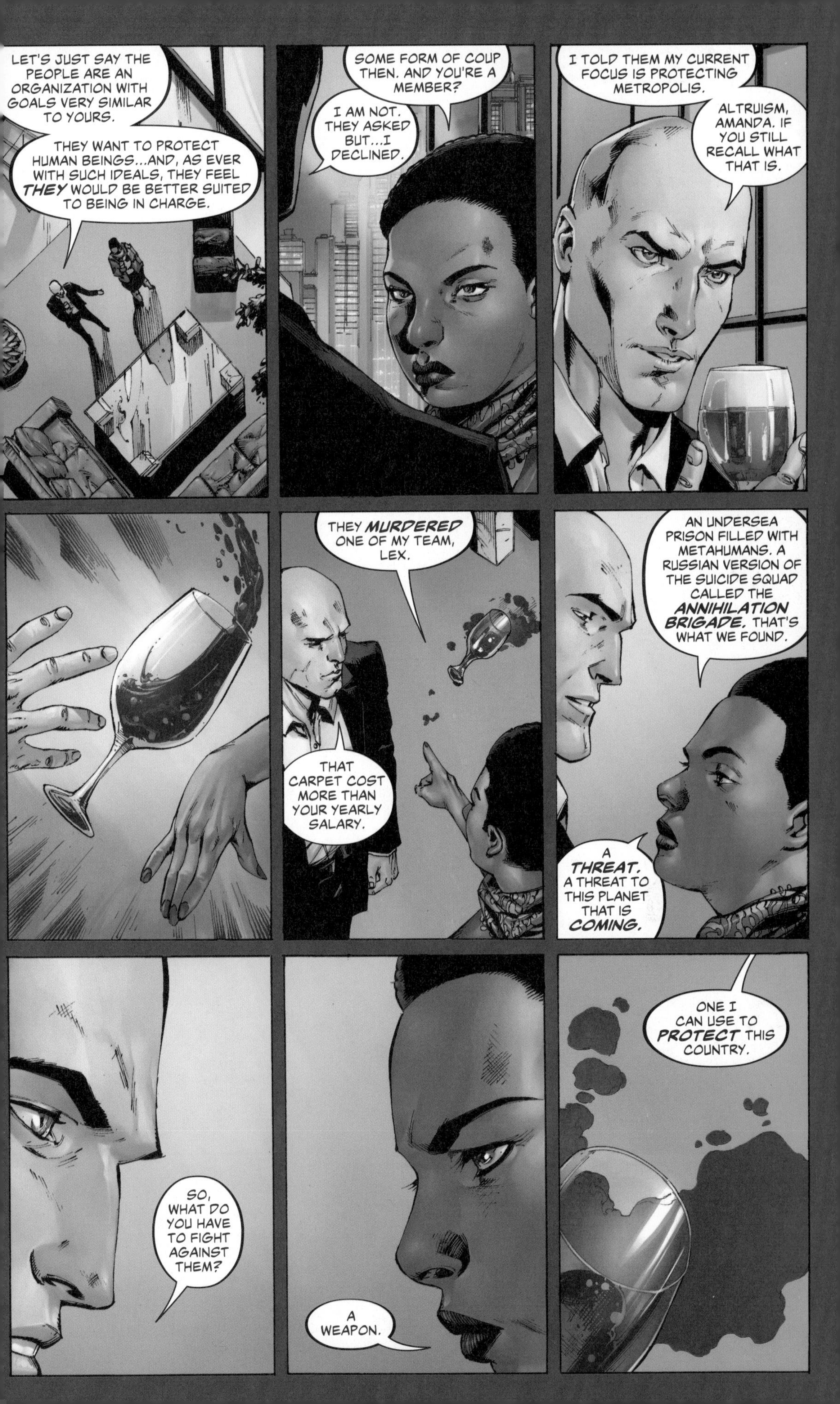
LET'S JUST SAY THE PEOPLE ARE AN ORGANIZATION WITH GOALS VERY SIMILAR TO YOURS.
THEY WANT TO PROTECT HUMAN BEINGS...AND, AS EVER WITH SUCH IDEALS, THEY FEEL *THEY* WOULD BE BETTER SUITED TO BEING IN CHARGE.
SOME FORM OF COUP THEN. AND YOU'RE A MEMBER?
I AM NOT. THEY ASKED BUT...I DECLINED.
I TOLD THEM MY CURRENT FOCUS IS PROTECTING METROPOLIS.
ALTRUISM, AMANDA. IF YOU STILL RECALL WHAT THAT IS.
THEY *MURDERED* ONE OF MY TEAM, LEX.
THAT CARPET COST MORE THAN YOUR YEARLY SALARY.
AN UNDERSEA PRISON FILLED WITH METAHUMANS. A RUSSIAN VERSION OF THE SUICIDE SQUAD CALLED THE *ANNIHILATION BRIGADE.* THAT'S WHAT WE FOUND.
A *THREAT.* A THREAT TO THIS PLANET THAT IS *COMING.*
SO, WHAT DO YOU HAVE TO FIGHT AGAINST THEM?
A WEAPON.
ONE I CAN USE TO *PROTECT* THIS COUNTRY.

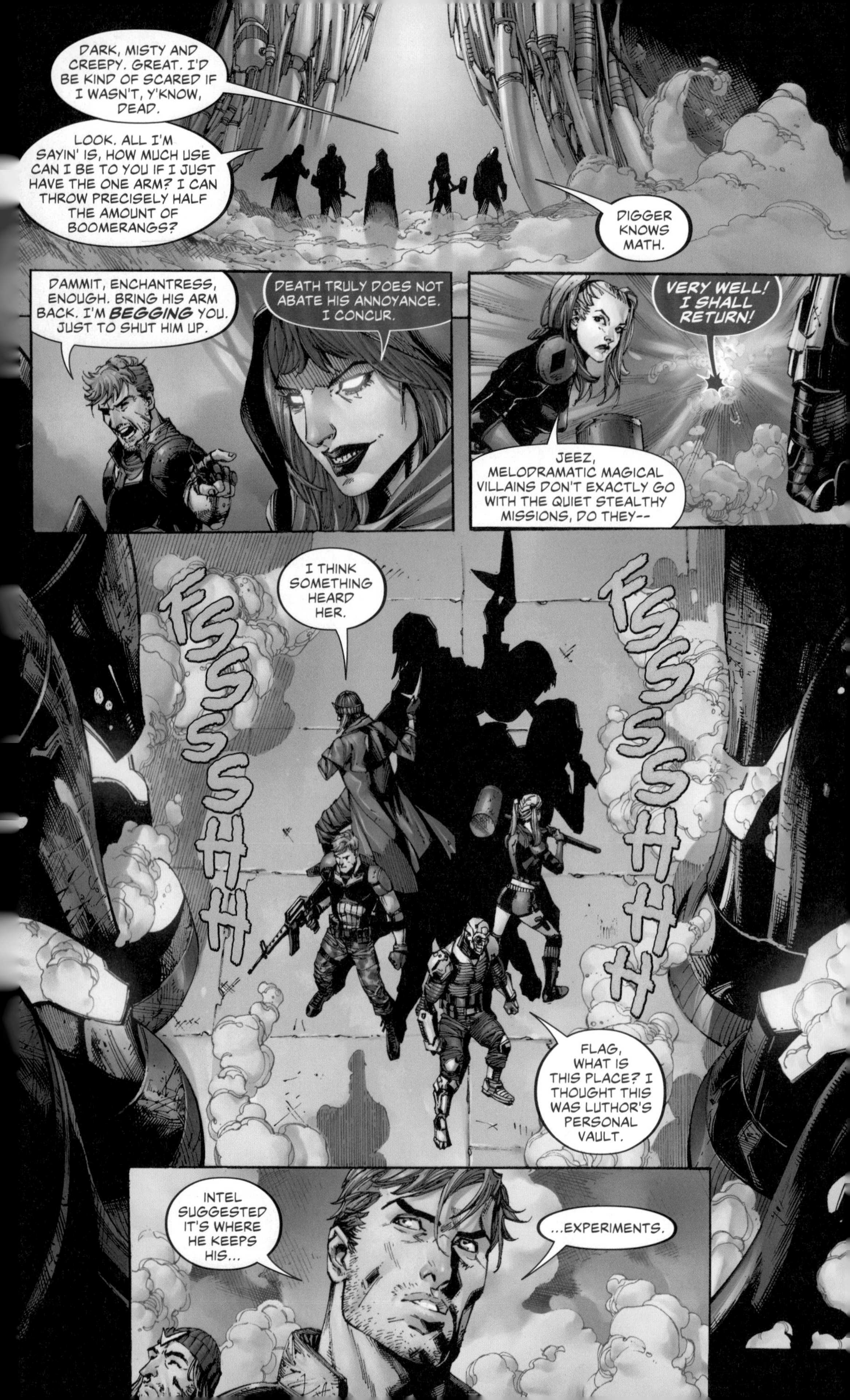
DARK, MISTY AND CREEPY. GREAT. I'D BE KIND OF SCARED IF I WASN'T, Y'KNOW, DEAD.
LOOK. ALL I'M SAYIN' IS, HOW MUCH USE CAN I BE TO YOU IF I JUST HAVE THE ONE ARM? I CAN THROW PRECISELY HALF THE AMOUNT OF BOOMERANGS?
DIGGER KNOWS MATH.
DAMMIT, ENCHANTRESS, ENOUGH. BRING HIS ARM BACK. I'M **BEGGING** YOU. JUST TO SHUT HIM UP.
DEATH TRULY DOES NOT ABATE HIS ANNOYANCE. I CONCUR.
VERY WELL! I SHALL RETURN!
JEEZ, MELODRAMATIC MAGICAL VILLAINS DON'T EXACTLY GO WITH THE QUIET STEALTHY MISSIONS, DO THEY--
FSSSSHHH
I THINK SOMETHING HEARD HER.
FSSSSHHHH
FLAG, WHAT IS THIS PLACE? I THOUGHT THIS WAS LUTHOR'S PERSONAL VAULT.
INTEL SUGGESTED IT'S WHERE HE KEEPS HIS...
...EXPERIMENTS.

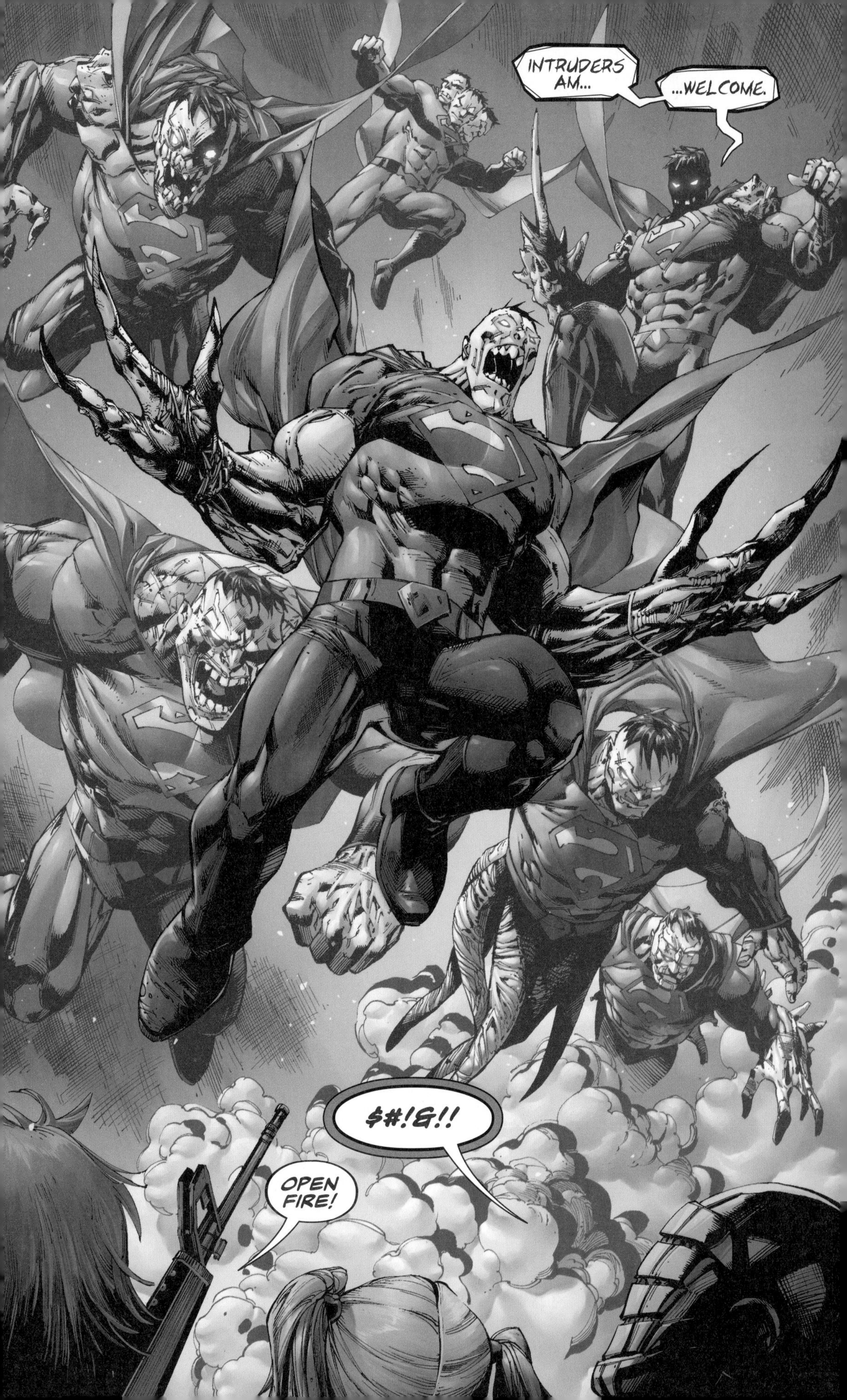
INTRUDERS AM...
...WELCOME.
$#!&!!
OPEN FIRE!

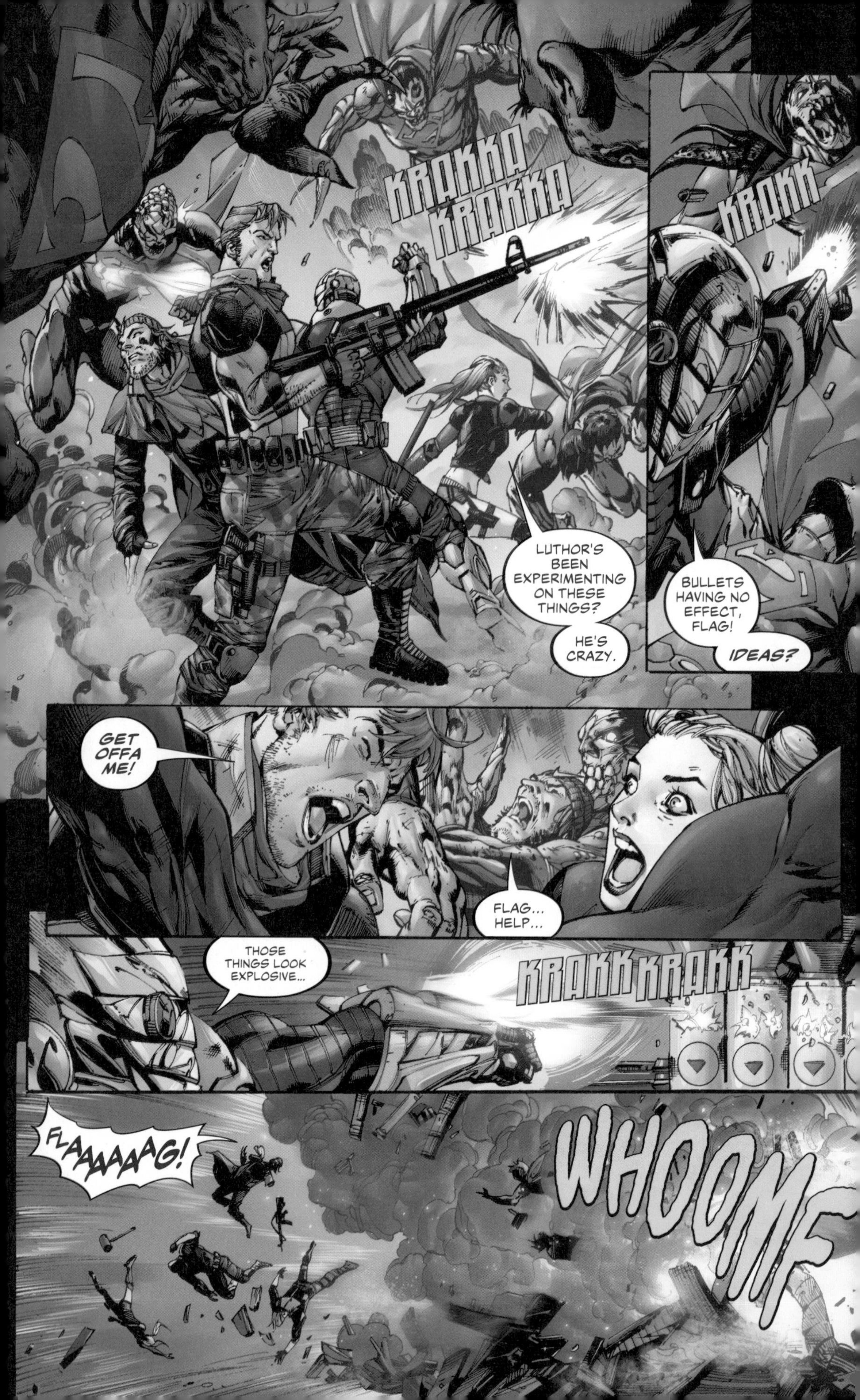
KRAKKA KRAKKA
KRAKK
LUTHOR'S BEEN EXPERIMENTING ON THESE THINGS?
HE'S CRAZY.
BULLETS HAVING NO EFFECT, FLAG!
IDEAS?
GET OFFA ME!
FLAG... HELP...
THOSE THINGS LOOK EXPLOSIVE...
KRAKK KRAKK
FLAAAAAAG!
WHOOMF

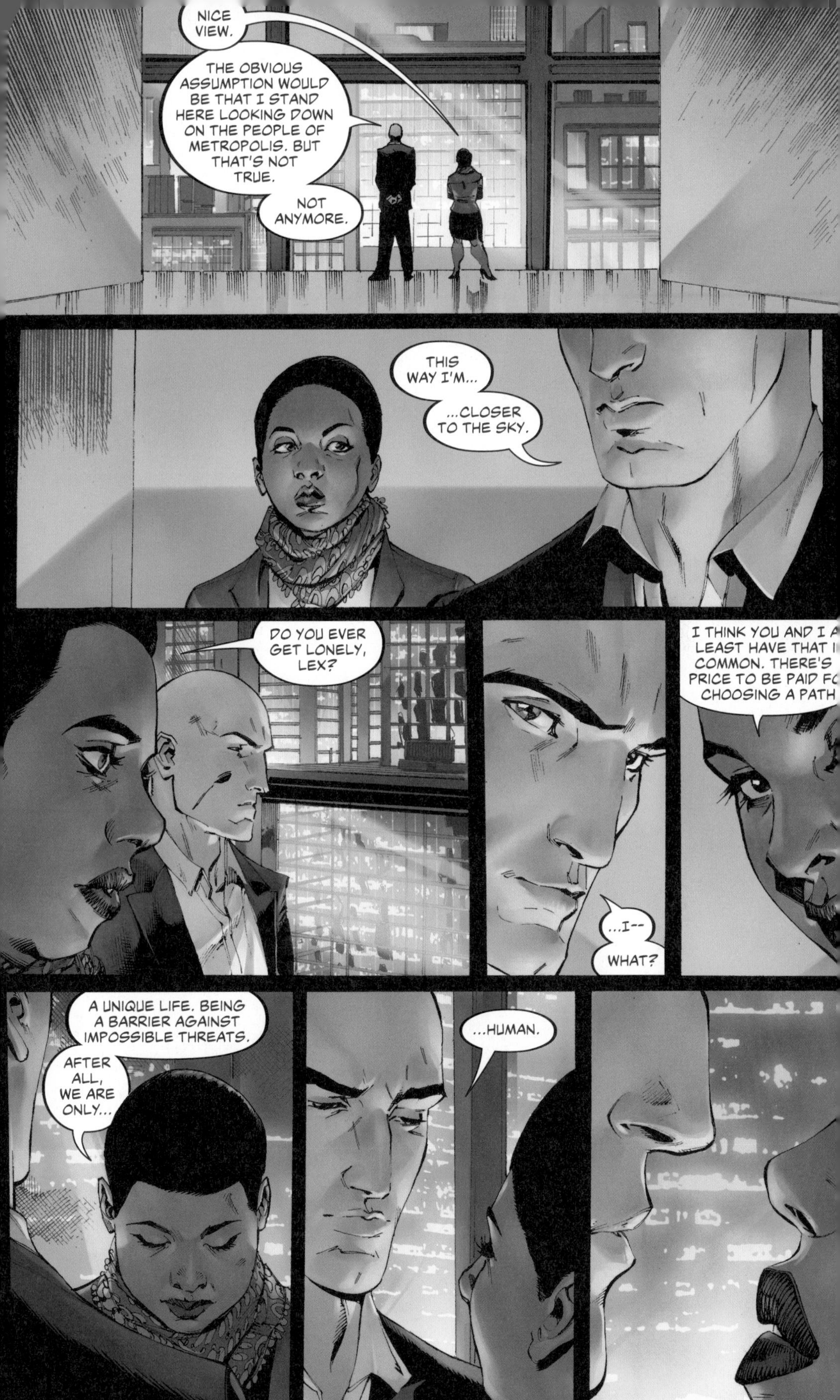
NICE VIEW.
THE OBVIOUS ASSUMPTION WOULD BE THAT I STAND HERE LOOKING DOWN ON THE PEOPLE OF METROPOLIS. BUT THAT'S NOT TRUE.
NOT ANYMORE.
THIS WAY I'M...
...CLOSER TO THE SKY.
DO YOU EVER GET LONELY, LEX?
I THINK YOU AND I A
LEAST HAVE THAT I
COMMON. THERE'S
PRICE TO BE PAID FO
CHOOSING A PATH
...I--
WHAT?
A UNIQUE LIFE. BEING A BARRIER AGAINST IMPOSSIBLE THREATS.
AFTER ALL, WE ARE ONLY...
...HUMAN.

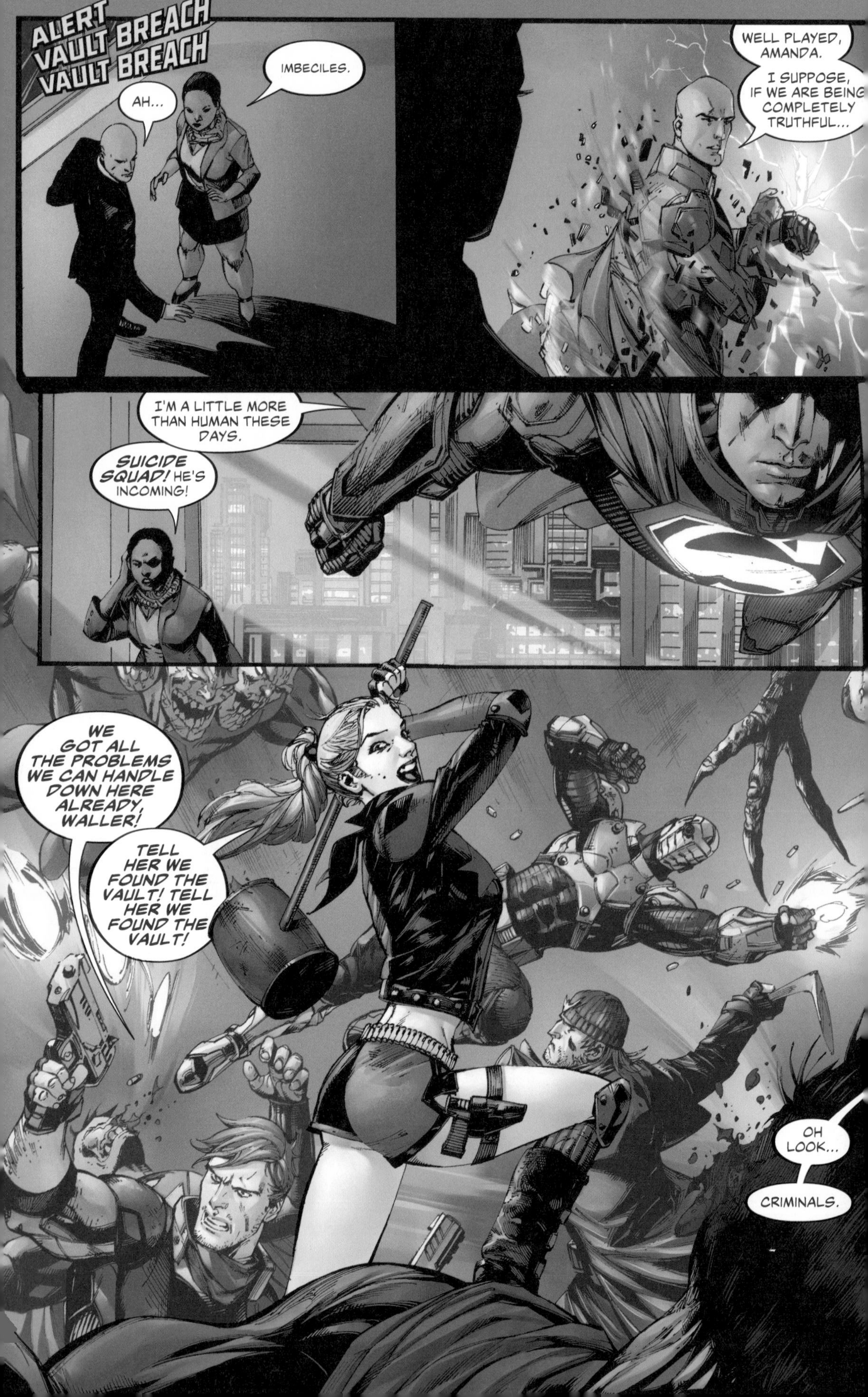
ALERT
VAULT BREACH
VAULT BREACH
AH...
IMBECILES.
WELL PLAYED, AMANDA.
I SUPPOSE, IF WE ARE BEING COMPLETELY TRUTHFUL...
I'M A LITTLE MORE THAN HUMAN THESE DAYS.
SUICIDE SQUAD! HE'S INCOMING!
WE GOT ALL THE PROBLEMS WE CAN HANDLE DOWN HERE ALREADY, WALLER!
TELL HER WE FOUND THE VAULT! TELL HER WE FOUND THE VAULT!
OH LOOK...
CRIMINALS.

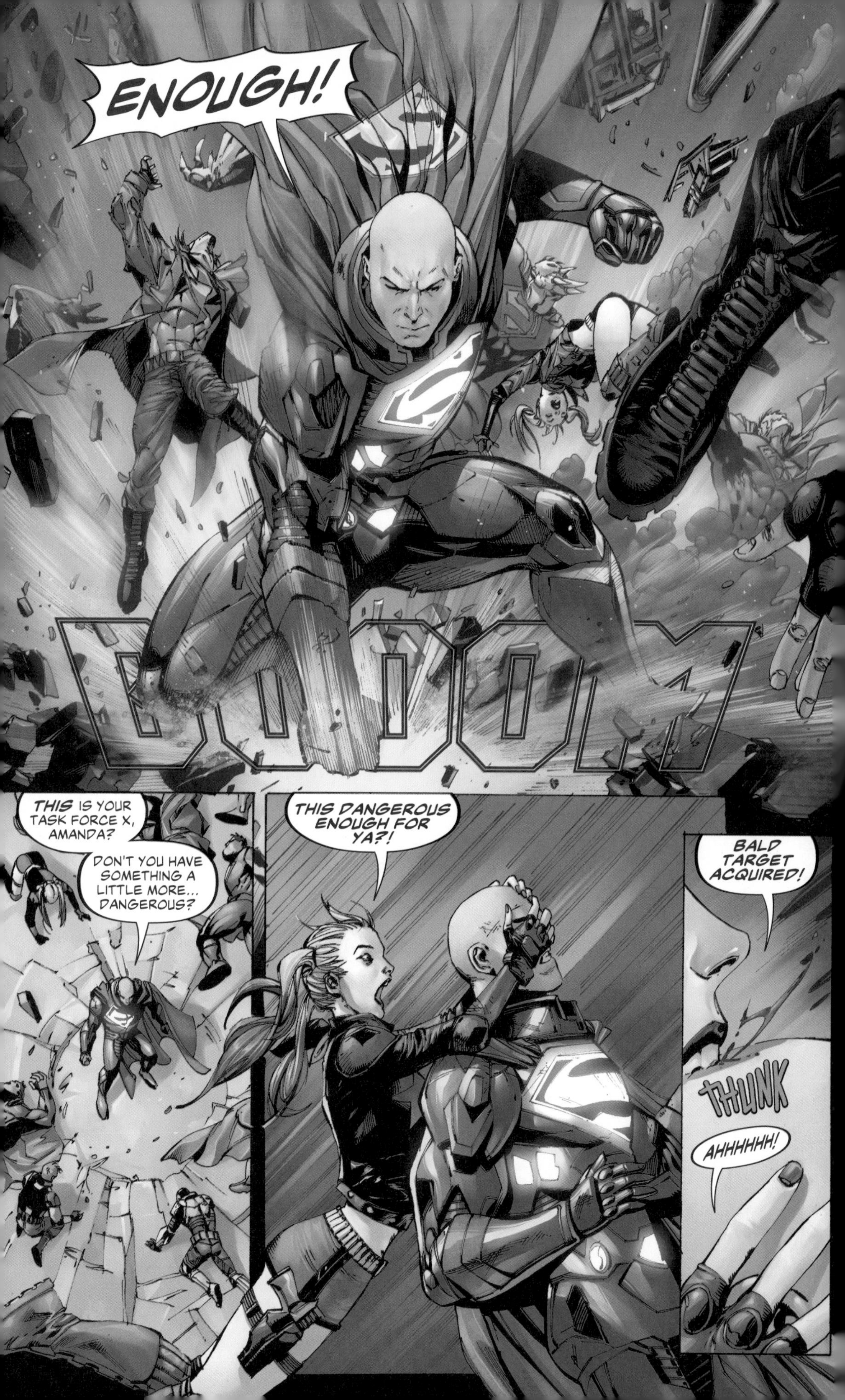
ENOUGH!
BOOOM
THIS IS YOUR TASK FORCE X, AMANDA?
DON'T YOU HAVE SOMETHING A LITTLE MORE... DANGEROUS?
THIS DANGEROUS ENOUGH FOR YA?!
BALD TARGET ACQUIRED!
THUNK
AHHHHHH!

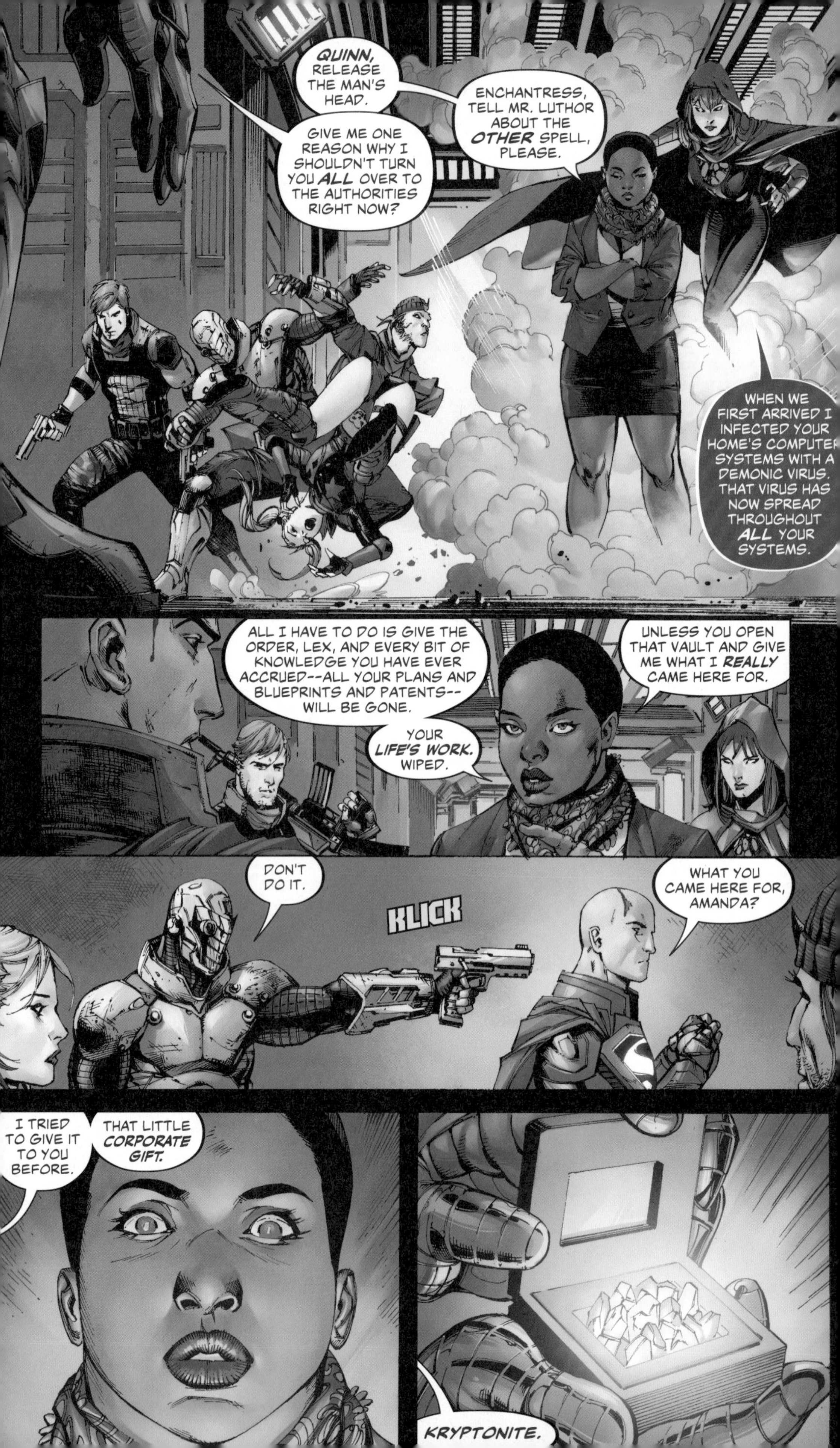
QUINN, RELEASE THE MAN'S HEAD.
GIVE ME ONE REASON WHY I SHOULDN'T TURN YOU ALL OVER TO THE AUTHORITIES RIGHT NOW?
ENCHANTRESS, TELL MR. LUTHOR ABOUT THE OTHER SPELL, PLEASE.
WHEN WE FIRST ARRIVED I INFECTED YOUR HOME'S COMPUTER SYSTEMS WITH A DEMONIC VIRUS. THAT VIRUS HAS NOW SPREAD THROUGHOUT ALL YOUR SYSTEMS.
ALL I HAVE TO DO IS GIVE THE ORDER, LEX, AND EVERY BIT OF KNOWLEDGE YOU HAVE EVER ACCRUED--ALL YOUR PLANS AND BLUEPRINTS AND PATENTS--WILL BE GONE.
YOUR LIFE'S WORK. WIPED.
UNLESS YOU OPEN THAT VAULT AND GIVE ME WHAT I REALLY CAME HERE FOR.
DON'T DO IT.
KLICK
WHAT YOU CAME HERE FOR, AMANDA?
I TRIED TO GIVE IT TO YOU BEFORE.
THAT LITTLE CORPORATE GIFT.
KRYPTONITE.

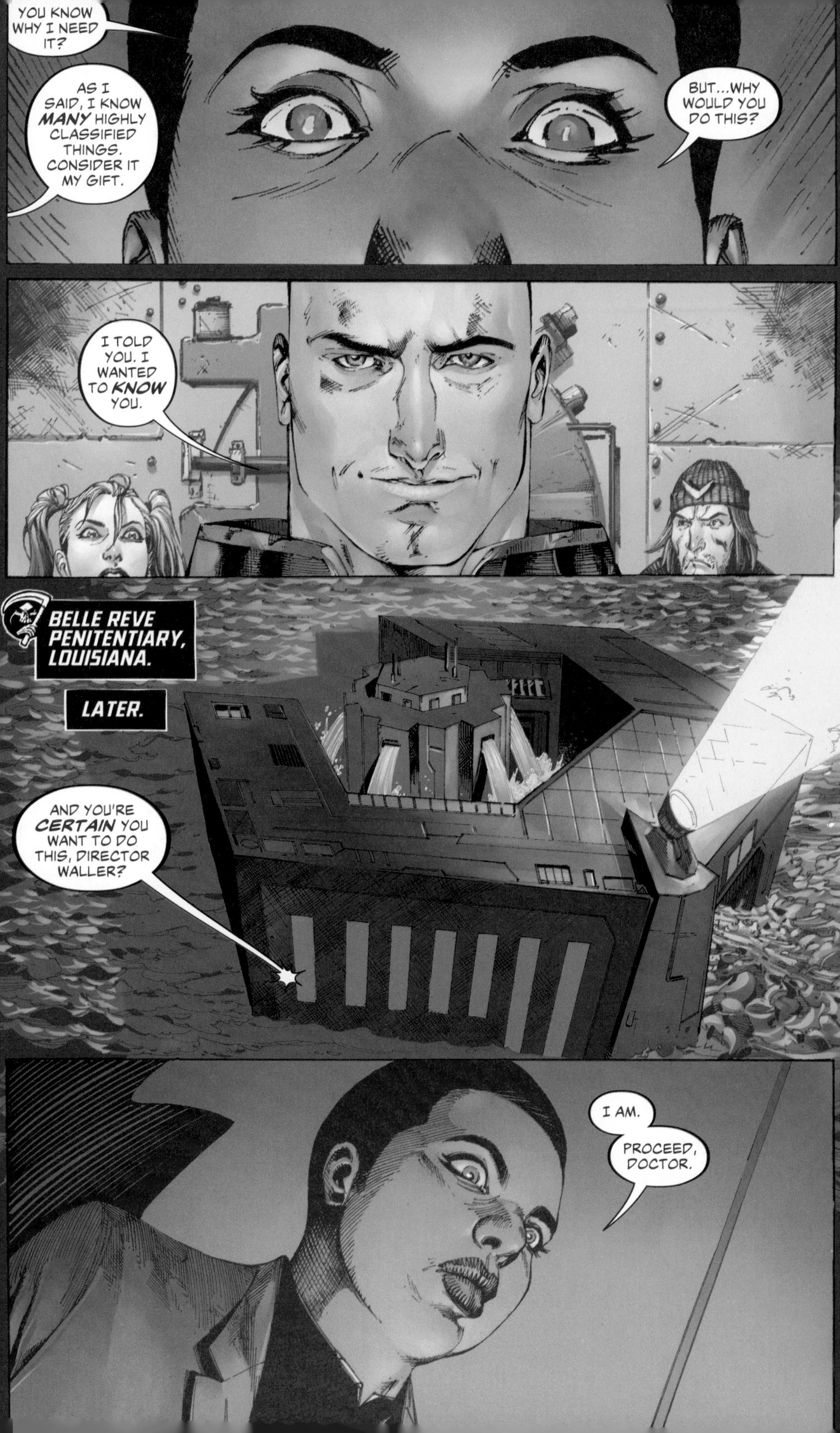
YOU KNOW WHY I NEED IT?
AS I SAID, I KNOW MANY HIGHLY CLASSIFIED THINGS. CONSIDER IT MY GIFT.
BUT...WHY WOULD YOU DO THIS?
I TOLD YOU. I WANTED TO KNOW YOU.
BELLE REVE PENITENTIARY, LOUISIANA.
LATER.
AND YOU'RE CERTAIN YOU WANT TO DO THIS, DIRECTOR WALLER?
I AM.
PROCEED, DOCTOR.

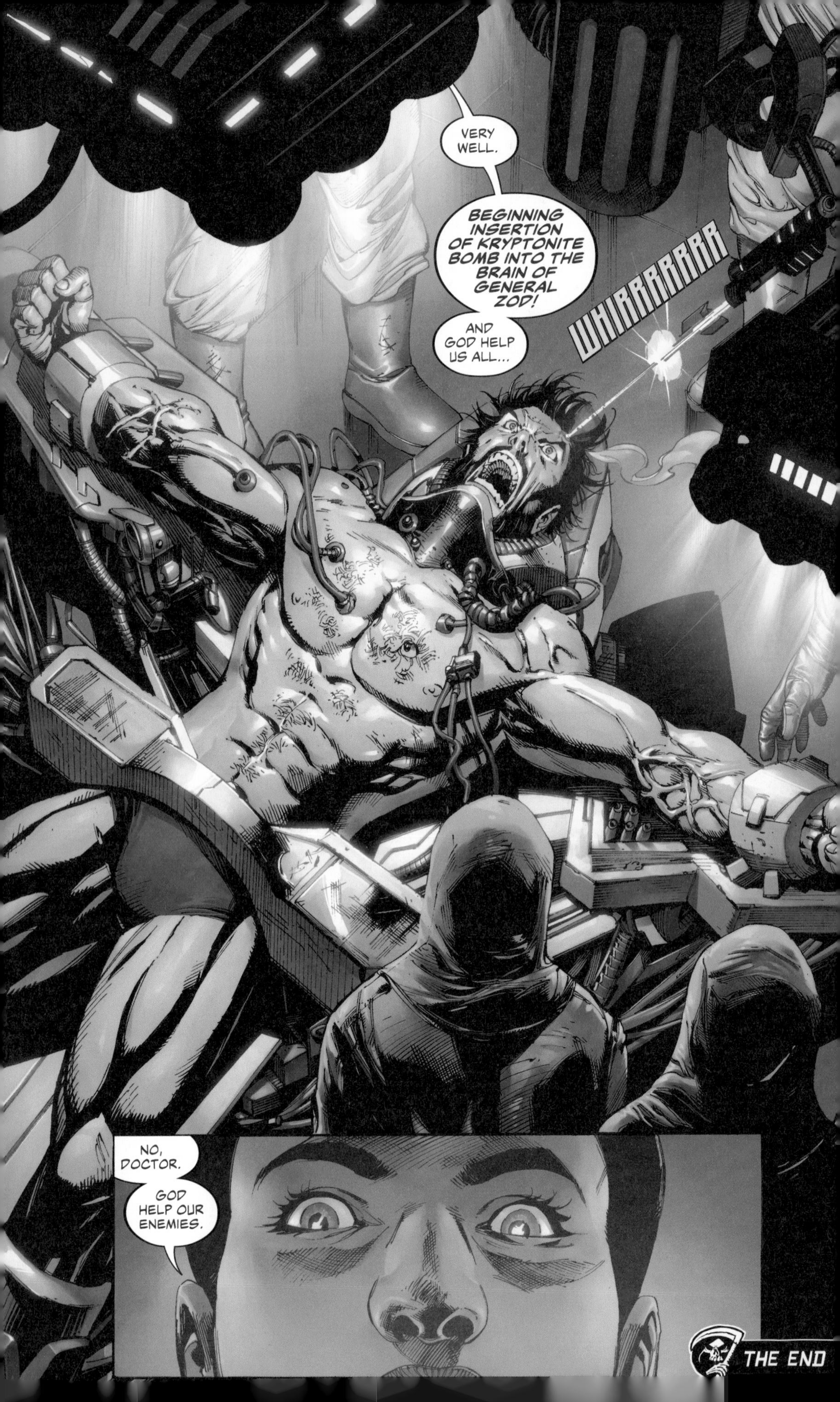
VERY WELL.
BEGINNING INSERTION OF KRYPTONITE BOMB INTO THE BRAIN OF GENERAL ZOD!
AND GOD HELP US ALL...
WHIRRRRRRR
NO, DOCTOR.
GOD HELP OUR ENEMIES.
THE END

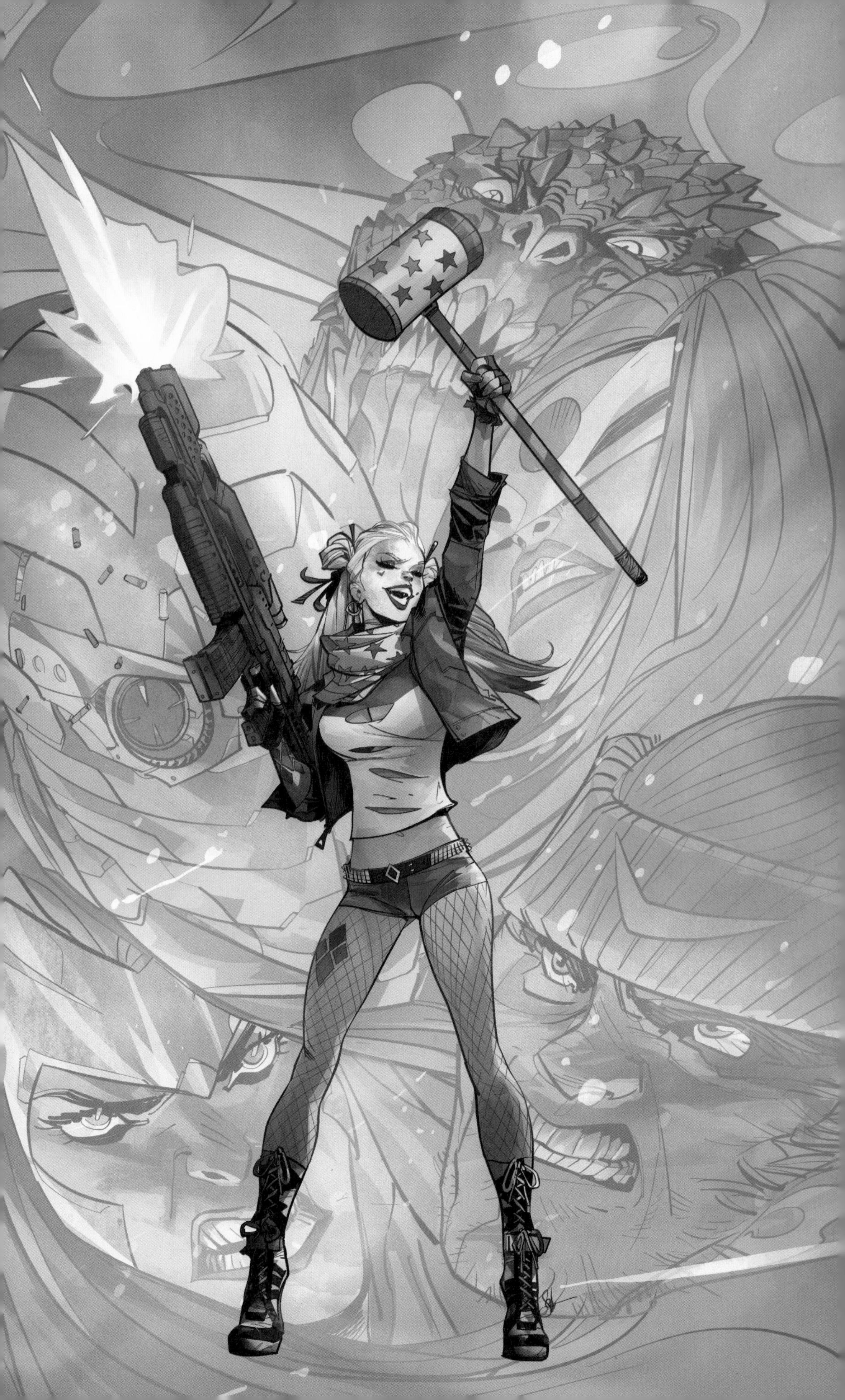

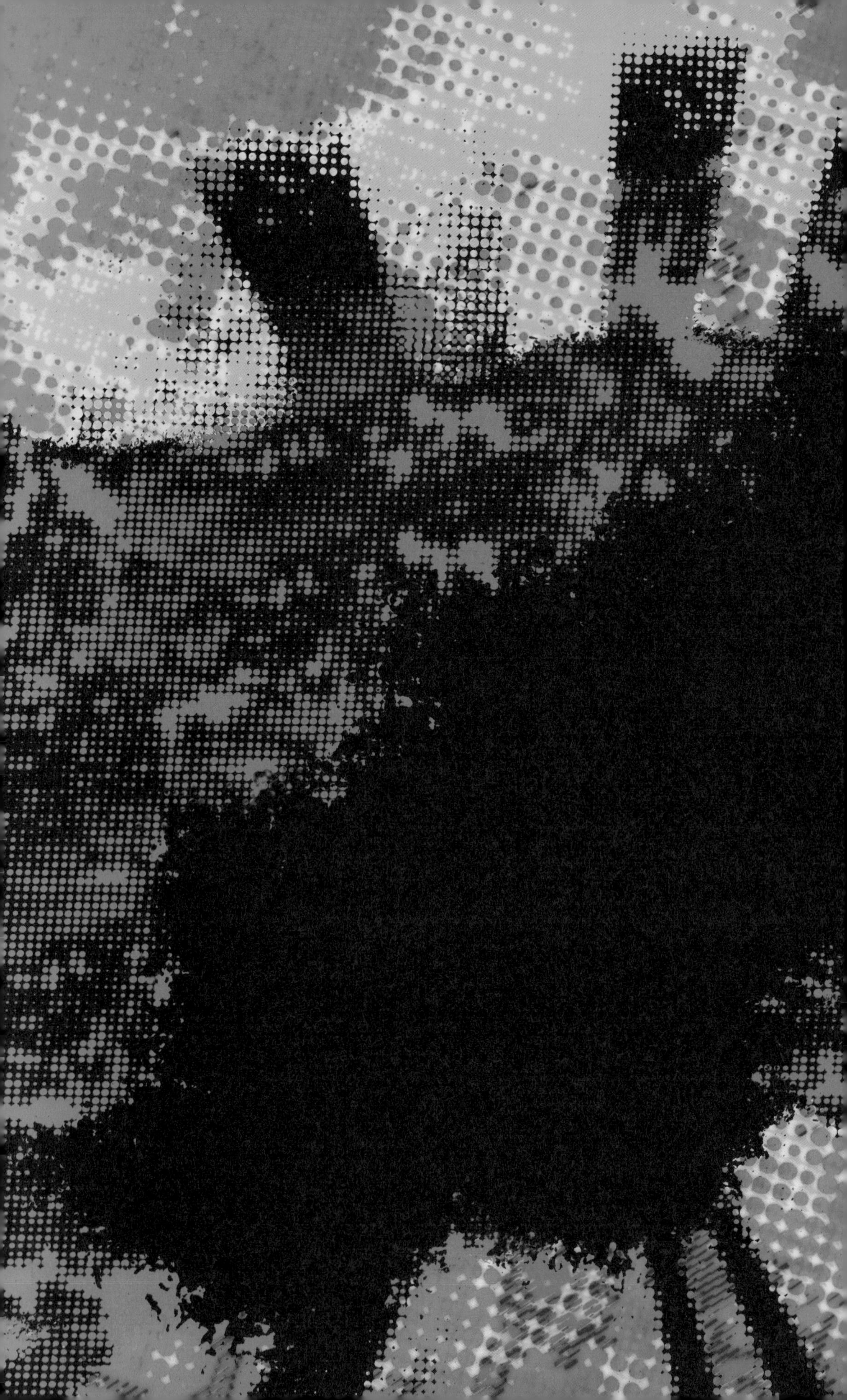

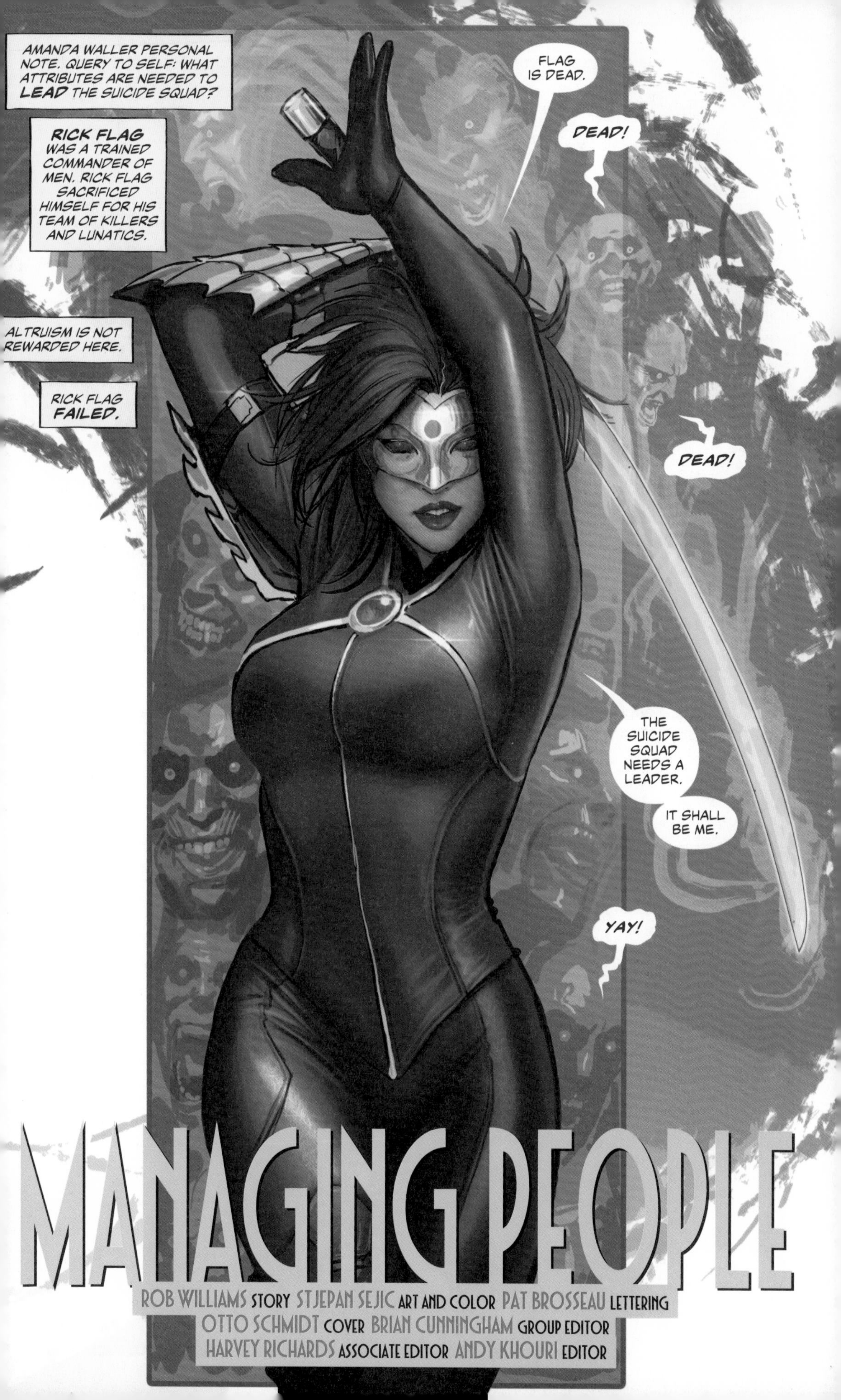
AMANDA WALLER PERSONAL NOTE. QUERY TO SELF: WHAT ATTRIBUTES ARE NEEDED TO LEAD THE SUICIDE SQUAD?
FLAG IS DEAD.
DEAD!
RICK FLAG WAS A TRAINED COMMANDER OF MEN. RICK FLAG SACRIFICED HIMSELF FOR HIS TEAM OF KILLERS AND LUNATICS.
ALTRUISM IS NOT REWARDED HERE.
RICK FLAG FAILED.
DEAD!
THE SUICIDE SQUAD NEEDS A LEADER.
IT SHALL BE ME.
YAY!
MANAGING PEOPLE
ROB WILLIAMS STORY STJEPAN SEJIC ART AND COLOR PAT BROSSEAU LETTERING
OTTO SCHMIDT COVER BRIAN CUNNINGHAM GROUP EDITOR
HARVEY RICHARDS ASSOCIATE EDITOR ANDY KHOURI EDITOR

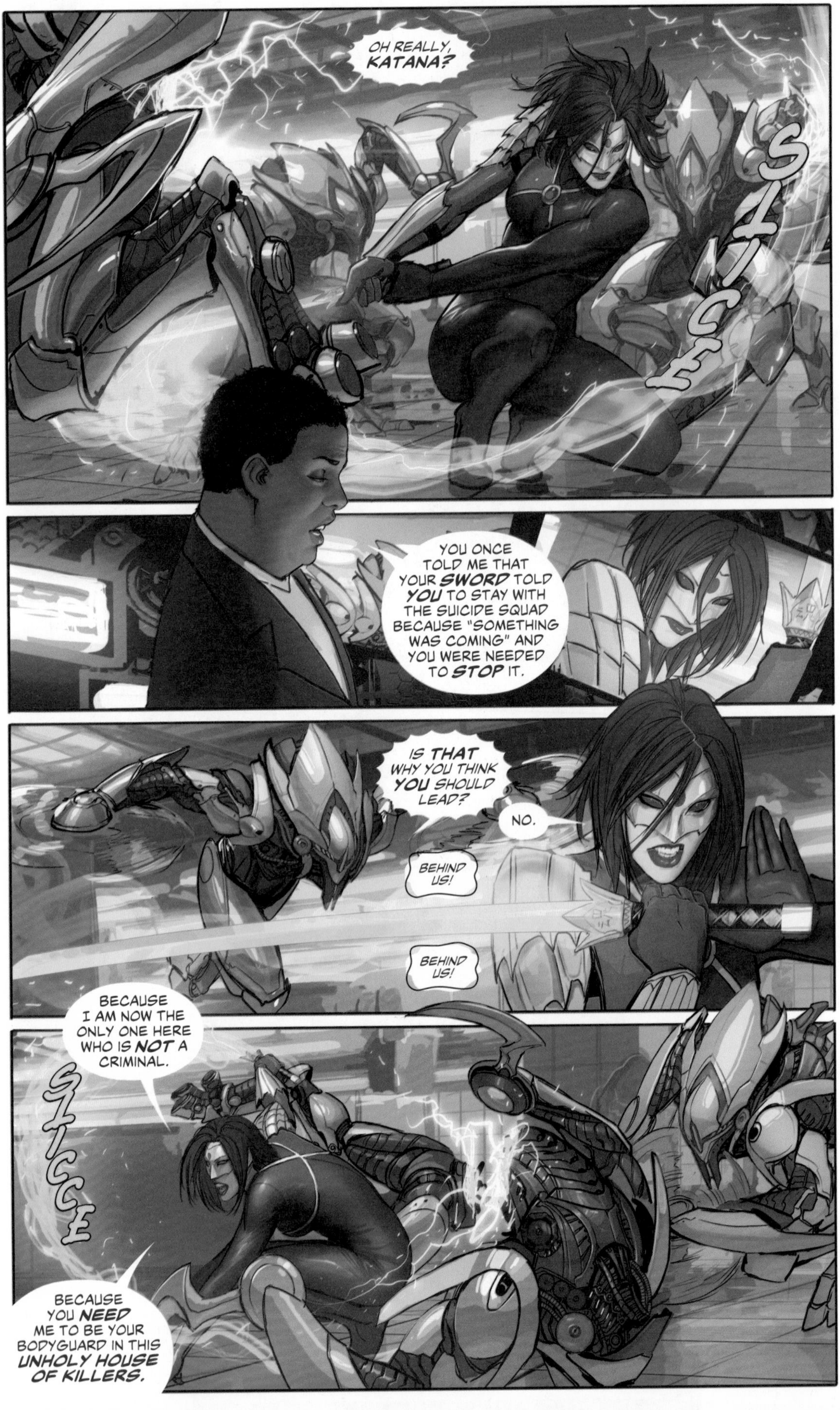

OH REALLY, KATANA?
SLICE
YOU ONCE TOLD ME THAT YOUR SWORD TOLD YOU TO STAY WITH THE SUICIDE SQUAD BECAUSE "SOMETHING WAS COMING" AND YOU WERE NEEDED TO STOP IT.
IS THAT WHY YOU THINK YOU SHOULD LEAD?
NO.
BEHIND US!
BEHIND US!
BECAUSE I AM NOW THE ONLY ONE HERE WHO IS NOT A CRIMINAL.
SLICE
BECAUSE YOU NEED ME TO BE YOUR BODYGUARD IN THIS UNHOLY HOUSE OF KILLERS.

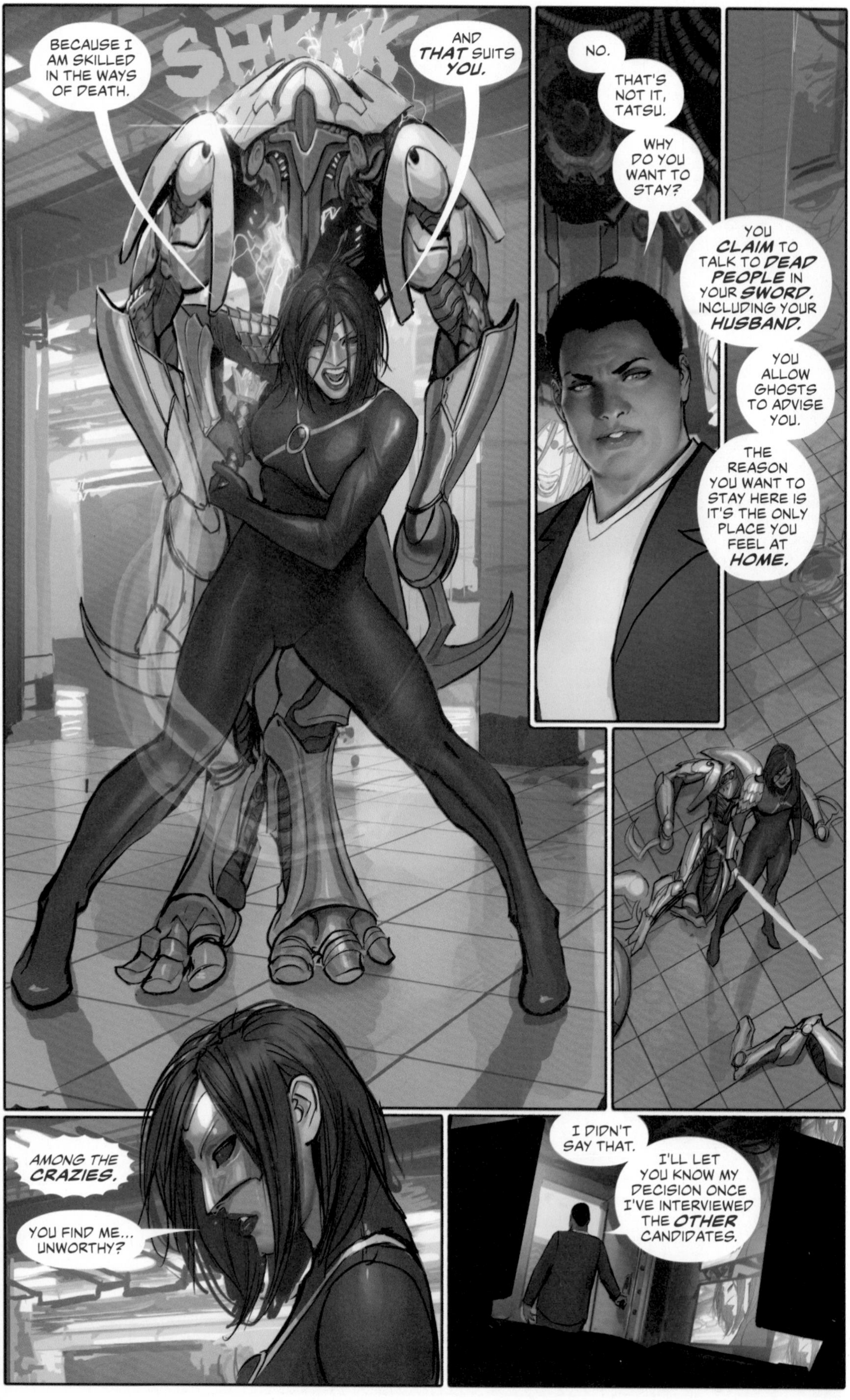
SHKKK
BECAUSE I AM SKILLED IN THE WAYS OF DEATH.
AND THAT SUITS YOU.
NO.
THAT'S NOT IT, TATSU.
WHY DO YOU WANT TO STAY?
YOU CLAIM TO TALK TO DEAD PEOPLE IN YOUR SWORD, INCLUDING YOUR HUSBAND.
YOU ALLOW GHOSTS TO ADVISE YOU.
THE REASON YOU WANT TO STAY HERE IS IT'S THE ONLY PLACE YOU FEEL AT HOME.
AMONG THE CRAZIES.
YOU FIND ME... UNWORTHY?
I DIDN'T SAY THAT.
I'LL LET YOU KNOW MY DECISION ONCE I'VE INTERVIEWED THE OTHER CANDIDATES.

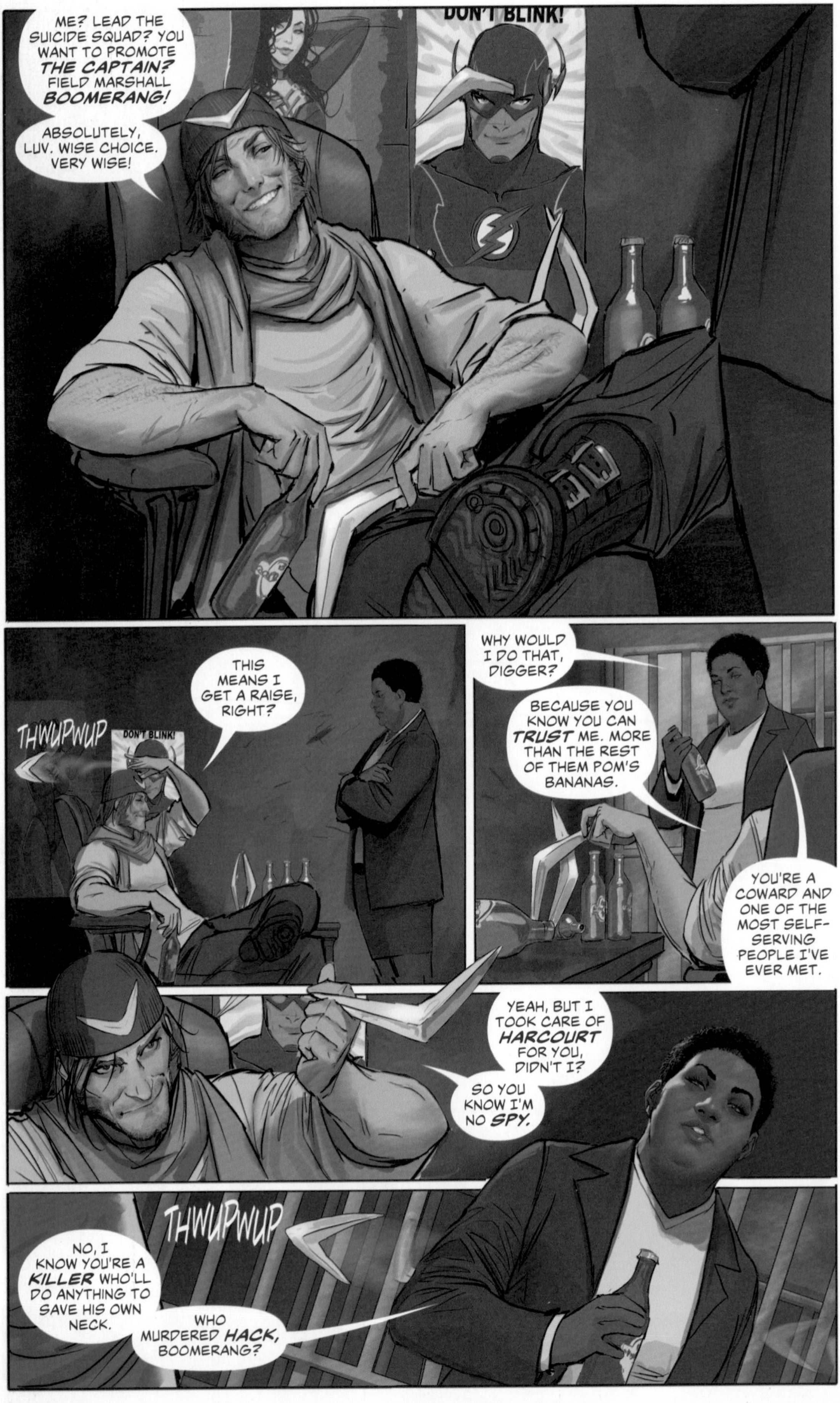
DON'T BLINK!
ME? LEAD THE SUICIDE SQUAD? YOU WANT TO PROMOTE THE CAPTAIN? FIELD MARSHALL BOOMERANG!
ABSOLUTELY, LUV. WISE CHOICE. VERY WISE!
THWUPWUP
DON'T BLINK!
THIS MEANS I GET A RAISE, RIGHT?
WHY WOULD I DO THAT, DIGGER?
BECAUSE YOU KNOW YOU CAN TRUST ME. MORE THAN THE REST OF THEM POM'S BANANAS.
YOU'RE A COWARD AND ONE OF THE MOST SELF-SERVING PEOPLE I'VE EVER MET.
YEAH, BUT I TOOK CARE OF HARCOURT FOR YOU, DIDN'T I?
SO YOU KNOW I'M NO SPY.
THWUPWUP
NO, I KNOW YOU'RE A KILLER WHO'LL DO ANYTHING TO SAVE HIS OWN NECK.
WHO MURDERED HACK, BOOMERANG?

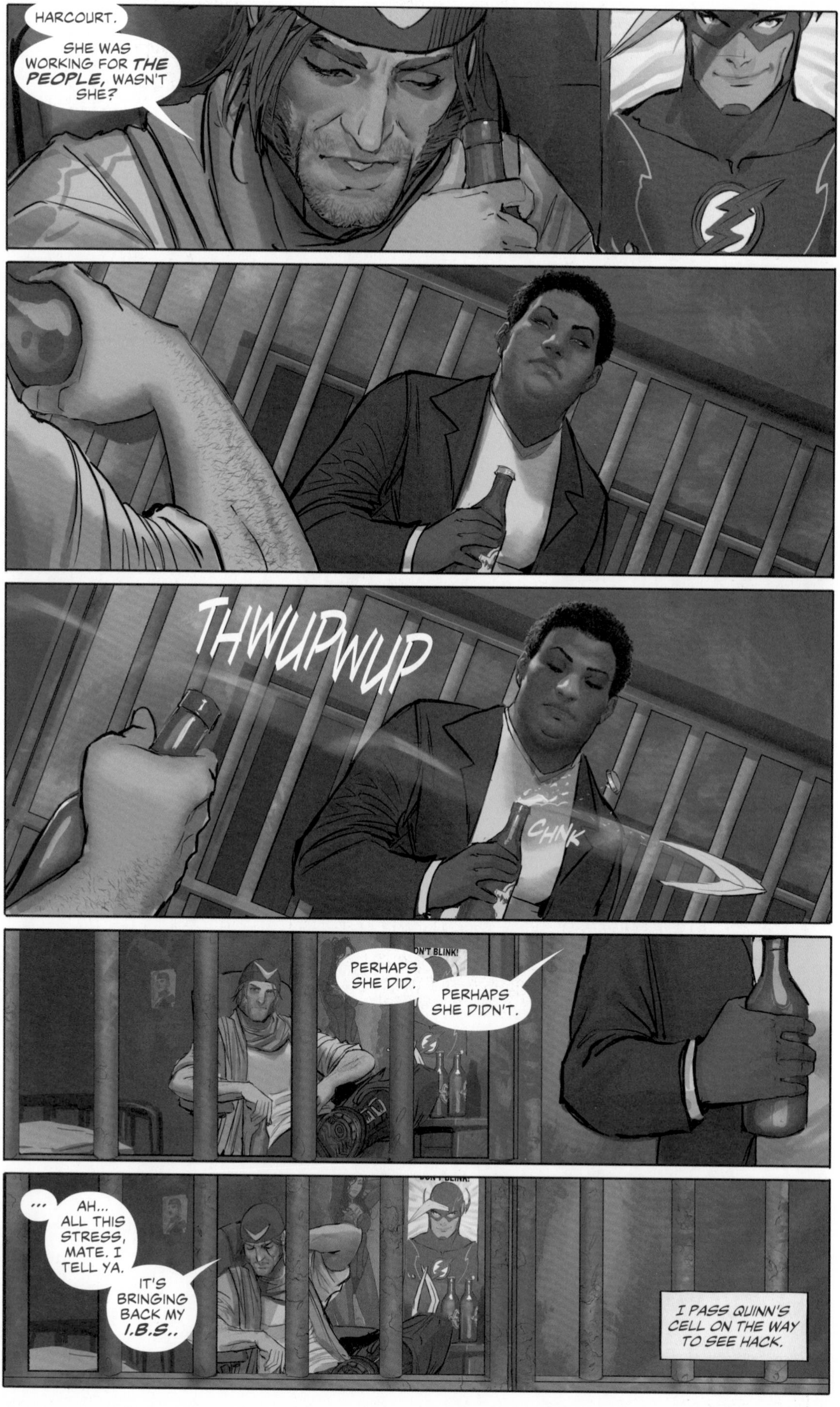
HARCOURT.
SHE WAS WORKING FOR THE PEOPLE, WASN'T SHE?
THWUPWUP
CHNK
PERHAPS SHE DID.
PERHAPS SHE DIDN'T.
...
AH... ALL THIS STRESS, MATE. I TELL YA.
IT'S BRINGING BACK MY I.B.S..
I PASS QUINN'S CELL ON THE WAY TO SEE HACK.

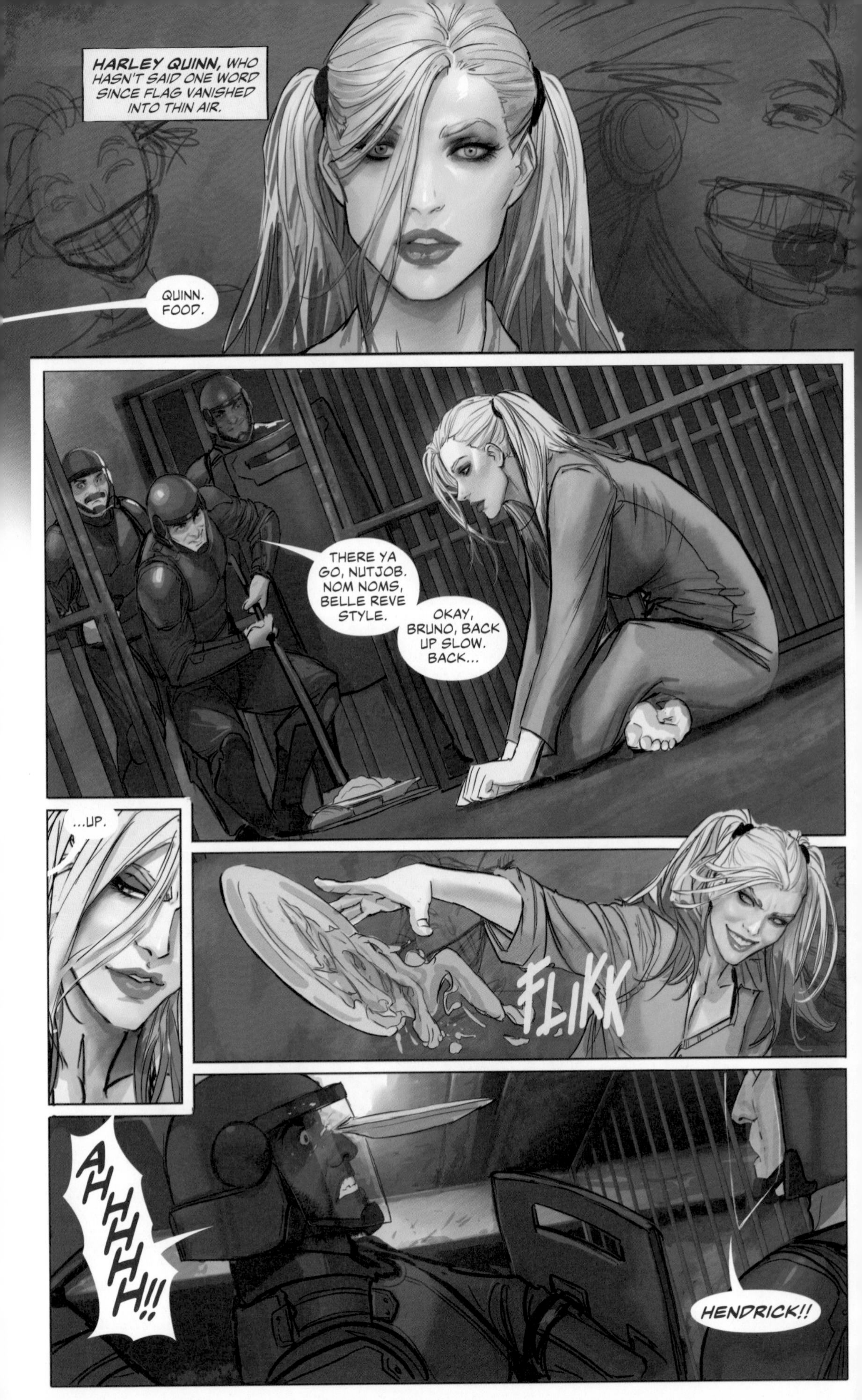
HARLEY QUINN, WHO HASN'T SAID ONE WORD SINCE FLAG VANISHED INTO THIN AIR.
QUINN. FOOD.
THERE YA GO, NUTJOB. NOM NOMS, BELLE REVE STYLE.
OKAY, BRUNO, BACK UP SLOW. BACK...
...UP.
FLIKK
AHHHHH!!
HENDRICK!!

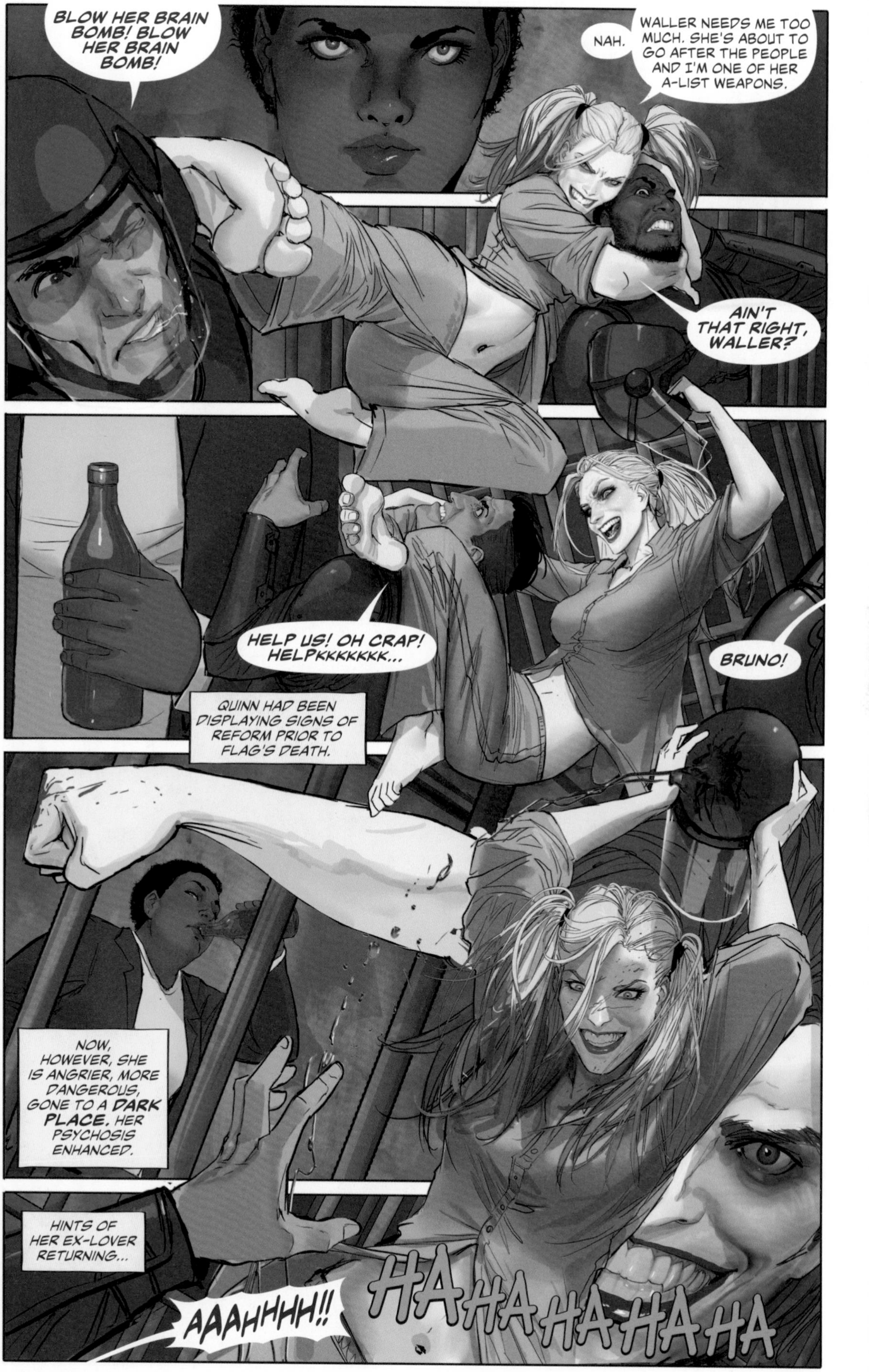
BLOW HER BRAIN BOMB! BLOW HER BRAIN BOMB!
NAH.
WALLER NEEDS ME TOO MUCH. SHE'S ABOUT TO GO AFTER THE PEOPLE AND I'M ONE OF HER A-LIST WEAPONS.
AIN'T THAT RIGHT, WALLER?
HELP US! OH CRAP! HELPKKKKKKK...
BRUNO!
QUINN HAD BEEN DISPLAYING SIGNS OF REFORM PRIOR TO FLAG'S DEATH.
NOW, HOWEVER, SHE IS ANGRIER, MORE DANGEROUS, GONE TO A DARK PLACE. HER PSYCHOSIS ENHANCED.
HINTS OF HER EX-LOVER RETURNING...
AAAHHHH!!
HA HA HA HA HA HA

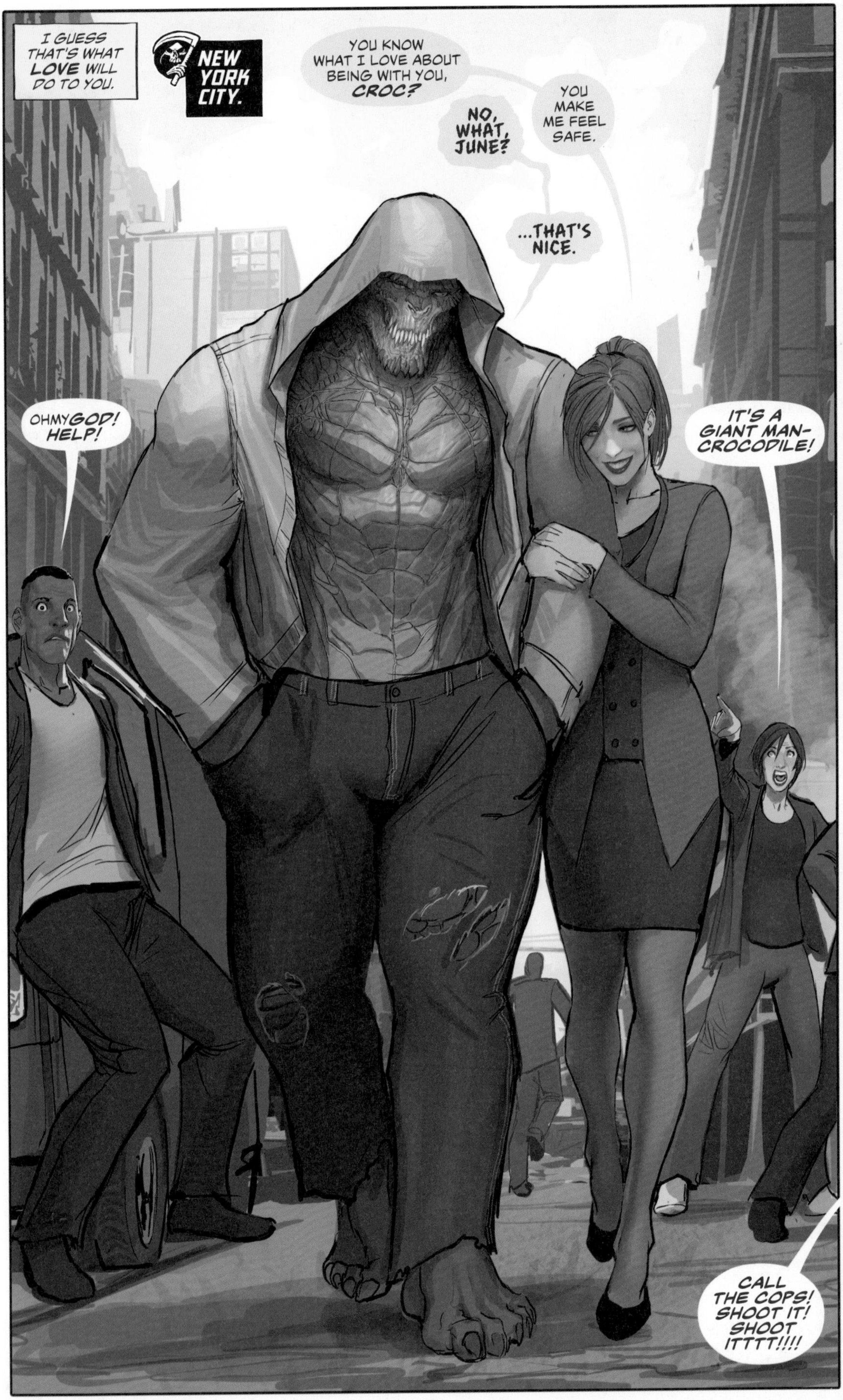
I GUESS THAT'S WHAT LOVE WILL DO TO YOU.
NEW YORK CITY.
YOU KNOW WHAT I LOVE ABOUT BEING WITH YOU, CROC?
NO, WHAT, JUNE?
YOU MAKE ME FEEL SAFE.
...THAT'S NICE.
OHMYGOD! HELP!
IT'S A GIANT MAN-CROCODILE!
CALL THE COPS! SHOOT IT! SHOOT ITTTT!!!!

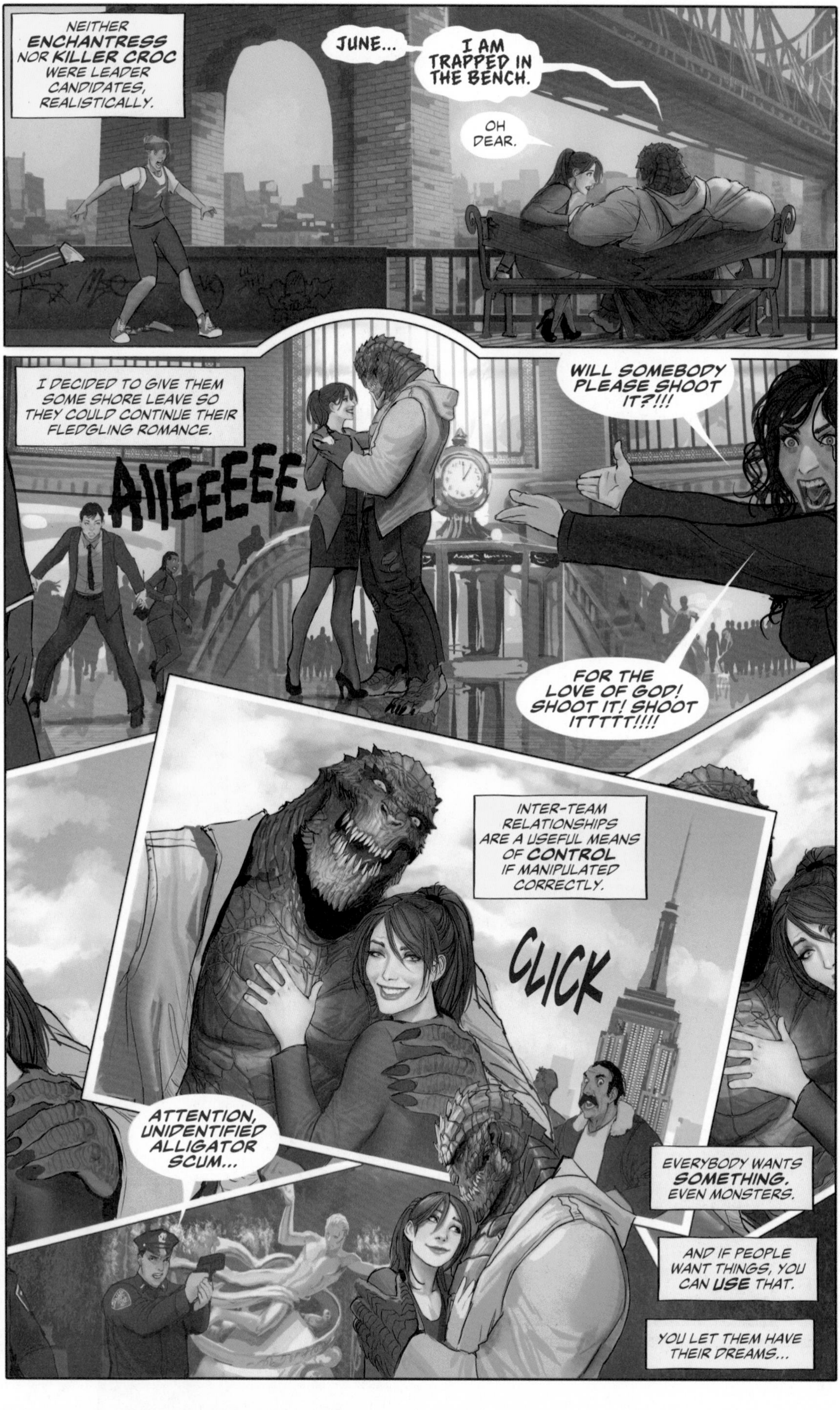
NEITHER ENCHANTRESS NOR KILLER CROC WERE LEADER CANDIDATES, REALISTICALLY.
JUNE...
I AM TRAPPED IN THE BENCH.
OH DEAR.
I DECIDED TO GIVE THEM SOME SHORE LEAVE SO THEY COULD CONTINUE THEIR FLEDGLING ROMANCE.
WILL SOMEBODY PLEASE SHOOT IT?!!!
AIIEEEEE
FOR THE LOVE OF GOD! SHOOT IT! SHOOT ITTTTT!!!!
INTER-TEAM RELATIONSHIPS ARE A USEFUL MEANS OF CONTROL IF MANIPULATED CORRECTLY.
CLICK
ATTENTION, UNIDENTIFIED ALLIGATOR SCUM...
EVERYBODY WANTS SOMETHING. EVEN MONSTERS.
AND IF PEOPLE WANT THINGS, YOU CAN USE THAT.
YOU LET THEM HAVE THEIR DREAMS...

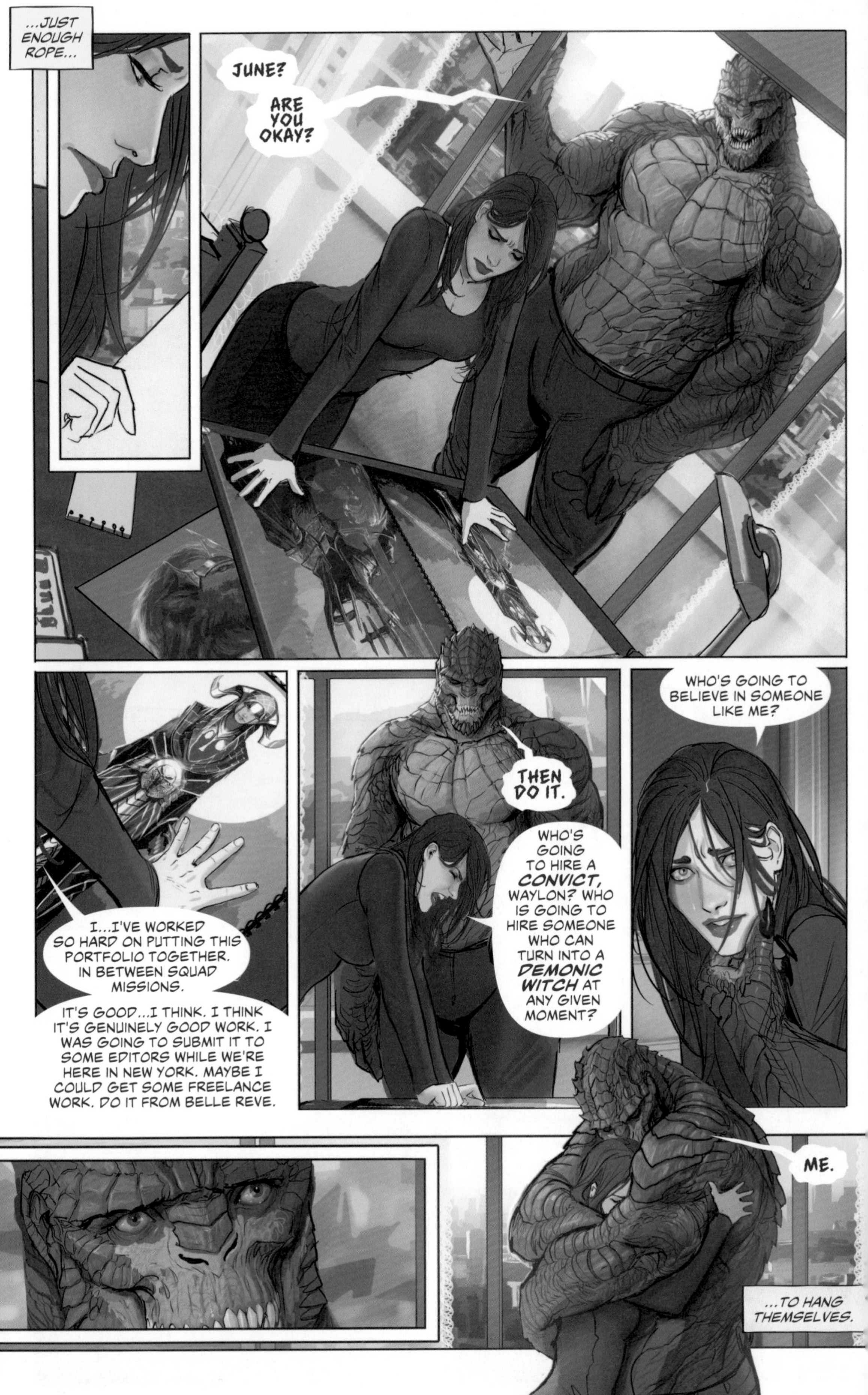
...JUST ENOUGH ROPE...
JUNE?
ARE YOU OKAY?
I...I'VE WORKED SO HARD ON PUTTING THIS PORTFOLIO TOGETHER. IN BETWEEN SQUAD MISSIONS.
IT'S GOOD...I THINK. I THINK IT'S GENUINELY GOOD WORK. I WAS GOING TO SUBMIT IT TO SOME EDITORS WHILE WE'RE HERE IN NEW YORK. MAYBE I COULD GET SOME FREELANCE WORK. DO IT FROM BELLE REVE.
THEN DO IT.
WHO'S GOING TO HIRE A CONVICT, WAYLON? WHO IS GOING TO HIRE SOMEONE WHO CAN TURN INTO A DEMONIC WITCH AT ANY GIVEN MOMENT?
WHO'S GOING TO BELIEVE IN SOMEONE LIKE ME?
ME.
...TO HANG THEMSELVES.

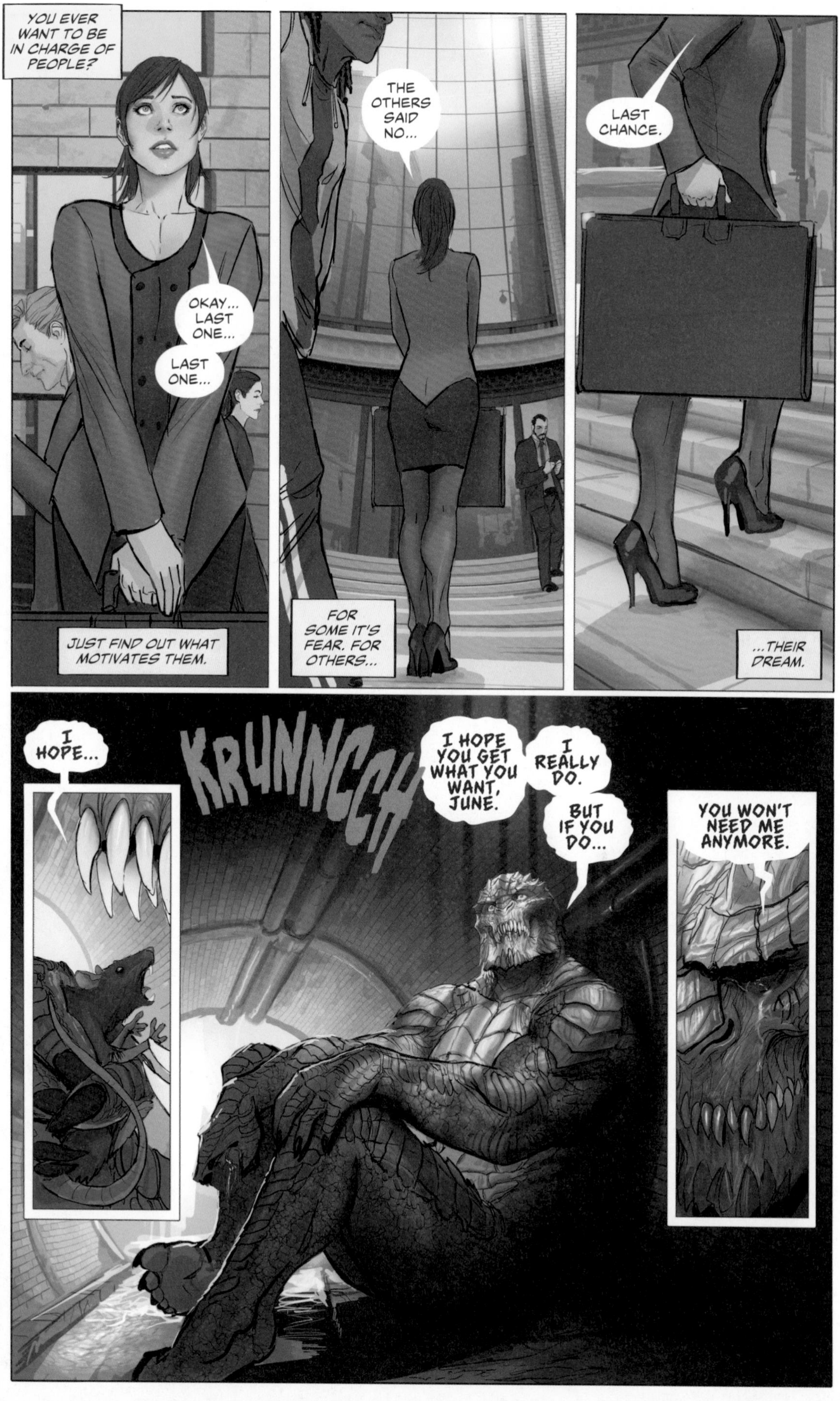
YOU EVER WANT TO BE IN CHARGE OF PEOPLE?
OKAY... LAST ONE...
LAST ONE...
JUST FIND OUT WHAT MOTIVATES THEM.
THE OTHERS SAID NO...
FOR SOME IT'S FEAR. FOR OTHERS...
LAST CHANCE.
...THEIR DREAM.
I HOPE...
KRUNNCCH
I HOPE YOU GET WHAT YOU WANT, JUNE.
I REALLY DO.
BUT IF YOU DO...
YOU WON'T NEED ME ANYMORE.

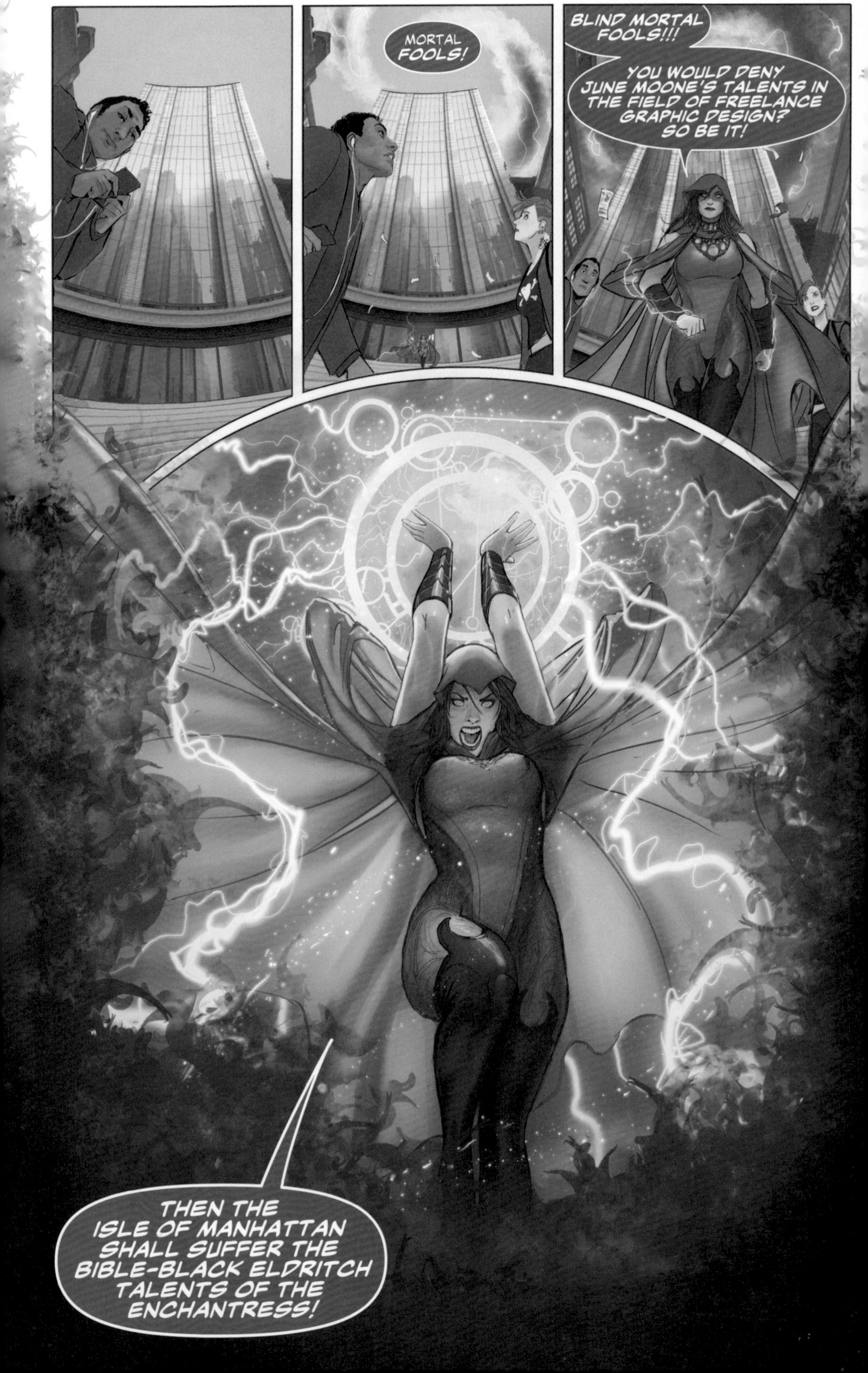
MORTAL FOOLS!
BLIND MORTAL FOOLS!!!
YOU WOULD DENY JUNE MOONE'S TALENTS IN THE FIELD OF FREELANCE GRAPHIC DESIGN? SO BE IT!
THEN THE ISLE OF MANHATTAN SHALL SUFFER THE BIBLE-BLACK ELDRITCH TALENTS OF THE ENCHANTRESS!

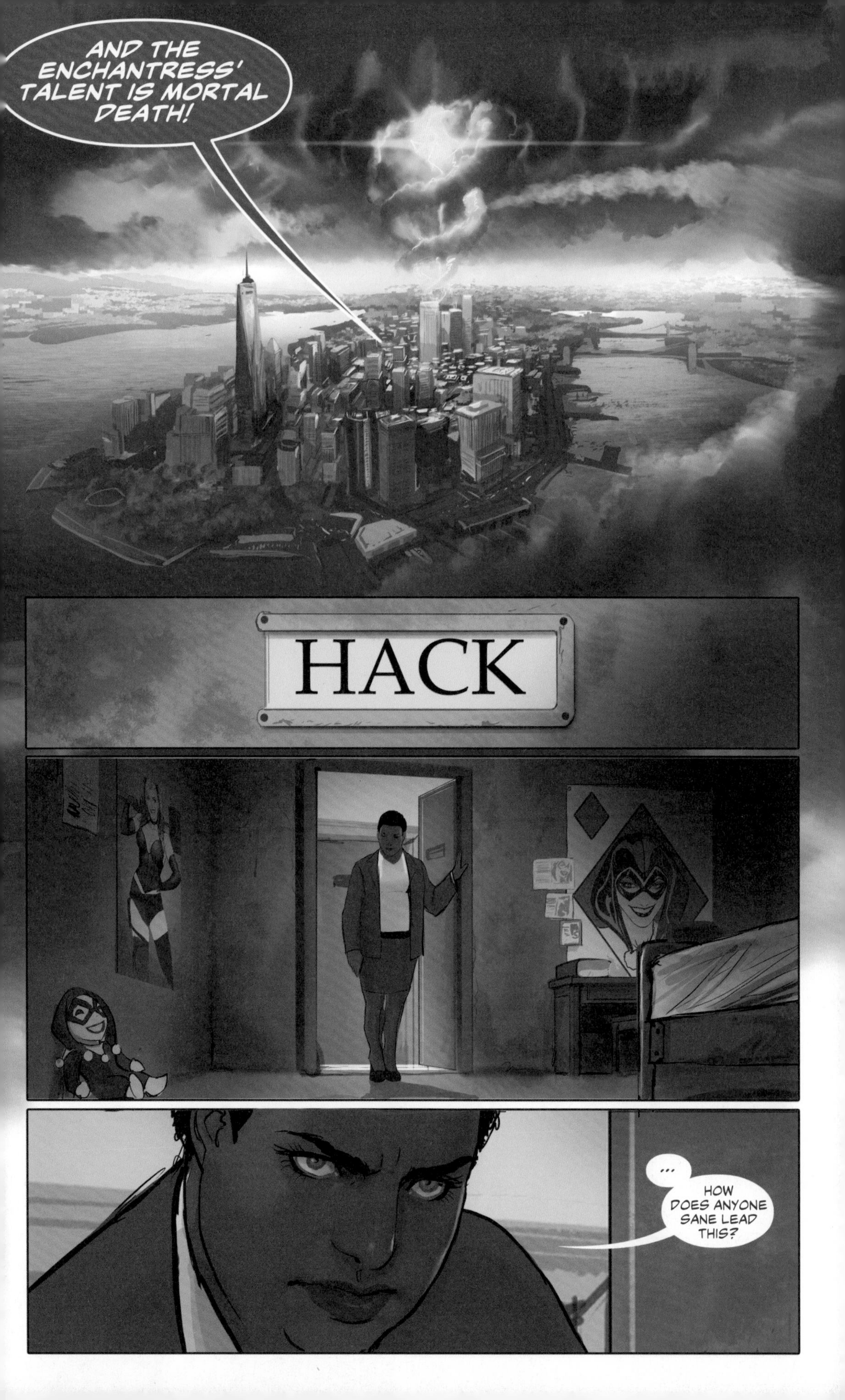
AND THE ENCHANTRESS' TALENT IS MORTAL DEATH!
HACK
...
HOW DOES ANYONE SANE LEAD THIS?

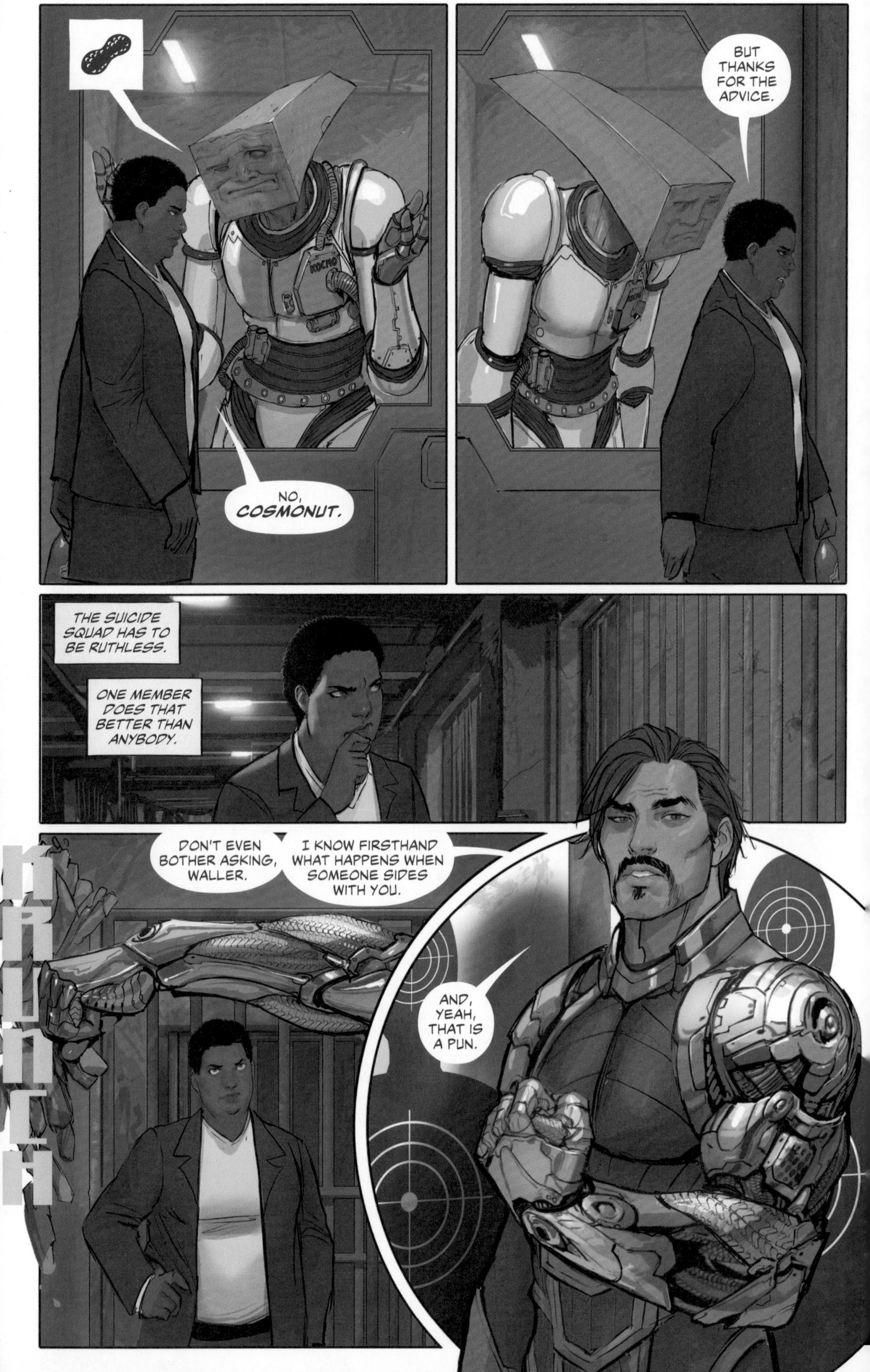
NO, COSMONUT.
BUT THANKS FOR THE ADVICE.
THE SUICIDE SQUAD HAS TO BE RUTHLESS.
ONE MEMBER DOES THAT BETTER THAN ANYBODY.
KRUNCH
DON'T EVEN BOTHER ASKING, WALLER.
I KNOW FIRSTHAND WHAT HAPPENS WHEN SOMEONE SIDES WITH YOU.
AND, YEAH, THAT IS A PUN.

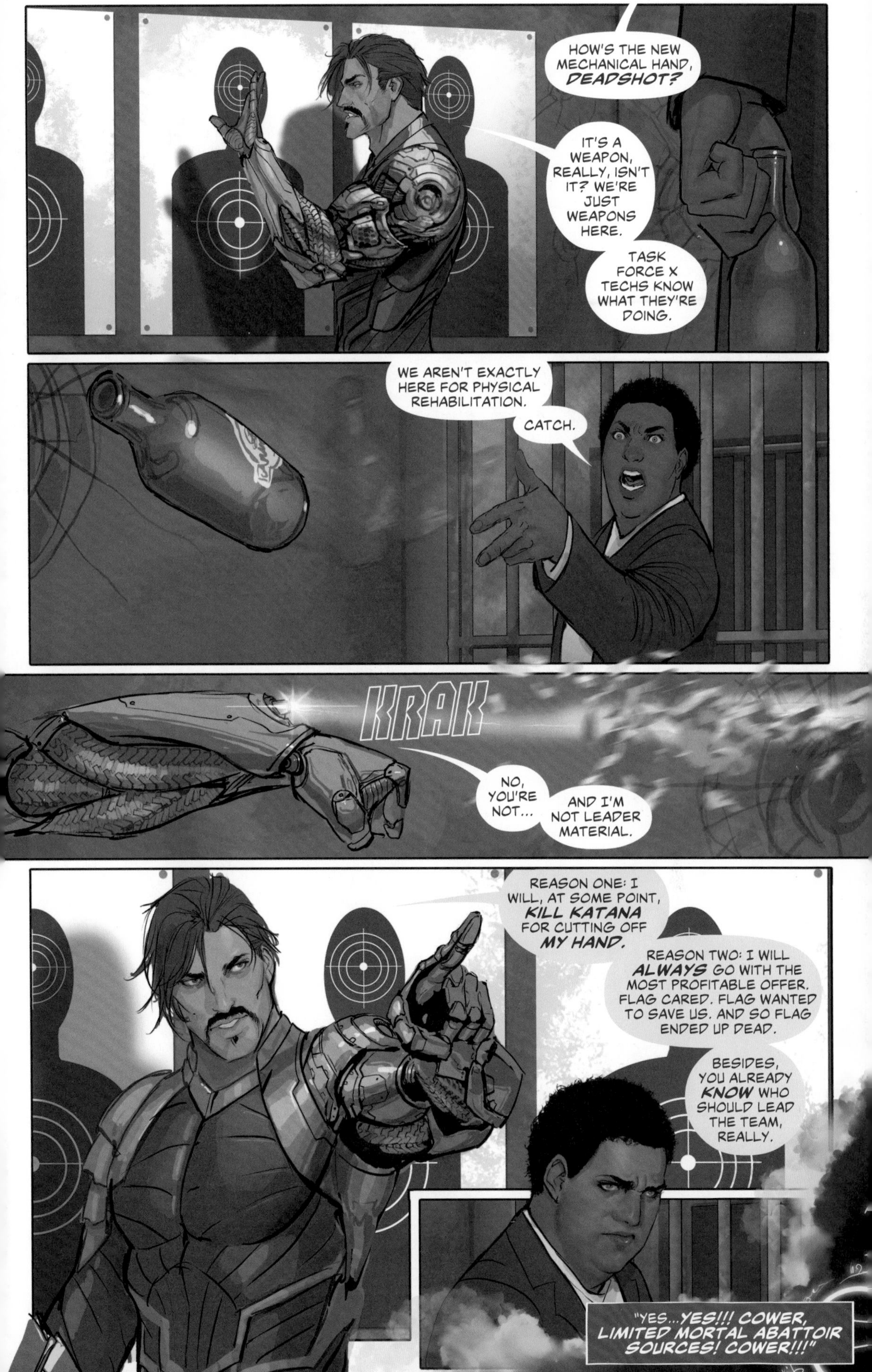
HOW'S THE NEW MECHANICAL HAND, DEADSHOT?
IT'S A WEAPON, REALLY, ISN'T IT? WE'RE JUST WEAPONS HERE.
TASK FORCE X TECHS KNOW WHAT THEY'RE DOING.
WE AREN'T EXACTLY HERE FOR PHYSICAL REHABILITATION.
CATCH.
KRAK
NO, YOU'RE NOT...
AND I'M NOT LEADER MATERIAL.
REASON ONE: I WILL, AT SOME POINT, KILL KATANA FOR CUTTING OFF MY HAND.
REASON TWO: I WILL ALWAYS GO WITH THE MOST PROFITABLE OFFER. FLAG CARED. FLAG WANTED TO SAVE US. AND SO FLAG ENDED UP DEAD.
BESIDES, YOU ALREADY KNOW WHO SHOULD LEAD THE TEAM, REALLY.
"YES...YES!!! COWER, LIMITED MORTAL ABATTOIR SOURCES! COWER!!!"

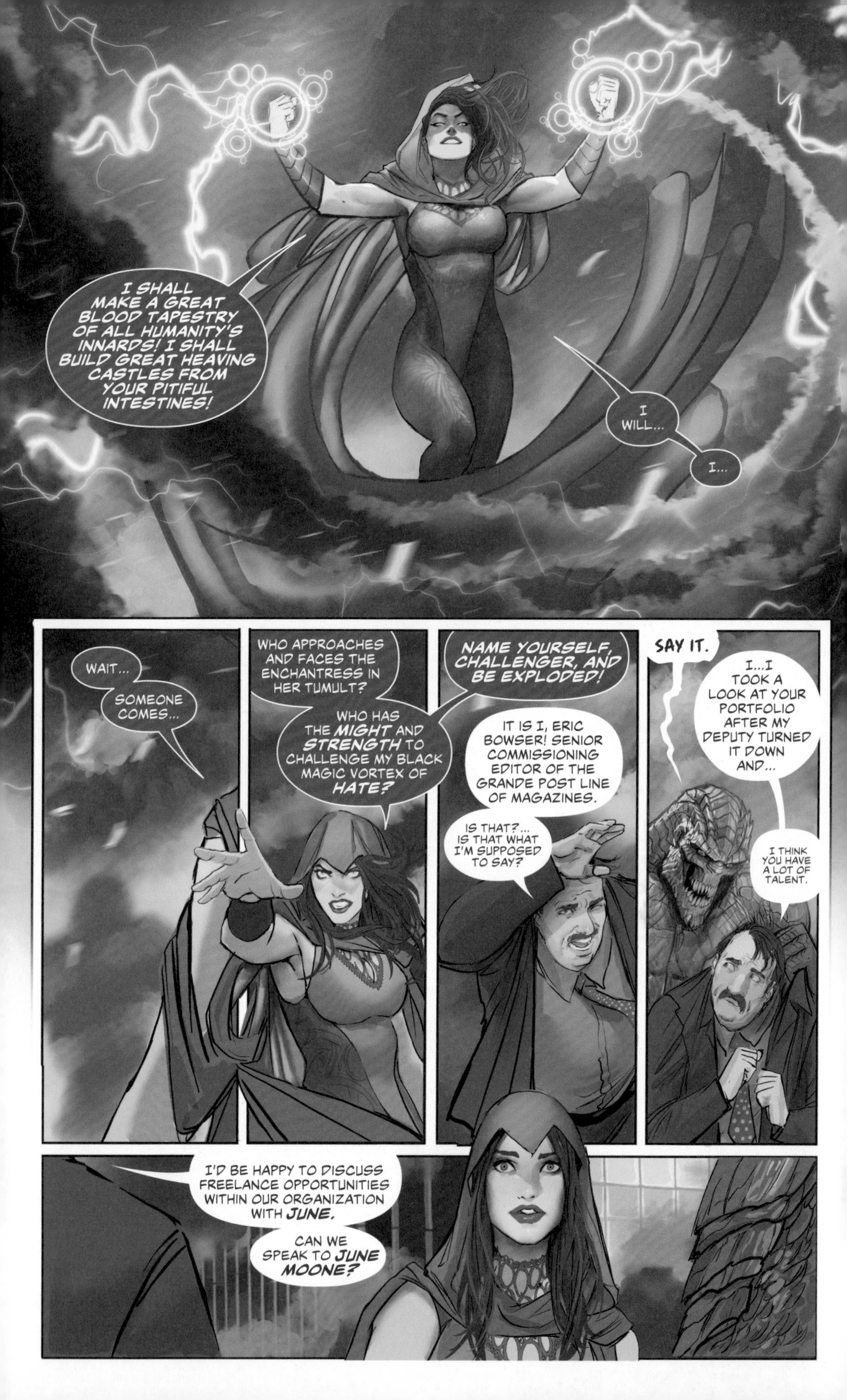
I SHALL MAKE A GREAT BLOOD TAPESTRY OF ALL HUMANITY'S INNARDS! I SHALL BUILD GREAT HEAVING CASTLES FROM YOUR PITIFUL INTESTINES!
I WILL...
I...
WAIT...
SOMEONE COMES...
WHO APPROACHES AND FACES THE ENCHANTRESS IN HER TUMULT?
WHO HAS THE MIGHT AND STRENGTH TO CHALLENGE MY BLACK MAGIC VORTEX OF HATE?
NAME YOURSELF, CHALLENGER, AND BE EXPLODED!
IT IS I, ERIC BOWSER! SENIOR COMMISSIONING EDITOR OF THE GRANDE POST LINE OF MAGAZINES.
IS THAT?... IS THAT WHAT I'M SUPPOSED TO SAY?
SAY IT.
I...I TOOK A LOOK AT YOUR PORTFOLIO AFTER MY DEPUTY TURNED IT DOWN AND...
I THINK YOU HAVE A LOT OF TALENT.
I'D BE HAPPY TO DISCUSS FREELANCE OPPORTUNITIES WITHIN OUR ORGANIZATION WITH JUNE.
CAN WE SPEAK TO JUNE MOONE?

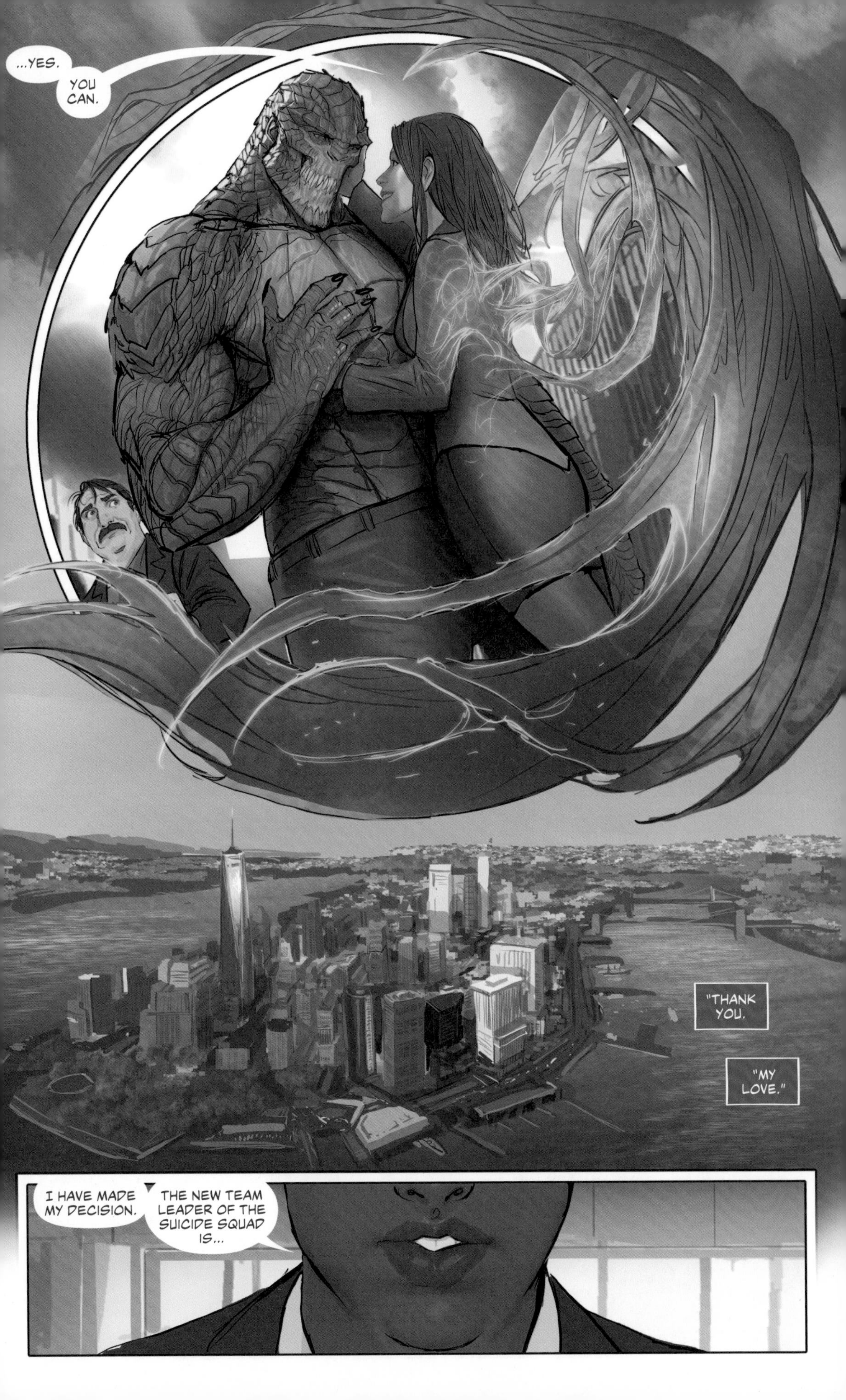
...YES. YOU CAN.
"THANK YOU.
"MY LOVE."
I HAVE MADE MY DECISION.
THE NEW TEAM LEADER OF THE SUICIDE SQUAD IS...

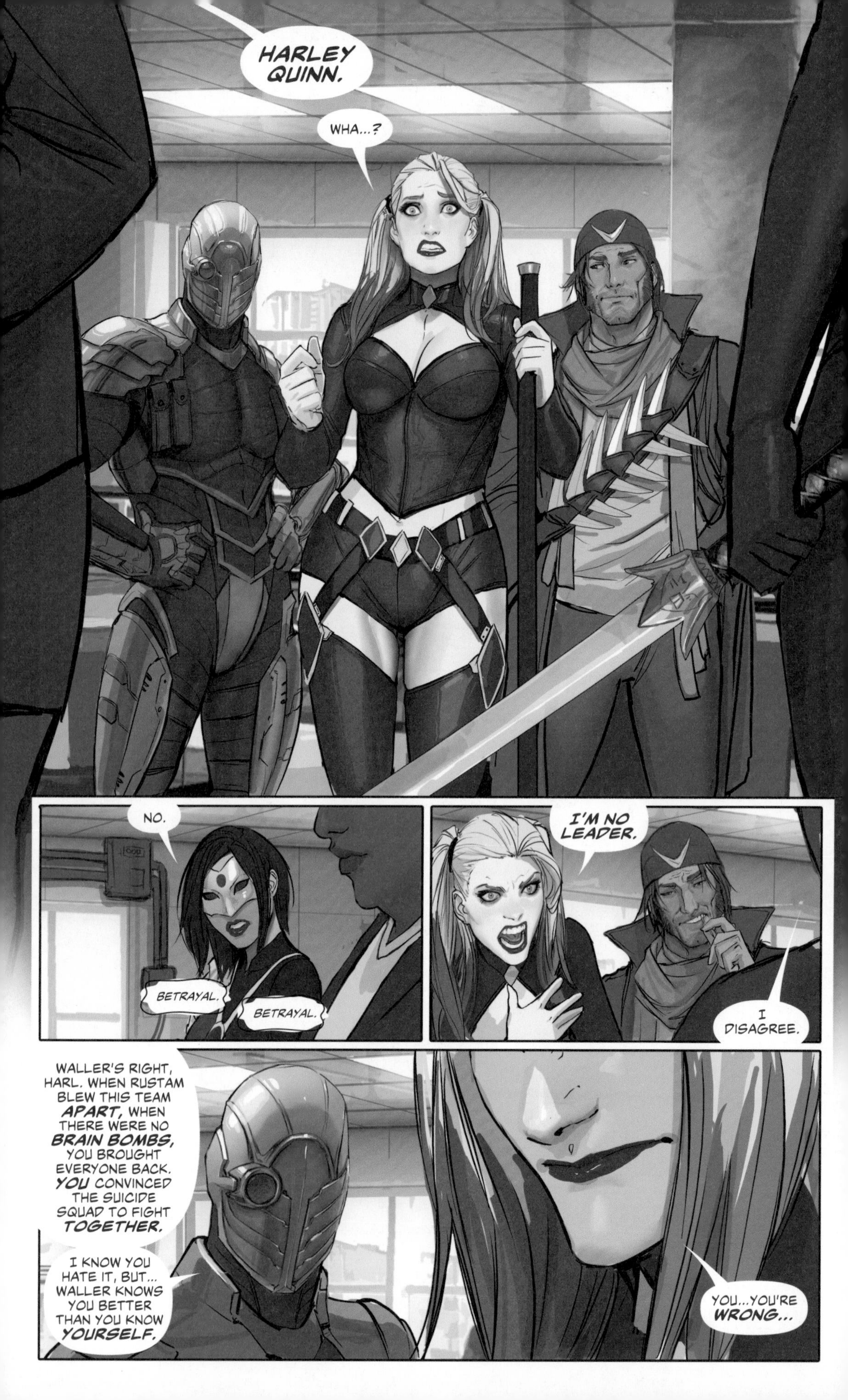

HARLEY QUINN.
WHA...?
NO.
BETRAYAL.
BETRAYAL.
I'M NO LEADER.
I DISAGREE.
WALLER'S RIGHT, HARL. WHEN RUSTAM BLEW THIS TEAM APART, WHEN THERE WERE NO BRAIN BOMBS, YOU BROUGHT EVERYONE BACK. YOU CONVINCED THE SUICIDE SQUAD TO FIGHT TOGETHER.
I KNOW YOU HATE IT, BUT... WALLER KNOWS YOU BETTER THAN YOU KNOW YOURSELF.
YOU...YOU'RE WRONG...

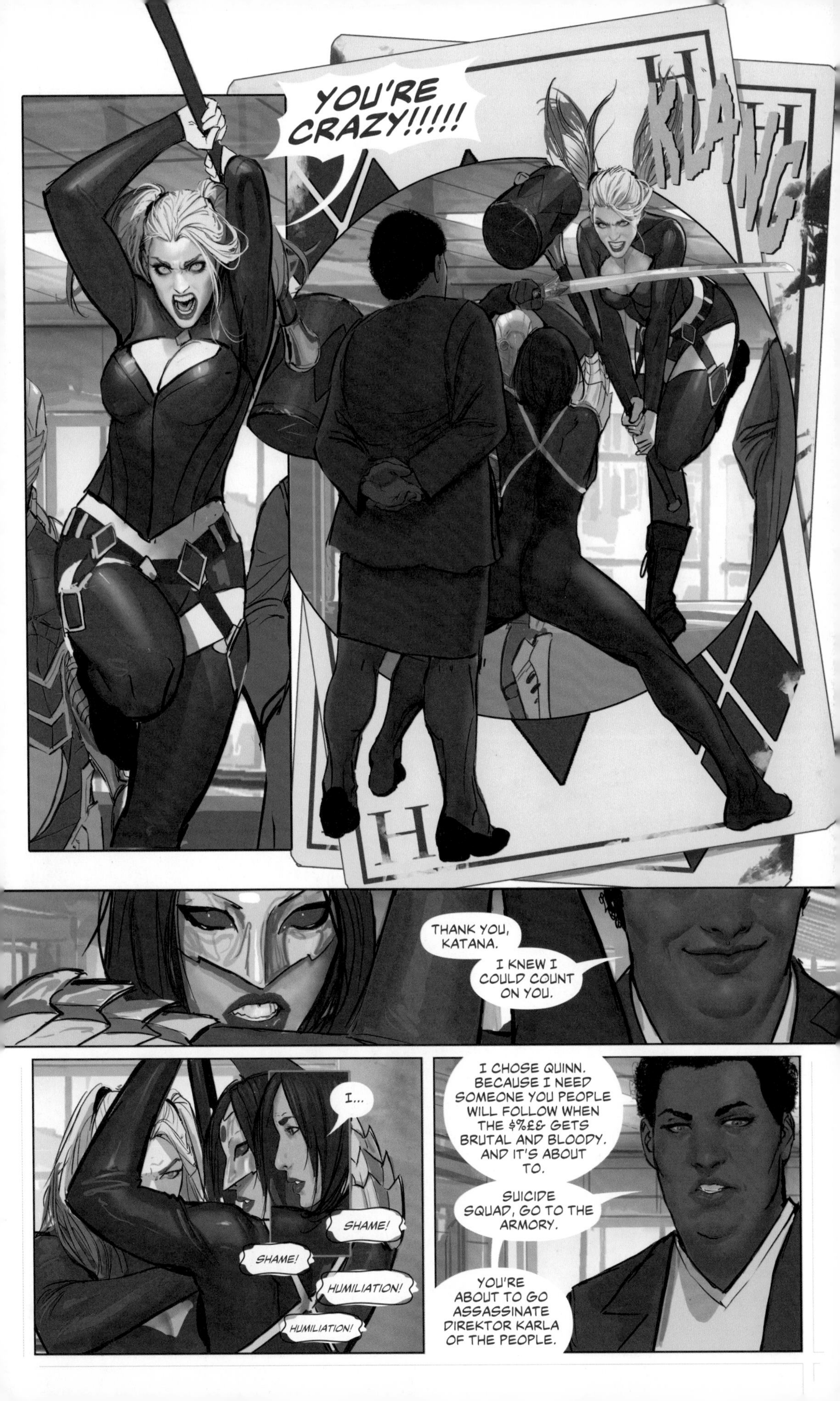
YOU'RE CRAZY!!!!!
KLANG
THANK YOU, KATANA.
I KNEW I COULD COUNT ON YOU.
I...
SHAME!
SHAME!
HUMILIATION!
HUMILIATION!
I CHOSE QUINN. BECAUSE I NEED SOMEONE YOU PEOPLE WILL FOLLOW WHEN THE $%£& GETS BRUTAL AND BLOODY. AND IT'S ABOUT TO.
SUICIDE SQUAD, GO TO THE ARMORY.
YOU'RE ABOUT TO GO ASSASSINATE DIREKTOR KARLA OF THE PEOPLE.

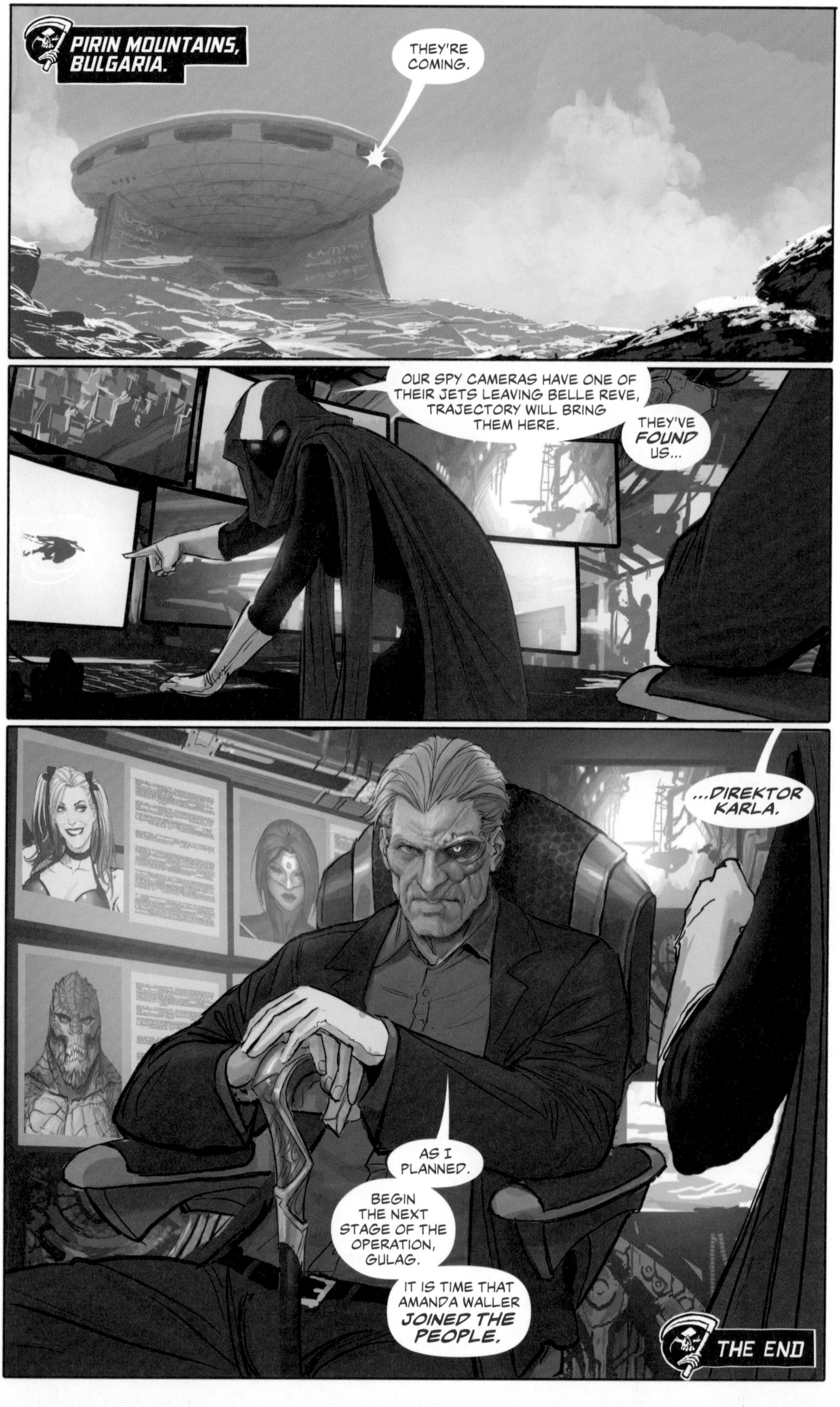
PIRIN MOUNTAINS, BULGARIA.
THEY'RE COMING.
OUR SPY CAMERAS HAVE ONE OF THEIR JETS LEAVING BELLE REVE, TRAJECTORY WILL BRING THEM HERE.
THEY'VE FOUND US...
...DIREKTOR KARLA.
AS I PLANNED.
BEGIN THE NEXT STAGE OF THE OPERATION, GULAG.
IT IS TIME THAT AMANDA WALLER JOINED THE PEOPLE.
THE END

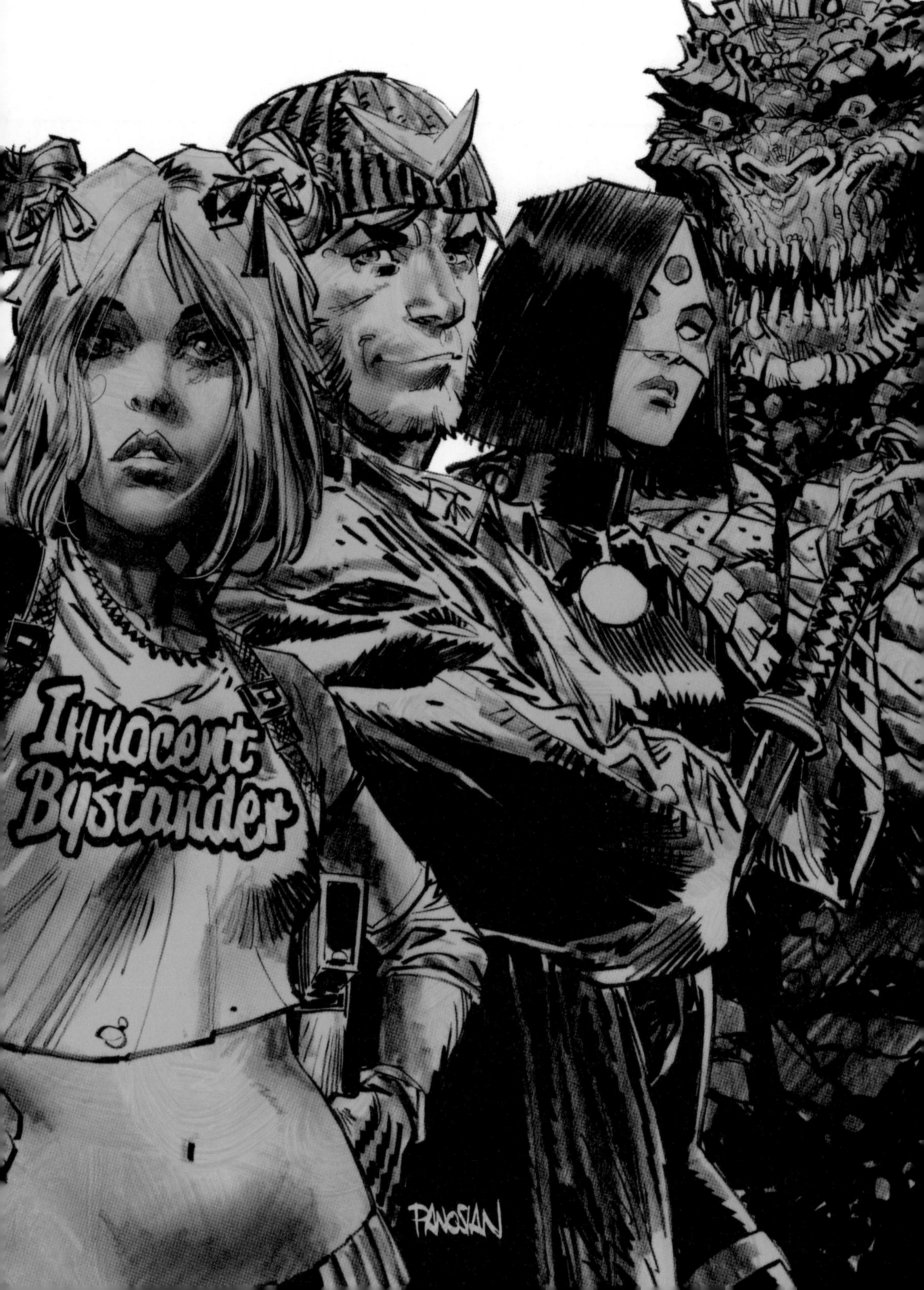
Innocent Bystander
PANOSIAN

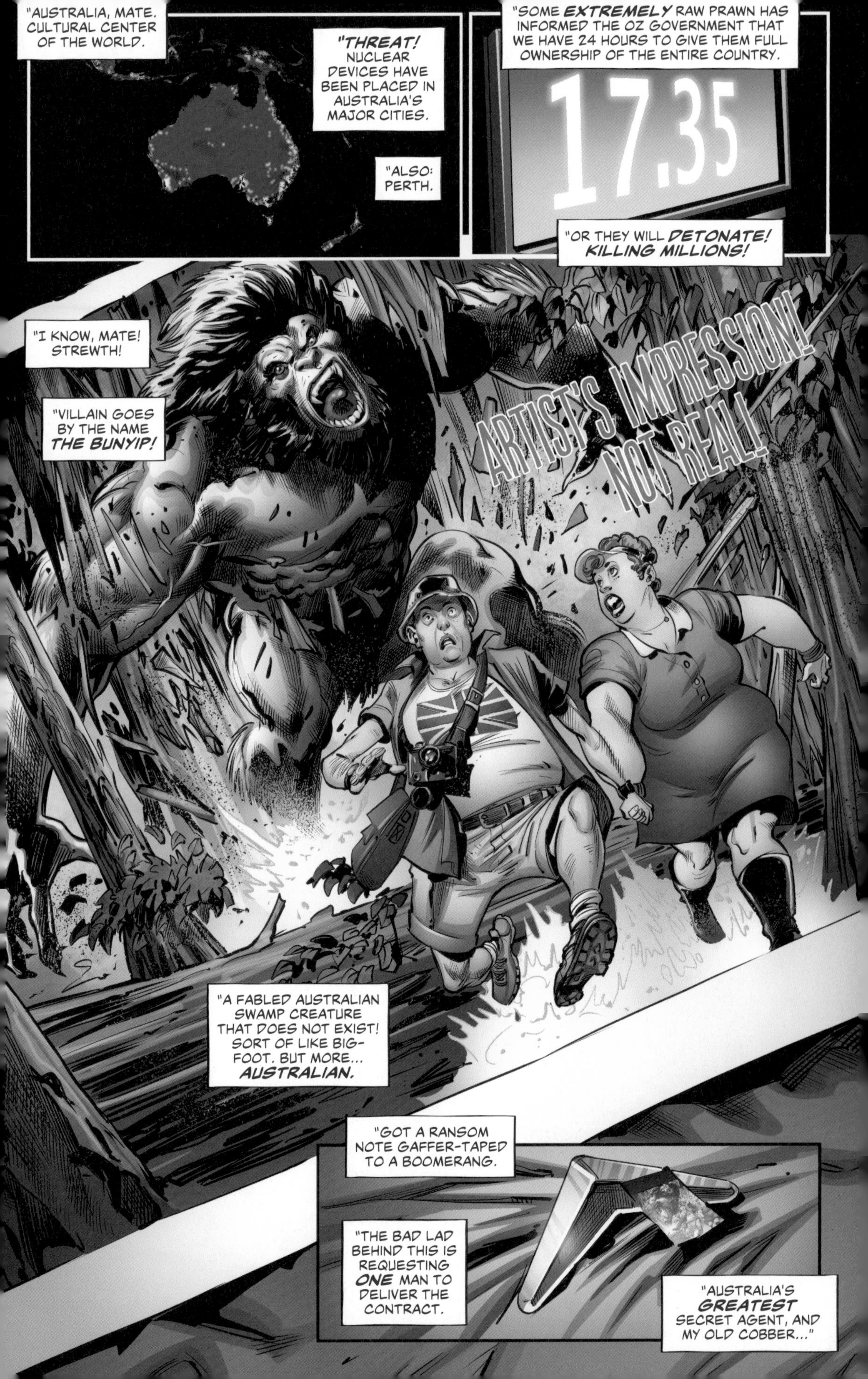
"AUSTRALIA, MATE. CULTURAL CENTER OF THE WORLD.
"THREAT! NUCLEAR DEVICES HAVE BEEN PLACED IN AUSTRALIA'S MAJOR CITIES.
"ALSO: PERTH.
"SOME EXTREMELY RAW PRAWN HAS INFORMED THE OZ GOVERNMENT THAT WE HAVE 24 HOURS TO GIVE THEM FULL OWNERSHIP OF THE ENTIRE COUNTRY.
17.35
"OR THEY WILL DETONATE! KILLING MILLIONS!
"I KNOW, MATE! STREWTH!
"VILLAIN GOES BY THE NAME THE BUNYIP!
ARTIST'S IMPRESSION! NOT REAL!
"A FABLED AUSTRALIAN SWAMP CREATURE THAT DOES NOT EXIST! SORT OF LIKE BIG-FOOT. BUT MORE... AUSTRALIAN.
"GOT A RANSOM NOTE GAFFER-TAPED TO A BOOMERANG.
"THE BAD LAD BEHIND THIS IS REQUESTING ONE MAN TO DELIVER THE CONTRACT.
"AUSTRALIA'S GREATEST SECRET AGENT, AND MY OLD COBBER..."

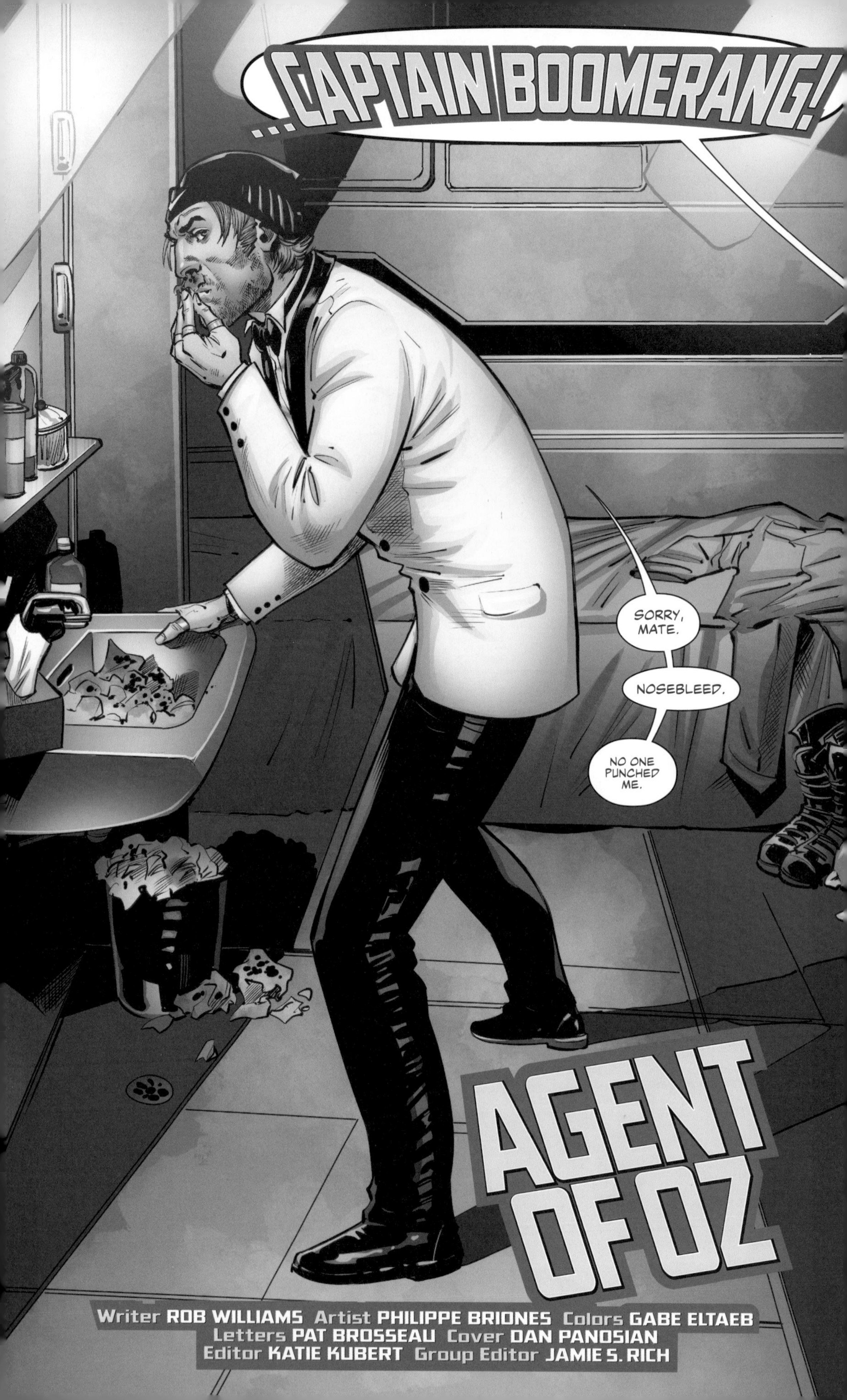
...CAPTAIN BOOMERANG!
SORRY, MATE.
NOSEBLEED.
NO ONE PUNCHED ME.
AGENT OF OZ
Writer ROB WILLIAMS Artist PHILIPPE BRIONES Colors GABE ELTAEB
Letters PAT BROSSEAU Cover DAN PANOSIAN
Editor KATIE KUBERT Group Editor JAMIE S. RICH

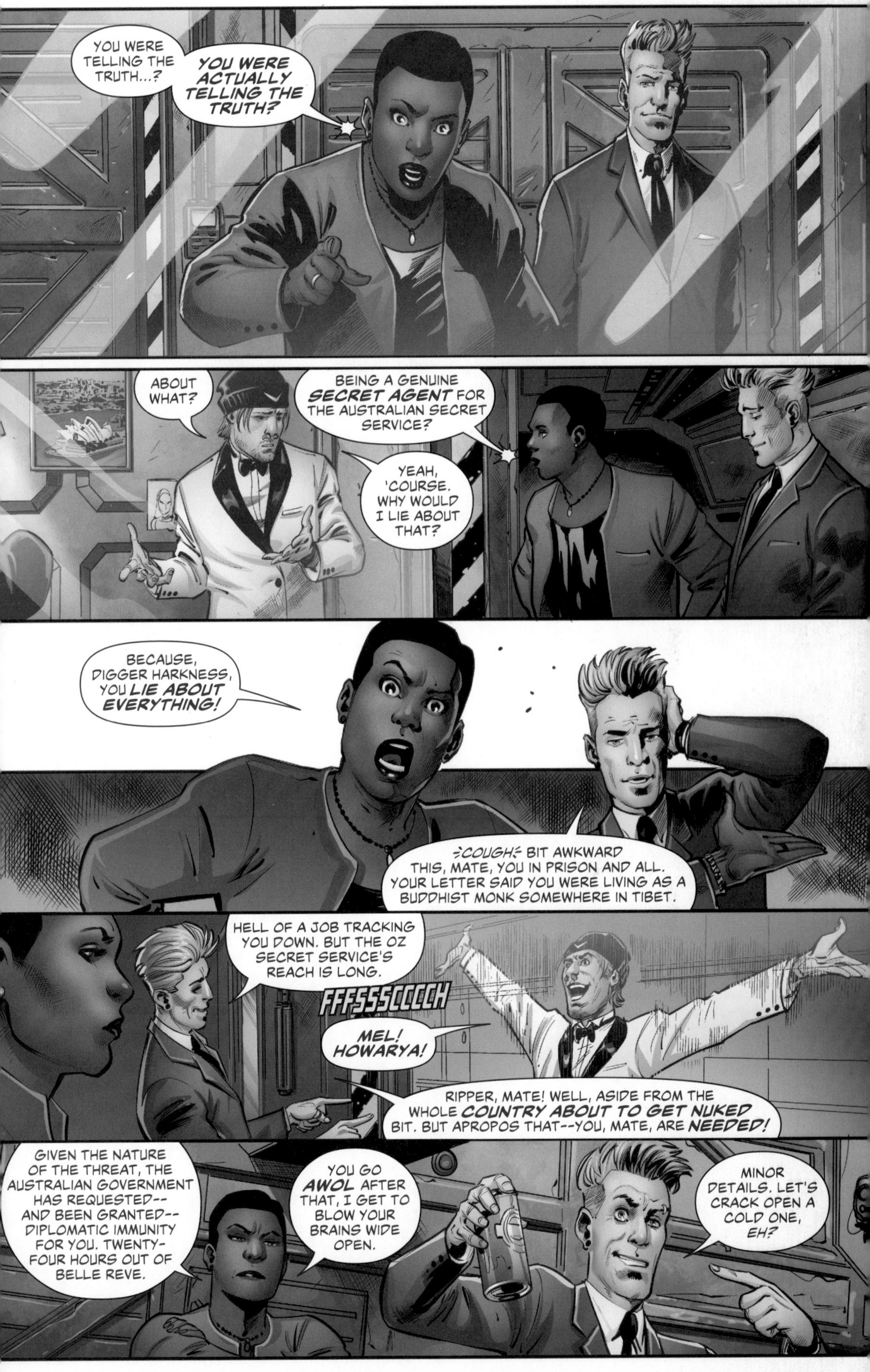
YOU WERE TELLING THE TRUTH...?
YOU WERE ACTUALLY TELLING THE TRUTH?
ABOUT WHAT?
BEING A GENUINE SECRET AGENT FOR THE AUSTRALIAN SECRET SERVICE?
YEAH, 'COURSE. WHY WOULD I LIE ABOUT THAT?
BECAUSE, DIGGER HARKNESS, YOU LIE ABOUT EVERYTHING!
=COUGH= BIT AWKWARD THIS, MATE, YOU IN PRISON AND ALL. YOUR LETTER SAID YOU WERE LIVING AS A BUDDHIST MONK SOMEWHERE IN TIBET.
HELL OF A JOB TRACKING YOU DOWN. BUT THE OZ SECRET SERVICE'S REACH IS LONG.
FFFSSSCCCCH
MEL! HOWARYA!
RIPPER, MATE! WELL, ASIDE FROM THE WHOLE COUNTRY ABOUT TO GET NUKED BIT. BUT APROPOS THAT--YOU, MATE, ARE NEEDED!
GIVEN THE NATURE OF THE THREAT, THE AUSTRALIAN GOVERNMENT HAS REQUESTED-- AND BEEN GRANTED-- DIPLOMATIC IMMUNITY FOR YOU. TWENTY-FOUR HOURS OUT OF BELLE REVE.
YOU GO AWOL AFTER THAT, I GET TO BLOW YOUR BRAINS WIDE OPEN.
MINOR DETAILS. LET'S CRACK OPEN A COLD ONE, EH?

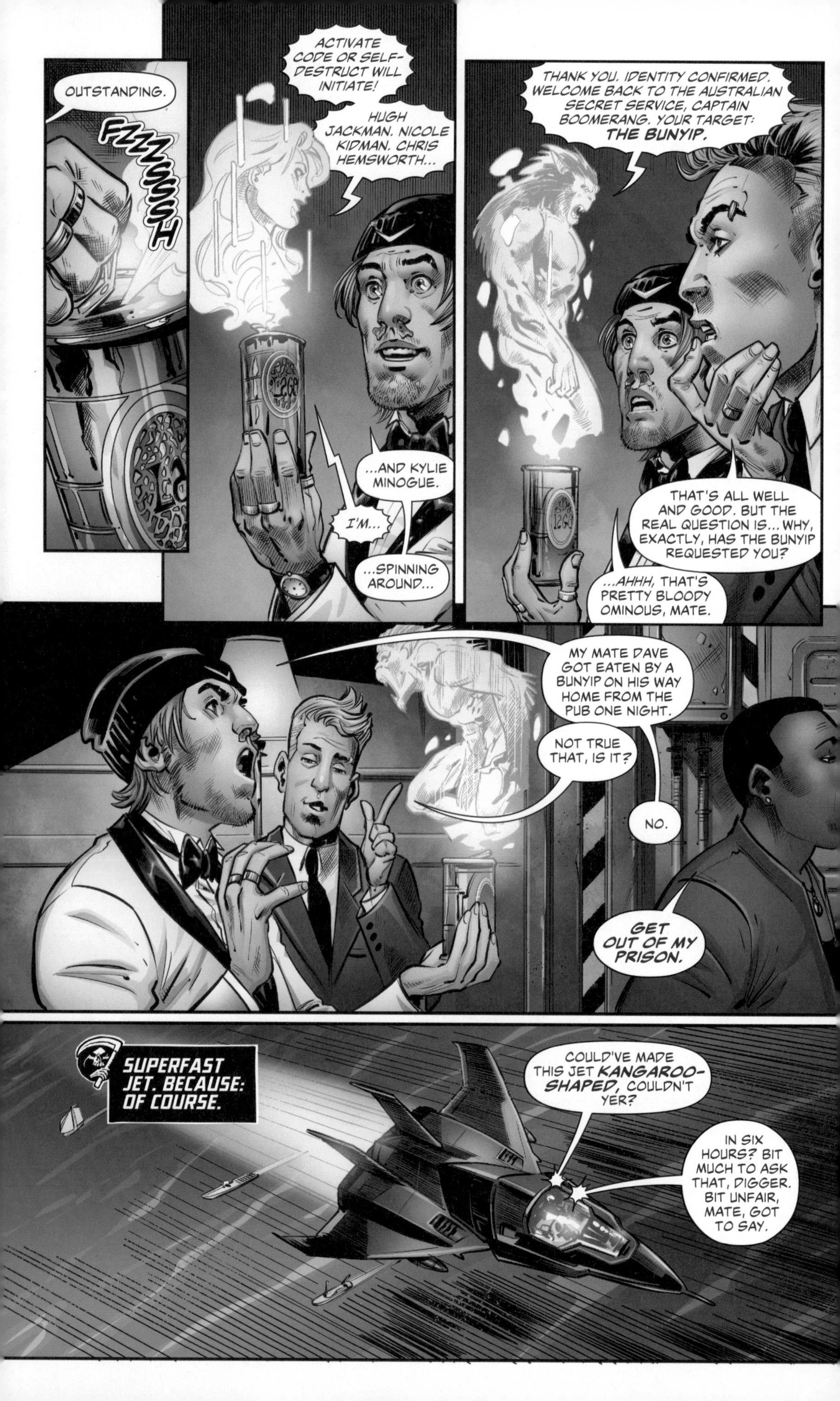
OUTSTANDING.
FZZZSSSH
ACTIVATE CODE OR SELF-DESTRUCT WILL INITIATE!
HUGH JACKMAN. NICOLE KIDMAN. CHRIS HEMSWORTH...
...AND KYLIE MINOGUE.
I'M...
...SPINNING AROUND...
THANK YOU. IDENTITY CONFIRMED. WELCOME BACK TO THE AUSTRALIAN SECRET SERVICE, CAPTAIN BOOMERANG. YOUR TARGET: THE BUNYIP.
THAT'S ALL WELL AND GOOD. BUT THE REAL QUESTION IS... WHY, EXACTLY, HAS THE BUNYIP REQUESTED YOU?
...AHHH, THAT'S PRETTY BLOODY OMINOUS, MATE.
MY MATE DAVE GOT EATEN BY A BUNYIP ON HIS WAY HOME FROM THE PUB ONE NIGHT.
NOT TRUE THAT, IS IT?
NO.
GET OUT OF MY PRISON.
SUPERFAST JET. BECAUSE: OF COURSE.
COULD'VE MADE THIS JET KANGAROO-SHAPED, COULDN'T YER?
IN SIX HOURS? BIT MUCH TO ASK THAT, DIGGER. BIT UNFAIR, MATE, GOT TO SAY.

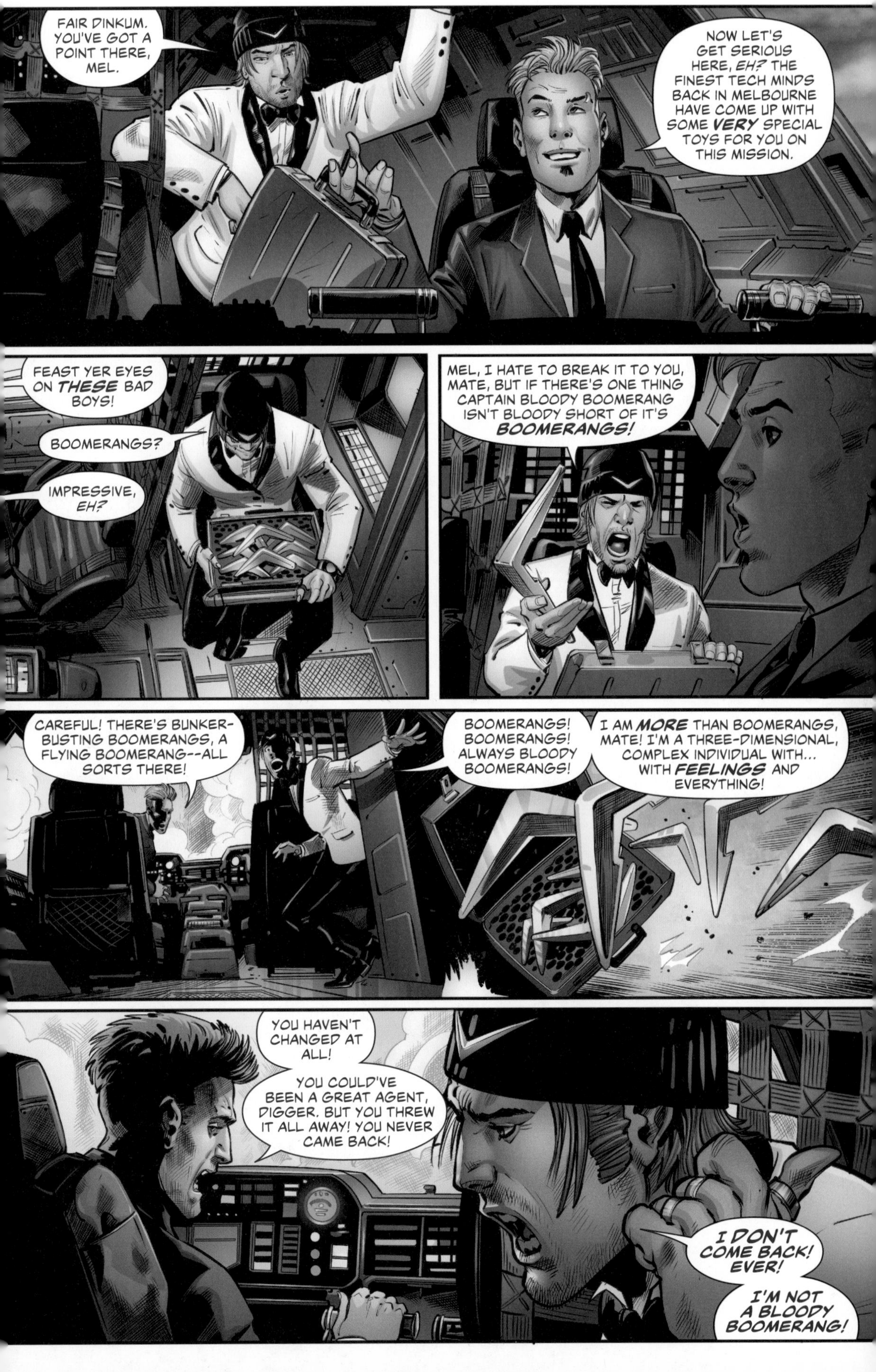
FAIR DINKUM. YOU'VE GOT A POINT THERE, MEL.
NOW LET'S GET SERIOUS HERE, EH? THE FINEST TECH MINDS BACK IN MELBOURNE HAVE COME UP WITH SOME VERY SPECIAL TOYS FOR YOU ON THIS MISSION.
FEAST YER EYES ON THESE BAD BOYS!
BOOMERANGS?
IMPRESSIVE, EH?
MEL, I HATE TO BREAK IT TO YOU, MATE, BUT IF THERE'S ONE THING CAPTAIN BLOODY BOOMERANG ISN'T BLOODY SHORT OF IT'S BOOMERANGS!
CAREFUL! THERE'S BUNKER-BUSTING BOOMERANGS, A FLYING BOOMERANG--ALL SORTS THERE!
BOOMERANGS! BOOMERANGS! ALWAYS BLOODY BOOMERANGS!
I AM MORE THAN BOOMERANGS, MATE! I'M A THREE-DIMENSIONAL, COMPLEX INDIVIDUAL WITH... WITH FEELINGS AND EVERYTHING!
YOU HAVEN'T CHANGED AT ALL!
YOU COULD'VE BEEN A GREAT AGENT, DIGGER. BUT YOU THREW IT ALL AWAY! YOU NEVER CAME BACK!
I DON'T COME BACK! EVER!
I'M NOT A BLOODY BOOMERANG!

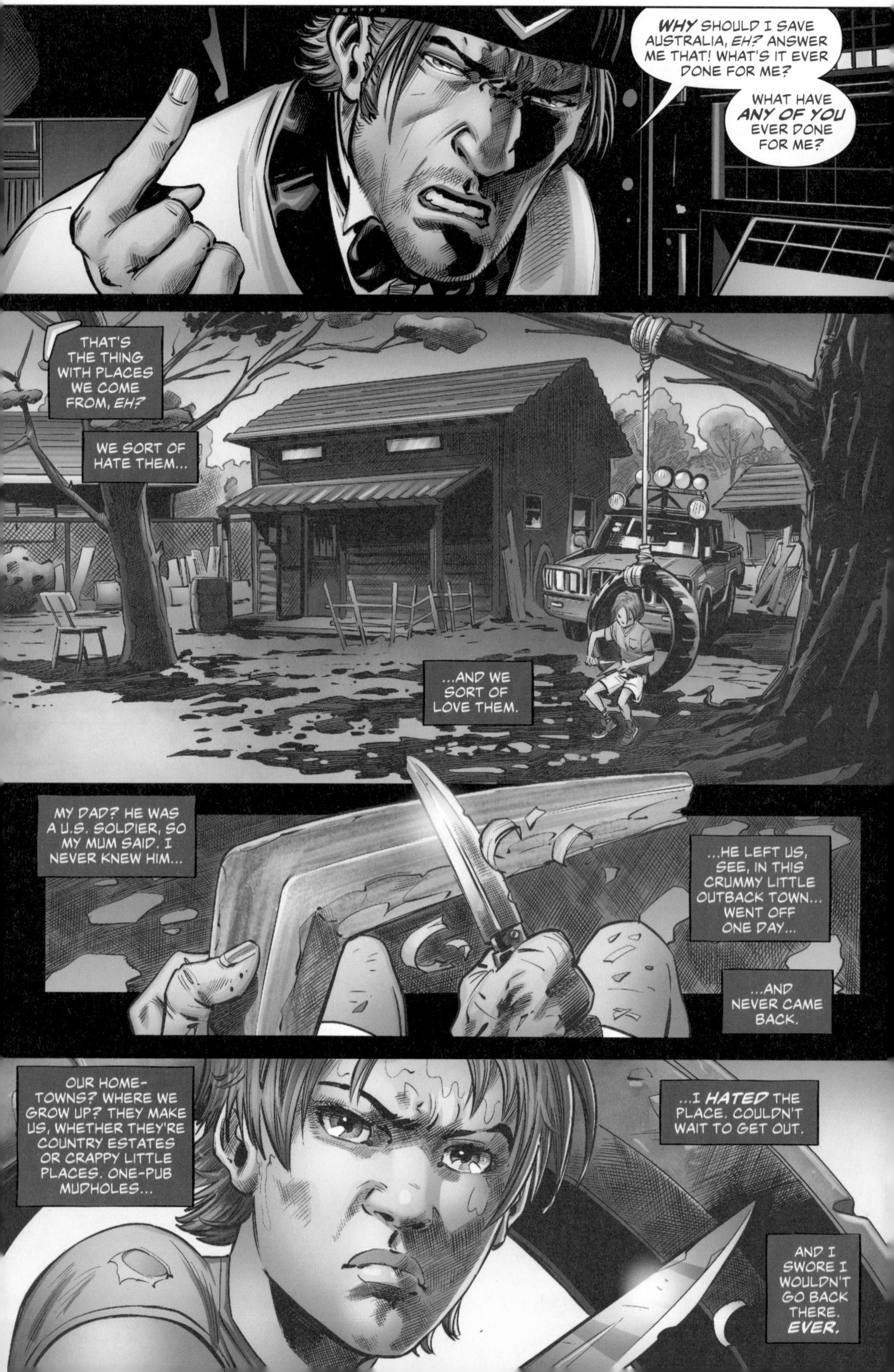
WHY SHOULD I SAVE AUSTRALIA, EH? ANSWER ME THAT! WHAT'S IT EVER DONE FOR ME?
WHAT HAVE ANY OF YOU EVER DONE FOR ME?
THAT'S THE THING WITH PLACES WE COME FROM, EH?
WE SORT OF HATE THEM...
...AND WE SORT OF LOVE THEM.
MY DAD? HE WAS A U.S. SOLDIER, SO MY MUM SAID. I NEVER KNEW HIM...
...HE LEFT US, SEE, IN THIS CRUMMY LITTLE OUTBACK TOWN... WENT OFF ONE DAY...
...AND NEVER CAME BACK.
OUR HOME-TOWNS? WHERE WE GROW UP? THEY MAKE US, WHETHER THEY'RE COUNTRY ESTATES OR CRAPPY LITTLE PLACES. ONE-PUB MUDHOLES...
...I HATED THE PLACE. COULDN'T WAIT TO GET OUT.
AND I SWORE I WOULDN'T GO BACK THERE. EVER.

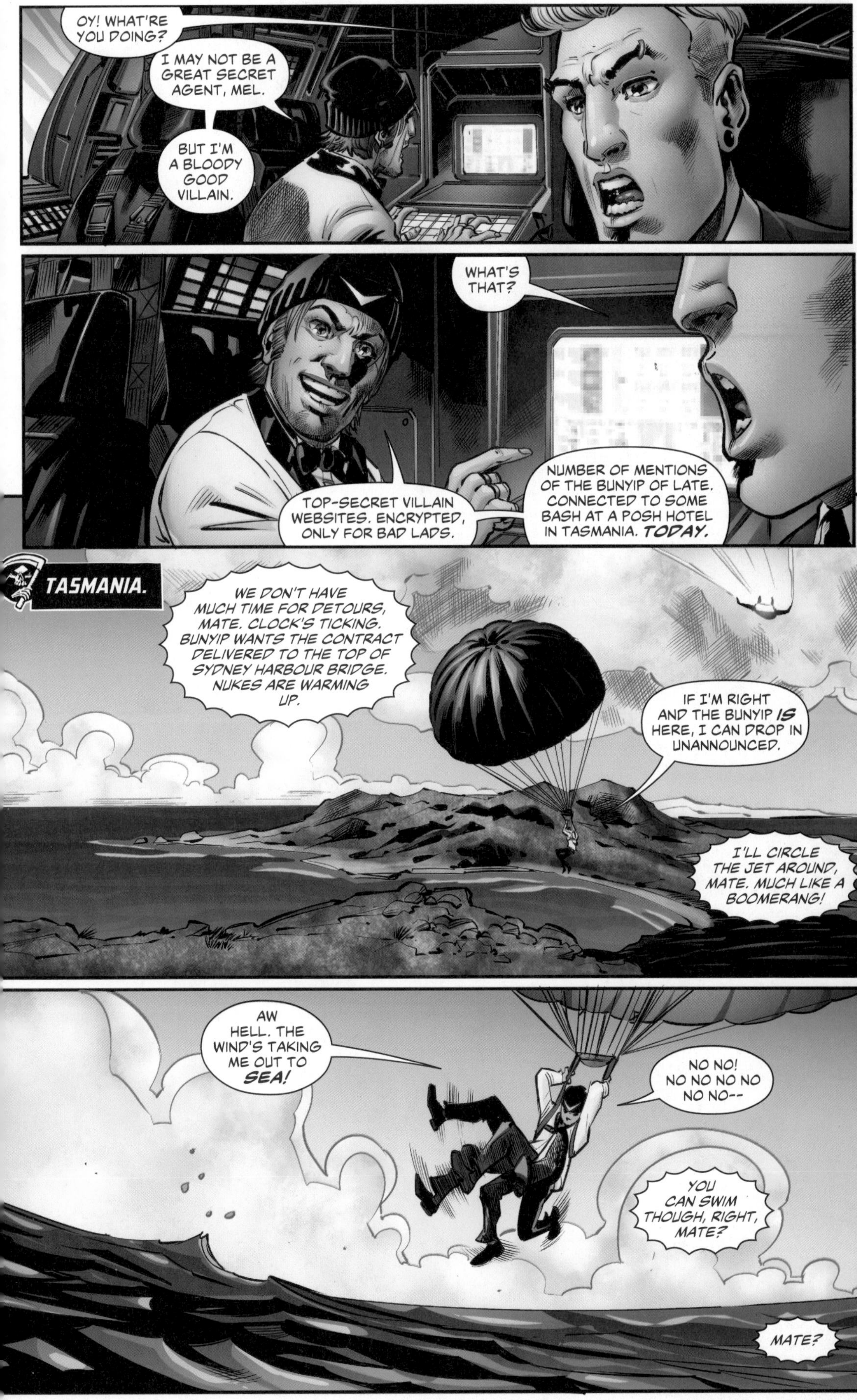
OY! WHAT'RE YOU DOING?
I MAY NOT BE A GREAT SECRET AGENT, MEL.
BUT I'M A BLOODY GOOD VILLAIN.
WHAT'S THAT?
TOP-SECRET VILLAIN WEBSITES. ENCRYPTED, ONLY FOR BAD LADS.
NUMBER OF MENTIONS OF THE BUNYIP OF LATE. CONNECTED TO SOME BASH AT A POSH HOTEL IN TASMANIA. TODAY.
TASMANIA.
WE DON'T HAVE MUCH TIME FOR DETOURS, MATE. CLOCK'S TICKING. BUNYIP WANTS THE CONTRACT DELIVERED TO THE TOP OF SYDNEY HARBOUR BRIDGE. NUKES ARE WARMING UP.
IF I'M RIGHT AND THE BUNYIP IS HERE, I CAN DROP IN UNANNOUNCED.
I'LL CIRCLE THE JET AROUND, MATE. MUCH LIKE A BOOMERANG!
AW HELL. THE WIND'S TAKING ME OUT TO SEA!
NO NO! NO NO NO NO NO NO--
YOU CAN SWIM THOUGH, RIGHT, MATE?
MATE?

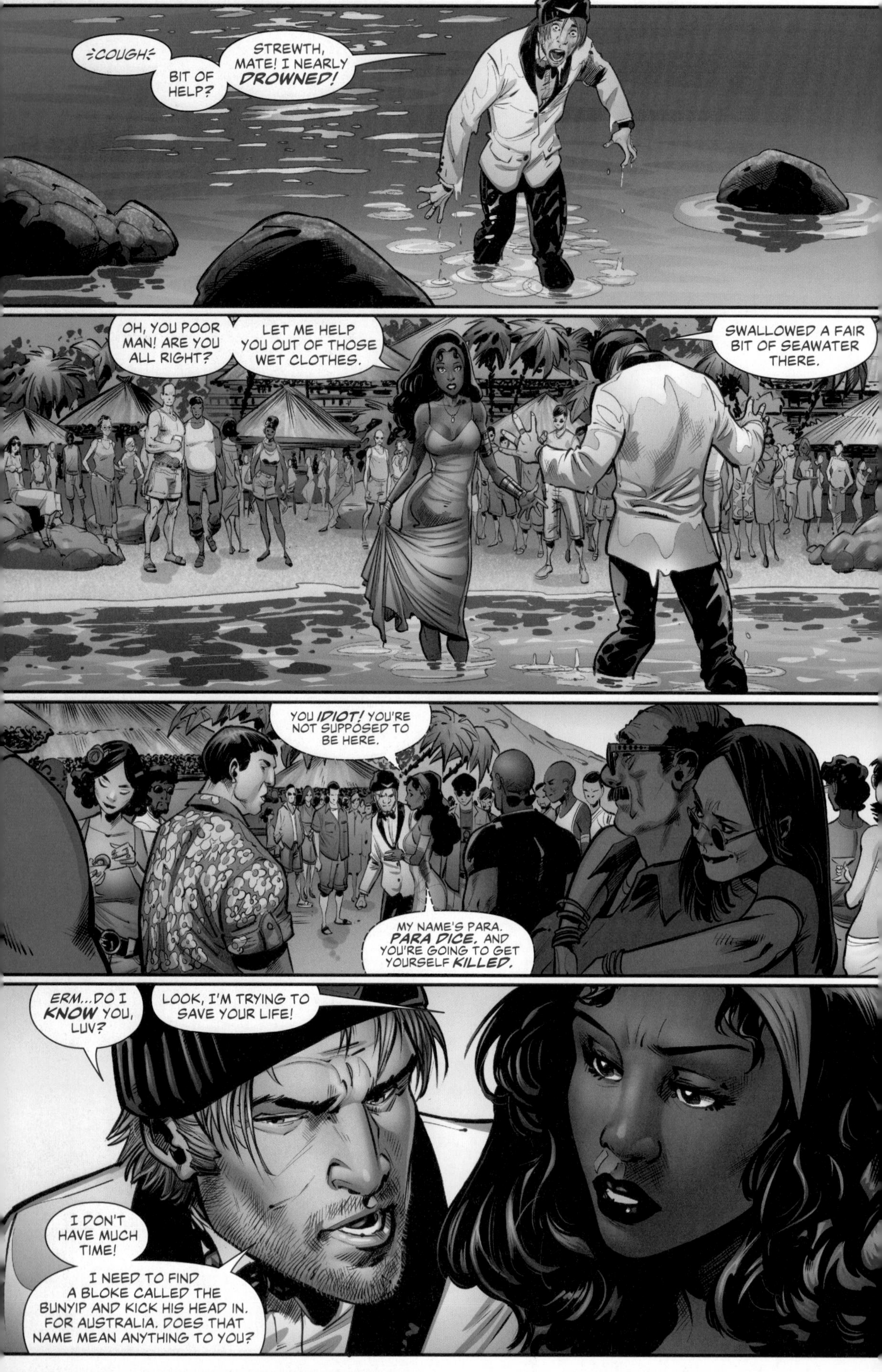

=COUGH=
BIT OF HELP?
STREWTH, MATE! I NEARLY DROWNED!
OH, YOU POOR MAN! ARE YOU ALL RIGHT?
LET ME HELP YOU OUT OF THOSE WET CLOTHES.
SWALLOWED A FAIR BIT OF SEAWATER THERE.
YOU IDIOT! YOU'RE NOT SUPPOSED TO BE HERE.
MY NAME'S PARA. PARA DICE. AND YOU'RE GOING TO GET YOURSELF KILLED.
ERM...DO I KNOW YOU, LUV?
LOOK, I'M TRYING TO SAVE YOUR LIFE!
I DON'T HAVE MUCH TIME!
I NEED TO FIND A BLOKE CALLED THE BUNYIP AND KICK HIS HEAD IN. FOR AUSTRALIA. DOES THAT NAME MEAN ANYTHING TO YOU?

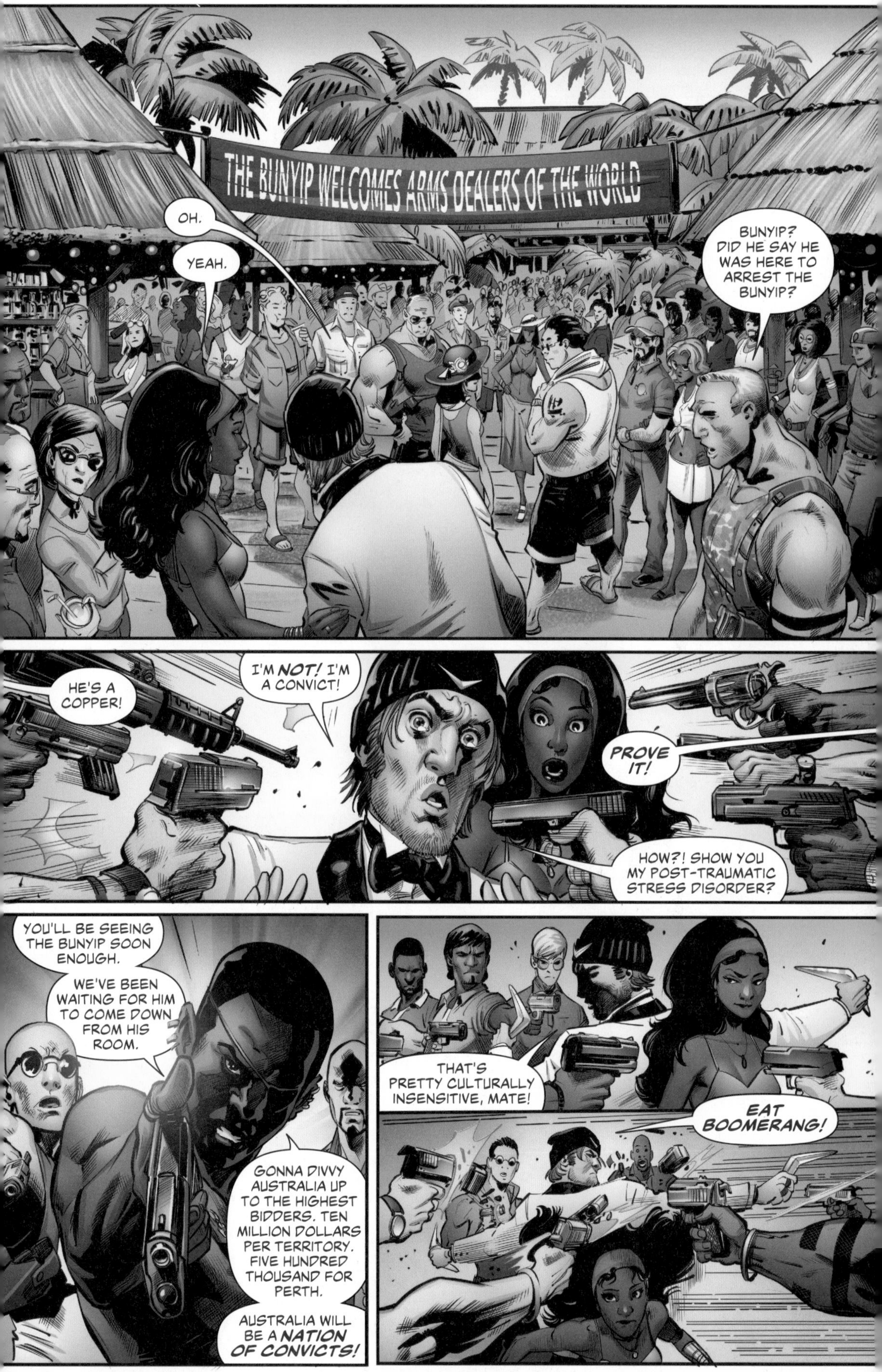
THE BUNYIP WELCOMES ARMS DEALERS OF THE WORLD
OH.
YEAH.
BUNYIP? DID HE SAY HE WAS HERE TO ARREST THE BUNYIP?
HE'S A COPPER!
I'M NOT! I'M A CONVICT!
PROVE IT!
HOW?! SHOW YOU MY POST-TRAUMATIC STRESS DISORDER?
YOU'LL BE SEEING THE BUNYIP SOON ENOUGH.
WE'VE BEEN WAITING FOR HIM TO COME DOWN FROM HIS ROOM.
GONNA DIVVY AUSTRALIA UP TO THE HIGHEST BIDDERS. TEN MILLION DOLLARS PER TERRITORY. FIVE HUNDRED THOUSAND FOR PERTH.
AUSTRALIA WILL BE A NATION OF CONVICTS!
THAT'S PRETTY CULTURALLY INSENSITIVE, MATE!
EAT BOOMERANG!

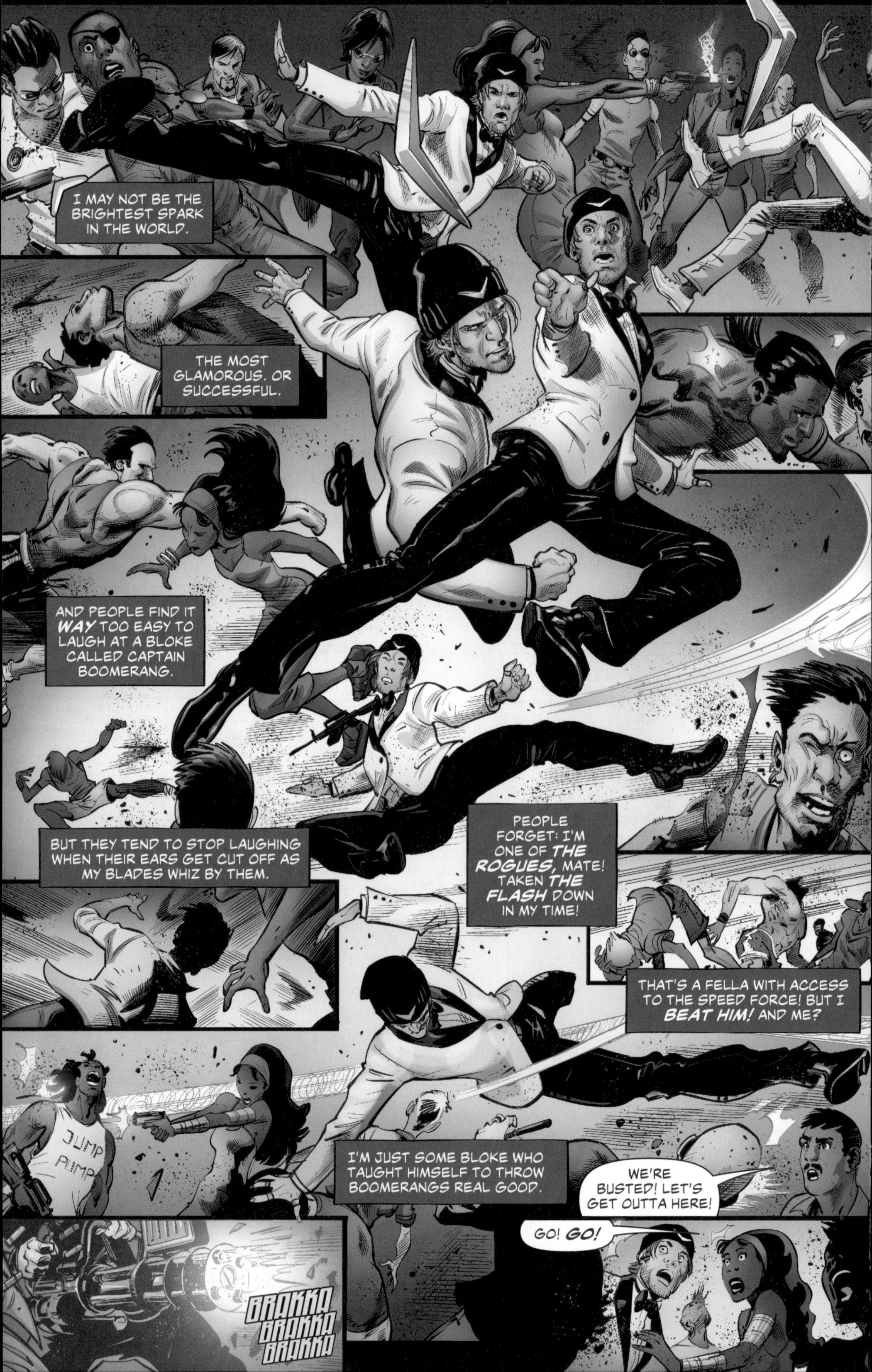
I MAY NOT BE THE BRIGHTEST SPARK IN THE WORLD.
THE MOST GLAMOROUS. OR SUCCESSFUL.
AND PEOPLE FIND IT WAY TOO EASY TO LAUGH AT A BLOKE CALLED CAPTAIN BOOMERANG.
BUT THEY TEND TO STOP LAUGHING WHEN THEIR EARS GET CUT OFF AS MY BLADES WHIZ BY THEM.
PEOPLE FORGET: I'M ONE OF THE ROGUES, MATE! TAKEN THE FLASH DOWN IN MY TIME!
THAT'S A FELLA WITH ACCESS TO THE SPEED FORCE! BUT I BEAT HIM! AND ME?
I'M JUST SOME BLOKE WHO TAUGHT HIMSELF TO THROW BOOMERANGS REAL GOOD.
JUMP PIMP
WE'RE BUSTED! LET'S GET OUTTA HERE!
GO! GO!
BRAKKA BRAKKA BRAKKA

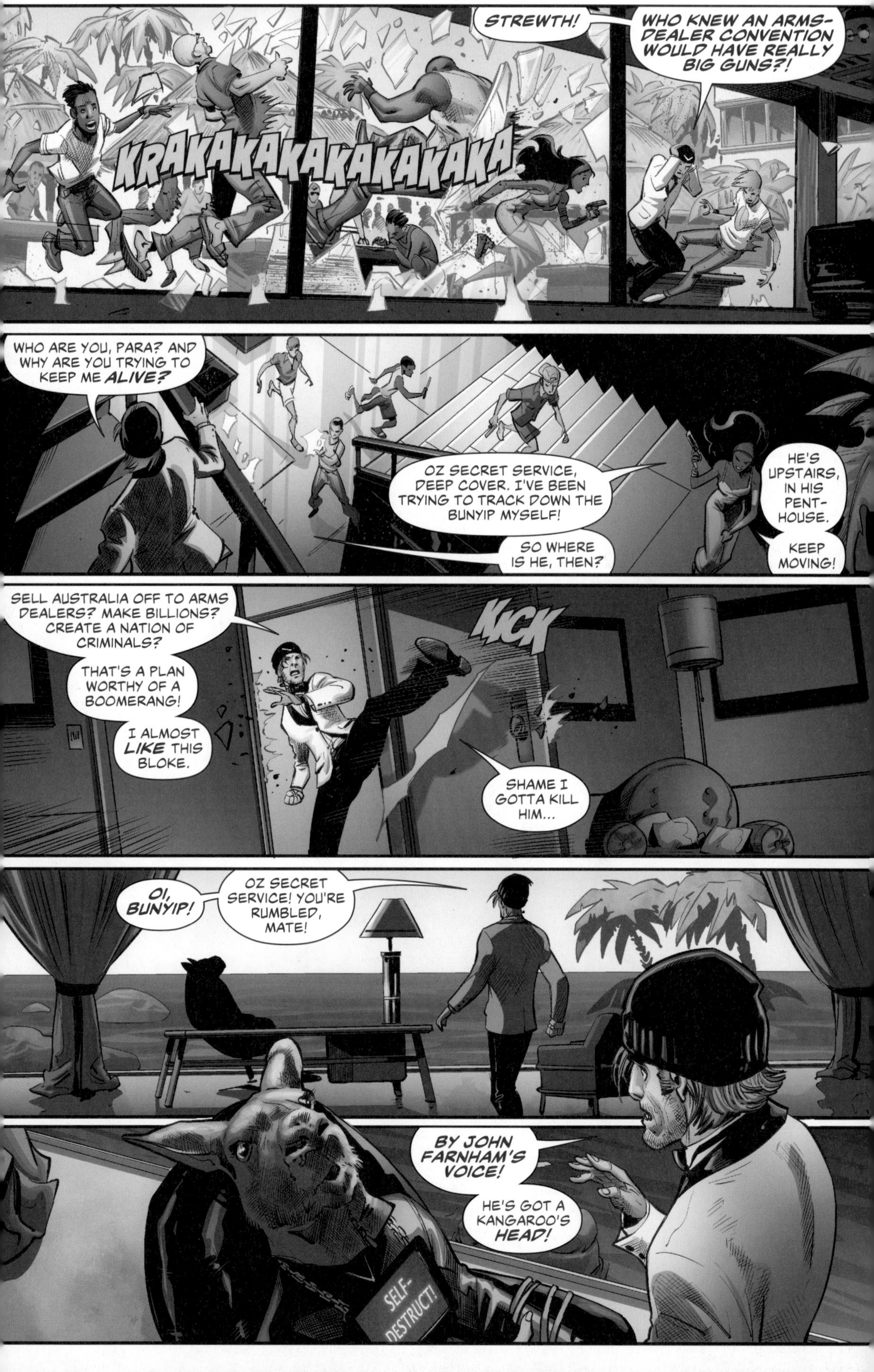
KRAKAKAKAKAKAKAKAKA
STREWTH!
WHO KNEW AN ARMS-DEALER CONVENTION WOULD HAVE REALLY BIG GUNS?!
WHO ARE YOU, PARA? AND WHY ARE YOU TRYING TO KEEP ME ALIVE?
OZ SECRET SERVICE, DEEP COVER. I'VE BEEN TRYING TO TRACK DOWN THE BUNYIP MYSELF!
SO WHERE IS HE, THEN?
HE'S UPSTAIRS, IN HIS PENT-HOUSE.
KEEP MOVING!
SELL AUSTRALIA OFF TO ARMS DEALERS? MAKE BILLIONS? CREATE A NATION OF CRIMINALS?
THAT'S A PLAN WORTHY OF A BOOMERANG!
I ALMOST LIKE THIS BLOKE.
KICK
SHAME I GOTTA KILL HIM...
OI, BUNYIP!
OZ SECRET SERVICE! YOU'RE RUMBLED, MATE!
BY JOHN FARNHAM'S VOICE!
HE'S GOT A KANGAROO'S HEAD!
SELF-DESTRUCT!

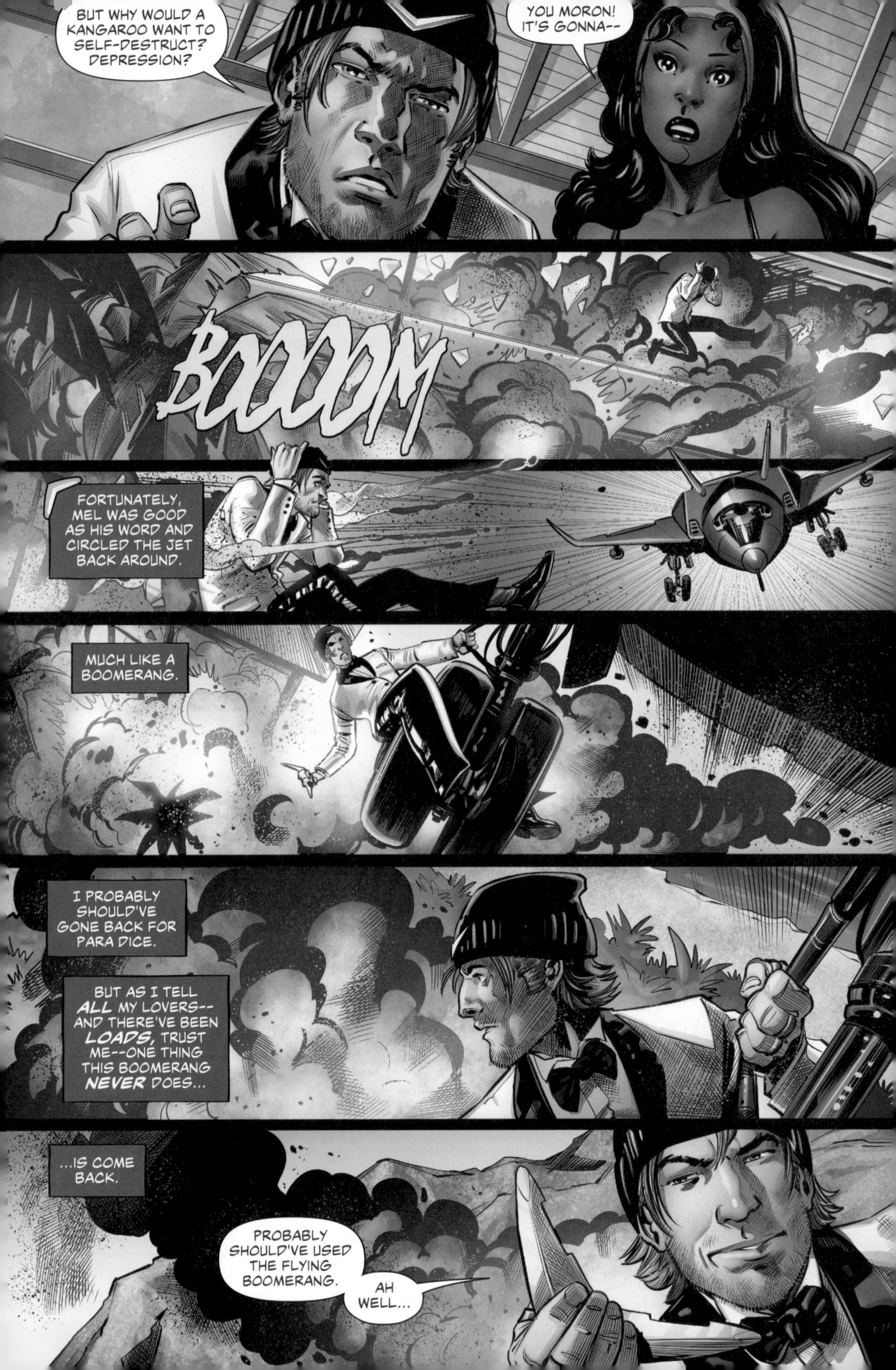
BUT WHY WOULD A KANGAROO WANT TO SELF-DESTRUCT? DEPRESSION?
YOU MORON! IT'S GONNA--
BOOOOM
FORTUNATELY, MEL WAS GOOD AS HIS WORD AND CIRCLED THE JET BACK AROUND.
MUCH LIKE A BOOMERANG.
I PROBABLY SHOULD'VE GONE BACK FOR PARA DICE.
BUT AS I TELL *ALL* MY LOVERS-- AND THERE'VE BEEN *LOADS*, TRUST ME--ONE THING THIS BOOMERANG *NEVER* DOES...
...IS COME BACK.
PROBABLY SHOULD'VE USED THE FLYING BOOMERANG.
AH WELL...

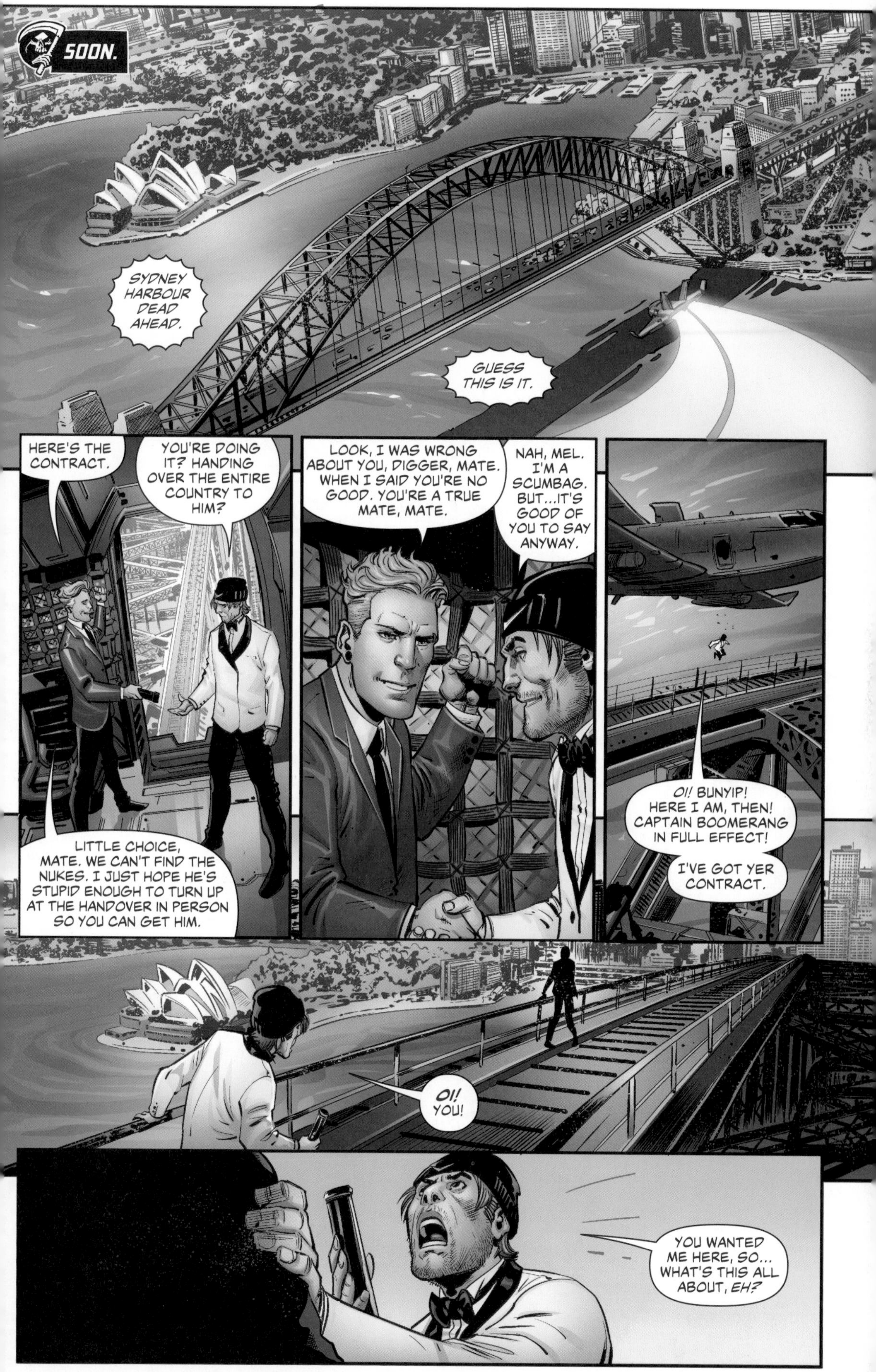
SOON.
SYDNEY HARBOUR DEAD AHEAD.
GUESS THIS IS IT.
HERE'S THE CONTRACT.
YOU'RE DOING IT? HANDING OVER THE ENTIRE COUNTRY TO HIM?
LITTLE CHOICE, MATE. WE CAN'T FIND THE NUKES. I JUST HOPE HE'S STUPID ENOUGH TO TURN UP AT THE HANDOVER IN PERSON SO YOU CAN GET HIM.
LOOK, I WAS WRONG ABOUT YOU, DIGGER, MATE. WHEN I SAID YOU'RE NO GOOD. YOU'RE A TRUE MATE, MATE.
NAH, MEL. I'M A SCUMBAG. BUT...IT'S GOOD OF YOU TO SAY ANYWAY.
OI! BUNYIP! HERE I AM, THEN! CAPTAIN BOOMERANG IN FULL EFFECT!
I'VE GOT YER CONTRACT.
OI! YOU!
YOU WANTED ME HERE, SO... WHAT'S THIS ALL ABOUT, EH?

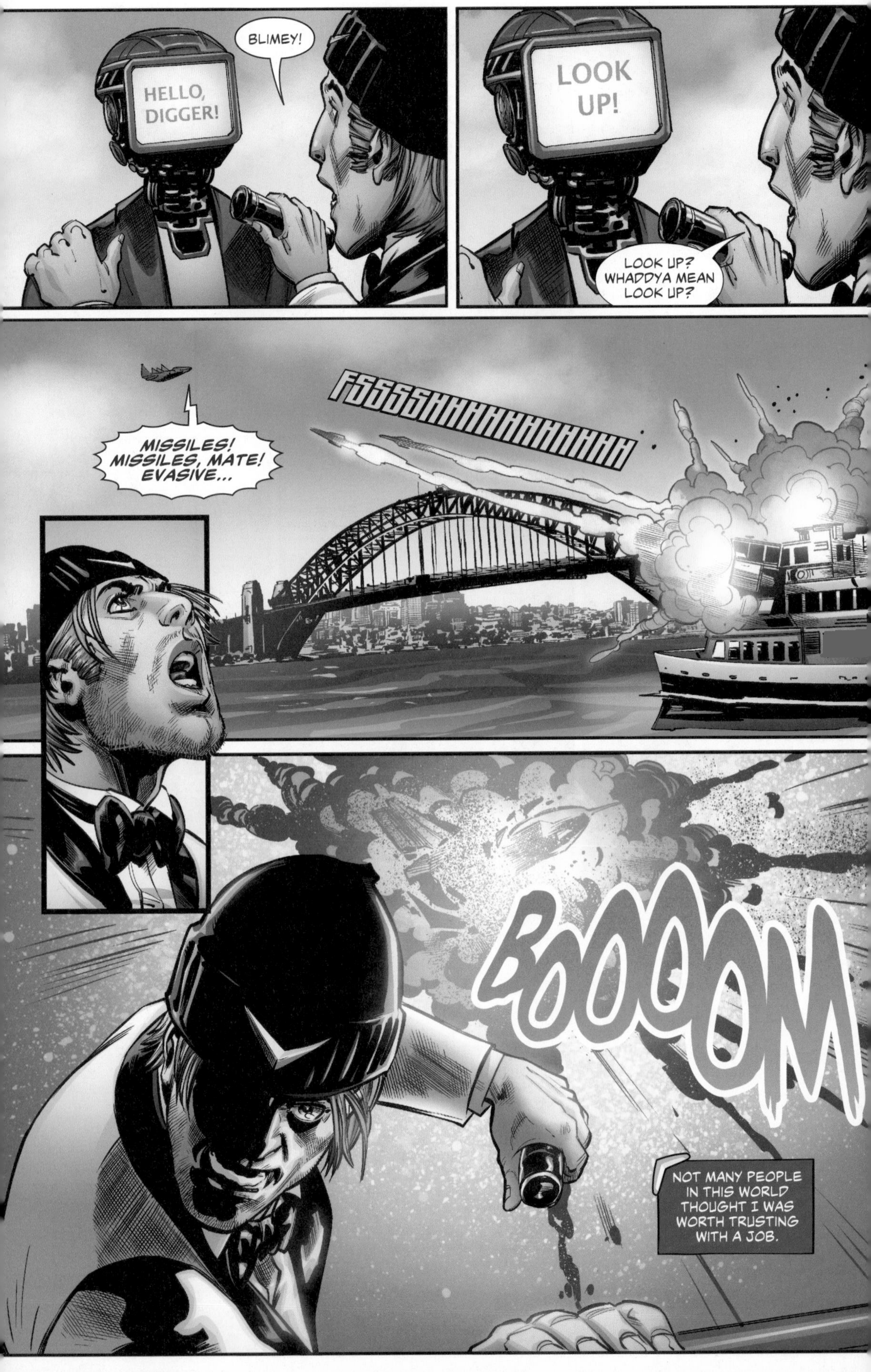
HELLO, DIGGER!
BLIMEY!
LOOK UP!
LOOK UP? WHADDYA MEAN LOOK UP?
FSSSSHHHHHHHHHHH
MISSILES! MISSILES, MATE! EVASIVE...
BOOOOM
NOT MANY PEOPLE IN THIS WORLD THOUGHT I WAS WORTH TRUSTING WITH A JOB.

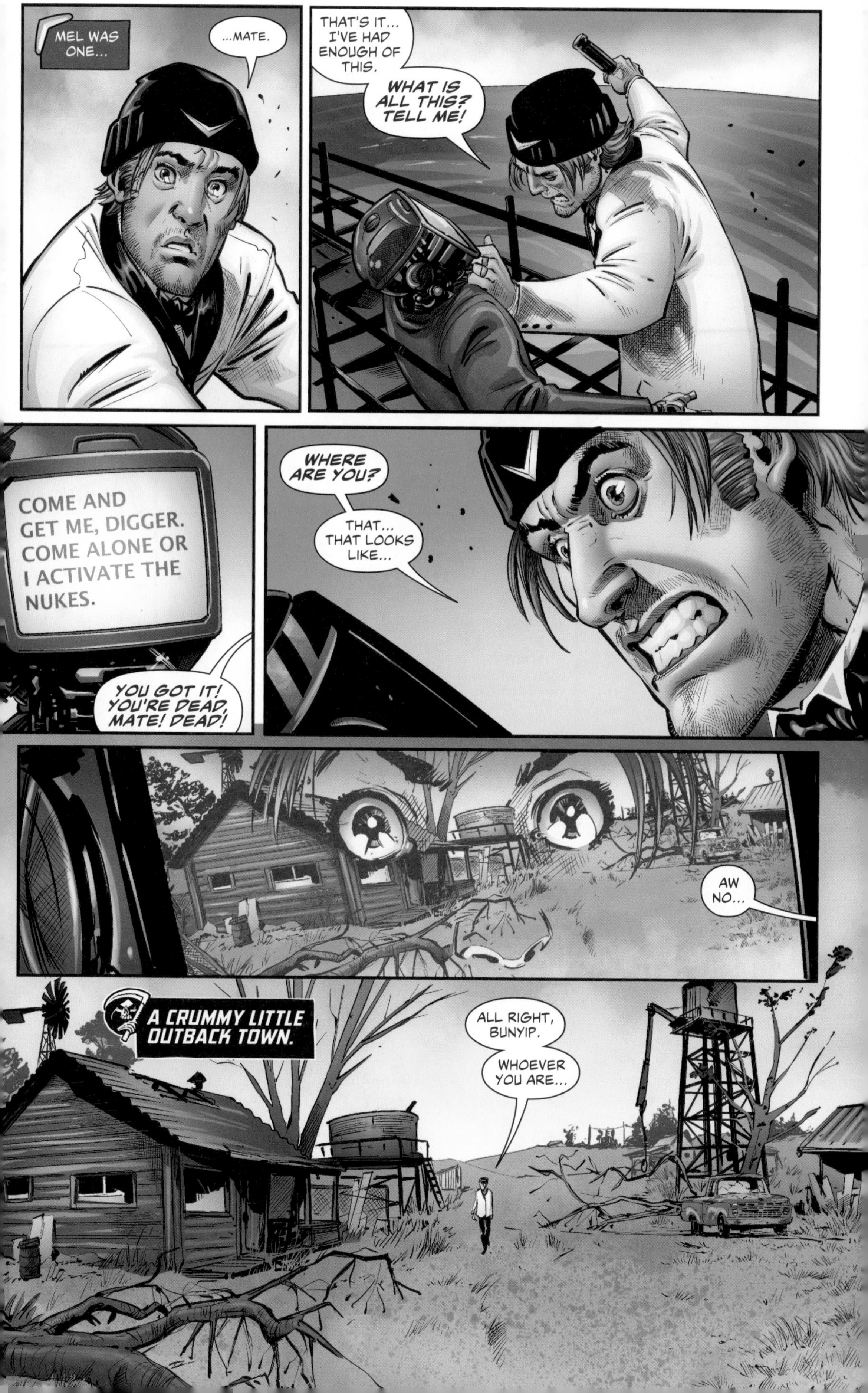

MEL WAS ONE...
...MATE.
THAT'S IT... I'VE HAD ENOUGH OF THIS.
WHAT IS ALL THIS? TELL ME!
COME AND GET ME, DIGGER. COME ALONE OR I ACTIVATE THE NUKES.
YOU GOT IT! YOU'RE DEAD, MATE! DEAD!
WHERE ARE YOU?
THAT... THAT LOOKS LIKE...
AW NO...
A CRUMMY LITTLE OUTBACK TOWN.
ALL RIGHT, BUNYIP.
WHOEVER YOU ARE...

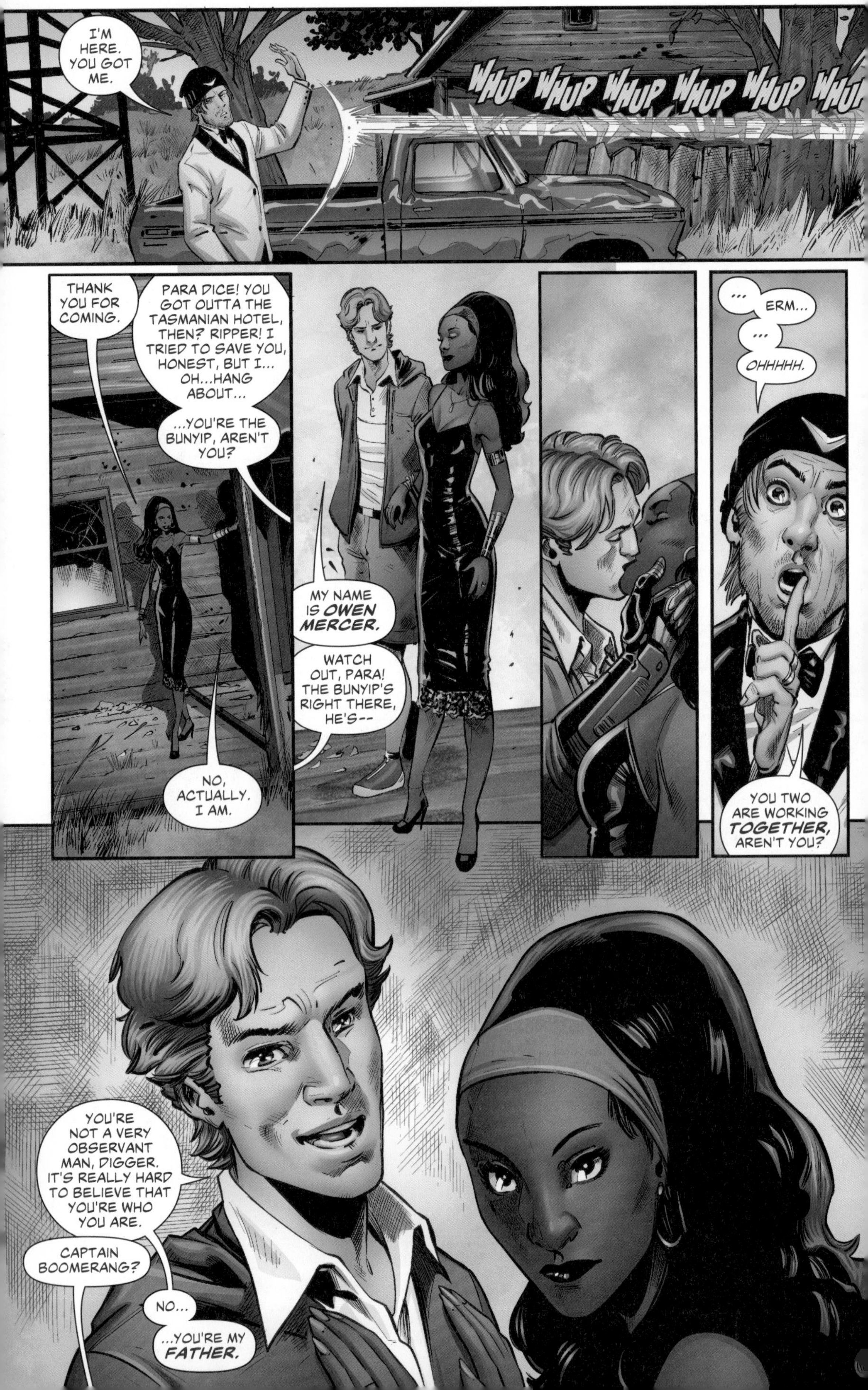
I'M HERE. YOU GOT ME.
WHUP WHUP WHUP WHUP WHUP WHU
THANK YOU FOR COMING.
PARA DICE! YOU GOT OUTTA THE TASMANIAN HOTEL, THEN? RIPPER! I TRIED TO SAVE YOU, HONEST, BUT I... OH...HANG ABOUT...
...YOU'RE THE BUNYIP, AREN'T YOU?
MY NAME IS OWEN MERCER.
WATCH OUT, PARA! THE BUNYIP'S RIGHT THERE, HE'S--
NO, ACTUALLY. I AM.
... ERM...
...
OHHHHH.
YOU TWO ARE WORKING TOGETHER, AREN'T YOU?
YOU'RE NOT A VERY OBSERVANT MAN, DIGGER. IT'S REALLY HARD TO BELIEVE THAT YOU'RE WHO YOU ARE.
CAPTAIN BOOMERANG?
NO...
...YOU'RE MY FATHER.

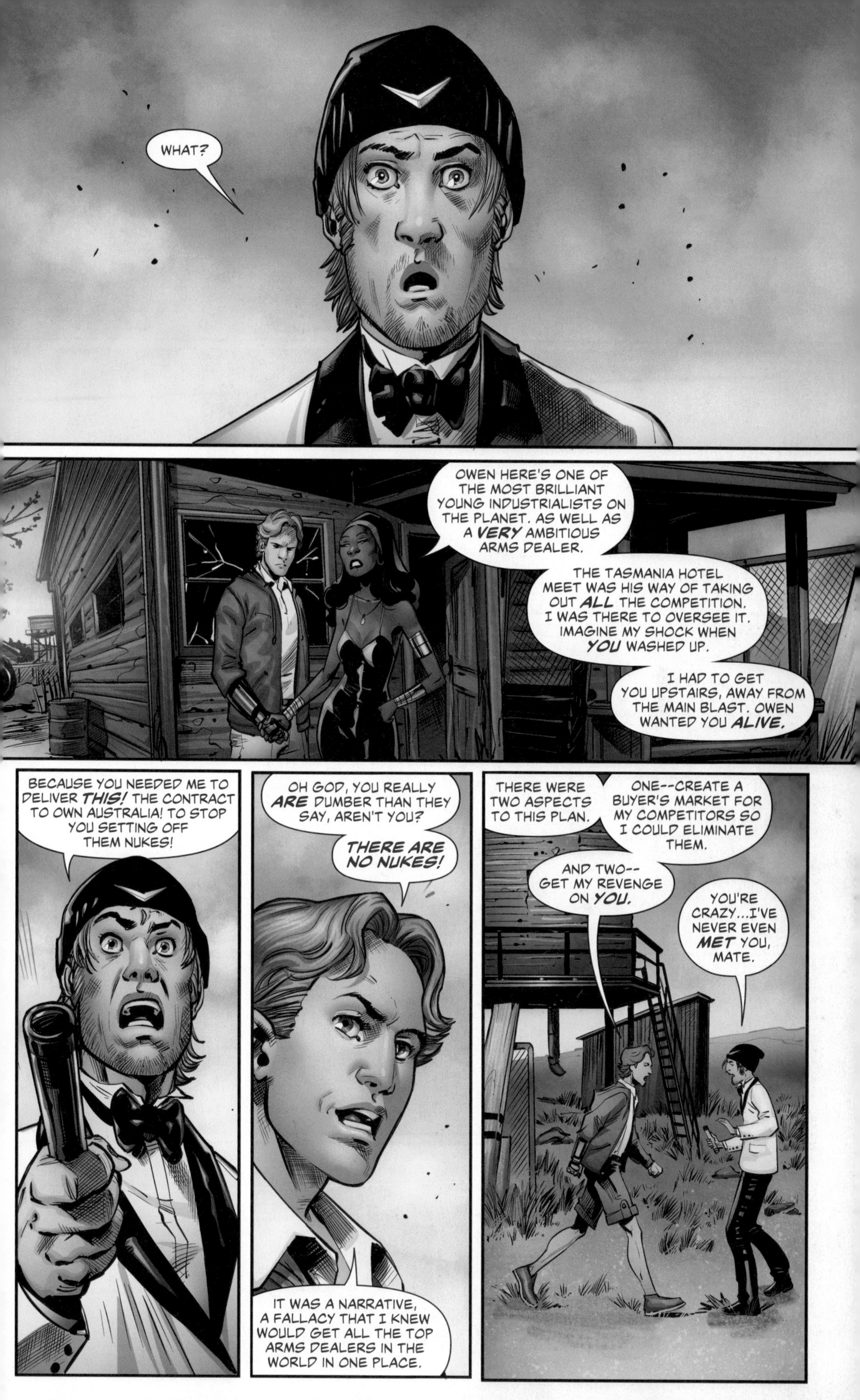
WHAT?
OWEN HERE'S ONE OF THE MOST BRILLIANT YOUNG INDUSTRIALISTS ON THE PLANET. AS WELL AS A VERY AMBITIOUS ARMS DEALER.
THE TASMANIA HOTEL MEET WAS HIS WAY OF TAKING OUT ALL THE COMPETITION. I WAS THERE TO OVERSEE IT. IMAGINE MY SHOCK WHEN YOU WASHED UP.
I HAD TO GET YOU UPSTAIRS, AWAY FROM THE MAIN BLAST. OWEN WANTED YOU ALIVE.
BECAUSE YOU NEEDED ME TO DELIVER THIS! THE CONTRACT TO OWN AUSTRALIA! TO STOP YOU SETTING OFF THEM NUKES!
OH GOD, YOU REALLY ARE DUMBER THAN THEY SAY, AREN'T YOU?
THERE ARE NO NUKES!
IT WAS A NARRATIVE, A FALLACY THAT I KNEW WOULD GET ALL THE TOP ARMS DEALERS IN THE WORLD IN ONE PLACE.
THERE WERE TWO ASPECTS TO THIS PLAN.
ONE--CREATE A BUYER'S MARKET FOR MY COMPETITORS SO I COULD ELIMINATE THEM.
AND TWO-- GET MY REVENGE ON YOU.
YOU'RE CRAZY...I'VE NEVER EVEN MET YOU, MATE.

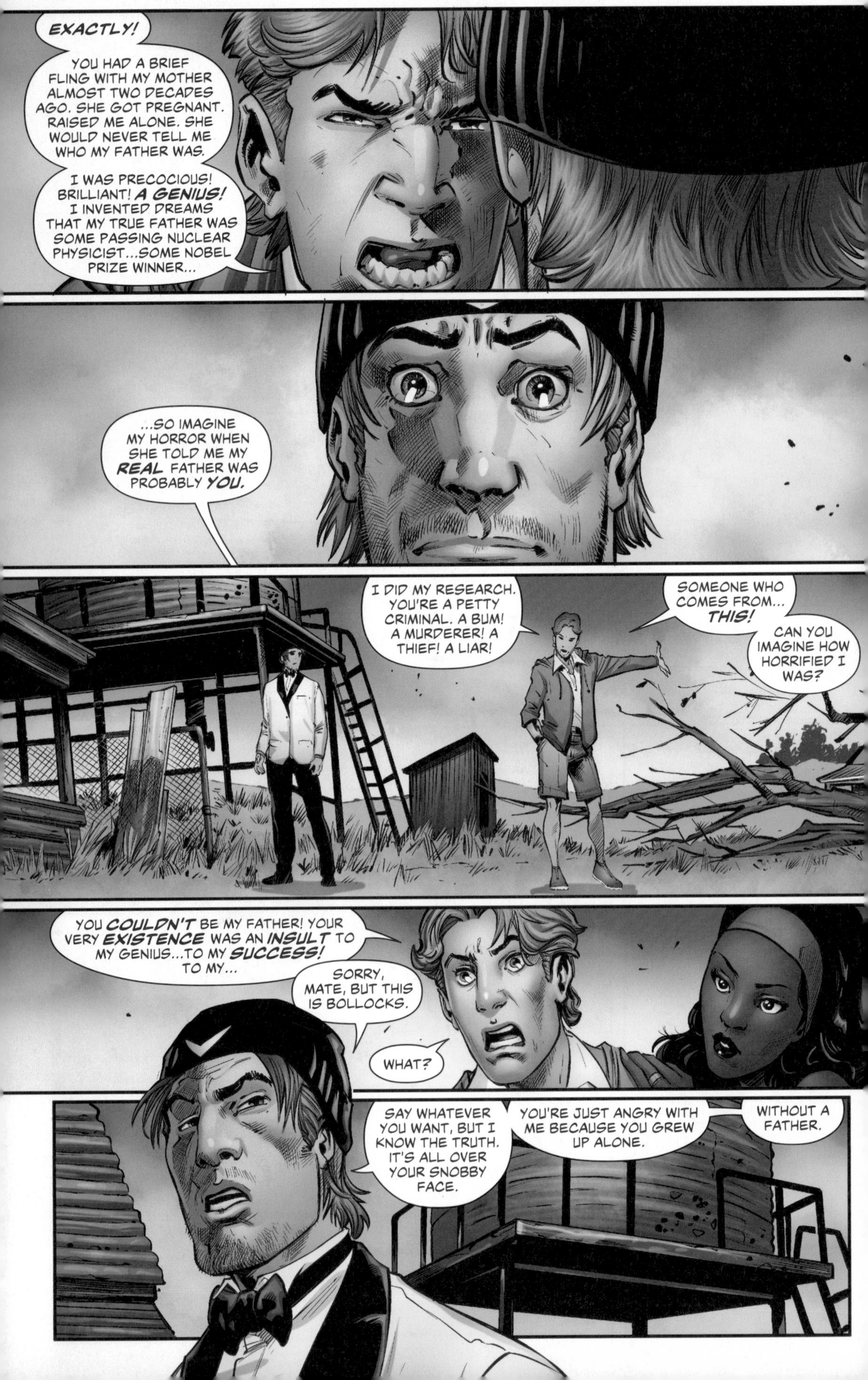
EXACTLY!
YOU HAD A BRIEF FLING WITH MY MOTHER ALMOST TWO DECADES AGO. SHE GOT PREGNANT. RAISED ME ALONE. SHE WOULD NEVER TELL ME WHO MY FATHER WAS.
I WAS PRECOCIOUS! BRILLIANT! A GENIUS! I INVENTED DREAMS THAT MY TRUE FATHER WAS SOME PASSING NUCLEAR PHYSICIST...SOME NOBEL PRIZE WINNER...
...SO IMAGINE MY HORROR WHEN SHE TOLD ME MY REAL FATHER WAS PROBABLY YOU.
I DID MY RESEARCH. YOU'RE A PETTY CRIMINAL. A BUM! A MURDERER! A THIEF! A LIAR!
SOMEONE WHO COMES FROM... THIS!
CAN YOU IMAGINE HOW HORRIFIED I WAS?
YOU COULDN'T BE MY FATHER! YOUR VERY EXISTENCE WAS AN INSULT TO MY GENIUS...TO MY SUCCESS! TO MY...
SORRY, MATE, BUT THIS IS BOLLOCKS.
WHAT?
SAY WHATEVER YOU WANT, BUT I KNOW THE TRUTH. IT'S ALL OVER YOUR SNOBBY FACE.
YOU'RE JUST ANGRY WITH ME BECAUSE YOU GREW UP ALONE.
WITHOUT A FATHER.

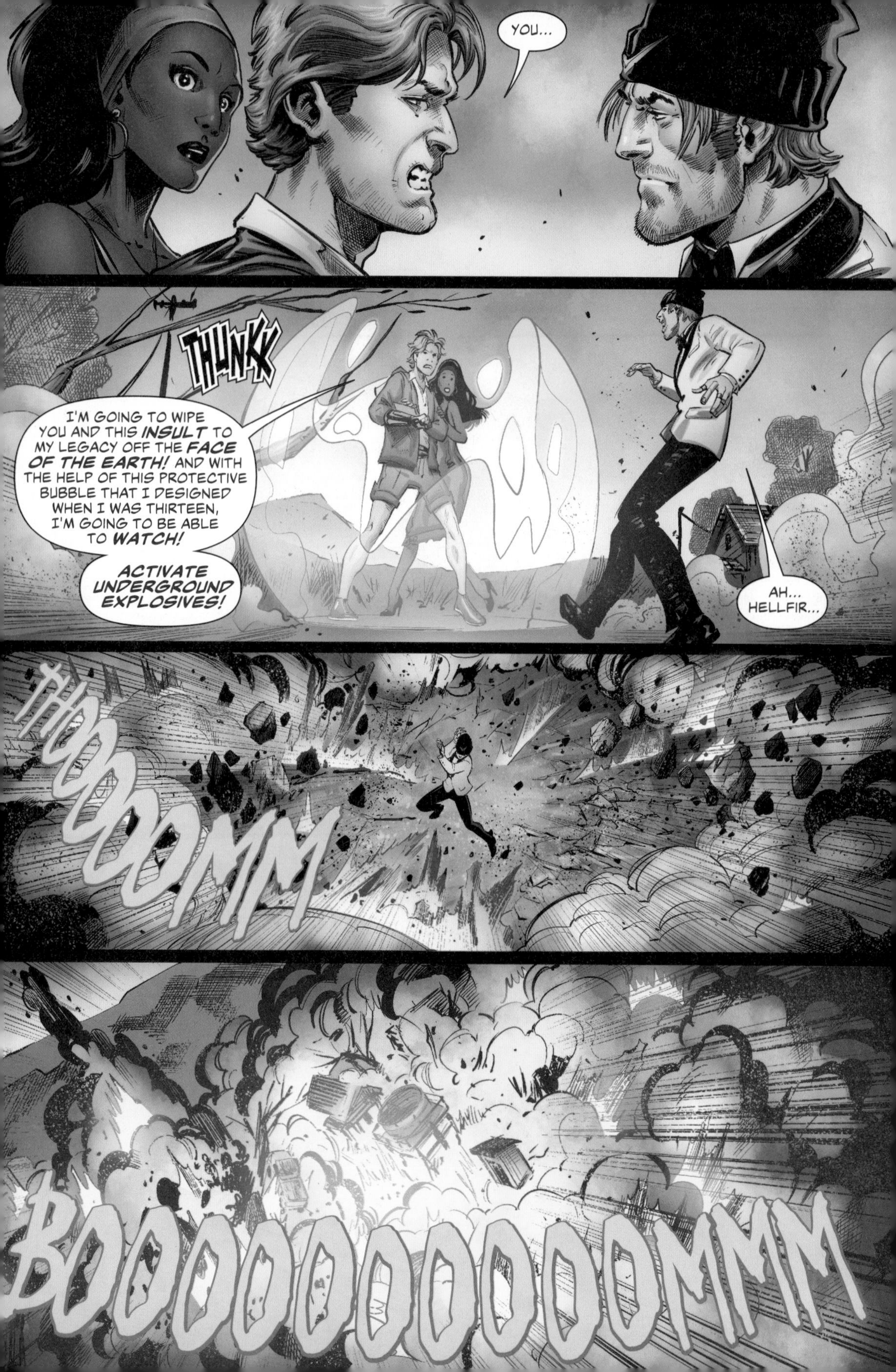
YOU...
THUNKK
I'M GOING TO WIPE YOU AND THIS INSULT TO MY LEGACY OFF THE FACE OF THE EARTH! AND WITH THE HELP OF THIS PROTECTIVE BUBBLE THAT I DESIGNED WHEN I WAS THIRTEEN, I'M GOING TO BE ABLE TO WATCH!
ACTIVATE UNDERGROUND EXPLOSIVES!
AH... HELLFIR...
THOOOOOMM
BOOOOOOOOOMMM

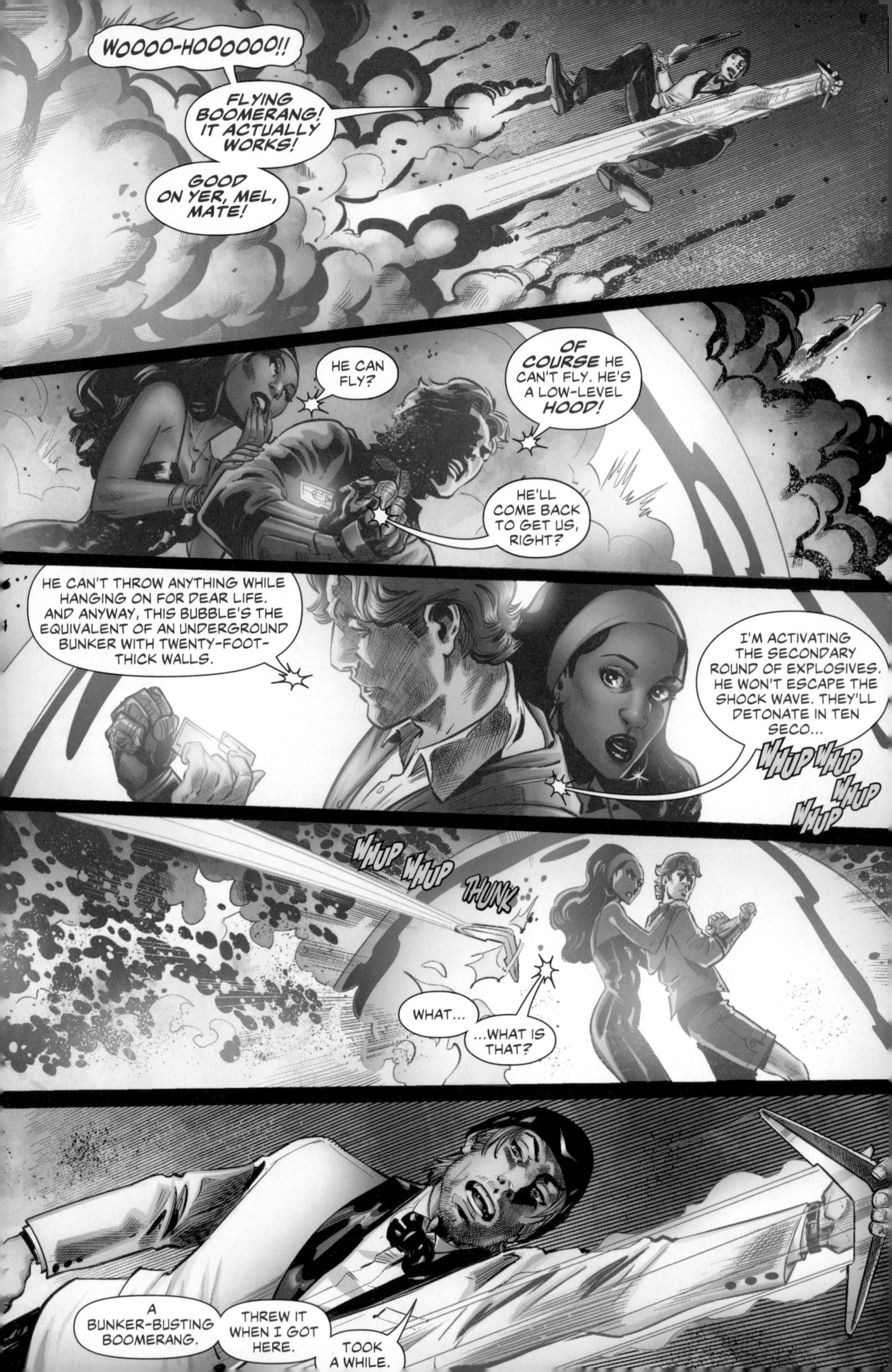
WOOOO-HOOOOOO!!
FLYING BOOMERANG! IT ACTUALLY WORKS!
GOOD ON YER, MEL, MATE!
HE CAN FLY?
OF COURSE HE CAN'T FLY. HE'S A LOW-LEVEL HOOD!
HE'LL COME BACK TO GET US, RIGHT?
HE CAN'T THROW ANYTHING WHILE HANGING ON FOR DEAR LIFE. AND ANYWAY, THIS BUBBLE'S THE EQUIVALENT OF AN UNDERGROUND BUNKER WITH TWENTY-FOOT-THICK WALLS.
I'M ACTIVATING THE SECONDARY ROUND OF EXPLOSIVES. HE WON'T ESCAPE THE SHOCK WAVE. THEY'LL DETONATE IN TEN SECO...
WHUP WHUP WHUP WHUP
WHUP WHUP
THUNK
WHAT...
...WHAT IS THAT?
A BUNKER-BUSTING BOOMERANG.
THREW IT WHEN I GOT HERE.
TOOK A WHILE.

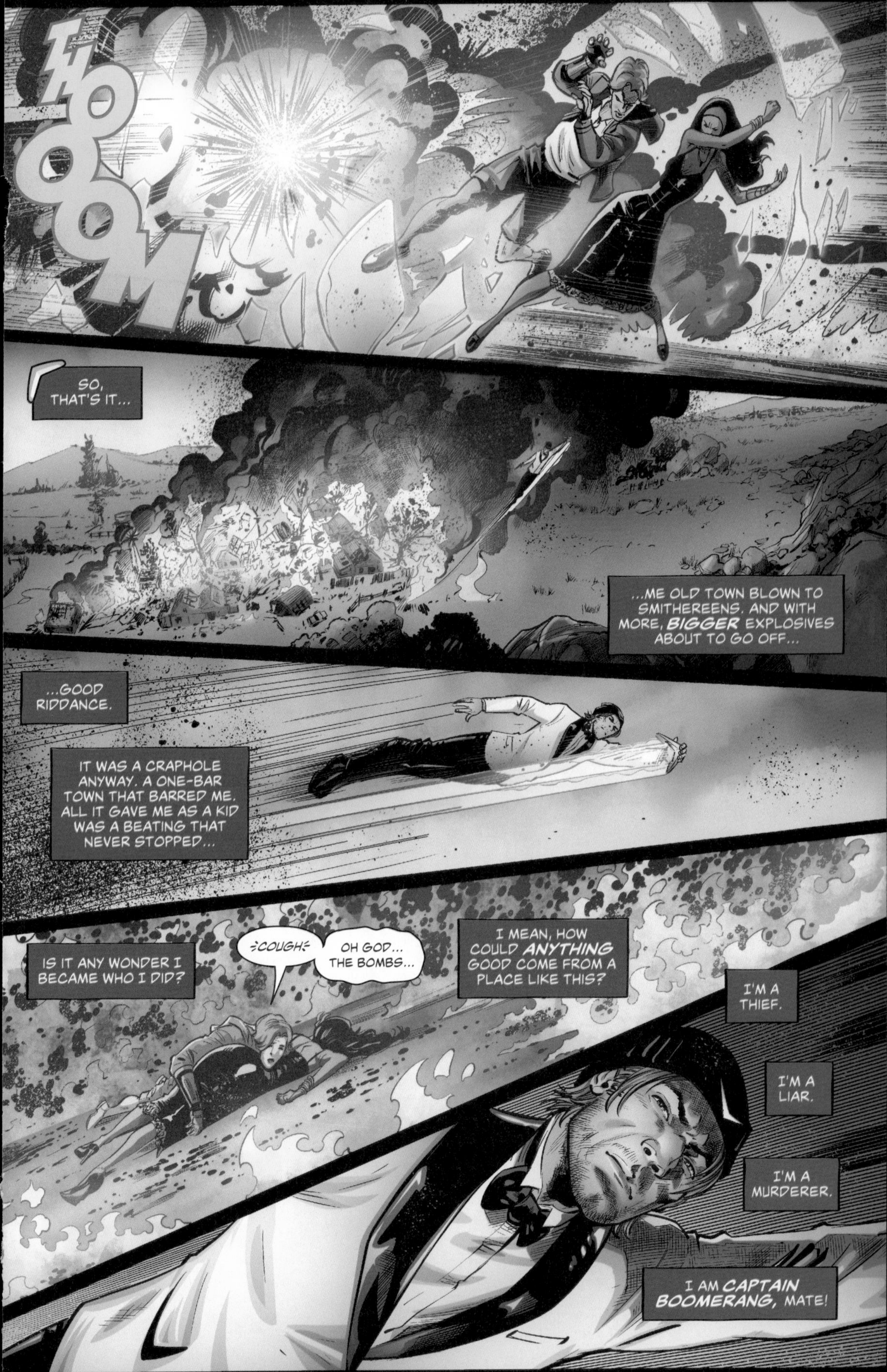
THOOOM
SO, THAT'S IT...
...ME OLD TOWN BLOWN TO SMITHEREENS. AND WITH MORE, BIGGER EXPLOSIVES ABOUT TO GO OFF...
...GOOD RIDDANCE.
IT WAS A CRAPHOLE ANYWAY. A ONE-BAR TOWN THAT BARRED ME. ALL IT GAVE ME AS A KID WAS A BEATING THAT NEVER STOPPED...
IS IT ANY WONDER I BECAME WHO I DID?
COUGH
OH GOD... THE BOMBS...
I MEAN, HOW COULD ANYTHING GOOD COME FROM A PLACE LIKE THIS?
I'M A THIEF.
I'M A LIAR.
I'M A MURDERER.
I AM CAPTAIN BOOMERANG, MATE!

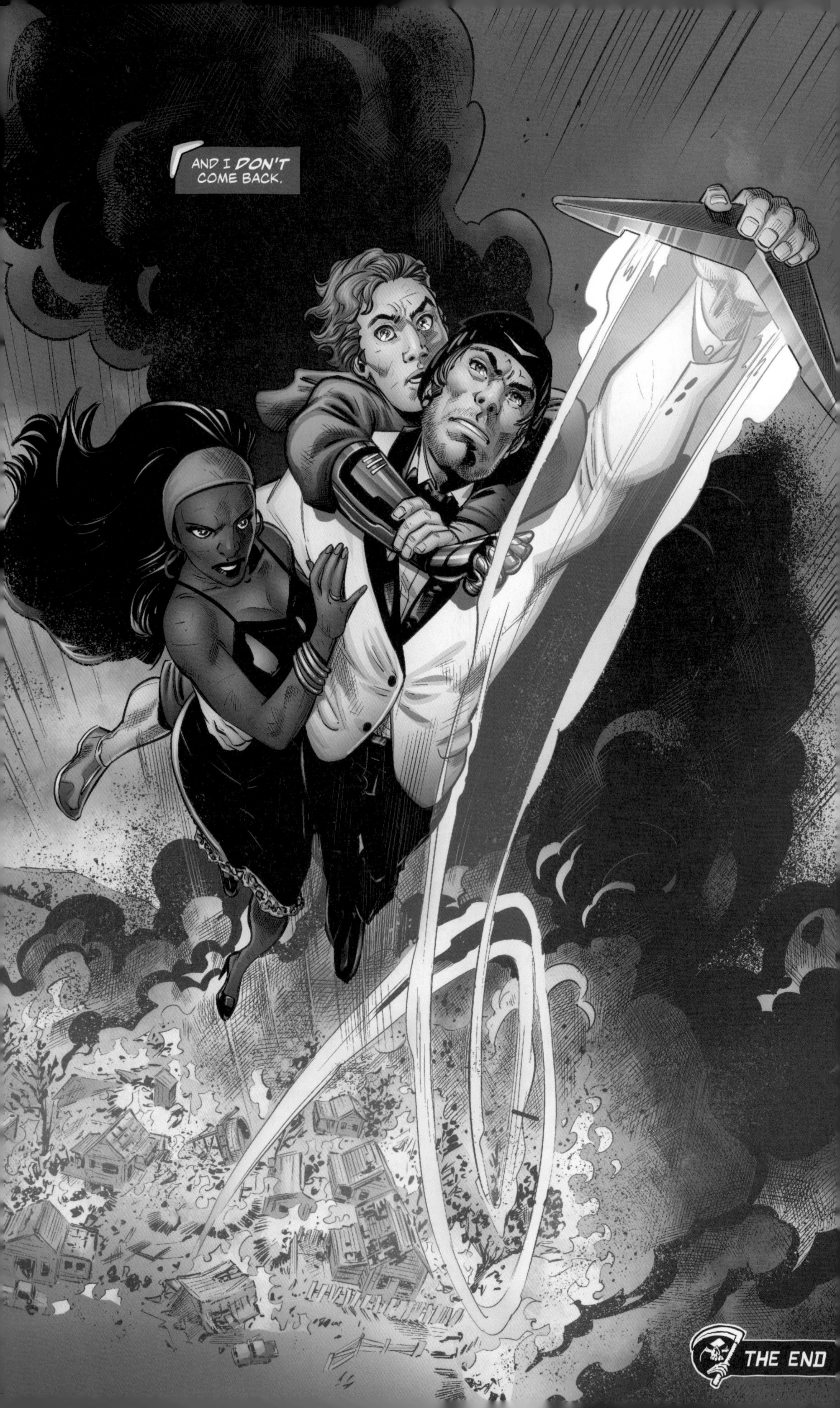
AND I DON'T COME BACK.
THE END